IMMORTALITY

IMMORTALITY

Edited by
PAUL EDWARDS

Prometheus Books

59 John Glenn Drive
Amherst, New York 14228-2197

Published 1997 by Prometheus Books

01 00 99 98 97   5 4 3 2 1

Library of Congress Cataloging-in-Publication Data

Immortality / edited, with an introduction, notes, and bibliographical essay by
    Paul Edwards.
        p.   cm.
    Originally published: New York : Macmillan Pub. Co., 1992.
    Includes bibliographical references.
    ISBN 1–57392–130–0 (pbk. : alk. paper)
    1. Immortality (Philosophy) 2. Mind and body. 3. Mind-brain identity
theory. 4. Individuality. 5. Reincarnation.
[BD421.I47   1997]
129—dc21   96–40309
                                                                    CIP

Printed in the United States of America on acid-free paper

We must needs believe in that other life in order
that we may live this life, and endure it, and give it
meaning and finality.

Unamuno

I have suffered too much in this life not to expect
another. All the subtleties of metaphysics will
never make me doubt for a minute the immortality
of the soul. I feel it, I believe it, I want it, I hope
for it. I will defend it to my last breath.

Rousseau

I believe that when I die I shall rot, and nothing of
my ego will survive.. . . . I should scorn to shiver
with terror at the thought of annihilation.
Happiness is nonetheless true happiness because it
must come to an end, nor do thought and love lose
their value because they are not everlasting.

Bertrand Russell

PREFACE

This book is not only about immortality but also about two of the most fascinating and difficult philosophical problems — the mind-body problem and the nature of personal identity. Immortality cannot be seriously discussed without an understanding of these problems and hence, both in my introduction and in the selections, I have covered all three issues. In making the selections I have been motivated by the desire to do justice to all viewpoints and arguments that deserve to be taken seriously. I believe that the selections do not exhibit any bias. However, in the introduction I have not refrained from occasionally expressing my own views. The temptation to do so proved irresistible, and, in any case, an introduction in which the editor takes sides is usually more interesting than one in which he tries to assume a pose of complete neutrality.

Many of the selections deal with immortality as it has been debated by Western philosophers and religious thinkers, but the book also contains extensive coverage of reincarnation. This theory has become extremely fashionable and is accepted or sympathetically considered by a great many people who are totally unaware of the case on the other side. This is particularly unfortunate when those involved are college students who ought to be better informed. The case for reincarnation is represented in several selections, but because I could not find a sufficiently compact statement of the case against it anywhere in the literature, I have summarized the major objections in the Introduction. Readers interested in a fuller presentation of the case against reincarnation are referred to my four-part series on the subject, which was published in *Free Inquiry* in 1986–1987.

The majority of the selections are well-known, but I have also included some pieces of great interest which are probably unfamiliar to most students of the subject. I would like to call special attention to Tertullian's critique of reincarnation, which is as simple as it is incisive; Voltaire's satirical treatment of all forms of belief in survival; Joseph Priestley's attempt to reconcile materialism with immortality; Hugh Elliot's defense of epiphenomenalism, here entitled "Tantalus," and Donald MacKay's ingenious argument that even if we regard consciousness as embodied in our brain, we need not abandon the hope for eternal life. John Beloff's "Is There Anything Beyond Death?—A Parapsychologist's Summation" is here published for the first time. Both believers and unbelievers will be grateful for this authoritative report of the work of psychical researchers.

I wish to thank the following friends and colleagues who read my introduction for criticism and suggestions: Victor Fernandez, Norbert Hoerster, Champe Ransom, Jerome Shaffer, and Michael Wreen.

Paul Edwards

CONTENTS

Immortality

INTRODUCTION CONTENTS

Introduction

WHEN BENJAMIN DISRAELI was on his deathbed Queen Victoria expressed a wish to visit him. Disraeli did not think this a good idea. "The Queen would only ask me," he is reported to have said, "to take a message to dear Albert." Except for Christian and Muslim fundamentalists, very few people today hold as confident and literal a belief in survival after death as Queen Victoria. However, the number of those who believe or half-believe in *some* kind of afterlife is still huge, and undoubtedly many who do not believe wish they could. What has been called the occultist explosion of recent decades and the interest in reincarnation are surely not due to the discovery of any new evidence, but rather to the reluctance to accept a purely naturalistic philosophy which teaches that death means total annihilation, that, in the words of *Ecclesiastes*, in the end "all is vanity," that just like animals men "are of the dust and will turn to dust again."

It can hardly be denied that a philosophy which maintains that the world is morally meaningful, that death is not the end, and that human beings—or at least some of them—will have another chance is emotionally more satisfying than naturalism. However, the question can hardly be avoided whether this emotionally more satisfying outlook is supported by adequate evidence; and it is this and related questions about what we may call the *logical* standing of the belief in life after death with which philosophers have concerned themselves. The selections which make up the bulk of this book deal with these logical issues, and not with the emotional effects of belief and unbelief. The same is

1

true of the Introduction. My aim here is to explain very fully the different forms which belief in immortality has taken and the arguments for and against each of them.

Some Preliminary Distinctions

Before going any further it will be helpful to call attention to several differences among believers in life after death. The first concerns the difference between what we may call the belief in "survival" and the belief in "immortality." As we shall use these terms, a believer in survival claims no more than that human beings will survive the death of their bodies, leaving it an open question whether they will go on existing forever. This view is entirely consistent with acceptance of eventual annihilation. A believer in immortality on the other hand makes the stronger claim that human beings will go on living for ever. It is worth observing that some of the evidence for life after death would, if cogent, merely prove survival. This is certainly true of all the evidence derived from parapsychology. Messages picked up by mediums would at the very most establish that certain dead persons still exist. They would not show that these individuals will go on existing forever. The same is of course true of "near death experiences" — deathbed visions and experiences during episodes when the heart stops beating. By contrast, metaphysical arguments of the sort found in Plato, the scholastic philosophers, and various rationalistic philosophers of the seventeenth and eighteenth centuries, would prove the indestructibility of human beings and hence their *eternal* life. It should be added that the division between those who reject any kind of life after death and those who believe either in survival or immortality is much more fundamental than the division between the two kinds of believers. It is safe to say that most of those who have a craving for continued existence after death would be quite happy to settle for survival — for five or ten million years or even just another thousand years — even if they were to be permanently extinguished after that.

Another difference among believers which deserves to be mentioned is between those who believe in *personal* survival and those who believe that human beings will not survive *as individuals* but will merge or be absorbed in some kind of "Universal Mind." Christians and those Jews who believe in immortality take the former view and so do non-denominational believers like Rousseau and Kant both of whom rejected Christianity but not life after death. Prominent among Western adherents of the latter view were the New England transcendentalists of the nineteenth century. William James, in a footnote in his lecture on immortality, quotes the following statement from Emerson's *Self-Reliance*:

> We lie in the lap of immense intelligence, which makes us receivers of its truth and organs of its activity. When we discern justice, when we discern truth, we do nothing of ourselves, but allow a passage to its beams.

It is this "immense intelligence" or Absolute Mind with which we become one after death.

James himself speaks of this Absolute Mind as "the mother sea" and "the great reservoir of consciousness." He does not explicitly endorse this position, but he writes about it with sympathy and respect. Among Western writers who have endorsed it are the physicist Erwin Schrödinger (1887–1961), known for his momentous contributions to quantum theory, and the influential novelist and political commentator Arthur Köstler (1905–1983). Schrodinger argued that contemporary physical theory which has abandoned the notion that particles are "identifiable individuals" naturally leads to the view taught in the Upanishads that the separation of individual minds is merely appearance and that "in truth there is only one mind." He suggests that at death "the veil of Maya," the deception of which makes us believe in a multiplicity of minds, will be lifted and we will realize that we are part of Brahman, the omnipresent, all-comprehending eternal self of Hinduism. Köstler believed that not only modern physics but also, and especially, the evidence of parapsychology support the view that there is a "psychic substratum," and "all-pervading mind-stuff," a "cosmic consciousness" out of which the "individual consciousnesses are formed and into which they dissolve again after three score years and ten."

It should be added that many Eastern reincarnationists combine both versions of survival belief. Hinduism teaches that after numerous incarnations individual minds will eventually be absorbed in Brahman, and Buddhists maintain that those who have lived sufficiently good lives will attain a state of enlightenment and reach Nirvana, which is not, as is frequently supposed, the absence of all consciousness, but a kind of Absolute or Cosmic Mind.

This book is primarily concerned with personal survival and there is next to no discussion of the impersonal variety. There are two reasons for this restriction. In the West, at least, those who believe or try to believe in survival because they find death and the world's injustice unbearable seem to derive comfort from the notion that they and those they care for will survive *as individuals*. With some notable exceptions, they seem to derive no comfort at all from the notion that they will be absorbed into the Absolute Mind when, at the same time, they will, in Köstler's phrase, become "depersonalized." Furthermore, while there is a vast literature offering arguments for belief in personal survival, there is next to nothing in the way of systematic defenses of impersonal survival. There is only one respect in which certain of our selections bear on the latter view. The mind–body dependence argument (selections 9, 10, and 33) would, if valid, not only rule out survival of a pure or disembodied individual mind, but equally that of a pure universal consciousness.

The last and most important preliminary distinction concerns what we may call the bearers or vehicles of survival. If a person is to survive after death there must be something in or relating to him that continues to be alive. It is important to distinguish between three vehicles. The first of these is the disembodied or pure mind. On this view a human being, while living on earth, is a body and a mind, and the mind will continue to exist after death without *any* body. This view has the support of several famous philosophers and of many of the more sophisticated religious believers. Plato certainly held this position and it also seems to have been the view of such diverse philosophers as Descartes, Locke, Kant, and Bergson. Some supporters of this view admit that life without any body may be an impoverished form of existence, but writers in the mystical tradition, who frequently despise matter in general and the human body (the "sinful flesh") in particular, teach the opposite. It is perhaps worth noting that many of the outstanding opponents of belief in survival (Hume and Russell for example) directed their criticisms at this conception, regarding the other versions as too absurd to warrant their attention.

The second vehicle of survival is the resurrected body. There are two significantly different versions of this view. On the more traditional and straightforward version, God will resurrect the very body that dies on the earth in much the same way as Jesus is said to have resurrected Lazarus. To avoid the obvious difficulties which such a position encounters, a number of philosophers and theologians maintain that God will create a new body. John Hick (selection 24) believes that this new body will be a replica of the one that died, but other theologians are not nearly so specific. In *I Corinthians*, chapter 15, St. Paul declares that the new "spiritual" body may differ from the physical one as much as a full grain of wheat differs from the wheat seed. In a well-known passage which was critically analyzed by Voltaire, Pascal also seemed to adopt the more sophisticated version of resurrectionism. "Is it more difficult," he asks, "to reproduce a man than to produce him at first?" Such a reproduction, he argued, is no more and no less miraculous than the creation of the universe, something that Voltaire disputed.

The third vehicle is the astral body. Until fairly recently few people other than the members of such esoteric cults as theosophy or anthroposophy had so much as heard of this vehicle, but with the occultist explosion of the last two decades the notions of the astral plane and astral projection have become quite familiar. Dr. Elisabeth Kübler-Ross's astral adventures have been described in some detail in such publications as *Newsweek* and Shirley MacLaine's best-selling books are full of reports of astral journeys. The basic idea is that human beings, contrary to what is usually believed, possess two bodies — the familiar physical body and also a "non-physical," "second" body that is the " 'double' or duplicate of the physical body." The last sentence is quoted from a programmatic article by Dr. Robert Crookall, a geologist by profession, who was probably the foremost astral theorist of the twentieth century. It is not easy to extract an intelligible explanation from the writings of astral believers of how the astral body is both "non-physical" and a double of the regular body. Perhaps one can construct something resembling a coherent account from the two kinds of evidence to which believers refer. The first of these are astral projections or out-of-body experiences (OBEs) in the course of which the person's regular body is in one place while his astral body is in another. During such projections the astral body is observed by the person himself but not by anybody else. The other evidence consists in the appearance of a person in two places at the same time. During these "bilocations" the astral body *is* publicly observable. It is maintained that after the death of their regular bodies, human beings will use their astral bodies as bearers of their consciousness. "For the first stage of our survival at least," to quote William Gerhardi, a prominent and much-admired novelist of the pre-War years, "we already have a body neatly folded away in our physical bodies, always at hand in case of death, or for special use."

Reincarnation and Karma

Traditional Western believers in survival, whether their vehicle is the pure mind or the resurrected body, have a special problem about just *where* one is supposed to survive. Believers in the disembodied mind are committed to the view that the next life does not occur anywhere. Pure minds do not occupy space and hence the next world cannot have any location. Even if some meaning can be attached to this statement, it is not easy to see that any worthwhile activities could be carried on in a "world" that is not in space. Believers in the resurrected body are not faced with this difficulty, but their problem — among many others — is to specify just where the resurrection world is located. Believers in reincarnation avoid this problem: survival takes place right here on earth and not in a world that has no location at all or in one whose location cannot be specified and which has never been seen or otherwise observed by anybody.

Reincarnation may be defined as the view that human beings do not, as most of us assume, live only once, but live many, perhaps an infinite number of times, acquiring a new body for each incarnation. An important difference between reincarnation and Western beliefs in survival is the view that human beings, or rather the souls that inhabit their bodies, did not have a beginning. Incarnations stretch infinitely into the past. In the *Bhagavad Gita*—which dates back to about 500 B.C. and thus precedes the rise of Buddhism—Krishna, the god of love, assures his as yet unenlightened companion Sanjaya that grief and sorrow are inappropriate emotions in relation to the death of somebody we loved. The reason is that a human being will live for ever and that "the eternal in man cannot die":

> We have all been for all time: I, and thou, and those kings of men. And we all shall be for all time, we all for ever and ever.

Belief in reincarnation comes in many forms. According to several Eastern versions the body from or into which a person migrates is not necessarily another human body: it can be that of an animal or a plant or even an inanimate object. Some nineteenth-century reincarnationists believed that sopranos were nightingales in a previous existence and that children with a talent for architecture had been beavers. The late Austrian conductor Herbert von Karajan did not claim to have been an animal in a previous life, but he was sure that he would return as an eagle. Bull terriers, the lovable little dogs whose noses look as though they had been bashed in, were probably prize fighters in a previous life and, as for New York City landlords, there can surely be no doubt that they once were sharks. According to a less fanciful version of the theory, human beings are incarnated only in human bodies. In the remainder of this discussion we shall concentrate on this latter version, but we will not entirely neglect its more imaginative alternative.

Most reincarnationists also believe that the universe is governed by the Law of Karma. This law maintains that the world is just, and justice is equated with retribution. Everything good that happens to a human being is a reward for some previous good deed, and everything bad is punishment for an evil deed. The following is the formulation of the Law of Karma by Rayner Johnson, a leading academic reincarnationist:

> Whatsoever a man sows, whether in the field of action or thought, sometime and somewhere the fruits of it will be reaped by him.

It is not of course denied that for many of their good acts human beings are not rewarded and for many of their evil deeds they are not punished in the present life, but in that case the appropriate rewards and punishments will come in a later life, just as the happiness and unhappiness in the present life are frequently rewards and punishments for deeds in earlier lives.

It is clear that one can believe in reincarnation without believing in Karma, but that the converse does not hold. To say that a human being will live again in other bodies does not by itself imply anything whatever about rewards and punishments. On the other hand, if somebody believes in Karma he must believe in reincarnation. For otherwise he could not account for the absence of any dependable correlation between the moral quality of acts on the one hand and rewards and punishments on the other. It would be difficult to find an Eastern believer who accepts reincarnation without also accepting Karma, but some of the best-known Western supporters of reincarnation (for example, the philosophers J. E. McTaggart and C. J. Ducasse, and Ian Stevenson, the psychiatrist whose research is claimed to have given reincarnation a scientific foundation) have not endorsed the Karmic doctrine.

It is evident that reincarnationists are committed to the controversial (but entirely respectable) philosophical theory known as "dualism." We already briefly met this theory when referring to the disembodied mind. If we include as dualists all those who agree that mental events and processes cannot be identified either with actual and possible behavior or with any bodily states or processes, then we may distinguish the more moderate variety, which holds that a person is *both* a mind and a body, from the extreme form, which maintains that a person *is* his mind and that the body is simply one of his possessions. It is clear that reincarnationists are committed to the latter of these views. A person's body is different in every incarnation, but he is the same since it is the same mind that animates all the different bodies. In the words of the *Bhagavad Gita*:

> As a man leaves an old garment and puts on the one that is new, the
> Spirit leaves his mortal body and then puts on one that is new.

Dualism is out of fashion at the moment, but there are still numerous philosophers who find it highly plausible. However, the *extreme* form of it to which reincarnationists are committed, is rejected by almost all contemporary philosophers; and if this extreme version is indeed untenable, reincarnation will have to be rejected along with it. We shall return to our discussion of the varieties of dualism in a later section.

The Case for Reincarnation

Undoubtedly some reincarnationists base their belief purely on faith. However, both Eastern and Western philosophers who have championed reincarnation maintain that their belief is based on solid evidence. It is asserted that reincarnation is the only theory which, in the words of the aforementioned Rayner Johnson, "carries with it the reasonable assurance that we live in a just world." In "Preexistence, Reincarnation and Karma" (selection 18) Dr. Johnson presents in some detail the argument for reincarnation based on the injustice found in the world. This argument is used by the great majority of the defenders of reincarnation, the more articulate and educated writers as well as the more primitive believers. It closely resembles the "moral" arguments for the existence of God and life after death found in Kant and numerous Christian and Jewish writers. I will not discuss it here because it is open to the same objections as the moral argument used by Western believers which will be considered in a later section (see pp. 63–64 below). In the remainder of this section I will concentrate on three more empirical lines of defense—the claim that certain well-known facts are best explained by the reincarnation-hypothesis, hypnotic regressions, and spontaneous memories of earlier lives, especially those studied by Ian Stevenson.

1. *Otherwise inexplicable empirical facts.* Reincarnationists constantly maintain that certain facts cannot be explained in terms of natural or, more specifically, biological causes. Only an explanation along reincarnationist lines is plausible. Existence in one or more previous lives is here advanced as an explanatory hypothesis. Since the structure of these arguments resembles that of many arguments in the sciences, it is tempting to call them "scientific," but since reincarnation is not a testable or falsifiable theory it would be more accurate to refer to them as "quasi-scientific." Among the facts frequently mentioned in this connection, by both Western and Eastern believers, are child geniuses like Mozart, Mendelssohn, and the Irish mathematician, William Hamilton; the so-called déjà vu experience; love at first sight; striking differences between children of the same parents; and many more.

In the case of some of the "otherwise inexplicable" facts, for example the déjà vu experience, it is by no means true that science has not been able to shed any light on them, but it may be granted that some of them have so far eluded anything like an adequate scientific explanation. Needless to say, this does not mean that they *cannot* be explained in terms of natural causes. Surely we have no grounds for supposing that in order to explain the extraordinary gifts of men like Mozart or Hamilton we have to go outside a study of the human brain. It should be remembered that in spite of the impressive progress of recent years, brain research is still in its infancy. Very few brain researchers have any serious doubts that with further improvements in our instruments we will be able to shed much light on these problems. It seems entirely plausible, for example, that Mozart's auditory cortex was in certain ways significantly different from that of people lacking his gifts. To foreclose further research in this area would be an utterly defeatist procedure. To substitute an explanation in terms of the acquisition of musical skill in an earlier life would be like abandoning medical research into the causes of cancer and substituting theological speculation on the ground that medical science has so far provided us with only a very limited understanding of cancer.

Reincarnationists are in the habit of talking very vaguely about the soul's acquiring skills and knowledge in a previous life and taking these along into the next incarnation. One must pin them down and inquire about the mechanics of this transmission. Let us assume that, before it came to inhabit the body of Wolfgang Amadeus, the soul of Mozart lived in the body of Heinrich Klapper and that it was during this incarnation that it acquired the knowledge passed on to the Mozart body. Reincarnationists who are not altogether lost to some fantastic form of occultism will admit that the transmission from the Klapper to the Mozart body must have occurred via the brain and nervous system of the new embryo. If they admit this they have tacitly admitted that Mozart's special ability was due to certain features of his brain that are not present in the brains of most other human beings. This does not, of course, show that reincarnation is false or, more specifically, that Mozart did not have a previous life. It does show that genetic causes are sufficient to explain Mozart's special gifts. It should be added that the authors of the quasi-scientific arguments evidently work with a pre-Mendelian, "common sense" theory of genetics that holds that all features in an offspring must have been exhibited in one or both parents. They do not seem to have heard either of recessive genes or of mutations.

2. *Hypnotic past-life regressions.* The general public is probably not familiar with any alleged evidence for reincarnation except the recollection of previous lives by hypnotic subjects. Such regressions are most impressive when the subject displays knowledge of historical details which—so it would seem—he could not have learned through normal channels.

This topic has been studied by a number of psychologists and it is now generally agreed that all such regressions are instances of what is known as cryptomnesia, or source amnesia, in which the hypnotic subjects did obtain their knowledge through normal channels but forgot the source. When they are rehypnotized and asked about the source, they usually reveal it without any resistance. Harold Rosen, a Canadian psychiatrist, describes the case of a patient who, under hypnosis, started writing in Oscan, a language spoken in Western Italy up to the first century B.C. The patient denied having ever seen the words he had written and also insisted that he had never so much as heard of Oscan. When rehypnotized, however, he recalled sitting in the library while somebody next to him opened a book on a page which contained the Oscan "Curse of Vibia." It was this Oscan curse that he had reproduced. Numerous similar cases are on record, one of them, that of Blanche Poynings, going back to 1906. It was investigated for the British Society for Psychical Research by the well-known classical scholar G. Lowes Dickinson who, after considerable effort, traced his subject's remarkably detailed knowledge of the personalities at the court of Richard II to her reading of a historical novel as a child. As a result of the work of Lowes Dickinson and the more recent research of

Edwin S. Zolik of Marquette University, the Finnish psychiatrist Reima Kampman, and the British television producer Melvin Harris, this phenomenon has been completely demystified. There is every reason to believe that the famous case of Bridey Murphy, which caused great excitement in the 1950s, was just such an instance of cryptomnesia.

3. *Spontaneous memories of past incarnations and the work of Ian Stevenson.* Throughout the ages claims have been made by or on behalf of certain individuals that they could recall previous lives. These memories or ostensible memories differ from hypnotic regressions in that they occur to the persons in their waking lives and are not provoked by artificial stimuli. "I have been born many times, Arjuna," says Krishna in the *Bhagavad Gita*,

> and many times hast thou been born. But I remember my past lives and thou hast forgotten thine.

It is widely believed by Buddhists that yogis have the power to remember entire past lives, namely, those in which they inhabited a human body. In his preface to the fourth edition of the *Tibetan Book of the Dead*, the editor, an American anthropologist by the name of W. Y. Evans-Wentz, who was a convert to Buddhism, insists that the belief in reincarnation need not be taken on faith. On the contrary, it has a "sound basis" in the "unequivocal testimony of yogis who claim to have died and reentered the human womb consciously." Similarly, Swami Nikhilananda, the able and well-informed editor of an abridged version of the *Upanishads*, rejects the theory of annihilation partly because it is inconsistent with "the intuitive and direct experience of the seers regarding the indestructibility of the soul." Not only yogis and "seers" but also emperors, poets, philosophers, and mystics are alleged to have remembered previous lives. The list usually includes Pythagoras, Empedocles, Ovid, Julian the Apostate, Swedenborg, Goethe, and Alexander Dumas Fils. On investigation most of these stories turn out to be false and, where the individuals really made assertions about a previous life, these could not be checked for their accuracy. They are therefore devoid of scientific value.

It is widely believed, however, that Ian Stevenson's studies of certain spontaneous memories do provide scientific evidence for reincarnation. Stevenson, a Canadian psychiatrist who has been associated with the University of Virginia medical school for over thirty years, is a major figure in parapsychology. He has occasionally written on topics other than reincarnation, but his fame rests on his reincarnation research. In his early publications he did not take a definite stand, but in more recent years he has come out as an ardent supporter of reincarnation. It should be remarked that he is an excellent writer and that the presentation of his cases is always lucid, systematic, and detailed. It will hardly come as a surprise that Stevenson has become a hero to believers in reincarnation all over the world. It is difficult to pick up a book or pamphlet defending reincarnation and published in the last twenty years or so that does not refer admiringly to Stevenson's work. What may be surprising is that his work has been praised and some of it also published in respectable journals. Reviewing the first volume of his *Cases of the Reincarnation Type*, the *Journal of the American Medical Association* praised his "painstakingly and unemotionally collected cases from India in which the evidence is difficult to explain on any assumption other than reincarnation." Two of Stevenson's articles were published in *Journal of Nervous and Mental Disease* whose editor, Eugene Brody, proudly told the *New York Post* that he had received three or four hundred requests for reprints from scientists in every discipline. In the volume *Psychic Voyages* in the Time-Life series on the occult — *Mysteries of the Unknown* (1987) — Stevenson's work is treated with great respect.

The bulk of Stevenson's cases which concern small children have a fairly uniform pattern. Between the ages of two and four these children usually begin making statements about coming from a home and place different from the one in which they are living. They recall altogether different parents and most of them speak of having lived as adolescents and adults. Some also recall their death, often a violent one, in their preceding life. Children vary greatly in the quantity of their utterances and the richness of the details they recall. The volume and clarity of the statements usually increase until between the ages of five and six. After that there is less and less mention of a previous life and by the age of eight the memories have in most cases faded completely. During the period when the children remember their earlier lives they often behave in strange ways. This strange behavior, according to Stevenson, is consistent with the character and occupation of the remembered person. In several cases, which form the subject matter of his books, there has been extensive corroboration. Research shows that the persons the children remember having been did in fact exist and many, although usually not all, descriptions of the experiences, acts, and relationships turn out to be correct. This at least is what Stevenson maintains, and if one reads his books and articles without knowing what the critics have to say, one can hardly fail to be impressed.

Stevenson repeatedly refers to himself as a scientist, but in handling criticisms of his research he does not act as a scientist should. He has never answered the more significant objections and he makes it a practice not even to mention their existence. *Children Who Remember Previous Lives* (1987), a summary of his work and a philosophical defense of reincarnation, contains a huge bibliography but not one item by any of his opponents. In the following remarks I will summarize four of the major criticisms.

1. Ian Wilson has emphasized that Stevenson generally dismisses on the flimsiest grounds the possibility of fraud on the part of the children, their parents, and other interested parties. Stevenson maintains that no motive for fraud exists, when such motives are only too evident. Wilson has pointed out that several of the children remembered belonging to a higher caste in their previous lives and seem to have been motivated by a wish for better living conditions. In one case, for example, a boy asked for one-third of the land of his past-life "father," but abruptly lost interest in his previous incarnation when this former father lost his fortune and became poorer than his father in the present life. Wilson also calls attention to the fact that Stevenson invariably tells us exceedingly little about the character and background of the parents, who are usually vital informants. In many cases, too, there was or easily could have been contact between the parents and persons connected with the "previous personality" about whose life the child had accurate recollections. The same criticism is found in an article by William G. Roll, a leading figure in American parapsychology, who, unlike Ian Wilson, is an admirer of Stevenson's work. Roll notes that in only seven of Stevenson's cases were the children's statements about previous lives recorded before the attempts at verification. Stevenson has himself admitted that where this is not done, subsequent developments may lead to embellishments of what the child is supposed to have said. Yet, in all these seven cases, the children lived "within the geographical or social circumference of the previous personality." This means that there could easily have been contact between the child's parents and the family of the dead individual whose personality is supposed to have surfaced in the child.

2. One of Stevenson's foremost critics is Professor Chari, an Indian philosopher who taught at Madras Christian University and who is not a Western materialist or positivist but a Hindu and a well-known parapsychologist. Chari does not reject reincarnation, but he believes that Stevenson is incredibly naive and that his reports have no evidential value. In a number of articles Chari has given us some insight into the way Indian cases "suggestive of reincarnation" are manufactured. He pointed out that cases of the kind Stevenson has collected occur mostly in cultures in which there is a deeply ingrained belief in reincarnation and, what is equally significant, in which the *type* of reincarnation claimed fits in with the form of reincarnation belief prevalent in a given area. Chari has himself studied cases quite similar to those reported by Stevenson and regards them as cultural artifacts, pure and simple. Chari proceeds to lament the "generally lax" standards of evidence prevailing in India. "Few bother about rigorous proofs of rebirth which is a cultural commitment (*pace* Stevenson) even without proofs."

3. Chari's conclusion is corroborated by the experiences of David Read Barker. Barker has a doctorate in anthropology and did the re-

search for his dissertation in India. Stevenson hired Barker to assist him in the analysis of some of his cases and also to investigate other cases in conjunction with Satwant Pasricha, a true and tried believer and disciple. Barker could not find a single case in which there was convincing evidence of the presence of a paranormal process. Two published items by Barker are relevant to our discussion. One of these is a letter in the *Journal of Parapsychology* (1979). The other is a joint publication with Pasricha, dealing with the case of Rakesh Gaur, in the *European Journal of Parapsychology* in 1981. In the letter, Barker described the Gaur case as "the most authentic, evidential and thoroughly investigated" of fifty-nine cases he had studied with Pasricha, and he concluded that it is "best interpreted as a result of Indian social psychology rather than parapsychology." There is no space to give an account of the 1981 article. It is most instructive because the case in question is so similar to those reported by Stevenson himself and because it describes in detail how the "verifications" of the child's memories were obtained.

4. Barker's two communications appeared in extremely specialized journals whose very existence is likely to be unknown to most of Stevenson's readers. Credit for calling attention to them belongs to Scott Rogo who, although himself a believer in reincarnation, is skeptical of the value of much of Stevenson's work. In the same book in which he quotes Barker's conclusions (*The Search for Yesterday*, 1985), Rogo also mentions the so-called Ransom report. He revealed that in the early 1970s Stevenson hired a lawyer by the name of Champe Ransom to assist him in the analysis of his data. According to Rogo, Ransom soon became highly critical of Stevenson's research methods. Rogo admitted that he had not been able to obtain a copy of Ransom's report but offered a description of its contents, which he conceded was based on hearsay. I mentioned Rogo's account in part 4 of my series on reincarnation, published in *Free Inquiry* in 1986–1987. To my surprise and pleasure Ransom turned out to be a reader of *Free Inquiry*. He kindly sent me a copy of his report which, with his consent, I plan to publish as an appendix to a book on reincarnation on which I am working. In a letter published in *Free Inquiry* (Fall 1987), Ransom wrote:

My experience as a research assistant at the Division of Parapsychology at the University of Virginia from 1970 to 1973 was an interesting but painful one. Eventually, I became disillusioned, mostly because of the zealous attitude of the researchers (as opposed to a more balanced one), the defensive attitude toward outside skepticism, and the weakness of the evidence. The more thoroughly I studied an alleged paranormal event, the less likely a paranormal explanation seemed right.

The following is a summary of Ransom's report supplied by him for the present volume:

The Report lists and discusses a number of methodological flaws in Stevenson's research. Three notable ones are that leading questions were asked, that the questioning period for each witness was quite brief, and that the time that elapsed between the alleged occurrence of an event and the investigation of it was quite long, frequently years. In addition, the Report details problems with Stevenson's reporting of the cases. Such problems include his presenting the conclusions of witnesses rather than the observational data that led them to their conclusions, and his failure to discuss any weaknesses in a witness's report except in a separate part of the book. (And even there weaknesses are discussed in a way that does not clearly refer back to individual cases.) Stevenson's cases then do not amount to even halfway decent evidence. In only 11 of the approximately 1,111 rebirth cases had there been no contact between the two families before an investigation was begun. Of those 11, seven were seriously flawed in some respect. What this means is that in the great majority of cases, the two families had met years before a scientific investigation began, and that the likelihood of independent testimony was quite small. The rebirth cases are anecdotal evidence of the weakest sort.

Although Rogo's account of the details of Ransom's report was mistaken, he was not at all wrong in suggesting that it undermines Stevenson's pretense of having provided genuinely scientific evidence for reincarnation.

The Case Against Reincarnation

It is one thing to say that there is no good evidence for reincarnation. It is another to maintain that reincarnation should be rejected as a false or perhaps an incoherent theory. In this section we shall look at some of the arguments which, if they are sound, would show that reincarnation is untenable. The first three arguments maintain that reincarnation is incompatible with certain obvious or well-established facts. The other considerations are of a more purely philosophical kind.

1. *Tertullian's objection.* This is a very simple argument and was concisely and forcefully stated by the early Church Father Tertullian (c. 160–220) in Chapter 31 of his *Treatise on the Soul* (*see* selection 3). "How happens it," he asks there, "that a man who dies in old age returns to life as an infant?" Whoever continues life in a new body might be expected to "return with the age he had attained at his death, that he might resume the precise life which he had relinquished." If "souls depart at different ages of human life," Tertullian continues, "how is it that they come back again at one uniform age?" John Hick, a Christian theologian who believes in the resurrection of the body (*see* selection 24) but who at the same time has a sympathetic interest in reincarnation, endorses this objection, pointing out that babies are not born with adult egos "as they would be if they were direct continuations of egos which had died at the end of a normal lifespan."

2. *Evolution and the recency of life.* It is difficult to see how reincarnation can be reconciled with evolutionary theory. In the first place, evolution teaches that the human race descends from nonhuman species and that there was a time when human bodies did not exist. However, the more sober version of reincarnationism with which we are primarily concerned here is committed to an infinite series of past incarnations in *human* bodies. Furthermore, evolution teaches that our consciousness developed gradually along with the brain and the nervous system. Reincarnationists are committed to holding that no *such* development occurred because it is the same soul that migrated from body to body. They may indeed concede that there has been *some* development—that some souls have gradually grown kinder and wiser and better informed. However, this is not the kind of development postulated by evolutionary theory. It may be thought that the wilder form of reincarnation which holds that human souls may have been incarnated in animal bodies escapes this objection. This is not so. Reincarnationists defending this version do *not* teach that the sequence of bodies in which a soul is incarnated is in any way parallel to the sequence postulated by evolutionists. A human being can become a dog or a gnat and, conversely, the soul may most recently have been in the body of a nightingale or a beaver.

Reincarnation is also inconsistent with what science has discovered about the relative recency of life. It is now generally accepted that for many billions of years after the Big Bang the universe contained no life at all. However, all forms of reincarnation postulate a series of incarnations stretching back into the past without limit. Pythagoras and the founders of Eastern religions can hardly be blamed for not knowing the science of the nineteenth and twentieth centuries, but this does not make the objection any less cogent.

3. *The population problem.* The next objection is based on the well-established fact that the human population of the earth has shown enormous increases throughout recorded history. In an article published in the July–August 1981 issue of *BioScience*, Arthur H. Westing of Amherst summarized the best available information about the number of human beings alive at various times. At the time at which he wrote, the population was estimated at 4.4 billion. In 1945 it had been 2.3 billion; in 1850, 1 billion; in 1650, 500 million; at the time of Christ, 200 million; and in 8000 B.C., approximately 5 million. Among other interesting calculations, Westing estimated that the 1981 population of 4.4 billion amounted to 9 percent of all human beings who ever lived, and that it was greater than the number of people who lived through the entire Paleolithic age, a period accounting for 86 percent of the duration of human life. It should be added that in spite of famines and wars the same trend has continued since 1981. According to figures supplied by the United Nations the earth's population reached 4.8

billion at the end of 1985, and on July 7, 1986, it passed the 5 billion mark. If current trends continue, the total human population will be 10 billion by the year 2016.

Most Eastern versions of reincarnationism teach that new souls are never added to the world. All souls have always existed. Every birth is a *rebirth*—the rebirth of a soul that has already existed. Reincarnationists who maintain that some souls are eventually allowed to give up their earthly existence and merge into the Absolute or Nirvana are committed to the view that in the long run the population must *decrease*. Other reincarnationists imply that the population is stationary. In either case, whether committed to a stationary or decreasing population, reincarnationism appears to be refuted by population statistics.

It is noteworthy that this argument has hardly ever been explicitly discussed by any of the academically respectable reincarnationists. One suspects that the reason for this is the great difficulty of finding an answer that would strike a sober person as even remotely credible. The less inhibited reincarnationists, however, have attacked the population argument with relish. Morey Bernstein, author of *The Search for Bridey Murphy*, has an easy answer. We can dispose of the objection by bringing in the population of the astral world:

> The total number of entities both in this and the afterworld can remain the same while the balance shifts between the numbers of entities on earth and the number in the unseen world.

V. F. Gunaratna, a Buddhist philosopher, reminds us that animals or gods may turn into human beings and the late K. N. Jayatilleke, another Buddhist philosopher, who had a master's degree from Cambridge, a doctorate from the University of London, and who was an admirer of A. J. Ayer, offers the reflection that the population increase may well be due to invasions of human embryos by souls from other planets.

Ian Stevenson has discussed this problem both in the article "Some Questions Related to Cases of the Reincarnation Type" and in *Children Who Remember Previous Lives*. In the former, published in 1974, he poses as neutral observer and remarks that if "the recent increase in the world's population" continues it will bring "difficulties for the reincarnation hypothesis." Since 1974 the increases have continued at an enormously accelerated pace, but this has not prevented Stevenson from becoming an ever more ardent believer. In the book that was published in 1987 he lists a number of "assumptions" that would dispose of the problem. The first such assumption is that "new individual human minds are created as needed and attached to human bodies." Stevenson tells us nothing about how or why these minds are created —do they simply come into existence without any cause or are they produced by a supernatural being? And why should so many new minds have been created in recent times? Apparently anything is better than the simple biological explanation adopted by most people in Western countries. The other "assumptions" Stevenson mentions are identical with those favored by such writers as Bernstein and Gunaratna. It may be that "minds presently incarnated in human bodies have been promoted from incarnation in non-human bodies." Another assumption is that "human minds may split or duplicate so that one mind can reincarnate in two or more bodies." The assumption Stevenson discusses most fully and which he seems to favor is that the interval between death and rebirth is not fixed but, on the contrary, "fluctuates from time to time." There may have been a period "when few minds were incarnated and many more were existing in the discarnate state, waiting for terrestrial incarnation, or perhaps hoping to avoid one." During a period when the interval is very great, "many discarnate minds may be awaiting reincarnation and could thus contribute to an even greater increase in the world's population than we have seen during the last two centuries."

The answer to all these solutions of the population problem is that they involve what may be called "noxious" *ad hoc* assumptions. Not all *ad hoc* assumptions are automatically objectionable, and it will be worthwhile to explain the distinction between those that are and those that are not. All of us constantly make perfectly reasonable *ad hoc* assumptions in everyday life and occasionally *ad hoc* assumptions have proved highly fruitful in the history of science. One of the most celebrated cases of this kind is the discovery of the planet Neptune. By the beginning of the nineteenth century Newtonian celestial mechanics enabled astronomers to calculate the orbits of most of the planets with very great accuracy. The orbits of two planets, however, those of Uranus and Mercury, defied all their calculations. To explain the discrepancy between the calculated and the observed orbits of Uranus, two astronomers, John Adams (1819–1892) and Urbain Leverrier (1811–1877), postulated the existence of a new planet having a certain size, shape, mass, and position in the sky. This was an *ad hoc* hypothesis in the sense that it was not based on any direct evidence and that its purpose was to "save" the Newtonian theory, that is, to retain it in spite of observations that seemed to contradict it. In 1846 Leverrier requested the Berlin astronomer Johann Galle to carry out the appropriate telescopic observations, and the result was the discovery of Neptune, one of the so-called giant planets with a mean diameter of approximately 28,000 miles and a mass 17.2 times that of Earth. The Adams-Leverrier hypothesis of a new planet was not "noxiously" *ad hoc* for two reasons: the theory that it was meant to save was itself powerfully supported by a vast array of observations and, although *ad hoc*, it was independently testable.

By contrast, the various rejoinders to the population argument are "noxiously" *ad hoc* because reincarnationism, unlike Newtonian mechanics, is not a theory for which there is powerful observational evidence and because the assumptions that are introduced are either, like mass immigrations from the astral world, not even in principle testable or, as in the case of population reductions on other planets, so vague as not to be testable in practice.

4. *The interregnum.* The difficulties mentioned so far are mild compared with the problems besetting reincarnationists in connection with what might be called the "interregnum"—the period between incarnations. The great majority of reincarnationists teach that death is not immediately followed by rebirth. The question at once arises as to just where and how people spend the interregnum and, more specifically, what they are like between incarnations.

There appear to be only two possible answers and neither is very alluring. The first is to say that a person exists as a disembodied or pure mind until he finds or chooses his new body. Such a position is faced with a number of serious logical and empirical problems which will be discussed later. There is also of course the question of how a pure mind, devoid of sense organs, could ever locate or choose the mother of his next incarnation.

The only alternative to the pure mind seems to be some sort of astral body; and this is in fact the view preferred by most reincarnationists. It is, for example, the position adopted in the *Tibetan Book of the Dead*, one of the sacred books of India, and a work much admired by such diverse figures as C. G. Jung, Paul Tillich, Stanislav Grof, Timothy Leary, and Raymond Moody, Jr. The *Tibetan Book* is primarily concerned with descriptions of the intermediate or "Bardo" world, and it offers detailed advice about how a person is to comport himself there. In the Bardo world human beings possess a "Bardo" body which is identical with the astral body or at least a close cousin. W. Y. Evans-Wentz, the editor of the English language version of the *Tibetan Book* whom we quoted earlier, describes the Bardo body as "an exact duplicate of the human body, from which it is separated in the process of death." It is "formed" of an unusual kind of matter, one that is invisible and "ethereal-like." The Bardo body, furthermore, possesses two of the supernatural attributes usually associated with astral travel. It can go anywhere instantaneously and it can pass through material objects as if they did not exist. The Bardo body cannot be perceived by live human beings, but at least for a short period after death it can see and hear "all the weeping and wailing of friends and relatives," although "they cannot hear him calling upon them." Substantially the same view is adopted by Ian Stevenson who is emphatic that the bearer of consciousness in the interregnum is a "non-physical body" and who believes that this body is composed of "some kind of matter," but a matter which "must be . . . quite different from what we ordinarily mean by the term." We shall see in the next section that there are overwhelmingly strong reasons for believing that no such entity exists. If a theory has to fall back on the introduction of something like the astral or Bardo body, this is sufficient to condemn it.

5. *The dependence of consciousness on the brain of the current body.* Some reincarnationists pride themselves on the empirical nature of their theory when it is compared with belief in the survival of the disembodied mind. The latter is said to clash with our experience that consciousness is found only in conjunction with certain physical entities, namely animal and human bodies. By contrast, the reincarnation theory accords perfectly well with this fact: although an individual's consciousness is connected with different bodies in different incarnations, it does always have a bodily substratum. A little reflection shows that this is an illusory advantage. If the mind–body dependence argument (pp. 51–53) is valid, it shows more than that a person's consciousness cannot exist without *a brain*; it shows that it cannot exist without the *current* brain, and this refutes reincarnation no less than the belief in the survival of the disembodied mind.

The Astral Body

In first introducing the notion of the astral body we briefly referred to the two kinds of evidence offered by believers in the astral body — bilocations and "astral projections," or out-of-body experiences (OBEs). It has been reported about a number of saints that they could appear in several places at the same time. Thus St. Anthony of Padua, whose sermon to the fishes has been immortalized in one of Gustav Mahler's *Wunderhorn* songs, knelt to pray on Holy Thursday of 1226 in the Church of St. Pierre du Queyrrix at Limoges and at that very moment also appeared at the other end of the town at another service. Sister Maria Coronel de Agreda, a seventeenth-century Spanish nun who modestly doubted her own gifts, had telepathic powers, was able to levitate, and experienced no less than five hundred bilocations. Just as saints and other members of religious orders no longer levitate, so they also have not engaged in bilocations in more recent centuries, but several secular cases have been reported during the past hundred and fifty years. One of those most frequently mentioned in the literature concerns Mme. Sagée, a schoolteacher in nineteenth-century France. Soon after her appointment, according to Crookall's account, rumors circulated that she had been seen far from the classroom where she was teaching. On one occasion when she was writing on the blackboard, Crookall writes, "all the girls saw not only her physical body but also her 'double' which made the same gestures." Perhaps the most distressing event occurred when she was helping to dress one of the girls, standing behind her. The girl happened to glance in the mirror and saw not one but two Mme. Sagées. She promptly fainted. After numerous complaints by parents the school authorities dismissed the luckless teacher. Some of these stories are delightful but unfortunately none of them is supported by proper documentation. The one case — that of Mr. and Mrs. Wilmot in nineteenth-century America — which on the face of it had impressive backing from eye-witnesses, totally collapsed when it was investigated by Susan Blackmore.

Bilocations are a myth. OBEs cannot be dismissed in the same way. They are quite real, but the question is whether they are evidence for the astral body. The term *"out-of-body experience"* has been simply and clearly defined by Blackmore as referring to "an experience in which one seems to perceive the world from a location outside the physical body." There is no question that many people in many countries at many different times have had such experiences. These experiences have certain common features reminiscent of the Bardo body of the *Tibetan Book of the Dead*: the person can travel at great speed and he can penetrate material objects like walls, roofs, and human bodies as if they were not there. Dr. Kübler-Ross, one of the outstanding astral travelers of our time, who has reported extraordinary journeys to the outer reaches of space, claims to have traveled at speeds greater than light. This remarkable feat conflicts with Einstein's special theory of relativity, which will presumably have to be abandoned. More modest travelers, who may have heard of Einstein's theory, merely claim that their speed was enormous. Certain further characteristics asserted to belong to all OBEs, both by Crookall and other astral theorists, are not in fact universal. By no means all subjects report that their vehicle was a duplicate of their regular human body. Celia Green, in her book *Out-of-Body Experiences*, reports many cases in which the person perceived himself as a blob or globe, a flare or a point of light, or in which he simply "looks" at his original body and has no sense of possessing another one in the place from which he is looking. Some astral travelers have reported seeing an extremely elastic silver cord connecting the astral body to the sleeping physical body. Many astral theorists also believe that, if the silver cord or "astral cable" is broken, the person must die. When a person dies, the cord breaks and this enables the astral body to leave for other regions. The supposed universality of the observation of the silver cord during OBEs has frequently been cited as conclusive evidence that they cannot be hallucinations. For this reason it should be emphasized that many reports of OBEs are on record without mention of a silver cord or, for that matter, any connecting link. Many of Celia Green's subjects do not report such a cord, and no astral cable appears in many of the OBEs reported in other cultures.

To speak of OBEs as "astral projections" is tendentiously misleading. It suggests that the only possible explanation of OBEs is the theory that a human being has a double and that it is this double which travels to the location from which the person believes himself to be perceiving the world. Susan Blackmore, who has probably studied the subject more exhaustively than anybody else, lists a number of possible explanations and treats the theory of the astral body as just one and in many ways the least plausible of the competing theories. If, as we shall see shortly, this theory can be independently shown to be absurd, it would at once be ruled out of court.

To most people who have not been caught up in the occult the notion of the astral body seems sheer lunacy, and reflection shows this impression to be entirely correct. One simple consideration relates to the clothes worn by astral travelers, whether they are engaged in a bilocation or merely in an OBE. I am not aware of a single case of bilocation in which an astral double was observed without clothes. When St. Anthony of Padua preached in two different churches in Limoges at the same time, he was wearing his usual clerical robes during both sermons. As for Mme. Sagée, the nineteenth-century French bilocationist, she surely shocked her students sufficiently by appearing in two places without being naked in either of her apparitions. In some reports of OBEs, in which the traveler's astral body is not publicly observable, the double was naked, but in most of them it did wear garments just like those worn by regular bodies. Now, the clothes worn by astral bodies cannot be ordinary, physical clothes: the astral bodies lack the solidity that would keep the clothes in place. The only alternative seems to be that they are astral clothes, but where are astral clothes manufactured and how do they suddenly appear on the scene when a bilocation or a private OBE occurs? Crookall and several leading theosophists were prepared to embrace the view that there are indeed astral duplicates of our clothes, as of all other regular physical objects, but this purely *ad hoc* assumption is not likely to commend itself to the sane segments of the human race.

Another problem for the astral believer is that of synchronization between the regular and the astral body. It will be remembered that the astral body is supposed to be an exact duplicate of the regular body. If the astral body leaves the regular body of a boy aged ten, it will look just like the boy looks then; if it leaves the body of the same person at the age of eighty, it will look like the regular body at the age of eighty. The astral bodies of men will look like the regular bodies of men and the astral bodies of women like the regular bodies of women. If a boxer has just been punched in the face resulting in a flattened nose and the loss of three front teeth, his astral body will show the same flattened nose and the same gap in his mouth. If the boxer retires and eats a great deal so that he becomes enormously fat, his astral body too will be enormous. If a woman in her prime, with soft and unblemished skin, were to take an astral trip, the skin of her astral body would be soft and unblemished. However, if the same woman were to take a trip many years later when her skin has become parched and wrinkled, this would also be true of her astral double. Astral believers prefer to state their theory in very general terms and usually flinch when such specific consequences are derived from it, but there is no doubt at all that these and similar statements about the appearance of astral doubles are really implied by the theory.

Now, the question that at once arises is how this exact synchronization is achieved. Except when it is released for a journey, the astral body resides inside the regular body. However, the exact state of the regular body at any given time is very largely the result of its movements and of influences upon it coming from its environment. To secure the synchronization required by astral theory we must postulate that corresponding to every physical act and movement there occurs an astral act and movement: corresponding to every ordinary breath, every normal meal, every physical exertion, every conversation, every injury, there must occur a corresponding astral process. Surely no sane person can believe that this happens. One would think that while it is safely tucked away inside the regular body, the astral body cannot do anything at all. But this is not all. One of the key propositions of astral theory makes most external influences on the astral body quite impossible. I am referring to all events in the person's life involving physical contact. According to the believer, the astral body cannot touch or be touched by another body, physical or astral. When our prize fighter had his nose flattened and three of his teeth knocked out, the corresponding damage to his astral body was not possible. Similarly, insofar as eating involves physical contact between various parts of the body and the food consumed, it cannot have an astral counterpart, and there is no way of explaining how the astral body becomes enormous if the regular body overeats.

Let us for the sake of argument assume that the objections just mentioned can somehow be answered and that all human beings possess astral doubles. A little reflection will show that the astral double cannot help the case of survival. Astral philosophy teaches that, except for its "lack of solidity," the astral body is an *exact* double of the regular one. Without this assumption the theory would not explain the facts — or alleged facts — of bilocation. However, if the astral body is an exact duplicate of the regular body it must die along with the regular body. This entirely reasonable conclusion seems to have escaped all astral theorists. If the secular body died as the result of a brain tumor or as the result of being shot through the heart, the astral brain and the astral heart must have been similarly injured. It is evident that if a person is to survive death he will need some other vehicle.

Dualism and Materialism

If the astral body is eliminated from further consideration we are left with two possible vehicles of survival: the disembodied mind and the resurrected body. Believers in survival of the disembodied mind are committed to dualism, a theory to which we have referred on several occasions. If dualism is true it does not by any means follow that human beings survive as disembodied minds or in any way whatever. The question, however, then remains open. If dualism is false, on the other hand, the theory of disembodied survival does not even get off the ground.

The most important alternative to dualism has always been a theory, or rather a family of theories, known as materialism which maintains that a person *is* his body and that what we call his mind is really a name for certain bodily phenomena. "Body am I entirely and nothing more," wrote Nietzsche, whose materialism is rarely mentioned in accounts of his philosophy, and " 'soul' is only the name of something in the body." According to Lucretius, who states not only his own view but also that of Democritus and Epicurus, the mind consists of atoms (selection 2). These atoms are finer and more mobile than the gross atoms which make up the rest of the world, but they are just as physical. According to Hobbes, the feeling of pleasure is "nothing really but motion about the heart, as conception is nothing but motion in the head." David Hartley (1705–1757), the founder of associationist psychology, whose materialism was wholeheartedly accepted by both Godwin and Shelley, maintained that sensations and thoughts consisted of vibrations of "medullary particles" in the brain. The "Idéologues," a group of French philosophers and scientists of the late eighteenth and nineteenth centuries (including such famous scientists as Lavoisier and La Place), held that the study of man must be reduced to physics and physiology. Human beings should be studied by the same methods used in the study of minerals and vegetables. "Just as the stomach and intestines are destined to operate digestion, the liver to filter bile, the parotid and maxillary glands to prepare the salivary juices," wrote Pierre Cabanis, one of the leaders of the Idéologues, "so the brain performs organically the secretion of thought." It may be noted in passing that Charles Darwin subscribed to the same view. "Why is thought being a secretion of the brain more wonderful than gravity a property of matter?," Darwin wrote in his private notebooks, which were not published until 1982. "It is our arrogance and admiration of ourselves," he went on, which keeps us from acknowledging the opposite. Echoing Cabanis, the nineteenth-century German biologist Carl Vogt wrote that "the relation between thought and the brain is roughly of the same order as that between bile and the liver or urine and the bladder." One obvious trouble with such theories is that while bile and urine can be seen, weighed and even bottled, this is unfortunately not possible in the case of the secretion called "thought."

One of the most radical forms of materialism which flourished in Great Britain and the United States during the years after the Second World War and in Central Europe a little earlier, is known as "logical" or "philosophical" behaviorism. A view of this kind was advanced in Gilbert Ryle's *Concept of Mind* and it was supported by the "left wing" of the logical positivists, notably Rudolf Carnap, Otto Neurath and Carl Hempel. The main idea of this theory is that psychological predicates —such expressions as "being frightened of dogs," "believing in God," "hating socialism,"—refer to the actual and possible behavior of human beings; and this behavior is of course publicly observable. To say that a given individual hates socialism is not a statement about his "inner" feelings, accessible only to himself, but about what he says and does and what he would say and do in various circumstances. It should be noted in passing that "psychological" behaviorists are not committed to this view. They do not, as a rule, deny the existence of "inner" mental states, but hold the less extreme view that a *scientific* psychology should concern itself exclusively with behavior. The statements of some psychological behaviorists suggest that they are really dualists, admitting the *existence* of mental states but denying that these states have any effect on human behavior.

A contemporary highly influential version of materialism, usually referred to as the "identity theory," also known as "central state materialism" and somewhat facetiously as the "Australian Heresy" (because two of its foremost exponents, J. J. C. Smart and David Armstrong, teach at Australian universities) maintains that sensations, and mental states and processes generally, are identical with states and processes of the brain. The contention is not merely that mental states are uniformly correlated with brain states—this is something a dualist can consistently admit—but that the two are identical. The authors of the theory emphasize that they do not assert a *logical* identity of sensations and brain processes but rather a *de facto* or empirical identity. Psychological and physicalistic predicates do not have the same significance or connotation but they have the same reference or denotation. Although they differ in meaning, experience shows that they refer to the same thing in much the same way as experience shows that the morning star is identical with the evening star or water with H_2O. As a parallel, Herbert Feigl (a well-known supporter of the theory) mentions the case of two explorers climbing the same mountain from different sides. We may suppose that they are in radio contact and that they are sending to each other very accurate descriptions of the mountain as it appears from their respective positions. The visual appearances may be so different that they believe to be climbing different mountains. Finally, however, when they meet on the top they realize that it was one and the same mountain all the time. In much the same way a person's sensations or dreams may be identical with brain processes, although what the individual experiences and what a brain physiologist would see are altogether different. On this view, the dualist is quite right in asserting that introspection discloses certain facts to us, but he is wrong in thinking that these facts are nonphysical. Whatever its own difficulties, the identity theory is much more sophisticated than earlier versions of materialism and escapes at least some of the objections commonly brought up against its predecessors in this tradition.

The Objections to Materialism

The identity theory is one of several versions of materialism that are extremely popular among contemporary philosophers who regard dualism as little more than a tissue of confusions. A number of philosophers, however, do not go along with this judgment and continue to support dualism. They do not deny that dualism involves some serious difficulties, but they insist that these pale into insignificance when compared with the objections to materialism. In the remainder of this section I will explain four of these objections.

1. *Privacy.* In the heyday of behaviorism a joke was current about a meeting of two behaviorists, one of whom says to the other, "You are fine — how am I?" This remark is so transparently absurd because mental states, at least those of which we are conscious, are directly available to the person and not to anybody else. This is what is often called their *privacy.* A person does not have to observe his behavior to know that he dislikes a piece of meat, or that he sees his cat lying on his desk, or that he has a throbbing toothache. Not only does he not need to observe his behavior in order to know these and a great many similar things, but he also does not need to observe what goes on in his brain. Indeed, he need not know anything about his brain or even that he has one. If a perfect correlation between dreams and brain states existed and were known, a brain physiologist would be able to infer what a person was dreaming on the basis of observing what was going on in his brain. The dreamer himself, however, does not need to engage in any inferences and, what is more, the perfect correlation could never have been established without introspective reports by people about their dreams. All this seems incompatible with logical behaviorism and most other forms of radical materialism. If thinking and dreaming were simply the movement of physical particles or secretions or events in the brain there would in principle be no reason why others could not observe the subject's mental states.

2. *Qualia.* Several philosophers have maintained that certain features of our experience are left out in any materialistic account of the world. The features in question are the so-called phenomenal qualities, the "raw feels", or qualia. Examples are sense qualities — colors, sounds, smells, tastes — and feelings — such as joy, sadness, or pain. No kind of physical information about a rose can capture the smell of a rose. This example is taken from the article "Epiphenomenal Qualities," by the Australian philosopher Frank Jackson, who proceeds to develop a set of

ingenious arguments to demonstrate this thesis to anybody who does not find it obvious. In discussing pain and the stimulation of C-fibers in the brain, the late John Mackie, another Australian philosopher, concedes that a person may be in pain when and only when his C-fibers are stimulated. Mackie observes that we may decide to use the word "pain" to refer to the C-fibre stimulation, adding that this would leave "untouched its phenomenal quality, how it feels to me, in fact its painfulness." The pain itself as felt "is an unreduced and irreducible feature of the situation."

3. *Intentionality.* Most, if not all, mental states possess a characteristic technically known as "intentionality." What is meant by this is that they are directed toward an object or "target." A story used to be told about a student of the German philosopher, Martin Heidegger, who, after reading the master's works, announced that he was now "resolved." When asked what he was resolved to do he said that this he did not know. ("Ich bin entschlossen, ich weiss nur nicht wozu!") Most of us would regard such a remark as absurd because one cannot just be resolved: one has to be resolved to do something or other — to leave one's job, enter a monastery, run for governor, or whatever. People are usually not just afraid, but they are afraid of this or that thing judged to be threatening and they do not just believe but they believe that something is or was or will be the case. The word "object" in the context of intentionality is used in a very broad sense to include what may not exist. People believe in fairies and witches and they are terrified of impending attacks which are not at all impending. Intentional objects may even include what existentialist writers refer to as "negative realities" and what we normally call absences, such as death, poverty, or loneliness. Some philosophers maintain that all facts are "positive," but this is clearly wrong if it is meant to include intentional objects. If I decide on early retirement, I may enjoy doing things I could not have done if I had not retired, but I may also enjoy *not* having to see or talk to certain people. These are two distinct pleasures. The negative intentional object of the second pleasure is not identical with any conjunction of positive intentional objects.

Now, it has been claimed by a number of philosophers that a materialistic scheme cannot accommodate intentionality. Mental states are about or point to objects beyond themselves, but it is not easy to see how material objects, even the neurons in the brain, can do this. How, asks John Searle, who in this context writes like a good dualist,

> can this stuff inside my head be *about* anything? How can it *refer* to anything? After all this stuff in the skull consists of "atoms in the void," just as all of the rest of material reality consists of atoms in the void. Now how, to put it crudely, can atoms in the void represent anything?

Rolland Puccetti, who, unlike Searle, really is a dualist, offers as an illustration the case when somebody is told that it is raining. Puccetti explains that the person cannot understand what he has been told until nerve impulses reach Wernicke's area in his left cerebral hemisphere. Now, clearly, a description of the "neuronal activity going on at the cortical juncture of parietal, occipital, and temporal lobes in his left hemisphere is itself not about the state of weather outside." Puccetti concludes that physical states and processes cannot be identical with mental acts because they "never point beyond themselves to anything else," the way mental acts do.

This objection has frequently been thought decisive against all forms of materialism. I will therefore point out that an identity-theorist could reply that although *sense* observation of the brain will not disclose the intentional object of a given brain state, introspection, which on his view is in fact an "inner" way of observing the brain state, does disclose the intentional object. The identity theory may not itself be plausible, but if its basic claim is allowed, then intentionality would not be a problem.

4. *Immateriality*. If materialism is true then mental states and processes should have mass, size, and shape, and occupy spatial positions. However, it seems absurd to regard them as having mass or size and shape or, for that matter, to be moving from one place to another at a given speed. It is not false but nonsense to say that one thought weighs more than or as much as or less than another. Again, to quote C. D. Broad, it is perfectly intelligible to ask whether a molecular movement is swift or slow, straight or circular, but such questions are nonsensical about the awareness of a red patch or of anything else. The question of location is somewhat more complicated because bodily sensations such as pains, itches, tremors, and cramps can be located in space (at least by the person who experiences them), but this is not true of other mental states. It is worth remembering that the classification of bodily sensations as "mental" is open to question: pains and cramps are admittedly private, but they also, on the face of it, seem very physical. Be this as it may, when it comes to thoughts and feelings it seems most implausible to regard them as occupying a spatial position or as having extension. In the section "Of the Immateriality of the Soul" in his *Treatise of Human Nature*, Hume observed that "a moral reflection cannot be placed on the right or on the left of a passion." A little earlier he had raised the question whether anybody could "conceive a passion of a yard in length, a foot in breadth, and an inch in thickness," implying that this was impossible, because passions, like other mental occurrences, have no extension. Hume concluded that "an object may exist and yet be nowhere." He would presumably have said that the opposite view — that whatever exists must have a location in space — is an *a priori* prejudice that is refuted by experience.

Hume's conclusion may be resisted on the ground that thoughts and images can be located "in the head," and there is no doubt that most of us do talk like this on some occasions. Saying that thoughts go on in the head is, of course, just a vague way of saying that they are located in the brain. This is not only the view of many ordinary people, but it has also won the support of some influential psychologists and philosophers. "Consciousness," in the words of Edwin C. Boring, a distinguished experimental psychologist of an earlier generation, "is *localized in the brain* in the sense that discriminative specificity originates there within the differential field that may be imposed by the periphery" (Boring's italics). Similarly, after claiming that "pains and other mental phenomena just are features of the brain (and perhaps the rest of the central nervous system)," the aforementioned John Searle goes on to assert that "our mental processes are biological phenomena located in our brains." It should be emphasized that these remarks are not put forward as recommendations to talk in certain ways but as *true statements* with the evident implication that anybody who thinks otherwise is mistaken. One may readily grant that mental processes are biological phenomena, but it does not follow either that they are features of the brain or that they are in the brain; and if the word "in" is used in either of its two natural senses, it is simply not true that they are in the brain. It is clear that mental states are not in the brain in the sense in which neurons are in the brain. A brain physiologist can see the neurons if the head is opened so as to make the brain visible, but he could not see the subject's mental states. Thomas Nagel has given the following amusing illustration. Suppose I am biting into a chocolate bar and have a certain taste experience. Let us imagine that a scientist was so crazy as to start licking my brain while I eat the chocolate. My brain would almost certainly not taste like chocolate, but even if it did the scientist would not have *my* taste experience (*see* H. H. Price, selection 21).

In the case of bodily sensations, the word "in" is used in a somewhat different sense. Here, to say that something (such as a pain or an itch) is in a certain location means no more than that it is felt to be there by the person who has the sensation. In this sense some few mental states may really be said to be in the brain, namely those resulting from brain injuries or tumors. However, the great majority of mental states are not experienced in the brain. If I feel a pain in the knee or a cramp in the foot, the pain and cramp are where I feel them and not in the brain.

Many, perhaps most, human beings find it incredible that anything should exist without having a location. The moment they regard something as real they at least tacitly assign a place to it. This includes the most devout believers in God, it includes occultists who identify the mind with the astral body and vaguely talk about "spirits," and it also includes respectable dualists in their less guarded moments. They then use language which amounts to an implicit retraction of their view that the mind is not in space. They constantly talk about thoughts, feelings, and sensations occurring "in" the mind as if the mind were a container or perhaps a little screen inside the brain on which the various mental events make their appearance. In 1967, *Philosophy and Phenomenological Research* published the text of a debate on "The Problem of Consciousness" between Brand Blanshard, one of the ablest defenders of dualism, and B. F. Skinner. In the opinion of all non-Skinnerians, Blanshard won the debate hands down, but even he was guilty of some backsliding. At one point Blanshard addressed himself to the question "Where are mental images?" and convincingly showed that a behaviorist has no plausible answer to this question. A dualist, he implied, has no problem with images since they are *"in* consciousness" (italics mine). One may fully agree with Blanshard that mental images do not present a problem for a dualist, but the correct answer from his dualistic point of view would have been that the images exist *nowhere*. Or else Blanshard should have said that for the dualist who is prepared to maintain that things may exist without being in space the question simply does not arise. It may be of interest to note that even Descartes, who so often and so emphatically denied that the mind has extension, nevertheless thought that it had a "seat," the seat being the pineal gland in the brain. In defense of Descartes it might be said that mathematical points and centers of gravity also have no extension and can nevertheless be assigned a spatial location. However, it is doubtful that Descartes attributed to the mind no greater reality than that possessed by mathematical points or centers of gravity.

Dualists maintain that the four sets of facts or alleged facts presented in the preceding survey can be explained only on the assumption that a human being is a mind as well as a body—that this mind has certain attributes that are radically different from those of the body, and that it is known directly by the person and cannot be known directly by anybody else. (It is left open here whether the mind is to be conceived as nothing more than a bundle or succession of mental states, or as an underlying subject of these states.) Many contemporary philosophers who are well aware of the facts in question do not subscribe to this conclusion. The last thirty years have witnessed the development of several new forms of materialism, some of them admittedly wild and not deserving serious attention, but others not wild at all and the work of subtle and brilliant minds. Contemporary materialists would claim either that the facts listed in our survey are entirely consistent with their theories or else they would deny that they *are* facts. It would lead too far to attempt a discussion of these theories here; but it is worth pointing out that many philosophers have not been won over by the arguments of the new materialists and that they continue to regard dualism as a viable theory.

One final comment. The word "mental" covers a very wide range of phenomena which differ in all kinds of ways among themselves. It covers thoughts, fantasies, dreams, feelings, and a multitude of sensations. In the dispute between dualism and materialism we may not be faced with an either-or situation. It might turn out that dualism is right for some mental phenomena and some form or forms of materialism for others. Speaking for myself, I find it grossly implausible to identify dreams or sensations with brain states. At the same time I am convinced that an identity theory is quite defensible for feelings, for example fear or rage. Fear and rage seem to be states of the organism: they are *felt* by the person who has them and they can be *observed* by others. The content of consciousness of the person who feels the fear is different from that of the person who observes the frightened individual, but it is arbitrary and unreasonable to confine the word "fear" to the experience of the subject. It seems much more natural to say that it is the same state, experienced in different ways by the subject and the observer. It should be noted that feelings are here identified with total states of the organism and not with brain events. Somebody who accepts dualism for some mental facts and materialism for others is committed to a view which lacks the neatness and "simplicity" of both the identity theory and of a thoroughgoing dualism; but, if it is true, this would be a small price to pay.

Interactionism

The survival of the disembodied mind does not just presuppose dualism. It presupposes a form of it known as dualistic *interactionism*. Dualistic interactionism has had many supporters among philosophers from Descartes right to the present and at least at first sight it seems eminently plausible. A dualistic interactionist maintains that there are causal connections between mind and body in both directions. Numerous illustrations readily suggest themselves. Wounds or injuries cause pain, stimulation of the sense organs produces sensations, indigestion may give rise to morbid feelings, and the consumption of drugs can seriously affect our moods. All these are instances of causal influence by the body on the mind, but there seems just as ample evidence of causal relations in the opposite direction: a person who is ill and has nothing to live for is far less likely to recover than one who has many interests and is filled with hope. Expectations of pleasant encounters affect our body in one way, expectations of unpleasant encounters in quite another. Embarrassment causes us to blush, fear to tremble, happiness to smile and sometimes to cry. Perhaps the plainest cases of mind-body causation are voluntary movements. A man decides to go to the opera. To obtain this result, he must go to the box office and buy a ticket. His decision to go to the opera thus produces a whole sequence of motions of his body—he leaves his apartment and hails a taxi, he walks from the cab to the box office, he stands in line, and ultimately purchases the ticket.

All this seems exceedingly plausible, but it has been questioned by both philosophers and scientists. Some philosophers, known as parallelists, of whom Leibniz is probably the most famous, have questioned the possibility of causal transactions in either direction. Some have questioned only the physical causation of mental states. This view, to which Ducasse gave the name of "hypophenomenalism," has not been widely held. A far larger number of philosophers and scientists have advanced the theory known as epiphenomenalism, which, admitting body–mind causation, holds that mental states are mere by-products of brain states and possess no causal power. One of the consequences of epiphenomenalism is the impossibility of mental states in the absence of a bodily foundation. If the disembodied mind is to have a chance we must assume that epiphenomenalism is false. We will shortly turn to a discussion of epiphenomenalism, but before we can do this it is necessary to explain in some detail a basic division among dualists concerning the nature of the mind.

Is the Mind a Substance or a Bundle?

I hope I have said enough to show that, right or wrong, dualism is not a wild theory and cannot be dismissed as obviously absurd. To be able to proceed, let us assume from now on that dualism is true. However, dualists differ greatly among themselves on certain issues and some forms of dualism are much more defensible than others. In this section we are concerned with the question of whether the mind should be regarded as a substance or as nothing more than a "bundle," or succession of experiences.

Dualists who maintain that the mind is a substance insist that it cannot simply be identified with the sequence or series of a person's experiences: it is their *subject* or *owner*. It is that which "has" or "owns" them, and unlike the experiences—which constantly change —it remains the same throughout all of them. There surely cannot be dreams without a dreamer, thoughts without a thinker, or feelings without a "feeler." "Motion is unthinkable," writes Michael Maher, S.J. (1860–1917), the author of an excellent textbook, *Psychology,* "without something that is moved," and in the same way "cognition and passion cannot inhere in nothing." It seems incontrovertible that the mind which thinks, feels, perceives, and dreams remains "abidingly" the same. This last phrase occurs in a book by the Scottish religious philosopher James McCosh, one of the most influential philosophers teaching in the United States during the second half of the nineteenth century. McCosh was a disciple of Thomas Reid, the founder of the Scottish school of Common Sense, who developed the same idea in great detail (selection 11). In conscious opposition to the views of Locke and Hume, Reid wrote:

> My thoughts, and actions, and feelings, change every moment; they have no continued, but a successive existence; but that *self* or *I*, to which they belong, is permanent and has the same relation to all the succeeding thoughts, actions, and feelings which I call mine.

The sameness of the substance-self is most evident in memories. The truth of many memory judgments is known with complete certainty. When these are analyzed, writes Father Maher, it is clear that they implicitly involve the identification of one's present self with the self of the remembered experiences. This identification would be impossible if a mind were "merely a succession of states" or if the person's body were the "substantial principle" in which the mental states "inhered." It is a well-established physiological fact that the constituents of the body are completely changed in a comparatively short time. As for the other alternative, it may be observed that "fleeting mental acts could as little result in this self-conscious recollection as could the disconnected cognitions of successive generations of men."

The spiritual substance is also usually said to be "simple." By this it is meant that the substance, unlike material objects, cannot be broken up or analyzed into parts. Monroe Beardsley remarked that it is regarded by its champions as a kind of "ultimate spiritual particle." This notion derives from Plato, who argued in the *Phaedo* (selection 1) that only things which are "compound" or "composite" can be destroyed, because destruction means the breaking up of a thing into its constituent parts. This argument was taken over by Aquinas (selection 4) and was also endorsed by Reid, Mendelssohn, and numerous other pro-religious philosophers. More recent religious philosophers (for example, Kant and Hick) have not found it convincing. However, it should be noted that a person can quite consistently be a champion of the spiritual substance without believing in its indestructibility; and our concern in this section is not with survival but with the question of whether the mind should be conceived as a substance or a bundle.

There is a division of opinion among substance theorists on whether the spiritual substance is known as a result of inference, or whether it is given in immediate experience. Some nineteenth-century philosophers, especially those who were influenced by Kant, tended to adopt the former view. According to Francis Wayland (1796–1865), who was president of Brown University, we know nothing "of the essence of Mind" since it is not given in experience. "All that we are able to affirm of it," Wayland wrote, "is that it is *something* which perceives, reflects, remembers, imagines, and wills; but what that something is which exerts these energies we know not." Much more commonly it has been held that the substance-self is something known in immediate experience, that it is no less an *empirical* reality than the various experiences it has. That "I am an Ego which is the center and source of my acts and states," writes Father Maher, "is forced upon me by constant, intimate, immediate self-experience, with the most irresistible evidence." Perhaps the most famous statement of this view is found in volume 2 of *Metaphysics*, by the influential nineteenth-century German philosopher Hermann Lotze (1807–1881) who protested against the doctrine of "sensationalism" advocated by Locke, Hume, and Mill, charging that it was *un*empirical:

> A mere sensation without a subject is nowhere to be met with as a fact. It is impossible to speak of a bare movement without thinking of the mass whose movement it is; and it is just as impossible to conceive a sensation existing without the accompanying of that which has it — or rather, of that which feels it, for this also is included in the given fact of experience that the relation of the feeling subject to its feeling, whatever its other characteristics may be, is in any case something different from the relation of the moved element to its movement. It is thus and thus only, that the sensation is a given fact; and we have no right to abstract from its relation to its subject because this relation is puzzling, and because we wish to obtain a starting-point which looks more convenient, but is utterly unwarranted by experience.

Substantially the same claims have been made by numerous more recent philosophers, including C. A. Campbell, R. M. Chisholm, H. D. Lewis, and Richard Swinburne.

One of the most concise statements of the bundle theory is presented by Bertrand Russell in a popular article entitled "Do We Survive Death?" (1936). "We think and feel and act," he writes

> but there is not, in addition to thoughts and feelings and actions, a bare entity, the mind or the soul, which does or suffers these occurrences.

A person is the same at different times not because he has or is an unchanging spiritual substance but because there is a continuity of habit and memory:

> There was yesterday one person whose feelings I can remember, and that person I regard as myself of yesterday; but in fact, myself of yesterday was only certain mental occurrences which are now remembered, and are regarded as part of the person who now recollects them.

"What we call a mind," writes Hume, who was the first philosopher to develop the bundle theory in any detail,

> is nothing but a heap or collection of different perceptions, united together by certain relations, and supposed, though falsely, to be endowed with a perfect simplicity and identity.

Elsewhere Hume likens the mind to a theater

where several perceptions successively make their appearance; pass, repass, glide away, and mingle in an infinite variety of postures and situations . . . the comparison of the theater must not mislead us. They are the successive perceptions only, that constitute the mind.

More famous than either of these passages is the one in which Hume explicitly describes the mind as a "bundle of perceptions":

> For my part, when I enter most intimately into what I call myself, I always stumble on some particular perception or other, of heat or cold, light or shade, love or hatred, pain or pleasure. I never catch myself at any time without a perception, and never can observe anything but the perception. . . . If anyone, upon serious and unprejudiced reflection, thinks he has a different notion of himself, I must confess I can reason no longer with him. All I can allow him is, that he may be in the right as well as I, and that we are essentially different in this particular. He may, perhaps, perceive something simple and continued, which he calls himself; though I am certain there is no such principle in me.

Hume is not of course serious when he allows the possibility that some people experience themselves as spiritual substances. They no doubt think they do but in this they are deluding themselves:

> Setting aside some metaphysicians of this kind, I may venture to affirm of the rest of mankind, that they are nothing but a bundle or collection of different perceptions, which succeed each other with an inconceivable rapidity, and are in a perpetual flux and movement.

Hume evidently regarded the substance theory as *false*. Some contemporary philosophers have gone further and declared it to be *meaningless*. The spiritual substance is not like a mythical animal which we could recognize if we came across it but which as a matter of fact does not exist. We don't even know what it would be like to come across it. "The point is not," in the words of A. J. Ayer,

> that the vast majority of men are unable to perform the difficult feat of experiencing themselves as substances. It is rather that such a feat is not conceivable. There is nothing that would count as stumbling upon oneself, as opposed to some particular perception.

Hume, Russell, and Ayer were frankly anti-religious philosophers and opposed to any kind of survival after death. However, versions of the bundle theory have also been endorsed by philosophers who, like Mill, were agnostics on the subject or who, like James (selection 15) and H. H. Price (selection 21) were highly sympathetic if not outright believers. It is of some interest to note that in his criticisms of the substance theory Hume's influence has not been confined to Anglo-Saxon philosophers. Wilhelm Wundt (1832–1920), the founder of the first psychological laboratory as well as a highly respected philosopher, followed Hume in advocating what his critics called a "psychology without a soul" and Nietzsche, too championed a Humean view, regarding the substance theory as a grammatical illusion [Bibliography, p. 322]. Something like a bundle theory can even be detected in existentialist writers like Sartre. Long before any of the philosophers just mentioned the Buddha advocated the bundle theory. As quoted by Derek Parfit (selection 34) he remarked that "there exists no Individual, it is only a conventional name given to a set of elements."

As noted earlier, the spiritual substance still has some defenders, but most contemporary philosophers who have written on the subject agree with Hume that we are here dealing with a vacuous notion. Its emptiness is hidden by the metaphors used in statements of the theory, and also by its being confused with other notions which are not empty. When it is maintained that the spiritual substance owns the experiences of a person, the word "own" is not used in its literal sense. The spiritual substance is obviously not an owner in the sense in which a landlord is the owner of a certain apartment complex. The latter may be described and identified independently of the buildings he owns. We might point him out as the man standing to the left of Mayor Koch or the person who is just entering the building. Again, he might be described as 56 years old, six feet two inches tall, having blue eyes, hard-working, a bad husband but devoted father, a lover of Italian opera and a patient in Jungian analysis. When asked, "Who owns this building?" one can enumerate these and other physical and psychological attributes of the owner, and one is not restricted to the answer that the building is owned by the person who owns it. In the case of the spiritual substance, on the other hand, all one can say is that it is the entity which owns, or has, the various mental states. It cannot be identified or described independently of them. We most emphatically have not been told what "it" is by the statement that it is that which owns the experiences. We are here dealing with a featureless owner, and hence an entity which is *not* an owner in the usual sense.

It should also be emphasized that, as the spiritual substance is conceived by its champions, it cannot possibly be identified with the personality of the individual. The spiritual substance is supposed to be unvaryingly the same throughout life, but this is clearly not true of an individual's personality. A person can be submissive at one time of his life and domineering at another, compassionate and generous early in life and cruel and indifferent many years later, passionately interested in politics at the age of twenty and bored by it in old age. Yet throughout these periods his spiritual substance has not changed. It follows that the substance is not identical with the personality, and in fact it is not what anybody means by "I." Lotze insisted that what I experience are not just "atomic" sensations or feelings but myself as having these sensations. I do not just experience pain but myself as being in pain. Perhaps so, but the "I" that is here experienced cannot be the unchanging spiritual substance, or the soul.

Contrary to what its champions maintain, the spiritual substance does not in any way enter into an analysis of what we mean by personal identity. This was brought out forcefully by Locke (selection 6), who did not deny the existence of what he called the "immaterial" substance. Let us assume that Henry Kissinger has been engaged to give a lecture on "Machiavelli and Metternich" to the Association of Retired Diplomats and that he has been offered a sizable fee. The lecture is just what the audience hopes for—scholarly, witty, and interlaced with recollections of the speaker's own diplomatic career. When the president of the association is about to hand over the check, the lecturer declines to accept it on the grounds that he is not Henry Kissinger. "It is true that I have the Kissinger-body, the Kissinger-memories and an awareness of the continuity of Kissinger-experiences, but I woke up with a different spiritual substance. As a disciple of Lotze and H. D. Lewis, I cannot regard myself as Henry Kissinger any longer." The president of the association is unlikely to accept this conclusion and there is no doubt that the judges of the Supreme Court, liberals and conservatives alike, would rule that in spite of his loss of the Kissinger-spiritual substance, the man who gave the lecture *is* Henry Kissinger.

Let us briefly consider a very different scenario. At the beginning of the talk, the lecturer looks like Henry Kissinger and speaks entertainingly about Machiavelli and Metternich as well as his own diplomatic service, but then during the next hour, to the consternation of the audience, the Kissinger body gradually changes into the body of Shirley MacLaine. Along with these changes there is a change in the voice and also in the subject and the personal recollections. After the physical transformation has been completed, the lecture is all about reincarnation, the occult, the astral body, Hollywood, and recollections of Shirley MacLaine's life. Now suppose that the president of the association refuses payment but that the lecturer, looking and talking just like Shirley MacLaine, insists on payment on the grounds that "he" is Henry Kissinger because, in spite of all the undeniable changes that have taken place, "he" is still aware of himself as the Kissinger spiritual substance. Payment would be refused on the ground (probably not the only one) that the lecturer is no longer Henry Kissinger. Such a refusal would be sustained in court even if it was allowed that the lecturer's protestations about possessing the Henry Kissinger spiritual substance are entirely sincere.

It will be replied that none of this answers the original challenge: there cannot be dreams without a dreamer or feelings without a feeler and hence our experiences require a subject, an "I" which possesses them. There are two possible answers to this retort. Some bundle theorists would flatly deny the need for a subject and it is not at all obvious that they are wrong. They would say that because we use the words "I" and "mind" as nouns and frequently as grammatical subjects, we are liable to assume that they designate things. Experience shows that they do not designate things any more than such words as "space" and "time" and many others that have puzzled philosophers. The mind is a "many" and not a "one" — it is a series or stream of experiences, and to say that a given experience such as a dream or a feeling of fear belongs to a certain mind is to say that it is a member of a *certain* class of experiences as contrasted with other classes of experiences that constitute other minds. Alexander Bain was one of the leading defenders of the bundle theory in the nineteenth century. F. H. Bradley in a much-quoted passage thought that he could show that the bundle theory involves an intolerable paradox. "Mr. Bain," he wrote, "thinks the mind is a collection. Has Mr. Bain reflected: who collects Mr. Bain?" Anthony Quinton, a contemporary bundle theorist, was ready with the answer that "the later Mr. Bain collects the earlier Mr. Bain by recollecting him." Alternatively, it may be replied that the body is entirely capable of fulfilling the role of a subject of experiences and dispositions. There is nothing absurd in holding that a human being is a body with both physical and mental attributes. As we shall see in the next section, precisely this view has been advocated by a number of influential philosophers.

It should be emphasized that the bundle theory is a plausible answer only to the question "What is a *mind*?" and not to the question "what is a *person*?" or "What is a human being?" No adequate answer to the latter question can leave out reference to the body. Unfortunately both Hume and several of his successors, who were in effect what we earlier called extreme dualists identifying a person with his mind, did not always clearly distinguish the two questions. "When my perceptions are removed for any time, as by sound sleep," Hume wrote, "so long am I insensible of *myself*, and may truly be said not to exist." This is clearly wrong since my body continues to exist at the time. The most that Hume had a right to say is that my mind then ceases to exist though even this may be disputed on the ground that, dreaming aside, my cognitive and emotional dispositions are not annihilated during sleep. However, this last issue — whether the mind continues to exist during dreamless sleep — is none of our concern and is in any event a purely verbal question.

Can Matter Think?

In the history of philosophy the word "materialism" has been used in several different senses. In the section on "Dualism and Materialism" it was used in the narrow sense, most common in contemporary philosophical discussions, in which it refers to any theory that identifies minds or mental facts with bodily phenomena of some kind. It has been customary to classify such theories as "reductive" or "monistic" materialism. However, "materialism" has also very commonly been used in a broader sense in which it refers to any theory that regards matter as the fundamental reality. Such a view may admit that some or all mental phenomena are *sui generis*. At the same time it holds that although the body can exist without the mind, the mind cannot exist without the body. Contemporary philosophers and scientists who are materialists in this broader sense usually also maintain that there was a time when matter did and mind did not exist and that in all probability there will again come a time when there will be no minds. In past centuries materialists confidently asserted that matter is eternal, but this view has recently been questioned by several cosmologists. When William James (selection 32) speaks of "cerebral materialism" he is obviously using the word in the broader sense. The scientists he has in mind did not maintain that consciousness is reducible to bodily phenomena but that it cannot exist without the brain.

In this and the next section I will briefly discuss two influential theories which are forms of materialism only in the broader sense. Both occupy an intermediate position between reductive materialism on one side and a full-fledged dualism on the other. The theory with which we are concerned in this section holds that there is only one substance or subject—the body—but that the body has mental as well as physical attributes, the mental attributes being irreducible to bodily states and processes. This view is perhaps best understood by briefly referring to an eighteenth-century dispute dealing with the question of whether matter could think. The leading participants in this debate took as their point of departure the observation in Locke's *Essay Concerning Human Understanding* that God could "give to certain systems of created senseless matter, put together as he thinks fit, some degrees of sense, perception and thought." It is "not much more remote from our comprehension," Locke went on, to conceive that "God can . . . superadd to matter a faculty of thinking than that he should superadd to it another substance with a faculty of thinking." Several British and French philosophers endorsed Locke's remark and proceeded to defend the view that in fact matter *does* think or, more precisely, that thinking and other mental processes are caused by the brain and may be regarded as attributes of the body. These included the leading English deists, John Toland and Anthony Collins, Voltaire (selection 10), Lamettrie, Holbach, and Priestley (selection 13). "Thought is so little incompatible with organized matter," wrote Lamettrie, "that it seems to be one of its properties on a par with electricity, the faculty of motion, impenetrability, and extension." Hume nowhere asserted that mental states are attributes of the body, but in his *Essay on Immortality* he observed that "nothing can be decided *a priori*," in support of the view that "matter, by its structure or arrangement, may not be the cause of thought" (selection 9). There is some doubt whether Priestley should be included in the above list. He seemed to waver, or rather not to be clear on the status of the mental attributes of the body. Although many of his remarks suggest that he regarded mental states as irreducible to anything physical, he also wrote that "man consists wholly of matter," which is most naturally interpreted as a form of reductive materialism. Voltaire was undoubtedly the most famous and influential advocate of this view, and I will therefore refer to it as "Voltairean materialism." Voltaire never called himself a materialist, but there is no doubt that he vigorously supported the view under discussion and realized its subversive implications. It is evident that, like reductive materialism, Voltairean materialism rules out survival of a disembodied mind but is entirely compatible with the resurrection of the body.

The main argument in favor of Voltairean materialism is that it is more economical than Cartesian dualism and dispenses with what is at best a highly obscure notion. "I am a body and I think," Voltaire wrote in his "Letter on Locke" — "shall I go and attribute to an unknown cause when I can so easily attribute it [thought] to a secondary one?" A human brain is an observable entity. If it produces thought, why also bring in a mysterious entity like the soul? Another argument is based on the similarity between human beings and animals. Many animals resemble human beings in having sense organs and a brain. We have every reason to believe that they have ideas and feelings, although the ideas and feelings of human beings are undoubtedly much more numerous and complex. Voltaire finds it incredible that animals are "mere machines," that is, beings devoid of ideas and feelings. Only a metaphysician is capable of believing something that so flagrantly contradicts common sense. Now, if the existence of ideas and feelings requires us to postulate a spiritual soul, then animals must also have spiritual souls. If people have spiritual souls, then so do dogs and moles and even fleas, worms, and mites. On the other hand, if we deny souls to animals, then we cannot make the possession of feelings and ideas a reason for postulating souls in human beings.

A number of twentieth-century philosophers — among them Ernest Nagel, John Dewey, Sidney Hook, and Antony Flew — subscribe to the same view. Flew in many places makes it clear that he is not a radical materialist, admitting that mental processes are irreducible to bodily phenomena. At the same time he insists that human beings are "creatures of flesh and blood" and these creatures of flesh and blood are the subjects of sensations, feelings, and thoughts. Perhaps the most forceful statement of Voltairean materialism occurs in a little-known and unjustly forgotten article, "Are Naturalists Materialists?" (1945), by Ernest Nagel. Nagel distinguishes between reductive and nonreductive materialism. The former, which he rejects, maintains that psychological terms are synonymous with "some expression or combination of expressions belonging to the class of physical terms." The latter, which he supports, makes the much milder claim that the occurrence of mental events is "contingent upon the occurrence of certain complex physico-chemico-physiological events and structures." No emotions, not even experiences of beauty or holiness, would exist unless "bodies appropriately organized were also present." Minds are not substances but "adjectival and adverbial of bodies." Mental states and processes are "properties . . . of spatio-temporal objects in their organized unity."

Voltairean materialism may or may not be true, but the most common objection to it is based on nothing but an *a priori* prejudice. In his contribution to *Life After Death*, from which we quoted earlier, Arthur Köstler opposes the view that the brain can "generate consciousness." Köstler bases himself on a lecture by Sir Cyril Burtt entitled "Psychology and Psychical Research," published in 1968 in the *Proceedings of the Society for Psychical Research*. There is no hope for life after death, writes Köstler,

> as long as we remain captives of that materialist philosophy which proclaimed—as Burtt ironically phrased it—that the chemistry of the brain "generates consciousness much as the liver generates bile."

This "naive materialism," however, must be rejected because it cannot explain "how the motions of particles could possibly generate this 'insubstantial pageant of images and ideas.' " Writing from a very different standpoint, the existential psychoanalyst Medard Boss, a disciple and close friend of Martin Heidegger, insists that "not a single human perception or thought . . . could ever be intelligibly derived from the physiological processes of the bodily metabolism, from any nerve functions, or from the so-called higher nervous activities which take place concommitantly." These words are put by Boss into the mouth of a patient whose reasoning he greatly admired. "How did the doctor," the patient went on, "picture such a transformation of physical processes into mental, immaterial phenomena? Perhaps as some kind of magic evaporation?" "It is inconceivable," Boss writes a little later, now speaking in the first person, "how blind particles and quanta of energy of a body can suddenly see and perceive things as the things they are with all their meaningful connotations."

Köstler, Burtt, and Boss were amateurs in philosophy, but exactly the same reasoning can be found in the writings of numerous professional philosophers. Thus Oswald Külpe (1862–1915), an eminent German psychologist and philosopher whose excessive love of his Kaiser resulted in his premature demise, insists that materialism "is incapable of explaining psychological facts." It does not allow us "to make even the simplest and most easily apprehended psychical processes intelligible." The sensation of red or a tone of a certain pitch are "in no way more intelligible from the fact that we may trace them back to some particular activity of the brain." In the same vein, the distinguished English theologian F. R. Tennant (1866–1957), whose ideas on immortality will be discussed later, maintained in his article "Materialism" in the *Hastings Encyclopedia of Religion and Ethics* that "materialism cannot explain even the simplest type of conscious process." According to Tennant there is an insuperable difficulty in conceiving "how a sensation or a feeling could be the necessary consequence or effect of . . . matter or mass-points." What agitates all these writers is shown very clearly in a passage from *Death and Consciousness* (1985), by the contemporary American philosopher David H. Lund:

> How can the brain, a material substance, produce something as radically different from it as consciousness is? How can the brain create out of its own material substance a reality that has no mass, no shape, no size, and is not even in space?

The answer to those questions is "Why not?" As Hume noted, only experience can tell us what causes what, and we possess no *a priori* evidence that the cause and effect cannot be "radically different." We have just as strong evidence for concluding that certain brain states bring about certain conscious states as we have for any number of causal relations between purely physical phenomena which are not questioned by any of the above-mentioned critics of materialism. If the production of mental states by the brain does not fit in with the *a priori* preconceptions of a given philosopher, this is simply too bad. It is certainly true that not *any* particles in *any* arrangement can bring about consciousness. The particles arranged as billiard balls or as cream puffs cannot do this, but apparently the particles of living brain tissues do bring it about.

All the writers quoted in the preceding paragraphs tacitly presuppose the scholastic maxim that any property possessed by an effect must have been present in its cause. They are of course dualists, but occasionally materialists also show themselves attached to this maxim. Thus Paul Churchland, best described as a "computational materialist," maintains that there is something objectionable in the contention that, although mental states are produced by the brain, they are not themselves physical:

> If that is how mental properties are produced, then one would expect a physical account of them to be possible. The simultaneous claim of evolutionary emergence and physical irreducibility is *prima facie* puzzling.

Köstler *et al.*, appeal to the scholastic maxim to show that mental states cannot be physically caused; Churchland appeals to it to show that, since they *are* physically caused, they must themselves be physical. Unfortunately for all these writers the scholastic maxim is glaringly false. Negative instances stare at one from all directions. J. S. Mill gave the example of water, which is a liquid although its components are gases, but perhaps the best negative instances come from evolution. If there were no mutations — if the offspring never possessed any new attributes — then natural selection would have nothing to operate on. If the scholastic maxim were true, then the amoeba would have to have been a mathematician.

Some of the computational philosophers harbor the illusion that if it were possible to produce robots whose behavior gave us as good a reason for inferring that they are thinking and feeling entities as we might have in the case of flesh-and-blood visitors from outer space, or indeed in the case of other members of our own species, this would prove reductive materialism. It would prove nothing of the kind. The creation of these beings would undoubtedly be a stunning technological achievement, but the fact that we had artificially produced thinking and feeling robots is entirely consistent with the view that their thoughts and feelings are irreducibly mental.

Epiphenomenalism

In the opinion of a number of philosophers and scientists, dualistic interactionism faces a serious, perhaps an insuperable problem in connection with the alleged causation of bodily phenomena by the mind. It is not the unlikeness between the mind and the body which presents the problem. We concluded in the last section that this unlikeness does not rule out causal influences by the body on the mind and it equally does not rule out causal influences in the opposite direction. The problem now under discussion arises because there seems to be no room for interventions in the brain by something nonphysical. If such an intervention occurred, the brain would no longer obey the laws of physics and chemistry, but all competent scientists agree that the brain is no different in this respect from other physical systems. "The will is not a material thing," wrote W. K. Clifford (1845–1879), the nineteenth-century mathematician and philosopher, and "it is not a mode of material motion." Anybody who asserts that the will influences matter is guilty of "nonsense." "Such an assertion," Clifford goes on, "belongs to the crude materialism of the savage. The only thing which influences matter is the position of surrounding matter or the motion of surrounding matter." "Mind *per se*," in the words of Sir Charles Sherrington, one of the most illustrious physiologists of the twentieth century, "cannot play the piano — mind *per se* cannot move a finger of a hand."

Occasionally a scientist or philosopher has asserted that the mind can create energy and that hence the Law of the Conservation of Energy is violated in the case of mind–body causation. The nineteenth-century astronomer Sir William Herschel (1792–1871) maintained that in a volitional act the will does originate some force, "though it may be no greater than is required to move a single material molecule through a space inconceivably minute." Similarly, J. B. Pratt, a prominent American philosopher of the first half of the twentieth century, regarded the mind as a "genuine creator of energy" and, unlike some other interactionists, openly admitted that mind–body interaction is incompatible with the Conservation of Energy. This violation, however, is minute from a cosmic perspective because it occurs only in that "tiny realm where matter comes into relation with personality." Neither Herschel nor Pratt gave indications of how their claim could be tested and, as far as I know, it is not supported by any scientific evidence.

Those who find it impossible to admit causal influences of the mind on the body but who also wish to retain the view that mental phenomena are *sui generis* have generally opted for a theory known as epiphenomenalism, which has been mentioned in several earlier discussions. "Our mental conditions," wrote T. H. Huxley, who coined the term "epiphenomenalism" and was one of its earliest champions,

> are simply symbols in consciousness of the changes which take place automatically in the organism; and, to take an extreme illustration, the feeling we call volition is not the cause of a voluntary act, but the symbol of that state of the brain which is the immediate cause of that act. We are conscious automata.

"Epiphenomenon" is the Greek word for "by-product." Mental states and processes on this view are by-products of brain events and they do not in turn influence the brain or any other part of the body. Shadworth Hodgson (1832–1912), another early supporter of the theory, likened consciousness to a "mere foam, aura or melody" and also to the colors laid on the surface of a mosaic whose stones correspond to the events in the brain. Santayana, a later epiphenomenalist, compared ideas to vestal virgins who were themselves born but did not have any offspring.

Definitions of epiphenomenalism do not usually contain any statement to the effect that mental events cannot give rise to other *mental* events, but Hodgson took the further step of depriving the mind of this power as well. A little reflection shows that this further denial is indeed implied by the initial claims of the theory. William James, who was a critic of epiphenomenalism, agreed with Hodgson that a consistent epiphenomenalist cannot allow any causal power at all to the mind. James offers the example of the relation between the learning of good news and the subsequent elation. We commonly regard the former as the cause of the latter, but if epiphenomenalism is true, the real causes of both of these conscious states are the underlying brain events. One brain event causes the awareness of good news. This brain event also causes another brain event which in turn causes the feeling of elation. It is the second brain event and not the awareness of the good news that causes the joy.

Epiphenomenalism may be regarded as a form of Voltairean materialism. Neither Voltaire nor any of the other Voltaireans mentioned in the last section concerned themselves with the question of the causal relation between mind and body. Voltaire would probably have preferred interactionism to epiphenomenalism, but there is nothing in Voltairean materialism which precludes an elaboration of the theory along epiphenomenalist lines. It is hardly surprising that believers in survival such as Tennant and Richard Swinburne should oppose epiphenomenalism, but the same is true of reductive materialists who have frequently used strong language in their denunciations. Churchland merely calls it "a strange view," but Richard Taylor remarks that, "when clearly conceived," epiphenomenalism "appears so bizarre a description of human nature as to make almost any alternative conception more acceptable." To this it should be added that most brain scientists favor epiphenomenalism. Some of them do so quite explicitly; others, who are not given to pronouncements on philosophical issues, implicitly favor epiphenomenalism in their practice. Among philosophers, epiphenomenalism is out of fashion, but some, including the present writer, are almost irresistibly drawn to it as the one theory which preserves what is sound in dualism while avoiding what they find incredible in mind–body interaction.

The following are some of the reasons why epiphenomenalism has been regarded as "strange," "bizarre," "unnatural," and "implausible." The last two epithets come from John Foster (selection 17), who is responsible for some of the most interesting and powerful objections.

1. There is, to begin with, what W. C. Kneale has referred to as "the great paradox of epiphenomenalism," the suggestion "that we are necessarily mistaken in all our ordinary thought about human action." The belief that "mental events are sometimes causes of physical events," Kneale regards as part of "the hard core of common sense" comparable to our belief in the reality of the external world. Kneale was writing against the epiphenomenalism of C. D. Broad, and he observes that when Broad is going to sit down "to reply to this criticism he will do so with no doubt at all about the possibility of determining by his thought what shall appear upon the paper." Belief in the efficacy of thought, Kneale adds, "is presupposed in all debates about the efficacy of thought."

2. It is argued that we have just as good evidence for supposing that the mind influences the body as that the body influences the mind. Somebody who rejects interaction in both directions is consistent, but the epiphenomenalist concedes that bodily processes can give rise to mental states. More specifically, the evidence that my volition to raise my arm causes it to go up is just as strong as that certain drugs will cause elation while others produce depression.

3. Epiphenomenalism is alleged to violate the theory of natural selection. From the fact that conscious states do not influence the body

and hence do not in any way help human beings to cope with the environment it follows that they have no survival value. However, according to natural selection, only traits with survival value evolve over time.

4. According to several critics, epiphenomenalism is incompatible with the role which logical reasoning plays in human behavior. This argument was employed in several places by Brand Blanshard. The brain states whose by-products our thoughts are alleged to be, Blanshard writes, "follow an order determined wholly by the laws of physics, such as those of motion, gravitation, and electric conduction." Direct inspection, however, shows that teleology and necessity do play a part in certain of our mental processes. If I reach a conclusion because it is logically implied by certain premises which I accept, teleology and necessity (or, more accurately, the recognition of necessity) determine the end result, and these are mental factors and not brain states. Brain states undoubtedly "provide the necessary condition of certain states of mind," but at least in the case of such activities as reasoning they are not the sufficient condition.

5. Closely connected with the preceding objection is the contention that epiphenomenalism is a "self-stultifying" theory. If it were true, we could never be *justified* in believing it to be true, for then all our beliefs would be entertained not because of any prior awareness of good grounds or adequate evidence but solely because of physical changes in the brain and nervous system. None of our conclusions, including epiphenomenalism itself, would be based on good evidence. Epiphenomenalism implies that the arguments offered by the epiphenomenalist "play no role in the formation of his beliefs or those of anyone else." The last sentence is quoted from Richard Swinburne, who proceeds to observe that "insofar as our beliefs which require reasons for their justification do not have acceptance of those reasons among their causes, they are unjustified."

6. A particularly ingenious argument is due to John Foster (selection 17). According to Foster, epiphenomenalism does not allow for introspective knowledge. We normally regard introspective reports as verbal utterances caused by the experiences which they report, but if epiphenomenalism is true this cannot be so since the mental states have "no causal access to our speech center."

7. Finally, there is a teaser due to Jerome Shaffer. Epiphenomenalism implies that if there had never been a single mental event, the whole of human history would have been the same. This means that

there still would have been developed a language with expressions for reporting mental events, and, incredibly, there would have been those verbal interchanges which constitute our arguments about the very existence of mental events.

This invites the question of how there could be no mental events

> and yet, to take the most incredible element in this story, men assert
> that they themselves certainly have them, wonder whether their fel-
> low men have them, and argue about the issue.

This is surely a staggering paradox. It should be noted parenthetically
that, in spite of working out this paradox to which he offered no reply,
Shaffer himself is an epiphenomenalist!

It would lead much too far to try and evaluate these objections here.
An intelligent epiphenomenalist could no doubt find plausible answers
to some of them ("Tantalus," by Hugh Elliot—selection 16—may be
regarded as an answer to the first two). It is not at all obvious, however,
that plausible answers are available to all of them—but it should be
remembered that all the rival theories in the field are also beset by
serious difficulties. What seems certain is that epiphenomenalism does
not deserve the contemptuous dismissal it has received from various
philosophers in recent years.

The Disembodied Mind and Its Critics

We can now turn to a discussion of the disembodied mind, the first of
the three vehicles of survival mentioned earlier. Throughout this discussion we will of course assume the truth of dualism and, more specifically, of dualistic interactionism. As H. H. Price points out (selection
21), the disembodied mind may be conceived either as an immaterial
substance or as a Humean bundle of experiences. "It is as easy to
conceive that a succession of feelings, a thread of consciousness may be
prolonged to eternity," J. S. Mill observes in *An Examination of Sir
William Hamilton's Philosophy*, "as that a spiritual substance for ever
continues to exist." A believer who wishes to avoid the serious difficulties in the notion of the immaterial substance explained earlier will
obviously prefer the bundle version. He would divide a human being's
existence into the premortem phase, when the bundle is associated
with a certain body, and the postmortem phase, when it is not associated with any body.

The survival of human beings as disembodied minds would of course
be undermined if dualism were false, but even if dualism is true the
believer is faced with several serious challenges. We shall here consider four of these. The first three, which are of relatively recent origin,
have prominently featured in the discussions of contemporary Anglo-
Saxon philosophers. The fourth, which in the opinion of many scientists
and philosophers is quite decisive, goes back at least as far as Lucretius.

1. *Are statements about disembodied minds intelligible?* In an article
on "Difficulties Confronting the Survival Hypothesis," the American
psychologist and psychical researcher Gardner Murphy insisted on

"the fact that bodies are the vehicles of personality and, that most people have no conception of personality except in such terms." He proceeded to challenge the reader "to try for a few minutes to imagine what his personal existence would be like if he were deprived of every device for making contact with his environment, except through the hypothetical use of continuous telepathy to and from other invisible minds." Antony Flew, who quotes these passages, approvingly remarks that "it is not just 'most people,' as Murphy modestly puts it, it is all of us whose conception of personality is grounded in the corporeal." We explain the meaning of "person words" to children "by some sort of direct or indirect pointing at members of that very special class of living physical objects to which we one and all belong." On several occasions Flew has forcefully conveyed his point by saying that human beings are "flesh-and-blood creatures." All the various activities of human beings "could only be predicated intelligibly of corporeal creatures." Just like Murphy, Flew is not a behaviorist or any other kind of reductive materialist. He would not dispute that a human being is more than his body but he would argue that, however much more than a body a human being may be, one cannot sensibly talk about this "more" without presupposing that he is a living organism.

Flew is by no means alone among contemporary philosophers to hold this view. In this book Geach (selection 23), Broad (selection 30), and Hospers (selection 31) support a similar position. It is of some interest to note that Geach, an ardent believer in the resurrection of the body, and Flew, an unbeliever in any kind of survival, are here united in their opposition to belief in the disembodied mind.

Among those who have spoken up in defense of the intelligibility of the notion of a disembodied mind are not only various traditional believers but also a number of well-known unbelievers, including Moritz Schlick, the founder of the Vienna Circle, C. Lewy, P. F. Strawson, A. J. Ayer and John Mackie. "Although all the persons we are acquainted with have bodies," Mackie writes,

> there is no great difficulty in conceiving what it would be for there to be a person without a body; for example, one can imagine oneself surviving without a body and, while at present one can act and produce results only by using one's limbs or one's speech organs, one can *imagine* having one's intentions fulfilled directly, without such physical means.

Unlike Mackie, Ayer shows some appreciation of the case of those who regard bodiless existence as incoherent. He concludes, however, that "the objections to the idea of there being disembodied streams of consciousness are in the end scientific rather than purely logical." In a passage that has frequently been quoted Ayer writes that one can imagine oneself waking to find oneself deprived of any bodily feeling or any perception of one's own body; one can imagine oneself seeming to wander about the world like a ghost, intangible to others and only occasionally visible and after a time not visible at all, a spectator of the world in which one does not participate.

The ideas here put forward by Mackie and Ayer have been developed in some detail in an exceptionally interesting and unjustly neglected article, "Disembodied Persons" (*Philosophy* 1986), by G. R. Gillett.

In attempting to decide this question one is well advised to heed one of Ayer's warnings. In the course of the discussion mentioned in the last paragraph, Ayer observes that it is not safe to trust one's linguistic intuitions here because they are likely to be the product and not the cause of one's philosophical views. Allowing for the possibility that one may easily be misled by one's linguistic intuitions, my own inclination is to side with those who regard statements about disembodied mental existence as intelligible. In certain conceivable (though highly fanciful) circumstances one might offer the intention of a disembodied mind as the most plausible explanation of a given range of events, and we would not fail to understand the reference to a disembodied mind in such a situation. To this it has to be added that the existence of such disembodied minds would be of an exceedingly diminished kind. So far from living on in paradise, a person deprived of his body and thus of all sense organs would, quite aside from many other gruesome deprivations, be in a state of desolate loneliness and eventually come to prefer annihilation. Aquinas showed great wisdom when he declared that somebody possessing a mind without a body would not be fully human.

2. *The problem of personal identity.* Let us assume, then, that statements about disembodied minds *are* intelligible. The believer is at once faced with another objection which many contemporary philosophers have regarded as fatal to his position. To see the full force of this objection let us remind ourselves that the believer in survival of human beings as disembodied minds does not merely assert the reality of another world inhabited by disembodied minds. He also asserts or implies that at least some of these disembodied minds are identical with human beings who once lived in embodied form on earth. He hopes or perhaps fears that after his death *he* will become a disembodied mind and also that some of the disembodied minds he will meet in the hereafter will be identical with people whom he knew on earth.

It is the justification of such identity assertions that has been questioned by a number of contemporary philosophers. They maintain that although memory is *a* criterion of personal identity, it is subordinate to the criterion of bodily continuity. People's memory claims are sometimes false. This may be due to lying but quite frequently people who make false memory assertions are entirely sincere. We must therefore distinguish between *really* remembering and only *seeming* to remember. The former does imply personal identity but the latter does not; and one can determine that a given claim constitutes real and not merely apparent memory only by appealing to bodily continuity. Conversely, showing the absence of bodily continuity is sufficient to refute a memory claim no matter how sincerely it may have been put forward (see Geach on the case of the Tichborne claimant, selection 23, p. 232). If the bodily criterion is in this way more fundamental than memory it follows that a disembodied mind could never know that it was identical with a disembodied mind existing at an earlier time or with a human being who lived on the earth.

If the objection just explained is sound, it also indirectly undermines the view that a continuously existing disembodied mind is a coherent notion. Terence Penelhum has pointed out that the ascription of most psychological predicates (such as "being in a state of panic," "thinking about Gorbachev's chances to stay in power," "watching the eclipse," and so forth) involves a lapse of time. The person to whom these mental states are attributed must of course remain the same throughout their duration, and if the bodily criterion of personal identity is fundamental it follows that such states cannot be meaningfully affirmed of a disembodied mind.

3. *The problem of individuation.* Let us suppose that both of the preceding difficulties can somehow be surmounted — that the notion of a disembodied mind is not incoherent and that we could identify disembodied survivors in the next world with human beings who once lived here on earth. There is another conceptual difficulty which has been stressed in recent years by a number of philosophers. On their view it is impossible to "individuate" human beings, to distinguish one from another, except by reference to their bodies. This objection was forcefully presented by Bernard Williams in a BBC discussion, "Life After Death," in which Anthony Quinton and H. D. Lewis were the other participants. Suppose, Williams writes, that "there are three rather than four persons existing at a given time." The only "comprehensible basis for distinguishing between them" would be that "there are three rather than four separate bodies, existing at the same time." Let us consider two persons whose minds are not just very similar but absolutely alike. This is of course not something that is likely to happen, but it is conceivable. "By some freak of nature," writes Keith Campbell, from whom this illustration is taken, "the course of their experience has been exactly alike and has worked in exactly the same way on the same innate tendencies. The minds of these two persons are alike in both history and contents." We would be entitled to say that there are two minds here and not just one because these two minds would be tied to two separate bodies. But what if one eliminated the two bodies? Would we still be entitled to say that there are two minds rather than one?

The same problem arises in connection with particular mental states or events. Let us suppose, writes Anthony Quinton,

> that two people, A and B, have qualitatively indistinguishable feelings of annoyance at a high whistling noise in their immediate neighborhood, beginning at the same time and existing for the same period.

We can justify our belief that in such a situation two experiences are going on and not merely one only if A and B are not disembodied minds. Quinton maintains that to individuate the experiences we must not only assign them to two different bodies but also regard the experiences themselves as having a location in space, but we are not here concerned with this additional claim. According to Quinton, people do not perceive the problem of individuation here because they tacitly attach the experiences in question "to some ghostly but really located surrogate, a shade or spectral voice, to carry out the indispensable positioning work ordinarily done by the body." The same suggestion is offered by Geach, who observes that people think it easy to individuate disembodied minds because they are "illegitimately ascribing" to them a kind of "differentiation — say, by existing *side by side* — that can be significantly ascribed only to bodies." Such illegitimate pictures, it should be noted, are commonly entertained not only by believers in the disembodied mind but also by the many unbelievers who grant that the believer has an intelligible position.

Both in the BBC discussion and in various of his publications, H. D. Lewis professes not to see a serious challenge to the disembodied mind here. In his article "Immortality and Dualism" he tells us that "this problem" has never worried him a great deal:

> It has always seemed evident to me that everyone knows himself to be the being that he is in just being so. We identify ourselves to ourselves in that way and not in the last resort on the basis of what we know about ourselves.

The same idea is presented in the BBC debate:

> My view, very sharply, is that everyone is aware of the being that he is in just being himself. He may, in loss of memory, forget his name, his home and much besides, but he still knows that he is himself. . . . There is something immediate and ultimate about the way in which I know that I am this being now whatever my experiences.

Lewis seems to be saying that as long as he is alive and sane, and perhaps even if he is not sane, he has what may be called the "I am — experience," and it is this experience and not his body that individuates him. Ronald Reagan has the Ronald Reagan-experience accompanying everything he does and thinks and in this way he knows that he is Ronald Reagan; George Bush has the George Bush-experience, H. D.

Lewis the H. D. Lewis-experience, and the same thing holds for all human beings.

Lewis deserves credit for being the only champion of the disembodied mind to take notice of the problem of individuation. It is doubtful, however, that he has succeeded in meeting the challenge. Allowing for the sake of argument that people really have the kind of experience that Lewis refers to, it is easy to see that it could not possibly serve as a basis for individuation. Let us assume that a double of H. D. Lewis suddenly appeared. How it was produced is irrelevant, but to simplify matters we may assume that it was created by God. What is important is that it should be an *exact* duplicate, physically and psychologically. Let us call this double "H. D. Lewis II." Now, if there is such a thing as the "I am so-and-so-experience," then H. D. Lewis II will have the same "I am H. D. Lewis-experience" as the original H. D. Lewis, and yet he would not be H. D. Lewis. Only the original H. D. Lewis, the person who debated with Quinton and Williams, is H. D. Lewis. If H. D. Lewis II were to claim the royalties for H. D. Lewis's books, Allen and Unwin would rightly refuse payment, and if the case ever came into court the original H. D. Lewis would undoubtedly prevail.

The appeal to individuation does not prove that disembodied mental existence is impossible. It only shows that we would not be able to justify believing in a plurality of disembodied minds as opposed to a single such mind; and Lewis rightly observes that it does not rule out the kind of Absolute Mind or Consciousness postulated by post-Hegelian idealists and certain Indian religions, or the "ocean of consciousness" of William James, Schrödinger, and Köstler referred to at the beginning of this Introduction. It is true that this ocean of consciousness theory has nothing to fear from the challenge of individuation, but two other very serious problems arise in connection with it. In the first place it is not clear that we are dealing with a genuine theory. We are given no more than a vague picture—individual minds are said to merge in the Absolute Mind after death, just as drops of water merge into the ocean. We certainly understand what is meant by an ocean composed of water. We also understand what would be meant by an ocean composed of some other liquid—milk, for example, or champagne. But what is an ocean composed of "mental stuff," to use an expression common among philosophers writing during the last decades of the nineteenth century? And even if this difficulty is waived and we concede that statements about an ocean of consciousness possess some literal significance, there are strong reasons for supposing that no such ocean exists. This will be explained at the end of the next section.

4. *The dependence of the mind on the brain.* The disembodied mind has already been so severely battered that a compassionate critic might wish to leave it in peace. Unfortunately, however, there is another extremely important and altogether formidable objection which cannot

be ignored. If the first three objections are classified as "conceptual," the one about to be explained may not inappropriately be regarded as scientific or empirical. It is based on the established dependence of mental states and processes on the body in general and the brain and central nervous system in particular. We already met this argument briefly at the end of our discussion of reincarnation. The basic idea has been stated very clearly by Bertrand Russell. "All the evidence goes to show," Russell writes, "that what we regard as our mental life is bound up with brain structure and organized bodily energy." At the same time we know that the brain is not immortal and that the organized energy of the living body becomes demobilized at death. Therefore "it is rational to suppose that mental life ceases when bodily life ceases." The three conceptual objections discussed earlier may weigh heavily with professional philosophers, but they are largely unknown to people in other fields. The empirical objection now under discussion, on the other hand, has a very wide public. After learning something about the way in which thoughts and feelings depend on the brain, a great many people, including psychologists and brain physiologists, find the notion of disembodied mental states utterly fantastic.

In this book the argument from the dependence of consciousness on the brain is defended by Hume (selection 9) and the present writer (selection 33). It is rejected by Bishop Butler (selection 7), who lived in an age when very little was known about the brain. However, it was also rejected by Mill (selection 14), James (selection 32), and Ducasse (selection 19), all of whom were familiar with some of the most notable results of brain physiology.

A little earlier we observed that believers in a universal or cosmic consciousness do not seem to be advocating a coherent theory. The argument now under discussion suggests that the theory would be in deep trouble even if it were coherent. A number of distinguished scientists of the late nineteenth century, who were hostile to belief in God, applied the argument to the question of a cosmic consciousness. "Can we regard the universe," asked W. K. Clifford, "or that part of it which immediately surrounds us, as a vast brain, and therefore the reality which underlies it as a conscious mind? This question has been considered by the great naturalist, Du Bois-Reymond, and has received from him that negative answer which I think we also must give." The naturalist in question, Emil Du Bois-Reymond (1818–1896), had written that before he could "allow a psychical principle to the universe" he needed to be shown "somewhere within it, embedded in neurine and fed with warm arterial blood under proper pressure, a convolution of ganglionic globules and nerve-tubes proportioned in size to the faculties of such a mind." But no such gigantic ganglionic globules or nerve-tubes are discoverable, and, hence, we should not allow a "psychical principle" to the universe. This argument does not of course have any bearing on belief in a God who is not equated with a cosmic or universal consciousness, but it is clearly relevant to the theory found in the *Upanishads* and championed by Schrödinger and Köstler.

The Resurrection of the Body

We have noted the powerful objections to belief in the astral body and the many difficulties faced by believers in the disembodied mind. Does the third vehicle of survival, the resurrected body, fare any better? It certainly has not been wanting in supporters. Belief in bodily resurrection was a tenet of the Pharisees (as opposed to the Sadducees, who did not believe in survival at all), it is universally accepted among Moslems, and it has the endorsement of most of the Christian churches. Both St. Paul and Thomas Aquinas believed in the resurrection of the body. "The trumpet shall sound," St. Paul proclaimed in one of the most famous passages of the New Testament, "and the dead shall be raised incorruptible." (*I Corinthians*, chapter 15). Aquinas emphatically believed in the resurrection of the body (selection 4), but his position is more complex than that of many other resurrectionists. He believed that for some time after death the soul continues to exist without the body, but he regarded such a state as falling short of a fully human existence. Eventually, however, the soul will be reunited with a resurrected body. Few Christian sects are as explicit about the details of the resurrection as Seventh Day Adventists, who are fundamentalists but reject the notion of hell. They believe that Christ will return to earth and, when the Second Coming occurs, the just will rise and live with Him for a thousand years. At the end of this millenium the unjust will also be raised, only to be extinguished along with Satan, the author of all sin. No date has been specified for the Second Coming but it is suggested that it will occur in the near future. Although individual Anglicans rebelled against what they considered a crude and offensive doctrine which played into the hands of the opponents of Christianity, the resurrection of the body has to this day remained part of the official theology of the Anglican Church. The Apostles' Creed, the baptismal creed of the Church, is quite specific on this issue and teaches the "Resurrection of the Flesh." To this account it must be added that the leading Christian existentialists, Rudolf Bultmann and Paul Tillich, who favor "demythologizing" Christian doctrines, reject the resurrection in any literal sense, but it is doubtful if they and their numerous followers believe in survival at all, at least in the straightforward sense in which we are concerned with it in this book. Several of the best-known Christian philosophers in Anglo-Saxon countries—Richard Swinburne, Thomas Geach, and John Hick—are supporters of this view, maintaining that it and not belief in the disembodied mind is the doctrine taught in the Bible.

Whatever its own difficulties, belief in resurrection of the body avoids many of the objections which have been leveled against belief in survival of the disembodied mind. To begin with, we have no individuation problem here: bodies are available to allow us to decide to whom a given experience or mental state belongs. Again, if a person survives with his body, it will be quite intelligible to say that he is sad or gay, that he sees and hears things and that he engages in various activities for which a body is required. Since resurrection bodies presumably possess brains, this doctrine is also quite consistent with the dependence of consciousness on the brain. Finally, survivors with resurrection bodies would not be condemned to the lonely existence of disembodied minds. Aquinas denied that there would be any sex or eating in Heaven, but a believer in the resurrected body is not committed to the pronouncements of Aquinas; and even without sex or food plenty of worthwhile activities would remain. It should also be pointed out that when believers think of their reunions with the dead in the next world they invariably imply that all those who participate in these reunions will have bodies and that these bodies will be the same as those they had on earth.

THE LITERAL VERSION

When first mentioning the resurrected body, we pointed out that this belief comes in two versions. The first, which may be described as the literal version, maintains that the vehicles of survival are the very bodies human beings had in this life. This is the view of Aquinas and several early Christian fathers. It also seems implied in numerous passages in the Bible. One of the most famous of these, set to music in Handel's *Messiah*, occurs in one of Job's speeches:

> For I know that my Redeemer liveth,
> And that he shall stand at the latter day upon the earth;
> And though after my skin worms destroy this body,
> yet in my flesh shall I see God. (*Job* 19; 25–26)

We are also told in the Book of Daniel that "many of them that sleep in the dust of the earth shall awake, some to everlasting life, and some to shame and everlasting contempt." The *Westminster Confession of Faith* of 1647, drawn up by the Puritan administrators and members of Parliament at the Westminster Assembly, is quite explicit on the subject. All the dead, according to this document, "shall be raised up with the self-same bodies, and none other" (chap. 32). In his Boyle lectures of 1704–1705, Samuel Clarke (1675–1729) supported the literal version of resurrection, as did Joseph Priestley (selection 13). Among contemporary philosophers, Peter van Inwagen and Peter Geach are ardent defenders of this view. Geach maintains that our bodies in the next life will be "materially continuous" with those we now have. "The traditional faith of Christianity, inherited from Judaism," Geach writes, "is that 'at the end of this age Messiah will come and men will rise from their graves to die no more' " (selection 23). Van Inwagen (selection 25) argues that unless the bodies we have on earth are somehow preserved until Judgment Day there can be no hope that *we* will be resurrected. It is of some interest that the opposition to cremation and dissection which prevailed in Christian countries until the end of the nineteenth century was in large measure the result of the widespread belief in resurrection in the literal sense. It was reasoned that if we have the skeletal remains it might be possible to resurrect the body on Judgment Day, but that this would be impossible if the remains had been completely destroyed by fire.

This simple and straightforward version of resurrectionism has been ridiculed by many writers, including some who were believers in survival. The late Professor C. J. Ducasse who spent a good deal of his life looking for evidence of survival and who ended up as a champion of reincarnation, was scathing in his dismissal of the resurrection doctrine. When the ideas of the Judeo-Christian religion are "viewed objectively," he wrote, "they are seen to be more paradoxical than the idea of reincarnation." This is particularly obvious in the case of the "resurrection of the flesh" in which Christians and Jews believed in spite of "the dispersion of the dead body's material by cremation or by incorporation of its particles into the living bodies of worms, sharks or vultures." Voltaire mercilessly ridiculed resurrectionism both in the *Philosophical Dictionary* and in the *Questions Concerning the Encyclopedia*. One of his favorite illustrations is derived from the practice of cannibalism (selection 10):

> A soldier from Brittany goes into Canada; there, by a very common chance, he finds himself short of food, and he is forced to eat an Iroquois whom he killed the day before. The Iroquois had fed on Jesuits for two or three months; a great part of his body had become Jesuit. Here, then, the body of a soldier is composed of Iroquois, of Jesuits, and of all that he had eaten before. How is each to take again precisely what belongs to him? And which part belongs to each?

These criticisms would be on target if the believers in resurrection did not also believe in an omnipotent and omniscient deity. In fact, however, all of them do, and an appeal to divine omnipotence and omniscience would take care of at least some of the difficulties. The standard retort is that God could collect all the particles of the old body and reassemble them in whatever way is required for resurrection. Nor, as both Aquinas and Priestley point out, is it necessary to collect *all* the particles. Cannibalism presents a special problem and the solution offered by Aquinas is not widely accepted, not even by theologians who agree with him on most other issues. Aquinas argues (selection 4) that what he called the "radical seed," by which he seems to mean the sperm, forms the essential bodily core around which God could rebuild a person's body. Richard Swinburne, who discusses this argument at some length, has pointed out that, contrary to what Aquinas believed, we now know that the sperm does not remain as a unit within the organism. There is no reason, to quote Swinburne, "why all the atoms which originally formed it should not be lost from the body" and "come to form parts of the original cells of many subsequent men." Swinburne concludes that the problem of cannibalism "remains without modern solution."

THE RESURRECTION REPLICA

The problems of cannibalism and several other difficulties besetting the literal form of resurrectionism are avoided by the more sophisticated version of the theory. Asserting the resurrection of the body, according to Bishop Charles Gore, an influential Anglican theologian of the early twentieth century, "does not mean that the particles of our former bodies, which were laid in the grave and which have decayed and passed into all sorts and forms of natural life, will be collected together again." "The resurrection of the dead," writes John Hick, one of the most articulate spokesmen of this position, "has nothing to do with the resuscitation of corpses in the cemetery" (selection 24). What it means is the creation of an "exact replica" of the dead body, a "resurrection replica." Perhaps because it would produce serious recognition difficulties, Hick does not go along with St. Paul's suggestion that the spiritual body of postmortem individuals may be as unlike the original as a full grain of wheat differs from the wheat seed. Hick favors the view of St. Irenaeus that the "resurrection body will have the same shape as the physical body." Hick postulates a "resurrection world inhabited only by resurrected persons." The resurrection world occupies "its own space," distinct from the space of the world in which we now live. Objects in both worlds occupy positions relative to those of other objects in the same world, but they are not "situated at any distance or at any direction" from objects in the other world. It is implied—although Hick nowhere explicitly asserts this—that a person in one world cannot perceive anything going on in the other one.

Aside from avoiding the problem of cannibalism, the more sophisticated version of resurrectionism has the advantage of not having to fall back at any stage on the disembodied mind. Anybody who maintains that God will resurrect our original bodies at the end of "this age," however, has to face the question of how individuals will exist during the period—which may be billions of years—between the moment of death and Judgment Day. This difficulty is quite similar to the interregnum problem of reincarnationists. The common talk about sleep in the grave is hardly acceptable, if only because it makes no sense to talk about skeletons, ashes, or dispersed atoms as sleeping. It is difficult to see how the defender of the literal version can avoid invoking the disembodied mind unless he wishes to postulate an astral body. Hick seems to hold that the next life begins immediately after the death of the original body and that the resurrection world exists right now. The transition from the present to the next life is likened to a journey from one country to another. The interregnum problem does not arise for this position.

So much for the advantages of the sophisticated version. It is, however, beset by many problems that are avoided by the literal version. For one thing, the postulation of a space distinct from the space of this world raises a great many questions. We will not pursue these here but will instead concentrate on the more basic difficulty which concerns the relation of the resurrection replica to the premortem individual. Are we justified in regarding them as identical? Antony Flew is one of those who maintain that we are not. "To produce even the most indistinguishably similar object after the first one has been totally destroyed and disappeared," he writes, "is to produce not the same object again, but a replica." Flew then points out how unjust it would be to punish or reward a replica for deeds performed by the original:

> To punish or reward a replica, reconstituted on Judgment Day, for the sins or the virtues of the old Antony Flew dead and cremated in 1984, is as inept and as unfair as it would be to reward or to punish one identical twin for what was in fact done by the other.

Flew could have added the observation that Hick is using the word "resurrection" in a highly misleading way. "Resurrection" in its original and literal sense means bringing a dead body back to life, and in such a case we would have no identity problem. If we accept the New Testament account, then Jesus resurrected Lazarus in this literal sense. If instead of bringing the body of Lazarus back to life Jesus had allowed it to remain a corpse and created a duplicate, this would no doubt have been a stunning miracle but it could hardly be counted as a resurrection.

Hick has answered his critics in several places (see, for example, the postscript to selection 24). He argues that in many hypothetical situations which diverge from "ordinary straight-forward identity" we are not faced with questions of fact but with "matters for decision." He mentions some of the ingenious thought experiments of Derek Parfitt, including one in which a "teletransporter" scans my body, records its states in complete detail, then destroys it and the next moment forms an exact replica on Mars. The replica's consciousness is continuous with that of the person on earth: Is it me? Have I been teletransported or has a new human being been created in my place? Hick maintains that this question is a matter for decision and that the same is true of the one concerning the identity of post- and premortem individuals. He then argues that the "best decision," by which he means "the one that best satisfies our intuitions and that gives rise to the fewest practical problems," is to say that the replica on Mars is me and equally that the postmortem replica in the next world is identical with the premortem person whose replica it is.

It does not appear that this is a valid answer to Hick's opponents. What we have here is a piece of willful self-deception. The following illustration supports the view that, unlike many of Parfitt's puzzle cases, the question raised by Hick's version of resurrectionism is quite adequately covered by existing rules, and that these rules require us to say that the replicas are *not* identical with the corresponding premortem persons. Let us assume that the great German baritone Dietrich Fischer-Dieskau is about to begin a recital of Schubert songs in Carnegie Hall. Just as he seems ready to launch into the first song, a replica appears on the stage — a person looking exactly like Fischer-Dieskau and, as subsequently develops, possessing a voice and a vocal style exactly like those of the master. It is also established that he completely resembles the original Fischer-Dieskau in character traits and has the same memories. Everybody, except for a handful of philosophers who had been working on the subject of personal identity, is dumbfounded. As if the appearance of the replica was not enough, the original Fischer-Dieskau collapses and, as is subsequently discovered, dies on the spot. After an intermission, Janet Kellerman, president of the Carnegie Hall Corporation, announces that although Mr. Fischer-Dieskau is indisposed, an exact replica has fortunately arrived in New York just in time and will sing the scheduled program. The replica then performs just as the original Fischer-Dieskau had been expected to do, receiving ovations from the audience and highly favorable notices in the press, with the usual reservations about the singer's tendency toward barking and shouting in dramatic songs. The original Fischer-Dieskau is buried in West Berlin, but both his family and the world of music accept the fiction that the replica *is* Fischer-Dieskau, that is, that it is identical with the singer who died on the stage of Carnegie Hall. For a few weeks indeed the replica is referred to as "Fischer-Dieskau II" in announcements of his appearances, but before long the "II" is dropped and he is announced as just Fischer-Dieskau.

Now, it seems clear that, however satisfying the fiction may be that the replica is identical with the late Fischer-Dieskau, it *is* a fiction. We do not have a case here calling for "decision." Our existing linguistic rules require us to describe the facts by saying that the double now universally treated as if he were the original Fischer-Dieskau is not in fact identical with the singer who collapsed on the stage of Carnegie Hall. And the same surely applies to Hick's case. Let us suppose that the double had appeared not on the stage of Carnegie Hall but in the resurrection world when Fischer-Dieskau was still alive and active on earth. The double would then no more be identical with Fischer-Dieskau than in the previously sketched situation. We will next suppose that the original Fischer-Dieskau died while the double continues to exist in the resurrection world. It is not clear why this should have the slightest effect on the identity question. Finally, we get to Hick's situation in which the double appears in the resurrection world *after* the original Fischer-Dieskau died. It is not apparent that this will affect the identity issue either. The inhabitants of the resurrection world may, indeed, to satisfy certain of their emotional needs, treat the replica as if he were the late Fischer-Dieskau, but this would just as much be a fiction as the one embraced by the earthly music lovers.

Another objection, directed primarily against the replica version but also with destructive implications for the literal version of the theory, is presented in van Inwagen's "The Possibility of Resurrection" (selection 25), an unjustly neglected paper containing many interesting observations on personal identity and the weaknesses of what van Inwagen calls "Aristotelian" attempts to defend resurrectionism. Readers convinced by van Inwagen's argument are liable to conclude that both forms of the resurrection doctrine are indefensible. He himself does not reach this conclusion and tries to salvage the literal version by the suggestion that "perhaps at the moment of each man's death God removes his corpse and replaces it with a simulacrum which is what is burnt or rots." Van Inwagen also considers the possibility that God is not quite so "wholesale." Perhaps "He removes for 'safekeeping' only the 'core person'—the brain and central nervous system—or even some special part of it." The removal of corpses is surely an observable process, even if the Remover is not observable, but, to the best of my knowledge, no undertaker or anybody else has ever observed such a removal. Van Inwagen does not help matters by failing to specify the location of the stolen corpses. If he is right, there should by now be quite a pile which could hardly escape detection. In any case, the notion of God as a chronic body-snatcher and arch-deceiver is not likely to commend itself to believers.

The Age Regression Problem

Both versions of resurrectionism are exposed to another difficulty to which no satisfactory answer seems available. Let us call it the "age regression" problem. This problem equally confronts the believer in the disembodied mind, but most of the theologians who recognized the problem and responded to it were resurrectionists. The following is a statement by W. T. Stace:

> When an old man dies, what kind of consciousness is supposed to survive? Is it his consciousness as it was just before death, which may perhaps have become imbecile? Or is it the consciousness of his mature middle age? Or is it the infant mind that he had when he was a baby? The point of these questions is not that we do not know the answers to them. The point is that all possible answers are equally senseless. Suppose we suggest that it is the mature consciousness which will survive because it is the best. Then will the old man who dies suddenly revert to his middle years after death? And will the infant who dies suddenly become mature?

Stace does not mean that the age-regression problem makes statements about survival meaningless. He does mean that it presents a serious difficulty in the way of getting a coherent or credible theory.

Dr. Kübler-Ross, who originally achieved fame for her work with dying patients, has in recent years spent much of her time defending belief in survival on "strictly scientific" grounds. She has the advantage over the rest of us of having met several visitors from the next world. On October 2, 1978, Kübler-Ross was interviewed by Roy Bonnisteel on a program broadcast on Canadian television. Bonnisteel had done his homework and was ready with questions about the likeness of our dead friends and relatives who are supposedly met in the course of near-death experiences and deathbed visions. The following exchange ensued:

> RB: Are they ever described in terms of what they are wearing? Are they wearing anything?
> KR: Only shortly after death they will appear like the physical bodies in order for you to recognize them. This is like an ethereal body. But you obviously know your child or your mother or father—
> RB: Yes, but you see, I'm wondering how they look, because a lot of people on their deathbed don't look very well. I mean, am I going to see—am I going to—
> KR: They look young and healthy.
> RB: They look young and healthy?
> KR: Yes.
> RB: At a younger age.
> KR: They look the way they feel would appeal to you the most.
> RB: Hmmm.
> KR: Like if you had a marvelous time with your mother when she was 50, she looked at her best, she would come to you the way she looked when she was 50 and you had the best time together. But that is their choice. They can appear any way that is the most appealing to you.

Surely not even Dr. Pangloss could have come up with a more cheerful solution. Ever since 1975 Kübler-Ross has announced a book in which all her evidence will be meticulously presented. We can only hope that its publication will not be delayed much longer.

St. Augustine and John Hick are two of the few serious philosophers who have offered detailed responses to our problem. Augustine maintains that the postmortem person will be about thirty years old, apparently regarding this as the physical and mental peak of life. Those who died in infancy nevertheless had the potentiality of adulthood and God will convert their potential into actual adulthood in the next life. Similarly, He will miraculously reverse the decline that set in after thirty. The main, but not the only, difficulty with this solution relates to the conversion of potential into actual adulthood in the case of children who died young. It is clear that Augustine did not consider certain of the complications involved in such conversions. What an individual becomes is obviously in large measure the result of interactions with other human beings. Let us assume that a child who in fact died at the age of six months would have interacted in a major way with twenty other people if he had lived to the age of thirty. These interactions would have had all kinds of effect not only on the child but also on the other twenty people. Will these twenty people be resurrected as they actually were at thirty or as they would have been if the child had not died in infancy? And what about effects on these people of other children who in fact died but are now assumed to have lived on? And what about the effects of the adults as they would have been on others? Will these others be resurrected as they actually were or as they would have been?

Hick understandably wishes to combine in the resurrection replicas the wisdom and maturity of age with the vigor and health of youth. We can conceive of the replica of the person "in the physical prime of his life," at around the age of thirty, but the price paid for health and vigor would be high. For such a replica will lose all the memories and character development that had accrued since he was thirty. On the whole it would be best to think of the replica as being like the original body as it was "at the last moment of conscious personal life." In that case, however, we must not allow the replica to die at once, as the original did. We will suppose that in the resurrection world it will be "subjected to processes of healing and repair which bring it into a state of health and activity." For people who died in old age we may go a step further and "conceive of a process of growing physically younger to an optimum age."

It is impossible not to admire the ingenuity with which Hick develops his Panglossian fantasies. We have obviously now reached a cloud-cuckoo land in which all the most delightful dreams will become reality. Hick resembles a pauper who imagines himself a millionaire and then debates with himself how he is going to spend his money. It is salutory to remind resurrectionists of all stripes that resurrections have never been observed and, by their own stipulation, cannot be observed in "this space." To bring the subject down to earth one is tempted to quote certain of Freud's comments in *The Future of an Illusion.* "What use to man," he writes, "is the illusion of a kingdom on the moon whose revenues have never yet been seen by anyone?" Let us leave the heavens, he then quotes his fellow-skeptic, Heinrich Heine, to the "angels and the sparrows."

Metaphysical and Moral Arguments

We noted earlier that reincarnationists generally support their belief by an appeal to various kinds of evidence. There is similarly a long history of attempts to justify the survival beliefs associated with Western religions by arguments of different kinds. Since Pascal and Rousseau, however, it has not been uncommon, especially among Protestant theologians, to declare that it is simply a matter of faith. "All the subtleties of metaphysics will never make me doubt for a moment the immortality of the soul and a beneficent providence," Rousseau wrote in a famous letter to Voltaire. "I feel it, I believe it, I want it, I hope for it. I will defend it to my last breath." Undoubtedly many believers feel just as Rousseau did. But this is only part of the story. For just as there is a hunger for immortality, so there is also a hunger for possessing evidence, as witnessed by the enormous popularity of books and articles about near-death experiences and similar phenomena. In this and the next two sections we will examine some of the major attempts to justify belief in survival on rational grounds. Evidence and arguments may not be what moves people and makes them into believers, but some of these arguments are of great interest and in any event they deserve to be considered in any reasonably comprehensive discussion of the case for and against survival.

F. R. Tennant, whose rejection of materialism was discussed earlier, has offered a helpful classification of the arguments in favor of survival. He first distinguishes those which presuppose theism, maintaining survival as one of its corollaries, from the arguments that are independent of assumptions about the existence and nature of God. He then subdivides the latter into three groups which he calls "empirical," "metaphysical" and "ethical" or "moral" respectively. By "empirical" arguments he means the evidence or alleged evidence from what is now called parapsychology. In this book the evidence from parapsychology is discussed in the piece by Paul and Linda Badham (selection 27) and John Beloff (selection 28). I have also included the account of A. J. Ayer's near-death experience in 1988 which attracted a great deal of attention because of the subject's fame and also because Ayer was known to be a total unbeliever in survival. In spite of subsequent protestations that he had been misunderstood, it is clear that at the time of writing his account Ayer thought that his experience had *some* evidential value.

The metaphysical and moral arguments will be briefly discussed in the present section. In the next section I will discuss the argument from the conservation of "spiritual energy" which does not neatly fit into Tennant's classification but may perhaps be regarded as "empirical" in a broad sense of this word. In the last section I will discuss the question of how far the assumption of an omnipotent and perfectly benevolent deity helps the case for survival. Tennant himself, it may be noted, rejected the metaphysical and moral arguments but maintained that theism allows us to derive a conclusion in favor of survival. Unlike more recent writers who have held the same view, Tennant believed that theism can be adequately supported by an appeal to teleology. His argument on this topic, incidentally, is much more careful and sophisticated than pre-Darwinian design arguments of the kind found in Voltaire and Paley.

All the best-known metaphysical arguments try to prove immortality by reflecting on the nature of the soul or spiritual substance and the meaning of such key terms as "destruction" and "annihilation." Tennant calls these arguments "metaphysical," but he might as well have described them as *"a priori"* since, as he puts it, they deal only with "a linkage of abstract ideas." Such arguments dominated philosophical discussion of immortality until the early eighteenth century and, in some places, even much later. They figure prominently, for example, in the writings of Ralph Cudworth (1617–1688), perhaps the most important of the Cambridge Platonists, and the aforementioned Samuel Clarke, who is best known for his defenses of free will and of absolute space and time in his correspondence with Leibniz. In Germany, whose Enlightenment was considerably tamer than its counterparts in France and Britain, such arguments were endorsed by Christian Wolff (1679–1754) and Moses Mendelssohn (1729–1786). Since the time of Hume and Kant the metaphysical arguments for immortality have lost most of their appeal and they are no longer taken very seriously, except perhaps as illustrations of a defective method of reasoning. In the present volume they are defended in the selections from Plato and Aquinas and they are criticized in those from Hume, Kant, Mill, and Hick.

One of the clearest statements of the ethical argument is found in Father Maher's *Psychology*:

Can it be equally well in the end for the successful swindler who amasses a fortune by the plunder of his clients, and for the upright man who struggles through a life of poverty, and resisting temptation, died in want? . . . Our whole rational moral nature affirms that this cannot be the final outcome of things: that it cannot in the last resort be as well or better for those who violate the principles of justice and those who faithfully observe the moral law. . . . *The first postulate of physical science is that the universe is rational. . . . Would it be a rational universe, if vice is to be rewarded and virtue to be punished in the end?* Is it a rational universe if the moral life of mankind be founded on an *illusion*? (Maher's italics.)

The objection to this admittedly moving argument which expresses a deeply felt need in many human beings is that it begs the main question. That the world is just is precisely what the skeptic does not allow. It cannot simply be assumed. From the fact that the universe is rational in the sense presupposed in science—that it contains regularities or uniformities—it does not at all follow that it is also rational in the moral sense. The moral argument contains, to quote Santayana, "a tremendous optimistic postulate, to the effect that what is requisite to moral rationality" must be realized; and this optimistic postulate is not supported by experience.

The Conservation of Spiritual Energy

The main idea of the argument to be discussed in this section is stated in a quotation from the rocket scientist Werner von Braun, which Thomas Pynchon placed at the head of his novel *Gravity's Rainbow*:

> Nature does not know extinction; all it knows is transformation. Everything science has taught me and continues to teach me, strengthens my belief in the continuity of life after death.

As far as I know Werner von Braun did not believe in reincarnation, but if his reasoning is sound it would also prove life before birth, and reincarnationists have in fact quite frequently appealed to the conservation of energy. Thus V. F. Gunaratna, a Buddhist philosopher, after informing his readers that "thought, like matter, is energy," proceeds to assert that since it is energy, it cannot be destroyed or annihilated. A few pages later in the same work we are again assured that, being a form of energy, thought "cannot be lost or destroyed." It goes on producing its results, and they in turn produce theirs, "though not necessarily in the same plane or sphere."

Unlike the metaphysical or moral arguments, the appeal to the conservation of spiritual energy cannot be described as a standard argument for immortality. However, it crops up again and again in popular literature and it is a staple of occultist ideology. Versions of it seem to have had some currency in the eighteenth century, quite a long time before the first formulation of conservation principles by physicists. We may infer this from the fact that Hume felt called upon to show one of its weaknesses. In any event, it is a fun argument if only because it commits more fallacies per square inch than almost any other argument known to man.

One of its least cryptic presentations is contained in "Ten Reasons for Believing in Immortality," a sermon delivered at the Community Church in New York in 1929 by John Haynes Holmes (1879–1964), one of the leading liberal Protestants of his time. Holmes begins by stating the conservation principle of physics in its pre-Einsteinian form, in which what is conserved is simply energy and not mass-energy. This is a detail which is of no consequence to our discussion. "The gist of this doctrine," Holmes writes, is "that nothing in the universe is ever lost. All energy is conserved." No matter what transformations take place, "the energy persists if not in the old form then in a new one" and the sum total remains the same. Holmes has no doubt that the conservation principle can be applied to the "spiritual world." Just as physical energy does not simply appear and disappear, so "intellectual or moral or spiritual energy" do not simply come and go:

> We would laugh at a man who contended that the heat in molten metal, which disappears under the cooling action of air or water, had thereby been destroyed. Why should we not similarly laugh at a man who argues that the personality of a human being, which disappears under the chilling influence of death, has thereby been annihilated?

The soul of man "is just as much a force in the world as magnetism or steam or electricity," and if the cosmic law of conservation "forbids the destruction of the latter," it must also "forbid the destruction of the former." In this way we are led to the conclusion that human beings must survive the death of their bodies:

> What prevails in the great realm of matter can be only an anticipation of what must equally prevail in the greater realm of spirit.

Before going any further it should be pointed out that just like the reincarnationists, Holmes and other Western writers who defend this argument are dualists. They are not talking about ordinary energy but about a special form of it that is not recognized by physicists. A materialist who regards thought as a secretion of the brain or who maintains that mental events are identical with brain states could quite consistently regard them as energy in the physical sense or at least as mass which is convertible into energy. Such a claim is not open to a dualist.

The most obvious objection to this argument is that there is no such thing as spiritual energy. If we accept dualism, as the defenders of the argument do, then thought is *not* a form of energy. It may be related to energy in various ways, but it must be *sui generis* or else we are back to some form of materialism. If the expression "spiritual energy" really referred to energy of some kind, it would have to be quantifiable. It would then be entirely possible to select a unit of this energy, say a "spir," and it would not be absurd to ask such questions as "Into how much heat or electricity can the spiritual energy now present in this person's mind be converted?" It would be possible to convert spiritual energy into kinetic or chemical energy and it would in principle be possible to establish appropriate transformation formulae.

Let us ignore this objection and grant for the sake of discussion that "spiritual energy" refers to something that is real but not physical. This would not be of any help to the supporters of the argument. The conservation principle has been shown by physicists to hold only for physical energy. If there is a non-physical energy we have no right whatever to say that the conservation principle applies to it. Incidentally, if we allow the concept of "spiritual energy," there would be no reason to disallow a concept of "spiritual entropy"; and just as *usable* physical energy is constantly lost, so the same might well be true of spiritual energy.

Even if we waive all these objections, the argument would still prove nothing to the point. The conservation of physical energy does not guarantee the continued, far less the eternal, existence of particular entities. It is quite consistent with the destruction of houses, mountains, stars and of course plants and animal bodies. What evidence is there that if our minds were indeed composed of spiritual energy, and if this energy were indestructible, that our *individual* minds exist for ever? "Admitting a spiritual substance to be dispersed throughout the universe," Hume wrote in his "Of the Immortality of the Soul," we have no right to exclude the possibility that it "may be continually dissolved by death" and take on forms or modifications which would be of no interest to us, that is, which would in no sense be continuations of *us* (selection 9).

It is of some interest to note that the aforementioned German psychologist and philosopher Wilhelm Wundt proposed a "law of the *increase* of spiritual energy." If we regard consciousness as "spiritual energy"—the mental counterpart of physical energy—Wundt is surely in a much stronger position than the believers in the *conservation* of spiritual energy. The population increase, the greater longevity and perhaps the more active mental life of human beings, surely support an increase rather than a constant amount of spiritual energy. William James, who approvingly refers to Wundt's proposed law, observes that "the amount of personal consciousness seems to be governed by no law analogous to that of the so-called conservation of energy in the material world." James illustrates his statement by noting that "when one man wakes up another does not have to go to sleep and when one is born another does not have to die in order to keep the consciousness of the universe in constant quantity."

As for von Braun's solemn pronouncement that "nature does not know extinction," the proper comment is that it is specious rhetoric. Nature "knows" plenty of extinctions. Dinosaurs are extinct and so are a great many other species. And what is true of "nature" equally holds for the human world. The library of Alexandria was burnt down by a mob of religious fanatics in A.D. 391 and many of the books in it, including all the works of Democritus, were lost forever. Similarly, many priceless art treasures were destroyed during the last war. And what about the Watergate tapes whose text had been erased and the documents shredded by Oliver North and his secretary? Examples can be multiplied indefinitely. Defenders of the argument occasionally say such things as, "If death is really the end, where does the consciousness of the individual go?" The skeptic can reply without any absurdity that consciousness goes nowhere — it just ceases to exist. Such an answer is entirely appropriate in a great many completely uncontroversial situations. As they age, singers frequently lose the special sheen of their voices. It clearly makes no sense to ask where the sheen has gone and the same is true of shadows which have disappeared. The fact that the sheen of a voice or a shadow has not gone anywhere does not entail that they still exist and are in fact indestructible.

God and Survival

Does human survival logically follow from the existence of God? Before dealing with this question let us summarize the four positions that have been held on the simultaneous truth (or otherwise) of these two beliefs:

1. The most familiar position in the West is belief in God as well as *human* survival. This is the view of traditional Christian believers, of Muslims and of many Jewish sects. Several of the authors represented in this book (Tertullian, Aquinas, Descartes, Priestley, MacKay, Geach, and Hick) adopt such a position.

It is of some interest to note certain of the disagreements among those who believe both in God and in human survival. The majority do not include animals, not even chimpanzees or dolphins, among creatures who will live after death, but some philosophers have been emphatic that animals cannot be excluded. Joseph Priestley, who was both a brilliant scientist and a kind and generous man, noted "the great misery" to which animals are frequently condemned. This fact "inclined" him to think that "a merciful and just God will make them some recompense for it hereafter." William James spoke up for a "democratic" view of immortality in opposition to the older "aristocratic" outlook which allowed survival only to a few outstanding members of the human race. He thought that the aristocratic view betrayed "the veriest lack and dearth of imagination" as well as a grave lack of compassion. "The universe, with every living entity which her resources create," he wrote, "creates at the same time a call for that entity, and an appetite for its continuance — creates it, if nowhere else, at least within the heart of the entity itself." James' listeners, who were mostly prosperous late-nineteenth-century Americans, presumably did not have a high opinion of the value of the Chinese. "Which of you here, my friends," James asked, "sees any fitness in their eternal perpetuation unreduced in numbers?" He then pointed out how these and other "aliens" were animated by an "inner joy of living as hot or hotter" than that "in the breasts" of his listeners. Survival after death should not only be postulated for all the numberless "Chinamen" but equally for our "half-brutish prehistoric brothers," for the "patient beasts," and even for "every leaf that ever grew in this world's forests and rustled in the breeze." It is perhaps reassuring to remember that James did not assert any of this as categorical truth. He never in fact declared himself a believer in survival at all. He merely regarded it as a possibility, defending it against certain objections. Perhaps even James would have balked at extending immortality to all the roaches who have ever lived. Although not very pleasant creatures, especially when they creep into a person's clothes, roaches may be excused on the ground that they are after all just doing "their thing," but if they continued to do their thing in Heaven they would once again have to be exterminated, unless of course they became purely spiritual or astral roaches.

It is doubtful that James convinced many of his listeners of the survival of "patient beasts" or of all the leaves that ever grew in the world's forests. They very probably agreed, however, that if Americans and Europeans survive, then so do "Chinamen." Very few educated believers at the present time would exclude any human beings for reasons of religion, race, or national origin, but there is serious disagreement over whether even those who have led worthless lives, and more especially those who have been filled with malice, will be allowed to survive. John Hick is convinced that all human beings will survive, even those who have done terrible harm. If there are "finally wasted lives" and "finally unredeemed suffering," Hick writes, then either God is not "perfect in love or He is not sovereign in rule over His creation." The life beyond death has to be conceived as a "state of exultant and blissful happiness," symbolized in the teaching of Jesus as "a joyous banquet in which all and sundry, having accepted God's gracious invitation, rejoice together."

Thomas Paine believed in God as ardently as Hick, but he did not think that all human beings will survive. In a posthumously published paper entitled "My Private Thoughts of a Future State" he observed that if "a man and a woman make a child," this does not impose on the Creator "the obligation of keeping the being so made in eternal existence." Some, namely those whose lives were spent "in doing good," will be happy hereafter, while "the very wicked will meet with some punishment." Some human beings will be neither rewarded nor punished: "those who are neither good nor bad" and also those "too insignificant for notice" will be "dropt entirely." Paine, who quite rightly regarded himself as an important person and also as a good one, was pleased to note that he was one of those who will be "continued" after death.

2. Some philosophers as well as many ordinary people, including some liberal Christians and Jews, believe in God without believing in survival. Voltaire and Mill among the writers represented in this book

fit this description. Voltaire believed in God on the basis of the design argument but he rejected survival as absurd in the light of the dependence of consciousness on the brain. Mill was less definite on the second issue, maintaining no more than that there is no clear-cut evidence either way.

3. There are some who believe in survival without believing in God. This view is not at all uncommon among Eastern reincarnationists, and some Western believers also adopt this position. We have already mentioned McTaggart and Ducasse, both of whom believed in reincarnation without believing in God. There are also atheists and agnostics among psychical researchers who are convinced that the evidence from parapsychology makes survival in another world highly probable.

4. There are philosophers and many others who reject both belief in God and in survival. Hume, Ayer, and Flew are among the authors represented in our book who belong to this group.

Let us now turn to what has been called the "theological argument" for survival — that the existence of God logically implies the survival of at least some human beings. Mill thought the argument to be invalid if we are talking about the only God whose existence is based on adequate evidence. He rejected all arguments for the existence of God except one version of the design argument which he regarded as supporting, with a considerable degree of probability, the existence of a *finite* deity. According to Mill we cannot deduce anything about human survival from the existence of such a God (selection 14). Mill allowed, however, that it is not unreasonable to infer survival from the existence of a "Being at once omnipotent and benevolent."

The latter conclusion — that we can deduce human survival from the existence of an omnipotent and benevolent deity — has won widespread but by no means universal endorsement from other philosophers, believers as well as unbelievers. Tennant, whose discussion is as comprehensive as it is sober and fair-minded, mentions "some theists" who deny that we can assert immortality to be an implication of theism since we do not know enough about God's purpose in creating the world. It may indeed be "the divine purpose in the world to produce moral personalities," but it is a further claim, and one that is not supported by any available evidence, that "the divine purpose includes the perfecting of finite moral persons, or provisions for the fulfillment of their aspirations." Tennant himself, however, regards this theological argument as valid. "God cannot be an ethically perfect Being," he writes, "and not respect the moral aspirations of the personalities which He has called into existence." If death were the end and if our love and all that is valuable in our personalities were finally extinguished, then we would not be able to ascribe righteousness to God.

Given his premises, Tennant's conclusion seems to be eminently reasonable, subject to one important proviso: the assertion that human beings will survive must be intelligible. If it is not, then God's omnipotence and perfect goodness would be of no avail. If a statement is meaningless God cannot suddenly make the same statement meaningful; and if a notion is incoherent God cannot make it coherent. In previous discussions we have noted several challenges to the intelligibility of the various forms of belief in survival. If these can be successfully rebutted, the theological argument works; if they cannot be answered, it does not work.

Let us assume that the difficulties concerning intelligibility and conceptual coherence can be overcome: what precisely does the theological argument show? It shows that the conclusion concerning the survival of human beings is as strong—that is, as certain or probable—as the assertion that there is an omnipotent and perfectly good God. To this conclusion it has to be added that, conversely, if we have strong reasons for disbelieving in survival so that there *will* be "finally wasted lives" and "finally unredeemed suffering," then we will have equally strong reasons for rejecting belief not indeed in any deity, but in one that is both omnipotent and benevolent.

There remains the problem of roaches, not to speak of sharks, barracudas, rattlesnakes, mosquitoes, and gnats. The history of theology undoubtedly contains some ingenious answers, but perhaps it would be wisest to wait for the solution until we ourselves reach the hereafter—provided of course that there is a hereafter and that we are among those who will reach it.

READINGS
ON
IMMORTALITY

1

PLATO

∞

The Release of the Soul from the Chains of the Body

∞

All the passages that make up the following selection are from the Phaedo, *in the translation of Benjamin Jowett. Socrates is speaking when the dialogue begins.*

The Separation of the Soul and Body

IN THIS PRESENT life, I reckon that we make the nearest approach to knowledge when we have the least possible intercourse or communion with the body, and are not surfeited with the bodily nature, but keep ourselves pure until the hour when God himself is pleased to release us. And thus having got rid of the foolishness of the body we shall be pure and hold converse with the pure, and know of ourselves the clear light everywhere, which is no other than the light of truth. For the impure are not permitted to approach the pure. These are the sort of words, Simmias, which the true lovers of knowledge cannot help saying to one another, and thinking. You would agree; would you not?

Undoubtedly, Socrates.

But, O my friend, if this be true, there is great reason to hope that, going whither I go, when I have come to the end of my journey, I shall attain that which has been the pursuit of my life. And therefore I go on my way rejoicing, and not I only, but every other man who believes that his mind has been made ready and that he is in a manner purified.

Certainly, replied Simmias.

And what is purification but the separation of the soul from the body, as I was saying before; the habit of the soul gathering and collecting herself into herself from all sides out of the body; the dwelling in her

73

own place alone, as in another life, so also in this, as far as she can; — the release of the soul from the chains of the body?

Very true, he said.

And this separation and release of the soul from the body is termed death?

To be sure, he said.

And the true philosophers, and they only, are ever seeking to release the soul. Is not the separation and release of the soul from the body their especial study?

That is true.

And, as I was saying at first, there would be a ridiculous contradiction in men studying to live as nearly as they can in a state of death, and yet repining when it comes upon them.

Clearly.

And the true philosophers, Simmias, are always occupied in the practice of dying, wherefore also to them least of all men is death terrible. Look at the matter thus: — if they have been in every way the enemies of the body, and are wanting to be alone with the soul, when this desire of theirs is granted, how inconsistent would they be if they trembled and repined, instead of rejoicing at their departure to that place where, when they arrive, they hope to gain that which in life they desired — and this was wisdom — and at the same time to be rid of the company of their enemy. Many a man has been willing to go to the world below animated by the hope of seeing there an earthly love, or wife, or son, and conversing with them. And will he who is a true lover of wisdom, and is strongly persuaded in like manner that only in the world below he can worthily enjoy her, still repine at death? Will he not depart with joy? Surely he will, O my friend, if he be a true philosopher. For he will have a firm conviction that there, and there only, he can find wisdom in her purity. And if this be true, he would be very absurd, as I was saying, if he were afraid of death. . . .

Recollection

. . . And shall we proceed a step further, and affirm that there is such a thing as equality, not of one piece of wood or stone with another, but that, over and above this, there is absolute equality? Shall we say so?

Say so, yes, replied Simmias, and swear to it, with all the confidence in life.

And do we know the nature of this absolute essence?

To be sure, he said.

And whence did we obtain our knowledge? Did we not see equalities of material things, such as pieces of wood and stones, and gather from them the idea of an equality which is different from them? For you will acknowledge that there is a difference. Or look at the matter in another way: — Do not the same pieces of wood or stone appear at one time equal, and at another time unequal?

That is certain.

But are real equals ever unequal? or is the idea of equality the same as of inequality?

Impossible, Socrates.

Then these (so-called) equals are not the same with the idea of equality?

I should say, clearly not, Socrates.

And yet from these equals, although differing from the idea of equality, you conceived and attained that idea?

Very true, he said.

Which might be like, or might be unlike them?

Yes.

But that makes no difference: whenever from seeing one thing you conceived another, whether like or unlike, there must surely have been an act of recollection?

Very true.

But what would you say of equal portions of wood and stone, or other material equals? and what is the impression produced by them? Are they equals in the same sense in which absolute equality is equal? or do they fall short of this perfect equality in a measure?

Yes, he said, in a very great measure too.

And must we not allow, that when I or any one, looking at any object, observes that the thing which he sees aims at being some other thing, but falls short of, and cannot be, that other thing, but is inferior, he who makes this observation must have had a previous knowledge of that to which the other, although similar, was inferior?

Certainly.

And has not this been our own case in the matter of equals and of absolute equality?

Precisely.

Then we must have known equality previously to the time when we first saw the material equals, and reflected that all these apparent equals strive to attain absolute equality, but fall short of it?

Very true.

And we recognize also that this absolute equality has only been known, and can only be known, through the medium of sight or touch, or of some other of the senses, which are all alike in this respect?

Yes, Socrates, as far as the argument is concerned, one of them is the same as the other.

From the senses then is derived the knowledge that all sensible things aim at an absolute equality of which they fall short?

Yes.

Then before we began to see or hear or perceive in any way, we must have had a knowledge of absolute equality, or we could not have referred to that standard the equals which are derived from the senses? — for to that they all aspire, and of that they fall short.

No other inference can be drawn from the previous statements.

And did we not see and hear and have the use of our other senses as soon as we were born?

Certainly.

Then we must have acquired the knowledge of equality at some previous time?

Yes.

That is to say, before we were born, I suppose?

True.

And if we acquired this knowledge before we were born, and were born having the use of it, then we also knew before we were born and at the instant of birth not only the equal or the greater or the less, but all other ideas; for we are not speaking only of equality, but of beauty, goodness, justice, holiness, and of all which we stamp with the name of essence in the dialectical process, both when we ask and when we answer questions. Of all this we may certainly affirm that we acquired the knowledge before birth?

We may.

But if, after having acquired, we have not forgotten what in each case we acquired, then we must always have come into life having knowledge, and shall always continue to know as long as life lasts — for knowing is the acquiring and retaining knowledge and not forgetting. Is not forgetting, Simmias, just the losing of knowledge?

Quite true, Socrates.

But if the knowledge which we acquired before birth was lost by us at birth, and if afterwards by the use of the senses we recovered what we precisely knew, will not the process which we call learning be a recovering of the knowledge which is natural to us, and may not this be rightly termed recollection? . . .

The Soul's Kinship with the Eternal

Then now let us return to the previous discussion. Is that idea or essence, which in the dialectical process we define as essence or true existence — whether essence of equality, beauty, or anything else — are these essences, I say, liable at times to some degree of change? or are they each of them always what they are, having the same simple self-existent and unchanging forms, not admitting of variation at all, or in any way, or at any time?

They must be always the same, Socrates, replied Cebes.

And what would you say of the many beautiful — whether men or horses or garments or any other things which are named by the same names and may be called equal or beautiful, — are they all unchanging and the same always, or quite the reverse? May they not rather be described as almost always changing and hardly ever the same, either with themselves or with one another?

The latter, replied Cebes; they are always in a state of change.

And these you can touch and see and perceive with the senses, but the unchanging things you can only perceive with the mind—they are invisible and are not seen?

That is very true, he said.

Well then, added Socrates, let us suppose that there are two sorts of existences—one seen, the other unseen.

Let us suppose them.

The seen is the changing, and the unseen is the unchanging?

That may be also supposed.

And, further, is not one part of us body, another part soul?

To be sure.

And to which class is the body more alike and akin?

Clearly to the seen—no one can doubt that.

And is the soul seen or not seen?

Not by man, Socrates.

And what we mean by "seen" and "not seen" is that which is or is not visible to the eye of man?

Yes, to the eye of man.

And is the soul seen or not seen?

Not seen.

Unseen then?

Yes.

Then the soul is more like to the unseen, and the body to the seen?

That follows necessarily, Socrates.

And were we not saying long ago that the soul when using the body as an instrument of perception, that is to say, when using the sense of sight or hearing or some other sense (for the meaning of perceiving through the body is perceiving through the senses)—were we not saying that the soul too is then dragged by the body into the region of the changeable, and wanders and is confused; the world spins round her, and she is like a drunkard, when she touches change?

Very true.

But when returning into herself she reflects, then she passes into the other world, the region of purity, and eternity, and immortality, and unchangeableness, which are her kindred, and with them she ever lives, when she is by herself and is not let or hindered; then she ceases from her erring ways, and being in communion with the unchanging is unchanging. And this state of the soul is called wisdom?

That is well and truly said, Socrates, he replied.

And to which class is the soul more nearly alike and akin, as far as may be inferred from this argument, as well as from the preceding one?

I think, Socrates, that, in the opinion of every one who follows the argument, the soul will be infinitely more like the unchangeable— even the most stupid person will not deny that.

And the body is more like the changing?

Yes.

Yet once more consider the matter in another light: When the soul and the body are united, then nature orders the soul to rule and govern, and the body to obey and serve. Now which of these two functions is akin to the divine? and which to the mortal? Does not the divine appear to you to be that which naturally orders and rules, and the mortal to be that which is subject and servant?

True.

And which does the soul resemble?

The soul resembles the divine, and the body the mortal—there can be no doubt of that, Socrates.

Then reflect, Cebes: of all which has been said is not this the conclusion?—that the soul is in the very likeness of the divine, and immortal, and intellectual, and uniform, and indissoluble, and unchangeable; and that the body is in the very likeness of the human, and mortal, and unintellectual, and multiform, and dissoluble, and changeable. Can this, my dear Cebes, be denied?

It cannot.

But if it be true, then is not the body liable to speedy dissolution? and is not the soul almost or altogether indissoluble?

Certainly.

And do you further observe, that after a man is dead, the body, or visible part of him, which is lying in the visible world, and is called a corpse, and would naturally be dissolved and decomposed and dissipated, is not dissolved or decomposed at once, but may remain for some time, nay even for a long time, if the constitution be sound at the time of death, and the season of the year favourable? For the body when shrunk and embalmed, as the manner is in Egypt, may remain almost entire through infinite ages; and even in decay, there are still some portions, such as the bones and ligaments, which are practically indestructible:—Do you agree?

Yes.

And is it likely that the soul, which is invisible, in passing to the place of the true Hades, which like her is invisible, and pure, and noble, and on her way to the good and wise God, whither, if God will, my soul is also soon to go,—that soul, I repeat, if this be her nature and origin, will be blown away and destroyed immediately on quitting the body, as the many say? That can never be, my dear Simmias and Cebes. The truth rather is, that the soul which is pure at departing and draws after her no bodily taint, having never voluntarily during life had connection with the body, which she is ever avoiding, herself gathered into herself; — and making such abstraction her perpetual study — which means that she has been a true disciple of philosophy; and therefore has in fact been always engaged in the practice of dying? For is not philosophy the study of death? —

Certainly —

That soul, I say, herself invisible, departs to the invisible world — to the divine and immortal and rational: thither arriving, she is secure of bliss and is released from the error and folly of men, their fears and wild passions and all other human ills, and for ever dwells, as they say of the initiated, in company with the gods. Is not this true, Cebes? . . .

The Transmigration of Souls

. . . the soul which has been polluted, and is impure at the time of her departure, and is the companion and servant of the body always, and is in love with and fascinated by the body and by the desires and pleasures of the body, until she is led to believe that the truth only exists in a bodily form, which a man may touch and see and taste, and use for the purposes of his lusts, — the soul, I mean, accustomed to hate and fear and avoid the intellectual principle, which to the bodily eye is dark and invisible, and can be attained only by philosophy; — do you suppose that such a soul will depart pure and unalloyed?

Impossible, he replied.

She is held fast by the corporeal, which the continual association and constant care of the body have wrought into her nature.

Very true.

And this corporeal element, my friend, is heavy and weighty and earthy, and is that element of sight by which a soul is depressed and dragged down again into the visible world, because she is afraid of the invisible and of the world below — prowling about tombs and sepulchres, near which, as they tell us, are seen certain ghostly apparitions of souls which have not departed pure, but are cloyed with sight and therefore visible.

That is very likely, Socrates.

Yes, that is very likely, Cebes; and these must be the souls, not of the good, but of the evil, which are compelled to wander about such places in payment of the penalty of their former evil way of life; and they continue to wander until through the craving after the corporeal which never leaves them, they are imprisoned finally in another body. And they may be supposed to find their prisons in the same natures which they have had in their former lives.

What natures do you mean, Socrates?

What I mean is that men who have followed after gluttony, and wantonness, and drunkenness, and have had no thought of avoiding them, would pass into asses and animals of that sort. What do you think?

I think such an opinion to be exceedingly probable.

And those who have chosen the portion of injustice, and tyranny, and violence, will pass into wolves, or into hawks and kites; — whither else can we suppose them to go?

Yes, said Cebes; with such natures, beyond question.

And there is no difficulty, he said, in assigning to all of them places answering to their several natures and propensities?

There is not, he said.

Some are happier than others; and the happiest both in themselves and in the place to which they go are those who have practised the civil and social virtues which are called temperance and justice, and are acquired by habit and attention without philosophy and mind.

Why are they the happiest?

Because they may be expected to pass into some gentle and social kind which is like their own, such as bees or wasps or ants, or back again into the form of man, and just and moderate men may be supposed to spring from them.

Very likely.

No one who has not studied philosophy and who is not entirely pure at the time of his departure is allowed to enter the company of the Gods, but the lover of knowledge only. And this is the reason, Simmias and Cebes, why the true votaries of philosophy abstain from all fleshly lusts, and hold out against them and refuse to give themselves up to them, — not because they fear poverty or the ruin of their families, like the lovers of money, and the world in general; nor like the lovers of power and honour, because they dread the dishonour or disgrace of evil deeds.

No, Socrates, that would not become them, said Cebes.

The Body as the Prison of the Soul

. . . they who have any care of their own souls, and do not merely live moulding and fashioning the body, say farewell to all this; they will not walk in the ways of the blind: and when philosophy offers them purification and release from evil, they feel that they ought not to resist her influence, and whither she leads they turn and follow.

What do you mean, Socrates?

I will tell you, he said. The lovers of knowledge are conscious that the soul was simply fastened and glued to the body—until philosophy received her, she could only view real existence through the bars of a prison, not in and through herself; she was wallowing in the mire of every sort of ignorance, and by reason of lust had become the principal accomplice in her own captivity. This was her original state; and then, as I was saying, and as the lovers of knowledge are well aware, philosophy, seeing how terrible was her confinement, of which she was to herself the cause, received and gently comforted her and sought to release her, pointing out that the eye and the ear and the other senses are full of deception, and persuading her to retire from them, and abstain from all but the necessary use of them, and be gathered up and collected into herself, bidding her trust in herself and her own pure apprehension of pure existence, and to mistrust whatever comes to her through other channels and is subject to variation; for such things are visible and tangible, but what she sees in her own nature is intelligible and invisible. And the soul of the true philosopher thinks that she ought not to resist this deliverance, and therefore abstains from pleasures and desires and pains and fears, as far as she is able; reflecting that when a man has great joys or sorrows or fears or desires, he suffers from them, not merely the sort of evil which might be anticipated—as for example, the loss of his health or property which he has sacrificed to his lusts—but an evil greater far, which is the greatest and worst of all evils, and one of which he never thinks.

What is it, Socrates? said Cebes.

The evil is that when the feeling of pleasure or pain is most intense, every soul of man imagines the objects of this intense feeling to be then plainest and truest: but this is not so, they are really the things of sight.

Very true.

And is not this the state in which the soul is most enthralled by the body?

How so?

Why, because each pleasure and pain is a sort of nail which nails and rivets the soul to the body, until she becomes like the body, and believes that to be true which the body affirms to be true; and from agreeing with the body and having the same delights she is obliged to have the same habits and haunts, and is not likely ever to be pure at her departure to the world below, but is always infected by the body; and so she sinks into another body and there germinates and grows, and has therefore no part in the communion of the divine and pure and simple. . . .

. . . A man of sense ought not to say, nor will I be very confident, that the description which I have given of the soul and her mansions is exactly true. But I do say that, inasmuch as the soul is shown to be immortal, he may venture to think, not improperly or unworthily, that something of the kind is true. The venture is a glorious one, and he ought to comfort himself with words like these, which is the reason why I lengthen out the tale. Wherefore, I say, let a man be of good cheer about his soul, who having cast away the pleasures and ornaments of the body as alien to him and working harm rather than good, has sought after the pleasures of knowledge; and has arrayed the soul, not in some foreign attire, but in her own proper jewels, temperance, and justice, and courage, and nobility, and truth—in these adorned she is ready to go on her journey to the world below, when her hour comes. You, Simmias and Cebes, and all other men, will depart at some time or other. Me already, as a tragic poet would say, the voice of fate calls. . . .

The Soul's Release

. . . We will do our best, said Crito: And in what way shall we bury you?

In any way that you like; but you must get hold of me, and take care that I do not run away from you. Then he turned to us, and added with a smile:—I cannot make Crito believe that I am the same Socrates who has been talking and conducting the argument; he fancies that I am the other Socrates whom he will soon see, a dead body—and he asks, How shall he bury me? And though I have spoken many words in the endeavour to show that when I have drunk the poison I shall leave you and go to the joys of the blessed,—these words of mine, with which I was comforting you and myself, have had, as I perceive, no effect upon Crito. And therefore I want you to be surety for me to him now, as at the trial he was surety to the judges for me: but let the promise be of another sort; for he was surety for me to the judges that I would remain, and you must be my surety to him that I shall not remain, but go away and depart; and then he will suffer less at my death, and not be grieved when he sees my body being burned or buried. I would not have him sorrow at my hard lot, or say at the burial, Thus we lay out Socrates, or, Thus we follow him to the grave or bury him; for false words are not only evil in themselves, but they infect the soul with evil. Be of good cheer then, my dear Crito, and say that you are burying my body only, and do with that whatever is usual, and what you think best. . . .

2

LUCRETIUS

⟅⟆

The Mind and the Spirit Will Die

⟆⟅

I HAVE ALREADY shown what the component bodies of everything are like; how they vary in shape; how they fly spontaneously through space, impelled by a perpetual motion; and how from these all objects can be created. The next step now is evidently to elucidate in my verses the nature of mind and of life. In so doing I shall drive out neck and crop that fear of Hell which blasts the life of man from its very foundations, sullying everything with the blackness of death and leaving no pleasure pure and unalloyed. I know that men often speak of sickness or of shameful life as more to be dreaded than the terrors of Hell; they profess to know that the mind consists of blood, or maybe wind, if that is how the whim takes them, and to stand in no need whatever of our reasoning. But all this talk is based more on a desire to show off than on actual proof, as you may infer from their conduct. . . .

I maintain that *mind and spirit are interconnected* and compose between them a single substance. But what I may call the head and the dominant force in the whole body is that guiding principle which we term mind or intellect. This is firmly lodged in the mid-region of the breast. Here is the place where fear and alarm pulsate. Here is felt the caressing touch of joy. Here, then, is the seat of intellect and mind. The rest of the vital spirit, diffused throughout the body, obeys the mind and moves under its direction and impulse. The mind by itself

This selection consists of extracts from book 3 of *De Rerum Natura*, in the translation by R. E. Latham, published in 1951 by Penguin Books, with whose permission they are here reprinted.

experiences thought and joy of its own at a time when nothing moves either the body or the spirit.

When our head or eye suffers from an attack of pain, our whole body does not share in its aching. Just so the mind sometimes suffers by itself or jumps for joy when the rest of the spirit, diffused through every limb and member, is not stirred by any new impulse. But, when the mind is upset by some more overwhelming fear, we see all the spirit in every limb upset in sympathy. Sweat and pallor break out all over the body. Speech grows inarticulate; the voice fails; the eyes swim; the ears buzz; the limbs totter. Often we see men actually drop down because of the terror that has gripped their minds. Hence you may readily infer a connexion between the mind and the spirit which, when shaken by the impact of the mind, immediately jostles and propels the body.

The same reasoning proves that *mind and spirit are both composed of matter*. We see them propelling the limbs, rousing the body from sleep, changing the expression of the face and guiding and steering the whole man — activities that all clearly involve touch, as touch in turn involves matter. How then can we deny their material nature? You see the mind sharing in the body's experiences and sympathizing with it. When the nerve-racking impact of a spear gashes bones and sinews, even if it does not penetrate to the seat of life, there ensues faintness and a tempting inclination earthwards and on the ground a turmoil in the mind and an intermittent faltering impulse to stand up again. The substance of the mind must therefore be material, since it is affected by the impact of material weapons.

My next task will be to demonstrate to you what sort of matter it is of which this mind is composed and how it was formed. First, I affirm that it is *of very fine texture and composed of exceptionally minute particles*. If you will mark my words, you will be able to infer this from the following facts. It is evident that nothing happens as quickly as the mind represents and sketches the happening to itself. Therefore the mind sets itself in motion more swiftly than any of those things whose substance is visible to our eyes. But what is so mobile must consist of exceptionally minute and spherical atoms, so that it can be set going by a slight push. The reason why water is set going and flowing by such a slight push is of course the smallness of its atoms and their readiness to roll. . . . In proportion as objects are smaller and smoother, so much the more do they enjoy mobility; the greater their weight and roughness, the more firmly are they anchored. Since, there-fore, the substance of the mind has been found to be extraordinarily mobile, it must consist of particles exceptionally small and smooth and round. . . .

Again, we are conscious that mind and body are born together, grow up together and together decay. With the weak and delicate frame of wavering childhood goes a like infirmity of judgement. The robust vigour of ripening years is accompanied by a steadier resolve and a maturer strength of mind. Later, when the body is palsied by the potent forces of age and the limbs begin to droop with blunted vigour, the understanding limps, the tongue falters and the mind totters: everything weakens and gives way at the same time. It is thus natural that the vital spirit should all evaporate like smoke, soaring into the gusty air, since we have seen that it shares the body's birth and growth and wearies with the weariness of age.

Furthermore, as the body suffers the horrors of disease and the pangs of pain, so we see the mind stabbed with anguish, grief and fear. What more natural than that it should likewise have a share in death? Often enough in the body's illness the mind wanders. It raves and babbles distractedly. At times it drifts on a tide of drowsiness, with drooping eyelids and nodding head, into a deep and endless sleep, from which it cannot hear the voices or recognize the faces of those who stand around with streaming eyes and tear-stained cheeks, striving to recall it to life. Since the mind is thus invaded by the contagion of disease, you must acknowledge that it is destructible. For pain and sickness are the artificers of death, as we have been taught by the fate of many men before us. . . .

When mind and spirit in the body itself are a prey to such violent maladies and suffer such distressing dispersal, how can you believe them capable of surviving apart from the body in the open air with the wild winds for company? . . .

Moreover, if the spirit is by nature immortal and can remain sentient when divorced from our body, we must credit it, I presume, with the possession of five senses. In no other way can we picture to ourselves departed spirits wandering through the Infernal Regions. So it is that painters and bygone generations of writers have portrayed spirits in possession of their senses. But eyes or nostrils or hand or tongue or ears cannot be attached to a disembodied spirit. Such a spirit cannot therefore be sentient or so much as exist. . . .

If the spirit is by nature immortal and is slipped into the body at birth, why do we retain no memory of an earlier existence, no impress of antecedent events? If the mind's operation is so greatly changed that all record of former actions has been expunged, it is no long journey, in my judgement, from this experience to annihilation. So you must admit that the pre-existent spirit has died and the one that is now is a new creation.

Let us suppose, for argument's sake, that the vital force of mind is introduced into us when the body is already fully formed, at the moment when we are born and step across the threshold of life. This theory does not square with the observed fact that the mind grows with the bodily frame and in the very blood. It would imply that the mind lived in solitary confinement, alone in its cell, and yet at the same time the whole body was shot through with sentience. Here then is proof upon proof that spirits are not to be regarded as birthless, nor yet as exempt from the law of death. If they were slipped into our bodies from outside, it cannot be supposed that the two would be so closely inter-locked as they are shown to be by the clearest evidence. For spirit so interpenetrates veins, flesh, sinews, bones, that our very teeth share in sensation—witness toothache and the shock of contact with icy water or a jagged stone buried in a loaf. Being thus interwoven, it does not seem possible that it should escape intact and extricate itself undam-aged from every sinew, bone and joint. Or, if you suppose that, after being slipped in from outside, the spirit oozes through our limbs, then it is all the more bound to perish with the body through which it is thus interfused. To ooze through something is to be dissolved in it and therefore to perish. We know that food, when it is rationed out amongst our limbs and members by diffusion through all the channels of the body, is destroyed and takes on a different nature. Just so, on the assumption that spirit and mind enter into the newly formed body as complete entities, they must be dissolved in oozing through it: our limbs must be interpenetrated through every channel by the particles composing this mind which lords it now in our body—this new mind born of the old one that must have perished in its diffusion through our limbs. It is thus evident that the human spirit is neither independent of a birthday nor immune from a latter end. . . .

Again, it is surely ludicrous to suppose that spirits are standing by at the mating and birth of animals—a numberless number of immortals on the look-out for mortal frames, jostling and squabbling to get in first and establish themselves most firmly. Or is there perhaps an estab-lished compact that first come shall be first served, without any trial of strength between spirit and spirit? . . . What can be imagined more incongruous, what more repugnant and discordant, than that a mortal object and one that is immortal and everlasting should unite to form a compound and jointly weather the storms that rage about them? . . .

If any feeling remains in mind or spirit after it has been torn from our body, that is nothing to us, who are brought into being by the wedlock of body and spirit, conjoined and coalesced. Or even if the matter that composes us should be reassembled by time after our death and brought back into its present state—if the light of life were given to us anew—even that contingency would still be no concern of ours once the chain of our identity had been snapped. We who are now are not concerned with ourselves in any previous existence: the sufferings of those selves do not touch us. When you look at the immeasurable extent of time gone by and the multiform movements of matter, you will readily credit that these same atoms that compose us now must many a time before have entered into the self-same combinations as now. But our mind cannot recall this to remembrance. For between then and now is interposed a breach in life, and all the atomic motions have been wandering far astray from sentience.

If the future holds travail and anguish in store, the self must be in existence, when that time comes, in order to experience it. But from this fate we are redeemed by death which denies existence to the self that might have suffered these tribulations. Rest assured, therefore, that we have nothing to fear in death. One who no longer is cannot suffer, or differ in any way from one who has never been born, when once this mortal life has been usurped by death the immortal.

When you find a man treating it as a grievance that after death he will either moulder in the grave or fall prey to flames or to the jaws of predatory beasts, be sure that his utterance does not ring true. Subconsciously his heart is stabbed by a secret dread, however loudly the man himself may disavow the belief that after death he will still experience sensation. I am convinced that he does not grant the admission he professes, nor the grounds of it; he does not oust and pluck himself root and branch out of life, but all unwittingly makes something of himself linger on. When a living man confronts the thought that after death his body will be mauled by birds and beasts of prey, he is filled with self-pity. He does not banish himself from the scene nor distinguish sharply enough between himself and that abandoned carcass. He visualizes that object as himself and infects it with his own feelings as an onlooker. That is why he is aggrieved at having been created mortal. He does not see that in real death there will be no other self alive to mourn his own decease — no other self standing by to flinch at the agony he suffers lying there being mangled, or indeed being cremated.

3

TERTULLIAN

⤳

The Refutation of the Pythagorean Doctrine of Transmigration

⤳

TERTULLIAN (C. 160–C.220), *an early Church Father, wrote extensively against Greek philosophers of antiquity as well as Gnostic heretics of his own time. Several chapters in* De Anima (On the Soul) *are devoted to reincarnation. The main targets of Tertullian's polemic here are Pythagoras and Plato. Tertullian repeatedly refers to the alleged thousand-year interval between incarnations. An interval of this duration had been mentioned by Plato in Book 10 of the* Republic. *In the* Phaedo *(selection 1), Plato was less specific, speaking of "many revolutions of ages." The selection that follows comprises chapters 30 and 31 of* De Anima. *The translation is by Peter Holmes.*

The Population Problem

(1) What answer can we give to the rest of their arguments? If, just as death follows life, life should follow death, the number of men in the human race must always remain the same, and that would be merely the number who first inaugurated human life. First, there were the living, and they died; from these dead came the living, and again the living from these dead men. Now, since this process was continually going on among the same group of people, no more came into the world than the original number. For, the men who died could not be more or less than those who had previously returned from death.

(2) In the ancient records of the human race, however, we learn that the number of men has gradually increased; either as aborigines, as

nomads, as exiles, or as conquerors, men have occupied new lands. The Scythians overran Parthia; the Temenidae, the Peloponnesus; the Athenians, in Asia; the Phrygians, in Italy: and the Phoenicians, Africa. Besides, many races have swarmed over unpopulated lands in large-scale migrations, in order to relieve the crowding of their cities. Native populations have remained in their original home or have loaned vast numbers of people to other lands.

(3) A glance at the face of the earth shows us that it is becoming daily better cultivated and more fully peopled than in olden times. There are few places now that are not accessible; few, unknown; few, unopened to commerce. Beautiful farms now cover what once were trackless wastes, the forests have given way before the plough, cattle have driven off the beasts of the jungle, the sands of the desert bear fruit and crops, the rocks have been ploughed under, the marshes have been drained of their water, and, where once there was but a settler's cabin, great cities are now to be seen. No longer do lonely islands frighten away the sailor nor does he fear their rocky coasts. Everywhere we see houses, people, stable governments, and the orderly conduct of life.

(4) The strongest witness is the vast population of the earth to which we are a burden and she scarcely can provide for our needs; as our demands grow greater, our complaints against nature's inadequacy are heard by all. The scourges of pestilence, famine, wars, and earthquakes have come to be regarded as a blessing to overcrowded nations, since they serve to prune away the luxuriant growth of the human race. Yet, when the sword of destruction has slaughtered vast hordes of men, the world has never yet been alarmed at the return from the dead of the masses that had died in that catastrophe of a thousand years before. Surely, the equalizing force of loss and gain would have long since become evident if men really returned to life from the grave.

(5) Why is it necessary to wait a thousand years for this return? Why does it not happen in a moment? There is a danger that the demand might exceed the supply if the deficiency is not made up in time. This brief period of our human life, compared to that one thousand years, seems to be very short; too short, in fact, when we consider that the spark of life is far more easily quenched than kindled. Finally, since the human race has not yet lived long enough to test the truth of this theory of transmigration of souls, we cannot agree that men come back to life from death.

The Problem of Identity

(1) Now if this recovery of life really takes place, personal individuality must be maintained. Hence, each of the souls which once inhabited a body must have returned each into a single body. Now, if two, three, or five souls all unite in the one womb, you will have no true return to

life, because they will not return as separate individuals. Yet, in this supposition, the original plan of creation would be followed out, since you would have several souls coming from one.

(2) Besides, since souls would have departed from this life at different ages, why do they all come back at the same age? At their birth, all men are imbued with the souls of infants; but, how comes it that a man who dies in old age returns to life as an infant? Far from slipping back in age during its exile of a thousand years, wouldn't it be more likely that is should return to life the richer for its millennial experience in the other world? At least, the soul ought to come back at the age it had when it departed, so as to resume life where it left off.

(3) If they did return as precisely the same souls, even though they might acquire different bodies and totally different fates in life, they ought to bring back with them the same characters, desires, and emotions they had before, since we should hardly have the right to pronounce them the same if they were lacking in precisely the characteristics which might prove their identity. You may ask me: "How can you be sure all this doesn't happen by some secret process? After all, why should *you* recognize those who come back, strangers to you, after a thousand years?" Ah, but when you tell me Pythagoras was once Euphorbus, I know that it doesn't!

(4) Take Euphorbus. It is clear that his was a military and warlike soul, if we can judge by the renown of his sacred shields. Compare him with the timorous and unwarlike Pythagoras who preferred to pass the time in Italy at geometry, astronomy, and music at a time when Greece was teeming with wars—the very opposite of Euphorbus in character and temperament. Pyrrhus spent his time in catching fish, and Pythagoras wouldn't eat a fish or any animal food. Beans were doubtless part of the ordinary fare of Aethalides and Hermotimus, but Pythogoras wouldn't even allow his disciples to walk through a bean-patch!

(5) Tell me, then, if you please, how can you say they can recover their own souls, if you can show no proof of identity of personality, habits, or way of living? And, out of all of Greece, only four souls are claimed to have returned. But, why should we restrict ourselves to Greece, as if there wouldn't have been transmigration of souls and even of bodies in every country, among all ages, conditions, and sexes, and that, every day, too? And why does Pythagoras alone experience these changes from one personality to another? Why hasn't this happened to me?

(6) However, if it is an exclusive privilege of philosophers, and Greek ones at that (as if there were no philosophers among the Scythians and Indians!), why didn't Epicurus recognize he had once been another person? Why didn't Chrysippus, or Zeno, or, in fact, Plato himself, whom we might well believe to have been Nestor, because of his honeyed eloquence?

4

ST. THOMAS AQUINAS

❧

The Resurrection of Man

❧

ALL SECTIONS OF *this selection other than the last are from the* **Summa** Theologica (A Summary of Theology) *in the translation of the Fathers of the English Dominican Province; the last section, from the* Summa Contra Gentiles (A Summary Against the Gentiles), *in the translation of Charles J. O'Neil. The* Summa Theologica *is a huge treatise consisting of three Parts as well as a Supplement. Each part is subdivided into "Questions" and most of these contain several "Articles." In the headings "Q" stands for "Question" and "A" for "Article." Aquinas begins each article with a statement of the objections to the doctrine he champions. He proceeds to expound his own view in the "body" or "corpus" of the article and concludes with replies to the objections.*

The selections from the Summa Theologica *are reprinted with the permission of Burns and Oates of Welwood, Tunbridge Wells; the section from the* Summa Contra Gentiles *with the permission of Doubleday, New York.*

The Immateriality of the Soul

WHETHER THE SOUL IS A BODY?

. . . To seek the nature of the soul, we must premise that the soul is defined as the first principle of life in those things which live; for we call living things *animate*, and those things which have no life, *inanimate*. Now life is shown principally by two actions, knowledge and movement. The philosophers of old, not being able to rise above their imagination, supposed that the principle of these actions was something corporeal: for they asserted that only bodies were real things; and that what is not corporeal is nothing: hence they maintained that the soul is something corporeal. This opinion can be proved to be false in many ways; but we shall make use of only one proof, based on universal and certain principles, which shows clearly that the soul is not a body.

It is manifest that not every principle of vital action is a soul, for then the eye would be a soul, as it is a principle of vision; and the same might be applied to the other instruments of the soul: but it is the *first* principle of life, which we call the soul. Now, though a body may be a principle of life, as the heart is a principle of life in an animal, yet nothing corporeal can be the first principle of life. For it is clear that to be a principle of life, or to be a living thing, does not belong to a body as such; since, if that were the case, every body would be a living thing, or a principle of life. Therefore a body is competent to be a living thing or even a principle of life, as *such* a body. Now that it is actually such a body, it owes to some principle which is called its act. Therefore the soul, which is the first principle of life, is not a body, but the act of a body; thus heat, which is the principle of calefaction, is not a body, but an act of a body. . . .

The Soul Is a Substance

WHETHER THE HUMAN SOUL IS SOMETHING SUBSISTENT?

. . . *Objection* 1. It would seem that the human soul is not something subsistent. For that which subsists is said to be *this particular thing.* Now *this particular thing* is said not of the soul, but of that which is composed of soul and body. Therefore the soul is not something subsistent.

. . . *Obj.* 3. Further, if the soul were subsistent, it would have some operation apart from the body. But it has no operation apart from the body, not even that of understanding: for the act of understanding does not take place without a phantasm, which cannot exist apart from the body. Therefore the human soul is not something subsistent. . . .

I answer that, It must necessarily be allowed that the principle of intellectual operation which we call the soul, is a principle both incorporeal and subsistent. For it is clear that by means of the intellect man can have knowledge of all corporeal things. Now whatever knows certain things cannot have any of them in its own nature; because that which is in it naturally would impede the knowledge of anything else. Thus we observe that a sick man's tongue being vitiated by a feverish and bitter humour, is insensible to anything sweet, and everything seems bitter to it. Therefore, if the intellectual principle contained the nature of a body it would be unable to know all bodies. Now every body has its own determinate nature. Therefore it is impossible for the intellectual principle to be a body. It is likewise impossible for it to understand by means of a bodily organ; since the determinate nature of that organ would impede knowledge of all bodies; as when a certain determinate colour is not only in the pupil of the eye, but also in a glass vase, the liquid in the vase seems to be of that same colour.

Therefore the intellectual principle which we call the mind or the intellect has an operation *per se* apart from the body. Now only that which subsists can have an operation *per se*. For nothing can operate but what is actual: wherefore a thing operates according as it is; for which reason we do not say that heat imparts heat, but that what is hot gives heat. We must conclude, therefore, that the human soul, which is called the intellect or the mind, is something incorporeal and subsistent. . . .

. . . *Reply Obj.* 3. The body is necessary for the action of the intellect, not as its organ of action, but on the part of the object; for the phantasm is to the intellect what colour is to the sight. Neither does such a dependence on the body prove the intellect to be non-subsistent; otherwise it would follow that an animal is non-subsistent, since it requires external objects of the senses in order to perform its act of perception.

Man Is Not Merely a Soul

WHETHER THE SOUL IS MAN?

. . . *I answer that*, The assertion, *the soul is man*, can be taken in two senses. First, that man is a soul; though this particular man, Socrates, for instance, is not a soul, but composed of soul and body. I say this, forasmuch as some held that the form alone belongs to the species; while matter is part of the individual, and not of the species. This cannot be true; for to the nature of the species belongs what the definition signifies; and in natural things the definition does not signify the form only, but the form and the matter. Hence in natural things the matter is part of the species; not, indeed, signate matter, which is the principle of individuality; but the common matter. For as it belongs to the notion of this particular man to be composed of this soul, of this flesh, and of these bones; so it belongs to the notion of man to be composed of soul, flesh, and bones; for whatever belongs in common to the substance of all the individuals contained under a given species, must belong also to the substance of the species.

It may also be understood in this sense, that this soul is this man; and this could be held if it were supposed that the operation of the sensitive soul were proper to it, apart from the body; because in that case all the operations which are attributed to man would belong to the soul only; and whatever performs the operations proper to a thing, is that thing;

wherefore that which performs the operations of a man is man. But it has been shown above . . . that sensation is not the operation of the soul only. Since, then, sensation is an operation of man, but not proper to him, it is clear that man is not a soul only, but something composed of soul and body. — Plato, through supposing that sensation was proper to the soul, could maintain man to be a soul making use of the body. . . .

WHETHER THE HUMAN SOUL IS INCORRUPTIBLE?

Objection 1. It would seem that the human soul is corruptible. For those things that have a like beginning and process seemingly have a like end. But the beginning, by generation, of men is like that of animals, for they are made from the earth. And the process of life is alike in both; because *all things breathe alike, and man hath nothing more than the beast*, as it is written (Eccles. iii. 19). Therefore, as the same text concludes, *the death of man and beast is one, and the condition of both is equal.* But the souls of brute animals are corruptible. Therefore, also, the human soul is corruptible.

Obj. 2. Further, whatever is out of nothing can return to nothingness; because the end should correspond to the beginning. But as it is written (Wisd. ii. 2), *We are born of nothing*; which is true, not only of the body, but also of the soul. Therefore, as is concluded in the same passage, *After this we shall be as if we had not been*, even as to our soul.

Obj. 3. Further, nothing is without its own proper operation. But the operation proper to the soul, which is to understand through a phantasm, cannot be without the body. For the soul understands nothing without a phantasm; and there is no phantasm without the body as the Philosopher* says (*De Anima* i. I). Therefore the soul cannot survive the dissolution of the body. . . .

I answer that, We must assert that the intellectual principle which we call the human soul is incorruptible. For a thing may be corrupted in two ways — *per se*, and accidentally. Now it is impossible for any substance to be generated or corrupted accidentally, that is, by the generation or corruption of something else. For generation and corruption belong to a thing, just as existence belongs to it, which is acquired by generation and lost by corruption. Therefore, whatever has existence *per se* cannot be generated or corrupted except *per se*; while things which do not subsist, such as accidents and material forms, acquire existence or lose it through the generation or corruption of composite things. Now it was shown above . . . that the souls of brutes are not self-subsistent, whereas the human soul is; so that the souls of brutes are corrupted, when their bodies are corrupted; while the human soul could not be corrupted unless it were corrupted *per se*. This, indeed, is

*By "the Philosopher" Aquinas always means Aristotle. [Ed.]

impossible, not only as regards the human soul, but also as regards anything subsistent that is a form alone. For it is clear that what belongs to a thing by virtue of itself is inseparable from it; but existence belongs to a form, which is an act, by virtue of itself. Wherefore matter acquires actual existence as it acquires the form; while it is corrupted so far as the form is separated from it. But it is impossible for a form to be separated from itself; and therefore it is impossible for a subsistent form to cease to exist. . . .

The Soul's Location Immediately After Death

I answer that, Even as in bodies there is gravity or levity whereby they are borne to their own place which is the end of their movement, so in souls there is merit or demerit whereby they reach their reward or punishment, which are the ends of their deeds. Wherefore just as a body is conveyed at once to its place, by its gravity or levity, unless there be an obstacle, so too the soul, the bonds of the flesh being broken, whereby it was detained in the state of the way, receives at once its reward or punishment, unless there be an obstacle. Thus sometimes venial sin, though needing first of all to be cleansed, is an obstacle to the receiving of the reward; the result being that the reward is delayed. And since a place is assigned to souls in keeping with their reward or punishment, as soon as the soul is set free from the body it is either plunged into hell or soars to heaven, unless it be held back by some debt, for which its flight must needs be delayed until the soul is first of all cleansed. This truth is attested by the manifest authority of the canonical Scriptures and the doctrine of the holy Fathers: wherefore the contrary must be judged heretical. . . .

The Destruction of the Sensitive Powers

I answer that, There are many opinions on this question. For some, holding the view that all the powers are in the soul in the same way as colour is in a body, hold that the soul separated from the body takes all its powers away with it: because, if it lacked any one of them, it would follow that the soul is changed in its natural properties, since these cannot change so long as their subject remains. But the aforesaid view is false, for since a power is so called because it enables us to do or suffer something, and since to do and to be able belong to the same subject, it follows that the subject of a power is the same as that which is agent or patient. Hence the Philosopher says (*De Somn. et Vigil.*) that *where we find power there we find action.* Now it is evident that certain operations, whereof the soul's powers are the principles, do not belong to the soul properly speaking but to the soul as united to the body, because they are not performed except through the medium of the body, — such as to see, to hear, and so forth. Hence it follows that suchlike powers belong to the united soul and body as their subject, but to the soul as their quickening principle, just as the form is the principle of the properties of a composite being. Some operations, however, are performed by the soul without a bodily organ, — for instance to understand, to consider, to will: wherefore, since these actions are proper to the soul, the powers that are the principles thereof belong to the soul not only as their principle but also as their subject. Therefore, since so long as the proper subject remains its proper passions must also remain, and when it is corrupted they also must be corrupted, it follows that these powers which use no bodily organ for their actions must needs remain in the separated body, while those which use a bodily organ must needs be corrupted when the body is corrupted: and such are all the powers belonging to the sensitive and the vegetative soul. . . .

The Resurection of the Body

I answer that, According to the various opinions about man's last end there have been various opinions holding or denying the resurrection. For man's last end which all men desire naturally is happiness. Some have held that man is able to attain this end in this life: wherefore they had no need to admit another life after this, wherein man would be able to attain to his perfection: and so they denied the resurrection. But this opinion is confuted with sufficient probability by the changeableness of fortune, the weakness of the human body, the imperfection and instability of knowledge and virtue, all of which are hindrances to the perfection of happiness, as Augustine argues at the end of *De Civ. Dei* (xix. 3). Hence others maintained that after this there is another life wherein, after death, man lives according to the soul only, and they held that such a life sufficed to satisfy the natural desire to obtain happiness: wherefore Porphyrius said as Augustine states (*De Civ. Dei,* xxi.): *The soul, to be happy, must avoid all bodies*: and consequently these did not hold the resurrection. This opinion was based by various people on various false foundations. For certain heretics asserted that all bodily things are from the evil principle, but that spiritual things are from the good principle: and from this it follows that the soul cannot reach the height of its perfection unless it be separated from the body since the latter withdraws it from its principle, the participation of which makes it happy. Hence all those heretical sects that hold corporeal things to have been created or fashioned by the devil deny the resurrection of the body. . . .

Others said that the entire nature of man is seated in the soul, so that the soul makes use of the body as an instrument, or as a sailor uses his ship: wherefore according to this opinion, it follows that if happiness is attained by the soul alone, man would not be baulked in his natural desire for happiness, and so there is no need to hold the resurrection.

But the Philosopher sufficiently destroys this foundation (*De Anima*, ii.), where he shows that the soul is united to the body as form to matter. Hence it is clear that if man cannot be happy in this life, we must of necessity hold the resurrection. . . .

The Resurrection of the Same Body

I answer that, On this point the philosophers erred and certain modern heretics err. For some of the philosophers allowed that souls separated from bodies are reunited to bodies, yet they erred in this in two ways. First, as to the mode of reunion, for some held the separated soul to be naturally reunited to a body by the way of generation. Secondly, as to the body to which it was reunited, for they held that this second union was not with the selfsame body that was laid aside in death, but with another, sometimes of the same, sometimes of a different species. Of a different species when the soul while existing in the body had led a life contrary to the ordering of reason: wherefore it passed after death from the body of a man into the body of some other animal to whose manner of living it had conformed in this life, for instance into the body of a dog on account of lust, into the body of a lion on account of robbery and violence, and so forth,*—and into a body of the same species when the soul has led a good life in the body, and having after death experienced some happiness, after some centuries began to wish to return to the body; and thus it was reunited to a human body. But this opinion arises from two false sources. The first of these is that they said that the soul is not united to the body essentially as form to matter, but only accidentally, as mover to the thing moved, or as a man to his clothes. Hence it was possible for them to maintain that the soul pre-existed before being infused into the body begotten of natural generation, as also that it is united to various bodies. The second is that they held intellect not to differ from sense except accidentally, so that man would be said to surpass other animals in intelligence, because the sensitive power is more acute in him on account of the excellence of his bodily complexion; and hence it was possible for them to assert that man's soul passes into the soul of a brute animal, especially when the human soul has been habituated to brutish actions. But these two sources are refuted by the Philosopher (*De Anima*, ii.), and in consequence of these being refuted, it is clear that the above opinion is false.

In like manner the errors of certain heretics are refuted. Some of them fell into the aforesaid opinions of the philosophers: while others held that souls are reunited to heavenly bodies, or again to bodies subtle as the wind. . . . Moreover these same errors of heretics may be refuted by the fact that they are prejudicial to the truth of resurrection

*See Plato, selection 1. [Ed.]

as witnessed to by Holy Writ. For we cannot call it resurrection unless the soul return to the same body, since resurrection is a second rising, and the same thing rises that falls: wherefore resurrection regards the body which after death falls rather than the soul which after death lives. And consequently if it be not the same body which the soul resumes, it will not be a resurrection, but rather the assuming of a new body. . . .

Objection. It would seem that it will not be identically the same man that shall rise again. For according to the Philosopher (*De Gener.* ii.): *Whatsoever things are changed in their corruptible substance are not repeated identically.* Now such is man's substance in his present state. Therefore after the change wrought by death the selfsame man cannot be repeated. . . .

I answer that, The necessity of holding the resurrection arises from this, — that man may obtain the last end for which he was made; for this cannot be accomplished in this life, nor in the life of the separated soul, as stated above (Q.LXXV., AA. 1, 2): otherwise man would have been made in vain, if he were unable to obtain the end for which he was made. And since it behoves the end to be obtained by the selfsame thing that was made for that end, lest it appear to be made without purpose, it is necessary for the selfsame man to rise again; and this is effected by the selfsame soul being united to the selfsame body. For otherwise there would be no resurrection properly speaking, if the same man were not reformed. Hence to maintain that he who rises again is not the selfsame man is heretical, since it is contrary to the truth of Scripture which proclaims the resurrection. . . .

The Problem of Cannibalism

The Objection. . . . It happens, occasionally, that some men feed on human flesh, and they are nourished on this nutrient only, and those so nourished generate sons. Therefore, the same flesh is found in many men. But it is not possible that it should rise in many. And the resurrection does not seem otherwise to be universal and entire if there is not restored to every man what he has had here. . . .

The Reply. . . . There is no obstacle to faith in the resurrection — even in the fact that some men eat human flesh. . . . For it is not necessary that whatever has been in man materially rise in him; further, if something is lacking, it can be supplied by the power of God. Therefore, the flesh consumed will rise in him in whom it was first perfected by the rational soul. But in the second man, if he ate not only human flesh, but other food as well, only that will rise in him which came to him materially from the other food, and which will be necessary to restore the quantity due his body. But, if he ate human flesh only, what rises in him will be that which he drew from those who generated him, and what is wanting will be supplied by the Creator's omnipotence. But let it be that the parents, too, have eaten only human flesh, and that as a result their seed—which is superfluity of nourishment—has been generated from the flesh of others; the seed, indeed, will rise in him who was generated from the seed, and in its place there will be supplied in him whose flesh was eaten something from another source. For in the resurrection this situation will obtain: If something was materially present in many men, it will rise in him to whose perfection it belonged more intimately. Accordingly, if something was in one man as the radical seed from which he was generated, and in another as the superfluity of nourishment, it will rise in him who was generated therefrom as from seed. If something was in one as pertinent to the perfection of the individual, but in another as assigned to the perfection of the species, it will rise in him to whom it belonged as perfection of the individual. Accordingly, seed will arise in the begotten, not in his generator; the rib of Adam will arise in Eve, not in Adam in whom it was present as in a principle of nature. But, if something was in both in the same degree of perfection, it will rise in him in whom it was the first time. . . .

5

RENÉ DESCARTES

The Incorporeal Soul and Its Body

The Absolute Certainty of My Own Existence

I DO NOT know whether I need tell you of my first meditations; for they are perhaps too metaphysical and uncommon for the general taste. At the same time I am in a way obliged to speak of them so as to make it possible to judge whether the foundation I have chosen is secure enough. I had noticed long before, as I said just now, that in conduct one sometimes has to follow opinions that one knows to be most uncertain just as if they were indubitable; but since my present aim was to give myself up to the pursuit of truth alone, I thought I must do the very opposite, and reject as if absolutely false anything as to which I could imagine the least doubt, in order to see if I should not be left at the end believing something that was absolutely indubitable. So, because our senses sometimes deceive us, I chose to suppose that nothing was such as they lead us to imagine. Because there are men who make

The passages comprising this selection are taken from sections 4 and 5 of the *Discourse on Method*, the second and sixth *Meditations*, the *Objections to the Second Meditation*, the *Principles of Philosophy*, and the *Passions of the Soul*. The selections from the *Discourse on Method*, the *Meditations*, and the *Objections to the Second Meditation* are in the translation by Elizabeth Anscombe and P. T. Geach and are reprinted with the permission of Thomas Nelson and Sons of Walton-on-Thames published in 1954. The translations of the sections from the *Principles of Philosophy* and the *Passions of the Soul* are by E. Haldane and G. R. T. Ross as they appear in *The Philosophical Works of Descartes*, published in 1931 by Cambridge University Press, with whose permission they are here reprinted. The headings of the first four sections are supplied by the editor, those of the last six sections by Descartes.

mistakes in reasoning even as regards the simplest points of geometry and perpetrate fallacies, and seeing that I was as liable to error as anyone else, I rejected as false all the arguments I had so far taken for demonstrations. Finally, considering that the very same experiences (*pensées*) as we have in waking life may occur also while we sleep, without there being at that time any truth in them, I decided to feign that everything that had entered my mind hitherto was no more true than the illusions of dreams. But immediately upon this I noticed that while I was trying to think everything false, it must needs be that I, who was thinking this (*qui le pensais*), was something. And observing that this truth "I am thinking (*je pense*), therefore I exist" was so solid and secure that the most extravagant suppositions of the sceptics could not overthrow it, I judged that I need not scruple to accept it as the first principle of philosophy that I was seeking.

I then considered attentively what I was; and I saw that while I could feign that I had no body, that there was no world, and no place existed for me to be in, I could not feign that I was not; on the contrary, from the mere fact that I thought of doubting (*je pensais à douter*) about other truths it evidently and certainly followed that I existed. On the other hand, if I had merely ceased to be conscious (*de penser*), even if everything else that I had ever imagined had been true, I had no reason to believe that I should still have existed. From this I recognised that I was a substance whose whole essence or nature is to be conscious (*de penser*) and whose being requires no place and depends on no material thing. Thus this self (*moi*), that is to say the soul, by which I am what I am, is entirely distinct from the body, and is even more easily known; and even if the body were not there at all, the soul would be just what it is. . . .

The Difference Between Men and Animals

I specially dwelt on showing that if there were machines with the organs and appearance of a monkey, or some other irrational animal, we should have no means of telling that they were not altogether of the same nature as those animals; whereas if there were machines resembling our bodies, and imitating our actions as far as is morally possible, we should still have two means of telling that, all the same, they were not real men. First, they could never use words or other constructed signs, as we do to declare our thoughts to others. It is quite conceivable that a machine should be so made as to utter words, and even utter them in connexion with physical events that cause a change in one of its organs; so that e.g. if it is touched in one part, it asks what you want to say to it, and if touched in another, it cries out that it is hurt; but not that it should be so made as to arrange words variously in response to the meaning of what is said in its presence, as even the dullest men can do. Secondly, while they might do many things as well as any of us or better, they would infallibly fail in others, revealing that they acted not from knowledge but only from the disposition of their organs. For while reason is a universal tool that may serve in all kinds of circumstances, these organs need a special arrangement for each special action; so it is morally impossible that a machine should contain so many varied arrangements as to act in all the events of life in the way reason enables us to act.

Now in just these two ways we can also recognise the difference between men and brutes. For it is a very remarkable thing that there are no men so dull and stupid, not even lunatics, that they cannot arrange various words and form a sentence to make their thoughts (*pensées*) understood; but no other animal, however perfect or well bred, can do the like. This does not come from their lacking the organs; for magpies and parrots can utter words like ourselves, and yet they cannot talk like us, that is, with any sign of being aware of (*qu'ils pensent*) what they say. Whereas men born deaf-mutes, and thus devoid of the organs that others use for speech, as much as brutes are or more so, usually invent for themselves signs by which they make themselves understood to those who are normally with them, and who thus have a chance to learn their language. This is evidence that brutes not only have a smaller degree of reason than men, but are wholly lacking in it. For it may be seen that a very small degree of reason is needed in order to be able to talk; and in view of the inequality that occurs among animals of the same species, as among men, and of the fact that some are easier to train than others, it is incredible that a monkey or parrot who was one of the most perfect members of his species should not be comparable in this regard to one of the stupidest children or at least to a child with a diseased brain, if their souls were not wholly different in nature from ours. And we must not confuse words with natural movements, the expressions of emotion, which can be imitated by machines as well as by animals. Nor must we think, like some of the ancients, that brutes talk but we cannot understand their language; for if that were true, since many of their organs are analogous to ours, they could make themselves understood to us, as well as to their fellows. It is another very remarkable thing that although several brutes exhibit more skill than we in some of their actions, they show none at all in many other circumstances; so their excelling us is no proof that they have a mind (*de l'esprit*), for in that case they would have a better one than any of us and would excel us all round; it rather shows that they have none, and that it is nature that acts in them according to the arrangements of their organs; just as we see how a clock, composed merely of wheels and springs, can reckon the hours and measure time more correctly than we can with all our wisdom.

I went on to describe the rational soul, and showed that, unlike the other things I had spoken of, it cannot be extracted from the potentiality of matter, but must be specially created; and how it is not enough for it to dwell in the human body like a pilot in his ship, which would only account for its moving the limbs of the body; in order to have in addition feelings and appetites like ours, and so make up a true man, it must be joined and united to the body more closely. Here I dwelt a little on the subject of the soul, as among the most important; for, after the error of denying God, (of which I think I have already given a sufficient refutation), there is none more likely to turn weak characters from the strait way of virtue than the supposition that the soul of brutes must be of the same nature as ours, so that after this life we have no more to hope or fear than flies or ants. Whereas, when we realise how much they really differ from us, we understand much better the arguments proving that our soul is of a nature entirely independent of the body, and thus not liable to die with it; and since we can discern no other causes that should destroy it, we are naturally led to decide that it is immortal.

I Am a Conscious Being

Yesterday's meditation plunged me into doubts of such gravity that I cannot forget them, and yet do not see how to resolve them. I am bewildered, as though I had suddenly fallen into a deep sea, and could neither plant my foot on the bottom nor swim up to the top. But I will make an effort, and try once more the same path as I entered upon yesterday; I will reject, that is, whatever admits of the least doubt, just as if I had found it was wholly false; and I will go on until I know something for certain—if it is only this, that there is nothing certain. Archimedes asked only for one fixed and immovable point so as to move the whole earth from its place; so I may have great hopes if I find even the least thing that is unshakably certain.

I suppose, therefore, that whatever things I see are illusions; I believe that none of the things my lying memory represents to have happened really did so; I have no senses; body, shape, extension, motion, place are chimeras. What then is true? Perhaps only this one thing, that nothing is certain.

How do I know, however, that there is not something different from all the things I have mentioned, as to which there is not the least occasion of doubt?—Is there a God (or whatever I call him) who gives me these very thoughts? But why, on the other hand, should I think so? Perhaps I myself may be the author of them.—Well, am I, at any rate, something?—"But I have already said I have no senses and no body—" At this point I stick; what follows from this? Am I so bound to a body and its senses that without them I cannot exist?—"But I have convinced myself that nothing in the world exists—no sky, no earth, no minds, no bodies; so am not I likewise non-existent?" But if I did convince myself of anything, I must have existed. "But there is some deceiver, supremely powerful, supremely intelligent, who purposely always deceives me." If he deceives me, then again I undoubtedly exist; let him deceive me as much as he may, he will never bring it about that, at the time of thinking (*quamdiu cogitabo*) that I am something, I am in fact nothing. Thus I have now weighed all considerations enough and more than enough; and must at length conclude that this proposition "I am," "I exist," whenever I utter it or conceive it in my mind, is necessarily true.

But I do not yet sufficiently understand what is this "I" that necessarily exists. I must take care, then, that I do not rashly take something else for the "I," and thus go wrong even in the knowledge that I am maintaining to be the most certain and evident of all. So I will consider afresh what I believed myself to be before I happened upon my present way of thinking; from this conception I will subtract whatever can be in the least shaken by the arguments adduced, so that what at least remains shall be precisely the unshakably certain element.

What, then, did I formerly think I was? A man. But what is a man? Shall I say "a rational animal"? No; in that case I should have to go on to ask what an animal is and what "rational" is, and so from a single question I should fall into several of greater difficulty; and I have not now the leisure to waste on such subtleties. . . . What am I to say now, when I am supposing that there is some all-powerful and (if it be lawful to say this) malignant deceiver, who has taken care to delude me about everything as much as he can? Can I, in the first place, say I have the least part of the characteristics that I said belonged to the essence of body? I concentrate, I think, I consider; nothing comes to mind; it would be wearisome and futile to repeat the reasons. Well, what of the properties I ascribed to the soul? Nutrition and locomotion? Since I have no body, these are mere delusions. Sensation? This cannot happen apart from a body; and in sleep I have seemed to have sensations that I have since realised never happened. Consciousness (*cogitare*)? At this point I come to the fact that there is consciousness (*or* experience: *cogitatio*); of this and this only I cannot be deprived. *I* am, *I* exist; that is certain. For how long? For as long as I am experiencing (*cogito*), maybe, if I wholly ceased from experiencing (*ab omni cogitatione*), I should at once wholly cease to be. For the present I am admitting only what is necessarily true; so "I am" precisely taken refers only to a conscious being; that is a mind, a soul (*animus*), an intellect, a reason— words whose meaning I did not previously know. I am a real being, and really exist; but what sort of being? As I said, a conscious being (*cogitans*). . . .

. . . I know that whatever I clearly and distinctly understand can be made by God just as I understand it; so my ability to understand one thing clearly and distinctly apart from another is enough to assure me that they are distinct, because God at least can separate them. (It is irrelevant what faculty enables me to think of them as separate.) Now I know that I exist, and at the same time I observe absolutely nothing else as belonging to my nature or essence except the mere fact that I am a conscious being; and just from this I can validly infer that my essence consists simply in the fact that I am a conscious being. It is indeed possible (or rather, as I shall say later on, it is certain) that I have a body closely bound up with myself; but at the same time I have, on the one hand, a clear and distinct idea of myself taken simply as a conscious, not an extended, being; and, on the other hand, a distinct idea of body, taken simply as an extended, not a conscious, being; so it is certain that I am really distinct from my body, and could exist without it. . . .

Consciousness Quite Different from Extension

To give a brief explanation of the real point: it is certain that experience (*cogitationem*) cannot exist apart from an experiencing being, nor in general can any act or accident exist apart from a substance to inhere in. Now we know substance, not immediately and in its own right, but only as the subject of certain acts; so it is very reasonable, and prescribed, by usage, to use different names for substances that we recognise as the subjects of quite different acts or accidents; we may then examine later on whether these different names stand for different things, or for one and the same thing. Now there are certain acts that we call *corporeal,* viz. size, shape, motion and all others that are inconceivable apart from extension in place; we call the substance in which they inhere a *body.* It is unimaginable that there is one substance to be the subject of shape, another to be the subject of local motion, and so on; all these acts fall under the common concept of extension. There are also other acts which we call *conscious* (*cogitativos*), e.g. understanding, willing, imagining, feeling; these all fall under the common concept of consciousness or perception or awareness; and we call the substance in which they inhere a *conscious being or mind.* The term used does not matter so long as we do not confuse this with corporeal substance; conscious acts have no affinity with corporeal acts, and the common concept of such acts, viz. *consciousness,* is quite different in kind from extension, the common concept of the other acts. . . .

What thought is

By the word thought I understand all that of which we are conscious as operating in us. And that is why not alone understanding, willing, imagining, but also feeling, are here the same thing as thought. For if I say I see, or I walk, I therefore am, and if by seeing and walking I mean the action of my eyes or my legs, which is the work of my body, my conclusion is not absolutely certain; because it may be that, as often happens in sleep, I think I see or I walk, although I never open my eyes or move from my place, and the same thing perhaps might occur if I had not a body at all. But if I mean only to talk of my sensation, or my consciously seeming to see or to walk, it becomes quite true because my assertion now refers only to my mind, which alone is concerned with my feeling or thinking that I see and I walk.

How we may know our mind better than our body.

But in order to understand how the knowledge which we possess of our mind not only precedes that which we have of our body, but is also more evident, it must be observed that it is very manifest by the natural light which is in our souls, that no qualities or properties pertain to nothing; and that where some are perceived there must necessarily be some thing or substance on which they depend. And the same light shows us that we know a thing or substance so much the better the more properties we observe in it. And we certainly observe many more qualities in our mind than in any other thing, inasmuch as there is nothing that excites us to knowledge of whatever kind, which does not even much more certainly compel us to a consciousness of our thought. To take an example, if I persuade myself that there is an earth because I touch or see it, by that very same fact, and by a yet stronger reason, I should be persuaded that my thought exists; because it may be that I think I touch the earth even though there is possibly no earth existing at all, but it is not possible that I who form this judgment and my mind which judges thus, should be non-existent; and so in other cases. . . .

The reason why everyone does not comprehend this in the same way.

Those who have not studied philosophy in an orderly way have held other opinions on this subject because they never distinguished their mind from their body with enough care. For although they had no difficulty in believing that they themselves existed, and that they had a greater assurance of this than of any other thing, yet because they did not observe that by themselves they ought merely to understand their minds [when metaphysical certainty was in question], and since on the contrary they rather meant that it was their bodies which they saw with their eyes, touched with their hands, and to which they wrongly attributed the power of perception, they did not distinctly comprehend the nature of the mind.

That the soul is united to all the portions
of the body conjointly.

But in order to understand all these things more perfectly, we must know that the soul is really joined to the whole body, and that we cannot, properly speaking, say that it exists in any one of its parts to the exclusion of the others, because it is one and in some manner indivisible, owing to the disposition of its organs, which are so related to one another that when any one of them is removed, that renders the whole body defective; and because it is of a nature which has no relation to extension, nor dimensions, nor other properties of the matter of which the body is composed, but only to the whole conglomerate of its organs, as appears from the fact that we could not in any way conceive of the half or the third of a soul, nor of the space it occupies, and because it does not become smaller owing to the cutting off of some portion of the body, but separates itself from it entirely when the union of its assembled organs is dissolved. . . .

That there is a small gland in the brain in which the
soul exercises its functions more particularly than
in the other parts.

It is likewise necessary to know that although the soul is joined to the whole body, there is yet in that a certain part in which it exercises its functions more particularly than in all the others; and it is usually believed that this part is the brain, or possibly the heart: the brain, because it is with it that the organs of sense are connected, and the heart because it is apparently in it that we experience the passions. But, in examining the matter with care, it seems as though I had clearly ascertained that the part of the body in which the soul exercises its functions immediately is in nowise the heart, nor the whole of the brain, but merely the most inward of all its parts, to wit, a certain very small gland which is situated in the middle of its substance and so suspended above the duct whereby the animal spirits in its anterior cavities have communication with those in the posterior, that the slightest movements which take place in it may alter very greatly the course of these spirits; and reciprocally that the smallest changes which occur in the course of the spirits may do much to change the movements of this gland.

How the soul and the body act on one another.

Let us then conceive here that the soul has its principal seat in the little gland which exists in the middle of the brain, from whence it radiates forth through all the remainder of the body by means of the animal spirits, nerves, and even the blood, which, participating in the impressions of the spirits, can carry them by the arteries into all the members. And recollecting what has been said above about the machine of our body, i.e. that the little filaments of our nerves are so distributed in all its parts, that on the occasion of the diverse movements which are there excited by sensible objects, they open in diverse ways the pores of the brain, which causes the animal spirits contained in these cavities to enter in diverse ways into the muscles, by which means they can move the members in all the different ways in which they are capable of being moved; and also that all the other causes which are capable of moving the spirits in diverse ways suffice to conduct them into diverse muscles; let us here add that the small gland which is the main seat of the soul is so suspended between the cavities which contain the spirits that it can be moved by them in as many different ways as there are sensible diversities in the object, but that it may also be moved in diverse ways by the soul, whose nature is such that it receives in itself as many diverse impressions, that is to say, that it possess as many diverse perceptions as there are diverse movements in this gland. Reciprocally, likewise, the machine of the body is so formed that from the simple fact that this gland is diversely moved by the soul, or by such other cause, whatever it is, it thrusts the spirits which surround it towards the pores of the brain, which conduct them by the nerves into the muscles, by which means it causes them to move the limbs.

6

JOHN LOCKE

Personal Identity, Consciousness and the Immaterial Substance

Corporeal and Spiritual Substances

WHEN WE TALK or think of any particular sort of corporeal substances, as horse, stone, etc., though the idea we have of either of them be but the complication or collection of those several simple ideas of sensible qualities, which we used to find united in the thing called horse or stone; yet, *because we cannot conceive how they should subsist alone, nor one in another,* we suppose them existing in and supported by some common subject; which support we denote by the name substance, though it be certain we have no clear or distinct idea of that thing we suppose a support.

The same thing happens concerning the operations of the mind, viz. thinking, reasoning, fearing, etc., which we concluding not to subsist of themselves, nor apprehending how they can belong to body, or be produced by it, we are apt to think these the actions of some other *substance,* which we call *spirit*; whereby yet it is evident that, having no other idea of notion of matter, but something wherein those many sensible qualities which affect our senses do subsist; by supposing a substance wherein thinking, knowing, doubting, and a power of moving, etc., do subsist, we have as clear a notion of the substance of spirit,

---

The first section of this selection is taken from chapter 23, all the others from chapter 27 of Book Two of Locke's *Essay Concerning Human Understanding.* The first edition of the *Essay* was published in 1690; chapter 27 appeared for the first time in the second edition in 1694.

as we have of body; the one being supposed to be (without knowing what it is) the *substratum* to those simple ideas we have from without; and the other supposed (with a like ignorance of what it is) to be the *substratum* to those operations we experiment in ourselves within. It is plain then, that the idea of *corporeal substance* in matter is as remote from our conceptions and apprehensions, as that of *spiritual substance*, or spirit: and therefore, from our not having any notion of the substance of spirit, we can no more conclude its non-existence, than we can, for the same reason, deny the existence of body; it being as rational to affirm there is no body, because we have no clear and distinct idea of the substance of matter, as to say there is no spirit, because we have no clear and distinct idea of the substance of a spirit. . . .

So that, in short, the idea we have of spirit, compared with the idea we have of body, stands thus: the substance of spirits is unknown to us; and so is the substance of body equally unknown to us. Two primary qualities or properties of body, viz. solid coherent parts and impulse, we have distinct clear ideas of: so likewise we know, and have distinct [and] clear ideas, of two primary qualities or properties of spirit, viz. thinking, and a power of action; i.e. a power of beginning or stopping several thoughts or motions. We have also the ideas of several qualities inherent in bodies, and have the clear distinct ideas of them; which qualities are but the various modifications of the extension of cohering solid parts, and their motion. We have likewise the ideas of the several modes of thinking viz. believing, doubting, intending, fearing, hoping; all which are but the several modes of thinking. We have also the ideas of willing, and moving the body consequent to it, and with the body itself too; for, as has been shown, spirit is capable of motion.

. . . If this notion of immaterial spirit may have, perhaps, some difficulties in it not easily to be explained, we have therefore no more reason to deny or doubt the existence of such spirits, than we have to deny or doubt the existence of body; because the notion of body is cumbered with some difficulties very hard, and perhaps impossible to be explained or understood by us. . . .

The Identity of Living Things

In the state of living creatures, their identity depends not on a mass of the same particles, but on something else. For in them the variation of great parcels of matter alters not the identity: an oak growing from a plant to a great tree, and then lopped, is still the same oak; and a colt grown up to a horse, sometimes fat, sometimes lean, is all the while the same horse: though, in both these cases, there may be a manifest change of the parts; so that truly they are not either of them the same masses of matter, though they be truly one of them the same oak, and the other the same horse. The reason whereof is, that, in these two cases, a mass of matter, and a living body, identity is not applied to the same thing.

IDENTITY OF VEGETABLES.

We must therefore consider wherein an oak differs from a mass of matter, and that seems to me to be in this, that the one is only the cohesion of particles of matter any how united, the other such a disposition of them as constitutes the parts of an oak; and such an organization of those parts as is fit to receive and distribute nourishment, so as to continue and frame the wood, bark, and leaves, etc., of an oak, in which consists the vegetable life. That being then one plant which has such an organization of parts in one coherent body, partaking of one common life, it continues to be the same plant as long as it partakes of the same life, though that life be communicated to new particles of matter vitally united to the living plant, in a like continued organization conformable to that sort of plants. For this organization being at any one instant in any one collection of matter, is in that particular concrete distinguished from all other, and is that individual life, which existing constantly from that moment both forwards and backwards, in the same continuity of insensibly succeeding parts united to the living body of the plant, it has that identity which makes the same plant, and all the parts of it, parts of the same plant, during all the time that they exist united in that continued organization, which is fit to convey that common life to all the parts so united.

IDENTITY OF ANIMALS.

The case is not so much different in brutes, but that any one may hence see what makes an animal and continues it the same. Something we have like this in machines, and may serve to illustrate it. For example, what is a watch?: It is plain it is nothing but a fit organization or construction of parts to a certain end, which, when a sufficient force is added to it, it is capable to attain. If we would suppose this machine one continued body, all whose organized parts were repaired, increased, or diminished by a constant addition or separation of insensible parts, with one common life, we should have something very much like the body of an animal; with this difference, that, in an animal the fitness of the organization, and the motion wherein life consists, begin together, the motion coming from within; but in machines, the force coming sensibly from without, is often away when the organ is in order, and well fitted to receive it.

THE IDENTITY OF MAN.

This also shows wherein the identity of the same man consists; vis., in nothing but a participation of the same continued life, by constantly fleeting particles of matter, in succession vitally united to the same organized body. He that shall place the identity of man in anything else, but like that of other animals, in one fitly organized body, taken in any one instant, and from thence continued, under one organization of life, in several successively fleeting particles of matter united to it, will find it hard to make an embryo, one of years, mad and sober, the same man, by any supposition, that will not make it possible for Seth, Ismael, Socrates, Pilate, Saint Austin, and Caesar Borgia, to be the same man. For, if the identity of soul alone makes the same man, and there be nothing in the nature of matter why the same individual spirit may not be united to different bodies, it will be possible that those men living in distant ages, and of different tempers, may have been the same man: which way of speaking must be, from a very strange use of the word man, applied to an idea, out of which body and shape are excluded. And that way of speaking would agree yet worse with the notions of those philosophers who allow of transmigration, and are of opinion that the souls of men may, for their miscarriages, be detruded into the bodies of beasts, as fit habitations, with organs suited to the satisfaction of their brutal inclinations. But yet I think nobody, could he be sure that the souls of Heliogabalus were in one of his hogs, would yet say that hog were a man or Heliogabalus.

IDENTITY SUITED TO THE IDEA.

It is not therefore unity of substances that comprehends all sorts of identity, or will determine it in every case; but to conceive and judge of it aright, we must consider what idea the word it is applied to stands for: it being one thing to be the same substance, another the same man, and a third the same person, if person, man, and substance, are three names standing for three different ideas; for such as is the idea belonging to that name, such must be the identity; which, if it had been a little more carefully attended to, would possibly have prevented a great deal of that confusion which often occurs about this matter, with no small seeming difficulties, especially concerning personal identity, which therefore we shall in the next place a little consider.

SAME MAN.

An animal is living organized body; and consequently the same animal, as we have observed, is the same continued life communicated to different particles of matter, as they happen successively to be united to that organized living body. And whatever is talked of other definitions, ingenious observation puts it past doubt, that the idea in our minds, of which the sound man in our mouths is the sign, is nothing else but of an animal of such a certain form: since I think I may be confident, that, whoever should see a creature of his own shape or make, though it had no more reason all its life than a cat or a parrot, would call him still a man; or whoever should hear a car or a parrot discourse, reason, and philosophize, would call or think it nothing but a cat or a parrot; and say, the one was a dull irrational man, and the other a very intelligent rational parrot. . . .

I presume it is not the idea of a thinking or rational being alone that makes the idea of a man in most people's sense, but of a body, so and so shaped, joined to it; and if that be the idea of a man, the same successive body not shifted all at once, must, as well as the same immaterial spirit, go to the making of the same man.

Consciousness and Personal Identity.

PERSONAL IDENTITY

This being premised, to find wherein personal identity consists, we must consider what person stands for; which, I think, is a thinking intelligent being, that has reason and reflection, and can consider itself as itself, the same thinking thing, in different times and places; which it does only by that consciousness which is inseparable from thinking, and, as it seems to me, essential to it: it being impossible for any one to perceive without perceiving that he does perceive. When we see, hear, smell, taste, feel, meditate, or will anything, we know that we do so. Thus it is always as to our present sensations and perceptions: and by this every one is to himself that which he calls self; it not being considered, in this case, whether the same self be continued in the same or divers substances. For, since consciousness always accompanies thinking, and it is that which makes every one to be what he calls self, and thereby distinguishes himself from all other thinking things: in this alone consists personal identity, i.e., the sameness of a rational being; and as far as this consciousness can be extended backwards to any past action or thought, so far reaches the identity of that person; it is the same self now it was then; and it is by the same self with this present one that now reflects on it, that that action was done.

CONSCIOUSNESS MAKES PERSONAL IDENTITY.

But it is further inquired, whether it be the same identical substance? This, few would think they had reason to doubt of, if these perceptions, with their consciousness, always remained present in the mind, whereby the same thinking thing would be always consciously present, and, as would be thought, evidently the same to itself. But that which seems to make the difficulty is this, that this consciousness being interrupted always by forgetfulness, there being no moment of our lives wherein we have the whole train of all our past actions before our eyes in one view, but even the best memories losing the sight of one part whilst they are viewing another; and we sometimes, and that the great-est part of our lives, not reflecting on our past selves, being intent on our present thoughts, and in sound sleep having no thoughts at all, or at least none with that consciousness which remarks our waking thoughts; I say, in all these cases, our consciousness being interrupted, and we losing the sight of our past selves, doubts are raised whether we are the same thinking thing, i.e., the same substance or no. Which, however reasonable or unreasonable, concerns not personal identity at all: the question being, what makes the same person, and not whether it be the same identical substance, which always thinks in the same person; which in this case, matters not at all: different substances, by the same consciousness (where they do partake in it) being united into one person, as well as different bodies by the same life are united into one animal, whose identity is preserved in that change of substances by the unity of one continued life. For it being the same consciousness that makes a man be himself to himself, personal identity depends on that only, whether it be annexed solely to one individual substance, or can be continued in a succession of several substances. For as far as any intelligent being can repeat the idea of an any past action with the same consciousness it had of it at first, and with the same consciousness it has of any present action; so far it is the same personal self. For it is by the consciousness it has of its present thoughts and actions, that it is self to itself now, and so will be the same self, as far as the same consciousness can extend to actions past or to come; and would be by distance of time, or change of substance, no more two persons, than a man be two men by wearing other clothes today than he did yesterday, with a long or a short sleep between: the same consciousness uniting those distant ac-tions into the same person, whatever substances contributed to their production.

Personal Identity in Change of Substances.

That this is so, we have some kind of evidence in our very bodies, all whose particles, whilst vitally united to this same thinking conscious self, so that we feel when they are touched, and are affected by, and conscious of good or harm that happens to them, are a part of ourselves; i.e., of our thinking conscious self. Thus, the limbs of his body are to every one a part of himself; he sympathizes and is concerned for them. Cut off a hand, and thereby separate it from that consciousness he had of its heat, cold, and other affections, and it is then no longer a part of that which is himself, any more than the remotest part of matter. Thus, we see the substance whereof personal self consisted at one time may be varied at another, without the change of personal identity; there being no question about the same person, though the limbs which but now were a part of it, be cut off. . . .

Personal Identity and the Immaterial Substance

But next, as to the first part of the question, "Whether if the same thinking substance (supposing immaterial substances only to think) be changed, it can be the same person?" I answer, that cannot be resolved, but by those who know what kind of substances they are that do think, and whether the consciousness of past actions can be transferred from one thinking substance to another. I grant, were the same consciousness the same individual action, it could not: but it being a present representation of a past action, why it may not be possible that that may be represented to the mind to have been, which really never was, will remain to be shown. And therefore how far the consciousness of past actions is annexed to any individual agent, so that another cannot possibly have it, will be hard for us to determine, till we know what kind of action it is that cannot be done without a reflex act of perception accompanying it, and how performed by thinking substances, who cannot think without being conscious of it. But that which we call the same consciousness, not being the same individual act, why one intellectual substance may not have represented to it, as done by itself, what it never did, and was perhaps done by some other agent; why, I say, such a representation may not possibly be without reality of matter of fact, as well as several representations in dreams are, which yet whilst dreaming we take for true, will be difficult to conclude from the nature of things. And that it never is so, will by us, till we have clearer views of the nature of thinking substances, be best resolved into the goodness of God, who, as far as the happiness or misery of any of his sensible creatures is concerned in it, will not, by a fatal error of theirs, transfer from one to another that consciousness which draws reward or punishment with it. How far this may be an argument against those who would place thinking in a system of fleeting animal spirits, I leave to be considered. But yet, to return to the question before us, it must be allowed, that, if the same consciousness (which, as has been shown, is quite a different thing from the same numerical figure or motion of body) can be transferred from one thinking substance to another, it will be possible that two thinking substances may make but one person. For the same consciousness being preserved, whether in the same or different substances, the personal identity is preserved.

As to the second part of the question, "Whether the same immaterial substance remaining, there may be two distinct persons?" which question seems to me to be built on this, whether the same immaterial being, being conscious of the action of its past duration, may be wholly stripped of all the consciousness of its past existence, and lose it beyond the power of ever retrieving it again; and so as it were beginning a new account from a new period, have a consciousness that cannot reach beyond this new state. All those who hold preexistence are evidently of this mind, since they allow the soul to have no remaining consciousness of what it did in that preexistent state, either wholly separate from body, or informing any other body; and if they should not, it is plain experience would be against them. So that personal identity reaching no further than consciousness reaches, a preexistent spirit not having continued so many ages in a state of silence, must needs make different persons. Suppose a Christian Platonist or a Pythagorean should, upon God's having ended all his works of creation the seventh day, think his soul hath existed ever since; and would imagine it has revolved in several human bodies, as I once met with one, who was persuaded his had been the soul of Socrates; (how reasonably I will not dispute; this I know, that in the post he filled, which was no inconsiderable one, he passed for a very rational man, and the press has shown that he wanted not parts or learning;) would any one say, that he, being not conscious of any of Socrates' actions or thoughts, could be the same person with Socrates? Let any one reflect upon himself, and conclude that he has in himself an immaterial spirit, which is that which thinks in him, and, in the constant change of his body keeps him the same: and is that which he calls himself: let him also suppose it to be the same soul that was in Nestor or Thersites, at the siege of Troy (for souls being, as far as we know anything of them, in their nature indifferent to any parcel of matter, the supposition has no apparent absurdity in it), which it may have been, as well as it is now the soul of any other man: but he now having no consciousness of any of the actions either of Nestor or Thersites, does or can be conceive himself the same person with either of them? Can he be concerned in either of their actions? Attribute them to himself, or think them his own, more than the actions of any other men that ever existed? So that this consciousness not reaching to any of the actions of either of those men, he is no more one self with either of them, than if the soul or immaterial spirit that now informs him had been created, and began to exist, when it began to inform his present body, though it were ever so true, that the same spirit that informed Nestor's or Thersites' body were numerically the same that now informs his. For this would no more make him the same person with Nestor, than if some of the particles of matter that were once a part of Nestor, were now a part of this man; the same immaterial substance, without the same consciousness, no more making the same person by being united to any body, than the same particle of matter, without consciousness united to any body, makes the same person. But let him once find himself conscious of any of the actions of Nestor, he then finds himself the same person with Nestor.

Memory and Personal Identity

And thus may we be able, without any difficulty, to conceive the same person at the resurrection, though in a body not exactly in make or parts the same which he had here, the same consciousness going along with the soul that inhabits it. But yet the soul alone, in the change of bodies, would scarce to any one but to him that makes the soul the man, be enough to make the same man. For should the soul of a prince, carrying with it the consciousness of the prince's past life, enter and inform the body of a cobbler, as soon as deserted by his own soul, every one sees he would be the same person with the prince, accountable only for the prince's actions: but who would say it was the same man? The body too goes to the making the man, and would, I guess, to everybody determine the man in this case; wherein the soul, with all its princely thoughts about it, would not make another man: but he would be the same cobbler to every one besides himself. I know that, in the ordinary way of speaking, the same person, and the same man, stand for one and the same thing. And indeed every one will always have a liberty to speak as he pleases, and to apply what articulate sounds to what ideas he thinks fit, and change them as often as he pleases. But yet, when we will inquire what makes the same spirit, man, or person, we must fix the ideas of spirit, man, or person in our minds, and having resolved with ourselves what we mean by them, it will not be hard to determine in either of them, or the like, when it is the same, and when not.

Consciousness Makes the Same Person.

But though the same immaterial substance or soul does not alone, wherever it be, and in whatsoever state, make the same man; yet it is plain, consciousness, as far as ever it can be extended, should it be to ages past, unites existences and actions, very remote in time into the same person, as well as it does the existences and actions of the immediately preceding moment: so that whatever has the consciousness of present and past actions, is the same person to whom they both belong. Had I the same consciousness that I saw the ark and Noah's flood, as that I saw an overflowing of the Thames last winter, or as that I write now; I could no more doubt that I who write this now, that saw the Thames overflowed last winter, and that viewed the flood at the general deluge, was the same self, place that self in what substance you please, than that I who write this am the same myself now whilst I write (whether I consist of all the same substance, material or immaterial, or no) that I was yesterday; for as to this point of being the same self, it matters not whether this present self be made up of the same or other substances; I being as much concerned, and as justly accountable for any action that was done a thousand years since, appropriated to me now by this self-consciousness, as I am for what I did the last moment.

Self Depends on Consciousness.

Self is that conscious thinking thing, whatever substance made up of (whether spiritual or material, simple or compounded, it matters not), which is sensible or conscious of pleasure and pain, capable of happiness or misery, and so is concerned for itself, as far as that consciousness extends. Thus every one finds, that, whilst comprehended under that consciousness, the little finger is as much a part of himself as what is most so. Upon separation of this little finger, should this consciousness go along with the little finger, and leave the rest of the body, it is evident the little finger would be the person, the same person, and self then would have nothing to do with the rest of the body. As in this case it is the consciousness that goes along with the substance, when one part is separate from another, which makes the same person, and constitutes this inseparable self; so it is in reference to substances remote in time. That with which the consciousness of this present thinking thing can join itself, makes the same person, and is one self with it, and with nothing else; and so attributes to itself, and owns all the actions of that thing as its own, as far as that consciousness reaches, and no further; as every one who reflects will perceive.

OBJECTS OF REWARD AND PUNISHMENT.

In this personal identity is founded all the right and justice of reward and punishment; happiness and misery being that for which every one is concerned for himself, and not mattering what becomes of any substance not joined to, or affected with that consciousness. For as it is evident in the instance I gave but now, if the consciousness went along with the little finger when it was cut off, that would be the same self which was concerned for the whole body yesterday, as making part of itself, whose actions then it cannot but admit as its own now. Though, if the same body should still live, and immediately from the separation of the little finger have its own peculiar consciousness, whereof the little finger knew nothing; it would not at all be concerned for it, as a part of itself, or could own any of its actions, or have any of them imputed to him.

This may show us wherein personal identity consists: not in the identity of substance, but, as I have said, in the identity of consciousness; wherein if Socrates and the present mayor of Queenborough agree, they are the same person: if the same Socrates waking and sleeping do not partake of the same consciousness. Socrates waking and sleeping is not the same person. And to punish Socrates waking for what sleeping Socrates thought, and waking Socrates was never conscious of, would be no more of right, than to punish one twin for what his brother-twin did, whereof he knew nothing, because their outsides were so like, that they could not be distinguished; for such twins have been seen.

But yet possibly it will still be objected, suppose I wholly lose the memory of some parts of my life, beyond a possibility of retrieving them, so that perhaps I shall never be conscious of them again; yet am I not the same person that did those actions, had those thoughts that I once was conscious of, though I have now forgot them? To which I answer, that we must here take notice what the word I is applied to; which, in this case, is the man only. And the same man being presumed to be the same person, I is easily here supposed to stand also for the same person. But if it be possible for the same man to have distinct incommunicable consciousness at different times, it is past doubt the same man would at different times make different persons; which, we see, is the sense of mankind in the solemnest declaration of their opinions; human laws not punishing the mad man for the sober man's actions, nor the sober man for what the mad man did, thereby making them two persons: which is somewhat explained by our way of speaking in English, when we say such an one is not himself, or is beside himself; in which phrases it is insinuated, as if those who now, or at least first used them, thought that self was changed, the selfsame person was no longer in that man. . . .

A Problem About Punishment

But is not a man drunk and sober the same person? why else is he punished for the fact he commits when drunk, though he be never afterwards conscious of it? Just as much the same person as a man that walks, and does other things in his sleep, is the same person, and is answerable for any mischief he shall do in it. Human laws punish both, with a justice suitable to their way of knowledge; because, in these cases, they cannot distinguish certainly what is real, what counterfeit: and so the ignorance in drunkenness or sleep is not admitted as a plea. For, though punishment be annexed to personality, and personality to consciousness, and the drunkard perhaps be not conscious of what he did, yet human judicatures justly punish him, because the fact is proved against him, but want of consciousness cannot be proved for him. But in the great day, wherein the secrets of all hearts shall be laid open, it may be reasonable to think, no one shall be made to answer for what he knows nothing of; but shall receive his doom, his conscience accusing or excusing him.

Consciousness Alone Makes Self

Nothing but consciousness can unite remote existences into the same person: the identify of substance will not do it; for whatever substance there is, however framed, without consciousness there is no person: and a carcass may be a person, as well as any sort of substance be so without consciousness.

Could we suppose two distinct incommunicable consciousnesses acting in the same body, the one constantly by day, the other by night;
and, on the other side, the same consciousness, acting by intervals, two
distinct bodies; I ask, in the first case, whether the day and the night
man would not be two as distinct persons as Socrates and Plato? And
whether, in the second case, there would not be one person in two
distinct bodies, as much as one man is the same in two distinct cloth-
ings? Nor is it at all material to say, that this same, and this distinct
consciousness, in the cases above mentioned, is owing to the same and
distinct immaterial substances, bringing it with them to those bodies;
which, whether true or no, alters not the case; since it is evident the
personal identity would equally be determined by the consciousness,
whether that consciousness were annexed to some individual immaterial substance or no. For, granting that the thinking substance in man
must be necessarily supposed immaterial, it is evident that immaterial
thinking thing may sometimes part with its past consciousness, and be
restored to it again, as appears in the forgetfulness men often have of
their past actions: and the mind many times recovers the memory of a
past consciousness, which it had lost for twenty years together. Make
these intervals of memory and forgetfulness to take their turns regu-
larly by day and night, and you have two persons with the same immaterial spirit, as much as in the former instance two persons with the
same body. So that self is not determined by identity or diversity or
substance, which it cannot be sure of, but only by identity of consciousness. . . .

7

JOSEPH BUTLER

Of a Future Life

Identity Can Survive Great Changes

. . . . LET US CONSIDER what the analogy of nature, and the several changes which we have undergone and those which we know we may undergo without being destroyed, suggest as to the effect which death may or may not have upon us; and whether it be not from thence probable that we may survive this change and exist in a future state of life and perception.

. . . From our being born into the present world in the helpless imperfect state of infancy and having arrived from thence to mature age, we find it to be a general law of nature in our own species that the same creatures, the same individuals, should exist in degrees of life and perception, with capacities of action, enjoyment and suffering in one period of their being greatly different from those appointed them in another period of it. And in other creatures the same law holds. For the difference of their capacities and states of life at their birth (to go no higher) and in maturity—the change of worms into flies and the vast enlargement of their locomotive powers by such change; and birds and insects bursting the shell, their habitation, and by this means entering into a new world, furnished with new accommodations for them, and finding a new sphere of action assigned them: these are instances of this general law of nature. Thus all the various and wonderful transforma-

This selection consists of chapter 1, part 1 (with some omissions) of *The Analogy of Religion* (1736).

tions of animals are to be taken into consideration here. But the state of life in which we ourselves existed formerly, in the womb and in our infancy, are almost as different from our present, in mature age, as it is possible to conceive any two states or degrees of life can be. Therefore, that we are to exist hereafter in a state as different (suppose) from our present as this is from our former is but according to the analogy of nature — according to a natural order or appointments of the very same kind as what we have already experienced.

Presumption of Survival

. . . We know we are endued with capacities of action, of happiness and misery, for we are conscious of acting, of enjoying pleasure and suffering pain. Now, that we have these powers and capacities before death is a presumption that we shall retain them through and after death, indeed a probability of it sufficient to act upon, unless there be some positive reason to think that death is the destruction of those living powers — because there is in every case a probability that all things will continue as we experience they are, in all respects except those in which we have some reason to think they will be altered. This is that kind of presumption or probability from analogy, expressed in the very word *continuance*, which seems our only natural reason for believing the course of the world will continue tomorrow as it has done so far as our experience or knowledge of history can carry us back. Nay, it seems our only reason for believing that any one substance now existing will continue to exist a moment longer — the self-existent substance only excepted. Thus, if men were assured that the unknown event, death, was not the destruction of our faculties of perception and of action, there would be no apprehension that any other power or event unconnected with this of death would destroy their faculties just at the instant of each creature's death — and therefore no doubt but that they would remain after it; which shows the high probability that our living powers will continue after death, unless there be some ground to think that death is their destruction. For if it would be in a manner certain that we should survive death, provided it were certain that death would not be our destruction, it must be highly probable that we shall survive it if there be no ground to think death will be our destruction.

No Evidence Against Survival

Now, though I think it must be acknowledged that prior to the natural and moral proofs of a future life commonly insisted upon, there would arise a general confused suspicion that in the great shock and alteration which we shall undergo by death we (that is, our living powers) might be wholly destroyed; yet even prior to these proofs there is really no particular distinct ground or reason for this apprehension at all, so far as I can find. If there be, it must arise either from *the reason of the thing* or from *the analogy of Nature*.

But we cannot argue from *the reason of the thing* that death is the destruction of living agents, because we know not at all which death is in itself, but only some of its effects, such as the dissolution of flesh, skin and bones. And these effects do in no wise appear to imply the destruction of a living agent. And besides, as we are greatly in the dark upon what the exercise of our living powers depends, so we are wholly ignorant what the powers themselves depend upon—the powers themselves as distinguished not only from their actual exercise but also from the present capacity of exercising them, and as opposed to their destruction; for sleep or . . . a swoon shows us not only that these powers exist when they are not exercised but shows also that they exist when there is no present capacity of exercising them, or that the capacities of exercising them for the present, as well as the actual exercise of them, may be suspended and yet the powers themselves remain undestroyed. Since, then, we know not at all upon what the existence of our living powers depends, this shows farther there can no probability be collected from the reason of the thing that death will be their destruction; because their existence may depend upon something in no degree affected by death—upon something quite out of the reach of this king of terrors—so that there is nothing more certain than that *the reason of the thing* shows us no connection between death and the destruction of living agents. Nor can we find anything throughout the whole *analogy of Nature* to afford us even the slightest presumption that animals ever lose their living powers, much less, if it were possible, that they lose them by death; for we have no faculties wherewith to trace any beyond or through it, so as to see what becomes of them. This event removes them from our view. It destroys the *perceptible* proof which we had before their death of their being possessed of living powers, but does not appear to afford the least reason to believe that they are then, or by that event, deprived of them. . . .

Our Bodies Are No Part of Ourselves

. . . . All presumptions of death's being the destruction of living beings must go upon supposition that they are compounded and so dissoluble; but since consciousness is a single and indivisible power it should seem that the subject in which it resides must be so too. For were the motion of any particle of matter absolutely one and indivisible so that it should imply a contradiction to suppose part of this motion to exist and part not to exist—that is, part of this matter to move and part to be at rest—then its power of motion would be indivisible and so also would the subject in which the power inheres, namely the particle of matter; for if this could be divided into two, one part might be moved and the other at rest, which is contrary to the supposition. In like manner it has been argued,[1] and, for anything appearing to the contrary, justly, that since the perception or consciousness which we have of our own existence is indivisible, so as that it is a contradiction to suppose one part of it should be here and the other there, the perceptive power or the power of consciousness is indivisible too, and consequently the subject in which it resides, that is, the conscious being. Now upon supposition that the living agent each man calls himself is thus a single being, which there is at least no more difficulty in conceiving than in conceiving it to be a compound, and of which there is the proof now mentioned, it follows that our organized bodies are no more ourselves or part of ourselves than any other matter around us. And it is as easy to conceive how matter, which is no part of ourselves, may be appropriated to us in the manner which our present bodies are, as how we can receive impressions from and have power over any matter. It is as easy to conceive that we may exist out of bodies as in them; that we might have animated bodies of any other organs and senses wholly different from these now given us and that we may hereafter animate these same or new bodies variously modified and organized; as to conceive how we can animate such bodies as our present. And lastly, the dissolution of all these several organized bodies, supposing ourselves to have successively animated them, would have no more conceivable tendency to destroy the living beings, ourselves, or deprive us of living faculties, the faculties of perception and action, than the dissolution of any foreign matter, which we are capable of receiving impressions from and making use of for the common occasions of life.

. . . The simplicity and absolute oneness of a living agent cannot, indeed, from the nature of the thing, be properly proved by experimental observations; but as these *fall* in with the supposition of its unity, so they plainly lead us to *conclude* certainly that our gross organized bodies, with which we perceive the objects of sense, and with which we act, are no part of ourselves, and therefore show us that we have no reason to believe their destruction to be ours, even without determining whether our living substances be material or immaterial. For we see by experience that men may lose their limbs, their organs of sense and even the greatest part of these bodies, and yet remain the same living agents. And persons can trace up the existence of themselves to a time when the bulk of their bodies was extremely small in comparison with what it is in mature age; and we cannot but think that they might then have lost a considerable part of that small body, and yet have remained the same living agents, as they may now lose great

1. *See* Dr. Clarke's letter to Mr. Dodwell and the defenses of it. Details of Clarke's publications are given in the bibliographical essay, p. 332 below (Ed.)

part of their present body and remain so. And it is certain that the bodies of all animals are in a constant flux from that never-ceasing attrition which there is in every part of them. Now things of this kind unavoidably teach us to distinguish between these living agents, ourselves, and large quantities of matter in which we are very closely interested: since these may be alienated and actually are in a daily course of succession and changing their owners, whilst we are assured that each living agent remains one and the same permanent being. . . .

Our Organs and Limbs Are Our Instruments

. . . If we consider our body somewhat more distinctly, as made up of organs and instruments of perception and motion, it will bring us to the same conclusion. Thus the common optical experiments show, and even the observation how sight is assisted by glasses shows, that we see with our eyes in the same sense as we see with glasses. Nor is there any reason to believe that we see with them in any other sense—any other, I mean, which would lead us to think the eye itself a percipient. The like is to be said of hearing; and our feeling distant solid matter by means of something in our hand, seems an instance of the like kind, as to the subject we are considering. All these are instances of foreign matter, or such as is no part of our body, being instrumental in preparing objects for and conveying them to the perceiving power, in a manner similar or like to the manner in which our organs of sense prepare and convey them. Both are, in a like way, instruments of our receiving such ideas from external objects, as the Author of Nature appointed those external objects to be the occasions of exciting in us. However, glasses are evidently instances of this: namely, of matter which is no part of our body preparing objects for and conveying them towards the perceiving power, in like manner as our bodily organs do. And if we see with our eyes only in the same manner as we do with glasses, the like may be justly concluded by analogy of all our other senses. . . .

So also with regard to our power of moving or directing motion by will or choice: upon the destruction of a limb, this active power remains, as it evidently seems, unlessened, so that the living being who has suffered this loss would be capable of moving as before had it another limb to move with. It can walk by the help of an artificial leg, just as it can make use of a pole or a lever to reach towards itself and to move things beyond the length and power of its natural arm: and this last it does in the same manner as it reaches and moves with its natural arm things nearer and of less weight. . . .

Thus a man determines that he will look at such an object through a microscope; or, being lame, suppose that he will walk to such a place with a staff a week hence. His eyes and feet no more determine in these cases than the microscope and staff. Nor is there any ground to think they any more put the determination in practice, or that his eyes are the seers or his feet the movers, in any other sense than as the microscope and the staff are. Upon the whole, then, our organs of sense and our limbs are certainly instruments which the living persons, ourselves, make use of to perceive and move with — there is not any probability that they are any more, nor, consequently, that we have any other kind of relation to them, than what we may have to any other foreign matter formed into instruments of perception and motion, suppose into a microscope or a staff . . . nor consequently is there any probability that the alienation or dissolution of these instruments is the destruction of the perceiving and moving agent.

And thus our finding that the dissolution of matter in which living beings were most closely interested is not their dissolution and that the destruction of several of the organs and instruments of perception and of motion belonging to them is not their destruction shows, demonstratively, that there is no ground to think that the dissolution of any other matter or destruction of any other organs and instruments will be the dissolution or destruction of living agents from the like kind of relation. And we have no reason to think we stand in any other kind of relation to anything which we find dissolved by death. . . .

The Immortality of Brutes

But it is said these observations are equally applicable to brutes; and it is thought an insuperable difficulty that they should be immortal and by consequence capable of everlasting happiness. Now this manner of expression is both invidious and weak; but the thing intended by it is really no difficulty at all, either in the way of natural or moral consideration. For (1) suppose the invidious thing, designed in such a manner of expression, were really implied, as it is not in the least, in the natural immortality of brutes — namely, that they must arrive at great attainments and become rational and moral agents — even this would be no difficulty, since we know not what latent powers and capacities they may be endued with. There was once, prior to experience, as great presumption against human creatures as there is against brute creatures arriving at that degree of understanding which we have in mature age — for we can trace up our own existence to the same origin as theirs. And we find it to be a general law of nature that creatures, endued with capacities of virtue and religion, should be placed in a condition of being in which they are altogether without the use of them for a considerable length of their duration, as in infancy and childhood. And a great part of the human species go out of the present world before they come to the exercise of these capacities in any degree at all.

But then (2), the natural immortality of brutes does not in the least imply that they are endued with any latent capacities of a rational or moral nature; and the economy of the universe might require that there should be living creatures without any capacities of this kind. And all difficulties as to the manner how they are disposed of are so apparently and wholly founded on our ignorance that 'tis wonderful they should be insisted upon by any but such as are weak enough to think they are acquainted with the whole system of things. . . .

Mortal Diseases Do Not Affect Our Intellectual Powers

. . . Human creatures exist at present in two states of life and perception different from each other, each of which has its own peculiar laws and its own peculiar enjoyments and sufferings. When any of our senses are affected or appetites gratified with the objects of them we may be said to exist or live in a state of sensation. When none of our senses are affected and yet we perceive and reason and act we may be said to exist or live in a state of reflection. Now it is by no means certain that anything which is dissolved by death is in any way necessary to the living being in this state of reflection, after ideas are gained; for though from our present constitution and condition of being our external organs are necessary for conveying in ideas to our reflecting powers, as carriages and levers and scaffolds are in architecture, yet when these ideas are brought in we are capable of reflecting in the most intense degree and of enjoying the greatest pleasure and feeling the greatest pain by means of that reflection, without any assistance from our senses, and without any at all which we know of from that body which will be dissolved by death. It does not appear, then, that the relation of this gross body to the reflecting being is in any degree necessary to thinking—to our intellectual enjoyments and sufferings—nor consequently that the dissolution or alienation of the former by death will be the destruction of those present powers which render us capable of this state of reflection. Further, there are instances of mortal diseases which do not at all affect our present intellectual powers; and this affords a presumption that those diseases will not destroy these present powers. Indeed, from the observations made above it appears that there is no presumption, from their mutually affecting each other, that the dissolution of the body is the destruction of the living agent. And by the same reasoning it must appear too that there is no presumption, from their mutually affecting each other, that the dissolution of the body is the destruction of our present reflecting powers; but instances of their not affecting each other afford a presumption to the contrary. Instances of mortal diseases not impairing our present reflecting powers evidently turn our thoughts even from imagining such diseases to be the destruction of them. Several things, indeed, greatly affect all our living powers and at length suspend the exercise of them—as for instance drowsiness, increasing till it ends in sound sleep; and from hence we might have imagined it would destroy them, till we found by experience the weakness of this way of judging. But in the diseases now mentioned there is not so much as this shadow of probability to lead us to any such conclusion as to the reflecting powers which we have at present; for in these diseases persons, the moment before death, appear to be in the highest vigour of life—they reveal apprehension, memory, reason, all entire, with the utmost force of affection, sense of a character, of shame and honour, and the highest mental enjoyments and sufferings, even to the last gasp; and these surely prove even greater vigour of life than bodily strength does. Now what pretence is there for thinking that a progressive disease, when arrived to such a degree, I mean that degree which is mortal, will destroy those powers which were not impaired, which were not affected by it, during its whole progress quite up to that degree? And if death by diseases of this kind is not the destruction of our present reflecting powers, 'twill scarce be thought that death by any other means is. . . .

Death May Put Us Into a Higher State of Life

. . . Death may, in some sort and in some respects, answer to our birth, which is not a suspension of the faculties which we had before it or a total change of the state of life in which we existed when in the womb, but a continuation of both, with such and such great alterations.

Nay, for aught we know of ourselves, of our present life and of death, death may immediately in the natural course of things put us into a higher and more enlarged state of life as our birth does: a state in which our capacities and sphere of perception and of action may be much greater than at present. For, as our relation to our external organs of sense renders us capable of existing in our present state of sensation, so it may be the only natural hindrance to our existing, immediately and of course, in a higher state of reflection. The truth is, reason does not at all show us in what state death naturally leaves us. But were we sure that it would suspend all our perceptive and active powers, yet the suspension of a power and the destruction of it are effects so totally different in kind—as we experience from sleep and a swoon—that we cannot in any wise argue from one to the other or conclude, even to the lowest degree of probability, that the same kind of force which is sufficient to suspend our faculties, though it be increased ever so much, will be sufficient to destroy them. . . .

The Future Life and the General Case for Religion

The credibility of a future life which has here been insisted upon, how little soever it may satisfy our curiosity, seems to answer all the purposes of religion in like manner as a demonstrative proof. Indeed a proof, even a demonstrative one, of a future life, would not be a proof of religion. For that we live hereafter is just as reconcilable with the scheme of atheism and as well to be accounted for by it as that we are now alive is; and therefore nothing can be more absurd than to argue from that scheme that there can be no future state. But as religion implies a future state, any presumption against such a state is a presumption against religion. And the foregoing observations remove all presumptions of this sort and prove, to a very considerable degree of probability, one fundamental doctrine of religion which, if believed, would greatly open and dispose the mind seriously to attend to the general evidence of the whole.

8

DAVID HUME

Of Personal Identity

We Are Nothing but Bundles of Perceptions

THERE ARE SOME philosophers who imagine we are every moment intimately conscious of what we call our *self*; that we feel its existence and its continuance in existence; and are certain, beyond the evidence of a demonstration, both of its perfect identity and simplicity. The strongest sensation, the most violent passion, say they, instead of distracting us from this view, only fix it the more intensely, and make us consider their influence on *self* either by their pain or pleasure. To attempt a further proof of this were to weaken its evidence; since no proof can be derived from any fact of which we are so intimately conscious; nor is there anything of which we can be certain if we doubt of this.

Unluckily all these positive assertions are contrary to that very experience which is pleaded for them; nor have we any idea of *self*, after the manner it is here explained. For, from what impression could this idea be derived? This question it is impossible to answer without a manifest contradiction and absurdity; and yet it is a question which must necessarily be answered, if we would have the idea of self pass for clear and intelligible. It must be some one impression that gives rise to every real

This selection consists of passages from section 6, part 4, book 1, of *A Treatise of Human Nature* (1739).

idea. But self or person is not any one impression, but that to which our several impressions and ideas are supposed to have a reference. If any impression gives rise to the idea of self, that impression must continue invariably the same, through the whole course of our lives; since self is supposed to exist after that manner. But there is no impression constant and invariable. Pain and pleasure, grief and joy, passions and sensations succeed each other, and never all exist at the same time. It cannot therefore be from any of these impressions, or from any other, that the idea of self is derived; and consequently there is no such idea.

But further, what must become of all our particular perceptions upon this hypothesis? All these are different, and distinguishable, and separable from each other, and may be separately considered, and may exist separately, and have no need of anything to support their existence. After what manner therefore do they belong to self, and how are they connected with it? For my part, when I enter most intimately into what I call *myself*, I always stumble on some particular perception or other, of heat or cold, light or shade, love or hatred, pain or pleasure. I never can catch *myself* at any time without a perception, and never can observe anything but the perception. When my perceptions are removed for any time, as by sound sleep, so long am I insensible of *myself*, and may truly be said not to exist. And were all my perceptions removed by death, and could I neither think, nor feel, nor see, nor love, nor hate, after the dissolution of my body, I should be entirely annihilated, nor do I conceive what is further requisite to make me a perfect nonentity. If any one, upon serious and unprejudiced reflection, thinks he has a different notion of *himself*, I must confess I can reason no longer with him. All I can allow him is, that he may be in the right as well as I, and that we are essentially different in this particular. He may, perhaps, perceive something simply and continued, which he calls *himself*; though I am certain there is no such principle in me.

But setting aside some metaphysicians of this kind, I may venture to affirm of the rest of mankind, that they are nothing but a bundle or collection of different perceptions, which succeed each other with an inconceivable rapidity, and are in a perpetual flux and movement. Our eyes cannot turn in their sockets without varying our perceptions. Our thought is still more variable than our sight; and all our other senses and faculties contribute to this change; nor is there any single power of the soul, which remains unalterably the same, perhaps for one moment. The mind is a kind of theater, where several perceptions successively make their appearance; pass, repass, glide away, and mingle in an infinite variety of postures and situations. There is properly no *simplicity* in it at one time, nor *identity* in different, whatever natural propension we may have to imagine that simplicity and identity. The comparison of the theater must not mislead us. They are the successive perceptions only, that constitute the mind; nor have we the most distant notion of the place where these scenes are represented, or of the materials of which it is composed. . . .

Causation, Memory, and Personal Identity

We now proceed to explain the nature of *personal identity*, which has become so great a question in philosophy, especially of late years, in England, where all the abstruser sciences are studied with a peculiar ardor and application. . . .

As to *causation*; we may observe that the true idea of the human mind, is to consider it as a system of different perceptions or different existences, which are linked together by the relation of cause and effect, and mutually produce, destroy, influence, and modify each other. Our impressions give rise to their correspondent ideas; and these ideas, in their turn, produce other impressions. One thought chases another, and draws after it a third, by which it is expelled in its turn. In this respect, I cannot compare the soul more properly to anything than to a republic or commonwealth, in which the several members are united by the reciprocal ties of government and subordination, and give rise to other persons who propagate the same republic in the incessant changes of its parts. And as the same individual republic may not only change its members, but also its laws and constitutions; in like manner the same person may vary his character and disposition, as well as his impressions and ideas, without losing his identity. Whatever changes he endures, his several parts are still connected by the relation of causation. And in this view our identity with regard to the passions serves to corroborate that with regard to the imagination, by the making our distant perceptions influence each other, and by giving us a present concern for our past or future pains or pleasures.

As memory alone acquaints us with the continuance and extent of this succession of perceptions, it is to be considered, upon that account chiefly, as the source of personal identity. Had we no memory, we never should have any notion of causation, nor consequently of that chain of causes and effects, which constitute our self or person. But having once acquired this notion of causation from the memory, we can extend the same chain of causes, and consequently the identity of our persons beyond our memory, and can comprehend times, and circumstances, and actions, which we have entirely forgot, but suppose in general to have existed. For how few of our past actions are there, of which we have any memory? Who can tell me, for instance, what were his thoughts and actions on the first of January 1715, the eleventh of March 1719, and the third of August 1733? Or will he affirm, because he has entirely forgot the incidents of these days, that the present self is not the same person with the self of that time; and by that means overturn all the most established notions of personal identity? In this view, therefore, memory does not so much *produce* as *discover* personal identity, by showing us the relation of cause and effect among our different perceptions. It will be incumbent on those who affirm that memory produces entirely our personal identity, to give a reason why we can thus extend our identity beyond our memory. . . .

9

DAVID HUME

⤜❧⤛

Of the Immortality of the Soul

⤜❧⤛

This essay could not be published in England during Hume's lifetime. It had been meant to be part of Five Dissertations, *to wit,* The Natural History of Religion. Of the Passions. Of Tragedy. Of Suicide. Of the Immortality of the Soul, *a book that was to be published by Andrew Millar in 1755. Several copies were actually printed, one of which reached Bishop William Warburton, a furious enemy of "infidels" in general and Hume in particular. Warburton urged the authorities to prosecute Millar and Hume, and the book was thereupon withdrawn. For the "obnoxious" dissertations on suicide and immortality Hume substituted an essay on the* Standard of Taste, *and a volume now entitled* Four Dissertations *was published in February 1757. One of the copies of the original book had reached Paris, however, and in 1770 the essays on suicide and immortality were published in a French translation. It appears that Hume, who was not mentioned as the author, never knew about this publication. In 1777, the year after Hume's death, the two pieces were published in London as* Two Essays, *without any mention of author or publisher. In 1783, there appeared a volume entitled* Essays on Suicide, and the Immortality of the Soul, Ascribed to the Late David Hume, Esq. Never before published. With remarks, intended as an Antidote to the Poison contained in these Performances. By the Editor. *This was the first occasion on which Hume's name appeared as author of the two essays. Hume had a violent loathing for Warburton and "his Flatterers." In his account of his own life, written shortly before his death, Hume referred to one of Warburton's abusive pamphlets as dis-*

playing "all of the illiberal petulance, arrogance, and scurrility, which distinguishes the Warburtonian School." He always refused to reply to Warburton on the ground that he would be "ashamed to engage with . . . such a low Fellow."

By the mere light of reason it seems difficult to prove the Immortality of the Soul. The arguments for it are commonly derived either from *metaphysical* topics, or *moral*, or *physical*. But in reality, it is the gospel, and the gospel alone, that has brought life and immortality to light.

I. Metaphysical topics suppose that the soul is immaterial, and that it is impossible for thought to belong to a material substance.

But just metaphysics teach us, that the notion of substance is wholly confused and imperfect, and that we have no other idea of any substance, than as an aggregate of particular qualities inhering in an unknown something. Matter, therefore, and spirit, are at bottom equally unknown; and we cannot determine what qualities inhere in the one or in the other.

They likewise teach us, that nothing can be decided *a priori* concerning any cause or effect; and that experience, being the only source of our judgments of this nature, we cannot know from any other principle, whether matter, by its structure or arrangement, may not be the cause of thought. Abstract reasonings cannot decide any question of fact or existence.

But admitting a spiritual substance to be dispersed throughout the universe, like the ethereal fire of the *Stoics*, and to be the only inherent subject of thought, we have reason to conclude from *analogy*, that nature uses it after the manner she does the other substance, matter. She employs it as a kind of paste or clay; modifies it into a variety of forms and existences; dissolves after a time each modification, and from its substance erects a new form. As the same material substance may successively compose the bodies of all animals, the same spiritual substance may compose their minds: their consciousness, or that system of thought, which they formed during life, may be continually dissolved by death; and nothing interests them in the new modification. The most positive assertors of the mortality of the soul, never denied the immortality of its substance. And that an immaterial substance, as well as a material, may lose its memory or consciousness, appears, in part, from experience, if the soul be immaterial.

Reasoning from the common course of nature, and without supposing any new interposition of the Supreme Cause, which ought always to be excluded from philosophy; what is incorruptible must also be ingenerable. The soul, therefore, if immortal, existed before our birth: And if the former existence noways concerned us, neither will the latter.

Animals undoubtedly feel, think, love, hate, will, and even reason, though in a more imperfect manner than man. Are their souls also immaterial and immortal?

II. Let us now consider the *moral* arguments, chiefly those derived from the justice of God, which is supposed to be further interested in the further punishment of the vicious and reward of the virtuous.

But these arguments are grounded on the supposition, that God has attributes beyond what he has exerted in this universe, with which alone we are acquainted. Whence do we infer the existence of these attributes?

'Tis very safe for us to affirm, that, whatever we know the Deity to have actually done, is best; but it is very dangerous to affirm, that he must always do what to us seems best. In many instances would this reasoning fail us with regard to the present world.

But, if any purpose of nature be clear, we may affirm, that the whole scope and intention of man's creation, so far as we can judge by natural reason, is limited to the present life. With how weak a concern, from the original, inherent structure of the mind and passions, does he ever look further? What comparison either for steadiness or efficacy, betwixt so floating an idea, and the most doubtful persuasion of any matter of fact, that occurs in common life?

There arise, indeed, in some minds, some unaccountable terrors with regard to futurity: but these would quickly vanish, were they not artificially fostered by precept and education. And those, who foster them: what is their motive? Only to gain a livelihood, and to acquire power and riches in this world. Their very zeal and industry, therefore, are an argument against them.

What cruelty, what iniquity, what injustice in nature, to confine thus all our concern, as well as all our knowledge, to the present life, if there be another scene still waiting us, of infinitely greater consequence? Ought this barbarous deceit to be ascribed to a beneficent and wise Being?

Observe with what exact proportion the task to be performed, and the performing powers, are adjusted throughout all nature. If the reason of man gives him a great superiority above other animals, his necessities are proportionably multiplied upon him. His whole time, his whole capacity, activity, courage, passion, find sufficient employment, in fencing against the miseries of his present condition. And frequently, nay almost always, are too slender for the business assigned them.

A pair of shoes, perhaps, was never yet wrought to the highest degree of perfection, which that commodity is capable of attaining. Yet it is necessary, at least very useful that there should be some politicians and moralists, even some geometers, poets, and philosophers among mankind.

The powers of men are no more superior to their wants, considered merely in this life, than those of foxes and hares are, compared to *their* wants and *their* period of existence. The inference from parity of reason is therefore obvious.

On the theory of the soul's mortality, the inferiority of women's capacity is easily accounted for: Their domestic life requires no higher faculties either of mind or body. This circumstance vanishes and becomes absolutely insignificant, on the religious theory: The one sex has an equal task to perform as the other: Their powers of reason and resolution ought also to have been equal, and both of them infinitely greater than at present.

As every effect implies a cause, and that another, till we reach the first cause of all, which is the *Deity*; everything that happens, is ordained by Him; and nothing can be the object of His punishment or vengeance.

By what rule are punishments and rewards distributed? What is the Divine standard of merit and demerit? Shall we suppose, that human sentiments have place in the Deity? However bold that hypothesis, we have no conception of any other sentiments.

According to human sentiments, sense, courage, good manners, industry, prudence, genius, etc., are essential parts of personal merits. Shall we therefore erect an elysium for poets and heroes, like that of the ancient mythology? Why confine all rewards to one species of virtue?

Punishment, without any proper end or purpose, is inconsistent with *our* ideas of goodness and justice; and no end can be served by it after the whole scene is closed.

Punishment, according to *our* conception, should bear some proportion to the offence. Why then eternal punishment for the temporary offences of so frail a creature as man? Can any one approve of *Alexander's* rage, who intended to exterminate a whole nation, because they had seized his favourite horse, Bucephalus?

Heaven and hell suppose two distinct species of men, the good and the bad. But the greatest part of mankind float betwixt vice and virtue.

Were one to go round the world with an intention of giving a good supper to the righteous and a sound drubbing to the wicked, he would frequently be embarrassed in his choice, and would find, that the merits and demerits of most men and women scarcely amount to the value of either.

To suppose measures of approbation and blame, different from the human, confounds every thing. Whence do we learn, that there is such a thing as moral distinctions, but from our own sentiments?

What man, who has not met with personal provocation (or what good-natur'd man who has), could inflict on crimes, from the sense of blame alone, even the common, legal, frivolous punishments? And does anything steel the breast of judges and juries against the sentiments of humanity but reflections on necessity and public interest?

By the Roman law, those who had been guilty of parricide, and confessed their crime, were put into a sack, along with an ape, a dog, and a serpent; and thrown into the river: Death alone was the punishment of those, who denied their guilt, however fully proved. A criminal was tried before *Augustus*, and condemned after a full conviction: but the humane emperor, when he put the last interrogatory, gave it such a turn as to lead the wretch into a denial of his guilt. "*You surely*, said the prince, *did not kill your father?*" This lenity suits our natural ideas of RIGHT, even towards the greatest of all criminals, and even though it prevents so inconsiderable a sufferance. Nay, even the most bigoted priest would naturally, without reflection, approve of it; provided the crime was not heresy or infidelity. For as these crimes hurt himself in his *temporal* interest and advantages; perhaps he may not be altogether so indulgent to them.

The chief source of moral ideas is the reflection on the interests of human society. Ought these interests, so short, so frivolous, to be guarded by punishments, eternal and infinite? The damnation of one man is an infinitely greater evil in the universe, than the subversion of a thousand millions of kingdoms.

Nature has rendered human infancy peculiarly frail and mortal; as it were on purpose to refute the notion of a probationary state. The half of mankind die before they are rational creatures.

III. The *physical* arguments from the analogy of nature are strong for the mortality of the soul: and these are really the only philosophical arguments, which ought to be admitted with regard to this question, or indeed any question of fact.

Where any two objects are so closely connected, that all alterations, which we have seen in the one, are attended with proportionable alterations in the other: we ought to conclude, by all rules of analogy, that, when there are still greater alterations produced in the former, and it is totally dissolved, there follows a total dissolution of the latter.

Sleep, a very small effect on the body, is attended with a temporary extinction: at least, a great confusion in the soul.

The weakness of the body and that of the mind in infancy are exactly proportioned; their vigour in manhood, their sympathetic disorder in sickness, their common gradual decay in old age. The step further seems unavoidable; their common dissolution in death.

The last symptoms, which the mind discovers, are disorder, weakness, insensibility, and stupidity; the forerunners of its annihilation. The further progress of the same causes, increasing the same effects, totally extinguish it.

Judging by the usual analogy of nature, no form can continue, when transferred to a condition of life very different from the original one, in which it was placed. Trees perish in the water; fishes in the air; animals in the earth. Even so small a difference as that of climate is often fatal.

What reason then to imagine, that an immense alteration, such as is made on the soul by the dissolution of its body, and all its organs of thought and sensation, can be effected without the dissolution of the whole?

Everything is in common betwixt soul and body. The organs of the one are all of them the organs of the other. The existence therefore of the one must be dependent on the other.

The souls of animals are allowed to be mortal: and these bear so near a resemblance to the souls of men, that the analogy from one to the other forms a very strong argument. Their bodies are not more resembling: yet no one rejects the argument drawn from comparative anatomy. The *Metempsychosis* is therefore the only system of this kind, that philosophy can hearken to.

Nothing in this world is perpetual; Everything, however seemingly firm, is in continual flux and change: The world itself gives symptoms of frailty and dissolution: How contrary to analogy, therefore, to imagine, that one single form, seeming the frailest of any, and subject to the greatest disorders is immortal and indissoluble! What a daring theory is that! How lightly, not to say how rashly, entertained!

How to dispose of the infinite number of posthumous existences ought also to embarrass the religious theory. Every planet, in every solar system, we are at liberty to imagine peopled with intelligent, mortal beings: At least we can fix on no other supposition. For these, then, a new universe must, every generation, be created beyond the bounds of the present universe: or one must have been created at first to prodigiously wide as to admit of this continual influx of beings. Ought such bold suppositions to be received by philosophy: and that merely on the pretext of a bare possibility?

When it is asked, whether *Agamemnon, Thersites, Hannibal, Nero,* and every stupid clown, that ever existed in *Italy, Scythia, Bactria, or Guinea,* are now alive; can any man think, that a scrutiny of nature will furnish arguments strong enough to answer so strange a question in the affirmative? The want of argument, without revelation, sufficiently establishes the negative. *Quanto facilius,* says Pliny, *certiusque sibi quemque credere, ac specimen accuritatis antegenitali sumere experimento.* * Our insensibility, before the composition of the body, seems to natural reason a proof of a like state after dissolution.

*Hume's quotation is the last sentence of a discussion of the belief in an after-life in Pliny's *Natural History*, Book VII, Section 55. It reads as follows: "All men are in the same state from their last day onward as they were before their first day, and neither body nor mind possesses any sensation after death, any more than it did before birth— for the same vanity prolongs itself also into the future and fabricates for itself a life lasting even into the period of death, sometimes bestowing on the soul immortality, sometimes transfiguration, sometimes giving sensation to those below, and worshipping ghosts and

(*Footnote continues on following page.*)

Were our horrors of annihilation an original passion, not the effect of our general love of happiness, it would rather prove the mortality of the soul: For as nature does nothing in vain, she would never give us a horror against an impossible event. She may give us a horror against an unavoidable event, provided our endeavours, as in the present case, may often remove it to some distance. Death is in the end unavoidable; yet the human species could not be preserved, had not nature inspired us with an aversion towards it. All doctrines are to be suspected which are favoured by our passions. And the hopes and fears which give rise to this doctrine, are very obvious.

'Tis an infinite advantage in every controversy, to defend the negative. If the question be out of the common experienced course of nature, this circumstance is almost, if not altogether, decisive. By what arguments or analogies can we prove any state of existence, which no one ever saw, and which no way resembles any that ever was seen? Who will repose such trust in any pretended philosophy, as to admit upon its testimony the reality of so marvelous a scene? Some new species of logic is requisite for that purpose; and some new faculties of the mind, that they may enable us to comprehend that logic.

Nothing could set in a fuller light the infinite obligations which mankind have to Divine revelation; since we find, that no other medium could ascertain this great and important truth.

---

making a god of one who has already ceased to be even a man—just as if man's mode of breathing were in any way different from that of the other animals, or as if there were not many animals found of greater longevity, for which nobody prophesies a similar immortality! But what is the substance of the soul taken by itself? What is its material? Where is its thought located? How does it see and hear, and with what does it touch? What use does it get from these senses, so what good can it experience without them? Next, what is the abode, or how great is the multitude of the souls or shadows in all these ages? These are fictions of childish absurdity and belong to a mortality greedy for life unceasing. . . . What repose are the generations ever to have if the soul retains permanent sensation in the upper world and the ghost in the lower? Assuredly this sweet but credulous fancy ruins nature's chief blessing, death, and doubles the sorrow of one about to die by the thought of sorrow to come hereafter also. . . . But how much easier and safer for each to trust in himself, and for us to derive our idea of future tranquility from our experience of it before birth!" The English translation just quoted is by H. Rackham. (Ed.)

10

VOLTAIRE

⤻

The Soul, Identity and Immortality

⤺

As a result of Voltaire's tendency to conceal his real views on various religious issues, his position on the question of survival has often been inaccurately described. In the 1760s he wrote a number of "Homilies" advocating natural religion, or deism, in opposition to both Christianity and atheism. In these he made numerous dire predictions about what would happen if people in general stopped believing in divine retribution in a hereafter. All the bonds of society would then be "sundered," "secret crimes" would inundate the world, and "like locusts" they would "spread over the earth." At the same time the question of whether we do in fact survive was left entirely open; survival had not been proven, but it was a distinct possibility. Yet Voltaire did not regard the question as open at all. He did believe in God, but he rejected any belief in survival as absurd and incredible. We know this from remarks he made to friends, from his correspondence, from works not published in his lifetime, and also from some that were published in his lifetime but in which he did not feel the need to conceal his real views. Unlike many others who have concluded that death is really the end, Voltaire did not regard such a philosophy as gloomy. "Death is nothing at all," he wrote; "the idea alone is sad." "To cease to love and be lovable," he wrote in a short poem addressed to Mme. du Châtelet, "is a death unbearable: to cease to live is nothing."

The first of the three selections reprinted here is taken from chapter 6 of the Traité de métaphysique, *which was written between 1734 and 1737 but not published until after Voltaire's death. The translation is by*

June Burnham. The second and third selections are from the Questions sur l'encyclopédie, *a multivolume work published between 1770 and 1772. In some editions the translation is attributed to "William F. Fleming," but there is no real evidence that a person by this name did the translation.*

Whether Man Is Immortal

This is not the place to examine whether God has, in fact, revealed the immortality of the soul. I am still assuming that I am a philosopher from another planet, who judges only according to my reason. This reason has taught me that all the ideas of men and animals come to them via their senses; I confess that I cannot help laughing when I am told that men will still have ideas when they no longer have senses. When a man loses his nose, the lost nose is no more a part of him than the pole star. When he loses all his parts and is no longer a man, isn't it then a little strange to say that he keeps the results of the organs which perished? I might just as well say that he eats and drinks after his death as say that he keeps his ideas after death; one is no more illogical than the other, and it certainly needed a fair number of centuries before anyone dared to make such an astonishing proposition. I know very well, I repeat, that as God has connected the ability to have ideas to a part of the brain, he can preserve this faculty only if he preserves this part of the brain; for preserving this faculty without the part would be as impossible as preserving a man's laugh or a bird's song after the death of the man or the bird. God could also have given men and animals a plain, immaterial soul, which he preserves independently of their bodies. For him, that is just as possible as creating a million worlds more than he did or giving me two noses and four hands, wings and claws; but if we are to believe that he has, in fact, done all these possible things, it seems to me that we would have to see them.

Seeing then no more than the extension and the feelings of man, let us assume he has something immortal. Who will prove to me that it is immortal? What! Me, even though I do not know its nature, I shall affirm that it is eternal! Me, though I know man did not exist yesterday, I shall affirm that there is in this man a part which is eternal by its nature! And while I shall refuse immortality to whatever animates the dog, the parrot, the lark, I shall award it to man just because he desires it!

It would indeed be very sweet to survive one's own self, to keep forever the most excellent part of one's being, while the other is destroyed, to live eternally with one's friends, etc. This fantasy (considered in that one sense) would be a consolation among real miseries. That is perhaps why the system of transmigration of souls was invented in earlier times; but is this system any more probable than the *Thousand*

and One Nights? And is it not just the fruit of the lively and absurd imagination of the majority of oriental philosophers? . . .

I do not assert that I have proofs against the spirituality and the immortality of the soul; but all the probabilities are against it; it is equally unjust and unreasonable to demand proof from an enquiry in which only conjectures are possible.

One must, however, anticipate the attitude of those who believe that the mortality of the soul would be contrary to the well-being of society and remind them that the ancient Jews, whose laws they admire, believed that the soul was material and mortal, not to mention the great schools of ancient philosophers who regarded the Jews highly and who were very honorable men.

Identity

This scientific term signifies no more than "the same thing." It might be correctly translated by "sameness." This subject is of considerably more interest than may be imagined. All agree that the guilty person only ought to be punished — the individual perpetrator, and no other. But a man fifty years of age is not in reality the same individual as the man of twenty; he retains no longer any of the parts which then formed his body; and if he has lost the memory of past events, it is certain that there is nothing left to unite his actual existence to an existence which to him is lost.

I am the same person only by the consciousness of what I have been combined with that of what I am; I have no consciousness of my past being but through memory; memory alone, therefore, establishes the identity, the sameness of my person.

We may, in truth, be naturally and aptly compared to a river, all whose waters pass away in perpetual change and flow. It is the same river as to its bed, its banks, its source, its mouth, everything, in short, that it not itself; but changing every moment its waters, which constitute its very being, it has no identity; there is no sameness belonging to the river.

Were there another Xerxes like him who lashed the Hellespont for disobedience, and ordered for it a pair of handcuffs; and were the son of this Xerxes to be drowned in the Euphrates, and the father desirous of punishing that river for the death of his son, the Euphrates might very reasonably say in its vindication: "Blame the waves that were rolling on at the time your son was bathing; those waves belong not to me, and form no part of me; they have passed on to the Persian Gulf; a part is mixed with the salt water of that sea, and another part, exhaled in vapor, has been impelled by a south-east wind to Gaul, and been incorporated with endives and lettuces, which the Gauls have since used in their salads; seize the culprit where you can find him."

It is the same with a tree, a branch of which broken by the wind might have fractured the skull of your great grandfather. It is no longer the same tree; all its parts have given way to others. The branch which killed your great grandfather is no part of this tree; it exists no longer.

It has been asked, then, how a man, who has totally lost his memory before his death, and whose members have been changed into other substances, can be punished for his faults or rewarded for his virtues when he is no longer himself? I have read in a well-known book the following question and answer:

"Question. How can I be either rewarded or punished when I shall no longer exist; when there will be nothing remaining of that which constituted my person? It is only by means of memory.that I am always myself; after my death, a miracle will be necessary to restore it to me—to enable me to re-enter upon my lost existence.

"Answer. That is just as much as to say that if a prince had put to death his whole family, in order to reign himself, and if he had tyrannized over his subjects with the most wanton cruelty, he would be exempted from punishment on pleading before God, 'I am not the offender; I have lost my memory; you are under a mistake; I am no longer the same person.' Do you think this sophism would pass with God?"

This answer is a highly commendable one; but it does not completely solve the difficulty.

It would be necessary for this purpose, in the first place, to know whether understanding and sensation are a faculty given by God to man, or a created substance; a question which philosophy is too weak and uncertain to decide.

It is necessary in the next place to know whether, if the soul be a substance and has lost all knowledge of the evil it has committed, and be, moreover, as perfect a stranger to what is has done with its own body, as to all the other bodies of our universe—whether, in these circumstances, it can or should, according to our manner of reasoning, answer in another universe for actions of which it has not the slightest knowledge; whether, in fact, a miracle would not be necessary to impart to this soul the recollection it no longer possesses, to render it consciously present to the crimes which have become obliterated and annihilated in its mind, and make it the same person that it was on earth; or whether God will judge it nearly in the same way in which the presidents of human tribunals proceed, condemning a criminal, although he may have completely forgotten the crimes he has actually committed. He remembers them no longer; but they are remembered for him; he is punished for the sake of the example. But God cannot punish a man after his death with a view to his being an example to the living. No living man knows whether the deceased is condemned or absolved. God, therefore, can punish him only because he cherished and accomplished evil desires; but if, when after death he presents himself before the tribunal of God, he no longer entertains any such desire; if for a period of twenty years he has totally forgotten that he did entertain such; if he is no longer in any respect the same person; what is it that God will punish in him?

These are questions which appear beyond the compass of the human understanding, and there seems to exist a necessity, in these intricacies and labyrinths, of recurring to faith alone, which is always our last refuge. . . .

Resurrection of the Ancients and the Moderns

RESURRECTION OF THE ANCIENTS

It has been asserted that the dogma of resurrection was much in vogue with the Egyptians, and was the origin of their embalmings and their pyramids. This I myself formerly believed. Some said that the resurrection was to take place at the end of a thousand years; others at the end of three thousand. This difference in their theological opinions seems to prove that they were not very sure about the matter.

Besides, in the history of Egypt, we find no man raised again; but among the Greeks we find several. Among the latter, then, we must look for the invention of resurrection.

But the Greeks often burned their bodies, and the Egyptians embalmed them, so that when the soul, which was a small, aerial figure, returned to its habitation, it might find it quite ready. This had been good if its organs had also been ready; but the embalmer began by taking out the brain and clearing the entrails. How were men to rise again without intestines, and without the medullary part by means of which they think? Where were they to find again the blood, the lymph, and other fluids?

You might conclude that it was still more difficult to rise again among the Greeks, where there was not left of you more than a pound of ashes at the utmost — mingled, too, with the ashes of wood, stuffs and spices.

Your objection is forceful, and I hold with you, that resurrection is a very extraordinary thing; but the son of Mercury did not the less die and rise again several times. The gods restored Pelops to life, although he had been served up as a ragout, and Ceres had eaten one of his shoulders. You know that Aesculapius brought Hippolytus to life again. This was a verified fact, of which even the most incredulous had no doubt; the name of "Virbius," given to Hippolytus, was a convincing proof. Hercules had resuscitated Alceste and Pirithous. Heres did, it is true — according to Plato — come to life again for fifteen days only. Still it was a resurrection; the time does not alter the fact.

Many grave schoolmen clearly see purgatory and resurrection in

Virgil. As for purgatory, I am obliged to acknowledge that it is expressly in the sixth book. This may displease the Protestants, but I have no alternative:

> *Non tamen omne malum miseris nec funditus omnes Corporea excedunt pestes, . . .* *

But we have already quoted this passage in the article on "Purgatory," which doctrine is here expressed clearly enough; nor could the people of that day obtain from the pagan priests an indulgence to abridge their sufferings for ready money. The ancients were much more severe and less corrupt than we are notwithstanding that they imputed so many foolish actions to their gods. What would you expect? Their theology was made up of contradictions, as the malignant say is the case with our own.

When their purgation was finished, these souls went and drank of the waters of Lethe, and instantly asked that they might enter fresh bodies and again see daylight. But is this a resurrection? Not at all; it is taking an entirely new body, not resuming the old one; it is a metempsychosis, without any relation to the manner in which we of the true faith are to rise again.

The souls of the ancients did, I must acknowledge, make a very bad bargain in coming back to this world, for seventy years at most, to undergo once more all that we know is undergone in a life of seventy years, and then suffer another thousand years' discipline. In my humble opinion there is no soul that would not tire of this everlasting vicissitude of so short a life and so long a penance.

RESURRECTION OF THE MODERNS

Our resurrection is quite different. Every man will appear with precisely the same body which he had before; and all these bodies will be burned for all eternity, except, at most, one in a hundred thousand. This is much worse than a purgatory of ten centuries, in order to live here again a few years.

When will the great day of this general resurrection arrive? This is not positively known; and the learned are much divided. Nor do they any more know how each one is to find his own body again. Hereupon they start many difficulties.

1. Our body, they say, is, during life, undergoing a continual change; at fifty years of age we have nothing of the body in which our soul was lodged at twenty.

2. A soldier from Brittany goes into Canada; there, by a very common chance, he finds himself short of food, and is forced to eat an

---

*"Nevertheless, for wretched men not every evil nor all bodily plagues depart completely [when they die]" . . . (*Aeneid* 6, 736–737).

Iroquois whom he killed the day before. This Iroquois had fed on Jesuits for two or three months; a great part of his body had become Jesuit. Here, then, the body of a soldier is composed of Iroquois, of Jesuits, and of all that he had eaten before. How is each to take again precisely what belongs to him? And which part belongs to each?

3. A child dies in its mother's womb, just at the moment that it has received a soul. Will it rise again foetus, or boy, or man? If foetus, to what good? If boy or man, where will the necessary material come from?

4. To rise again — to be the same person as you were — you must have your memory perfectly fresh and present; it is memory that makes your identity. If your memory is lost, how will you be the same man?

5. There are only a certain number of earthly particles that can constitute an animal. Sand, stone, minerals, metals, contribute nothing. It is only the soils favorable to vegetation that are favorable to the animal species. When, after the lapse of many ages, every one is to rise again, where shall be found the earth adapted to the formation of all these bodies?

6. Imagine an island, the vegetative part of which will support a thousand men, and five or six thousand animals for the nourishment and service of those thousand men; at the end of a hundred thousand generations we shall have to raise again a thousand millions of men. It is clear that matter will be wanting: "*Materies opus est, ut crescunt postera saecla.*"*

7. And lastly, when it is proved, or thought to be proved, that a miracle as great as the universal deluge, or the ten plagues of Egypt, will be necessary to work the resurrection of all mankind in the valley of Jehoshaphat, it is asked: What becomes of the souls of all these bodies while awaiting the moment of returning into their cases?

Fifty rather knotty questions might easily be put; but the theologians would easily find answers to them all.

---

*"There is need of matter, as future generations grow" (Lucretius).

11

THOMAS REID

Of the Nature and Origin of Our Notion of Personal Identity

Of Identity in General

THE CONVICTION WHICH every man has of his identity, as far back as his memory reaches, need no aid of philosophy to strengthen it; and no philosophy can weaken it, without first producing some degree of insanity.

The philosopher, however, may very properly consider this conviction as a phenomenon of human nature worthy of his attention. If he can discover its cause, an addition is made to his stock of knowledge; if not, it must be held as a part of our original constitution, or an effect of that constitution produced in a manner unknown to us.

That we may form as distinct a notion as we are able of this phenomenon of the human mind, it is proper to consider what is meant by identity in general, what by our own personal identity, and how we are led into that invincible belief and conviction which every man has of his own personal identity, as far as his memory reaches.

Identity in general I take to be a relation between a thing which is known to exist at one time, and a thing which is known to have existed at another time. If you ask whether they are one and the same, or two different things, every man of common sense understands the meaning

---

This selection is made up of chapter 4 and parts of chapter 6 of essay 3 as well as a passage from chapter 5 of essay 6 of Reid's *Essays on the Intellectual Powers of Man*, a work first published in 1785.

of your question perfectly. Whence we may infer with certainty, that every man of common sense has a clear and distinct notion of identity.

If you ask a definition of identity, I confess I can give none; it is too simple a notion to admit of logical definition: I can say it is a relation, but I cannot find words to express the specific difference between this and other relations, though I am in no danger of confounding it with any other. I can say that diversity is a contrary relation, and that similitude and dissimilitude are another couple of contrary relations, which every man easily distinguishes in his conception from identity and diversity.

I see evidently that identity supposes *an uninterrupted continuance of existence*. That which has ceased to exist cannot be the same with that which afterwards begins to exist; for this would be to suppose a being to exist after it ceased to exist, and to have had existence before it was produced, which are manifest contradictions. Continued uninterrupted existence is therefore necessarily implied in identity. Hence we may infer, that identity cannot, in its proper sense, be applied to our pains, our pleasures, our thoughts, or any operation of our minds. The pain felt this day is not the same individual pain which I felt yesterday, though they may be *similar* in kind and degree, and have the same cause. The same may be said of every feeling, and of every operation of mind. They are all successive in their nature, like time itself, no two moments of which can be the same moment. It is otherwise with the parts of absolute space. They always are, and were, and will be the same. So far, I think, we proceed upon clear ground in fixing the notion of identity in general.

Of Our Idea of Personal Identity

It is perhaps more difficult to ascertain with precision the meaning of *personality*; but it is not necessary in the present subject: it is sufficient for our purpose to observe, that all mankind place their personality in something that *cannot be divided, or consist of parts*. A part of a person is a manifest absurdity. When a man loses his estate, his health, his strength, he is still the same person, and has lost nothing of his personality. If he has a leg or an arm cut off, he is the same person he was before. The amputated member is no part of his person, otherwise it would have a right to a part of his estate, and be liable for a part of his engagements. It would be entitled to a share of his merit and demerit, which is manifestly absurd. A person is something indivisible, and is what Leibnitz calls a *monad*.

My personal identity, therefore, implies the continued existence of that indivisible thing which I call *myself*. Whatever this self may be, it is something which thinks, and deliberates, and resolves, and acts, and suffers. I am not thought, I am not action, I am not feeling; I am something that thinks, and acts, and suffers. My thoughts, and actions, and feelings, change every moment; they have no continued, but a successive, existence; but that *self*, or *I*, to which they belong, is permanent, and has the same relation to all the succeeding thoughts, actions, and feelings which I call mine.

Such are the notions that I have of my personal identity. But perhaps it may be said, this may all be fancy without reality. How do you know — what evidence have you — that there is such a permanent self which has a claim to all the thoughts, actions, and feelings which you call yours?

To this I answer, that the proper evidence I have of all this is *remembrance*. I remember that twenty years ago I conversed with such a person; I remember several things that passed in that conversation: my memory testifies, not only that this was done, but that it was done by me who now remembers it. If it was done by me, I must have existed at that time, and continued to exist from that time to the present: if the identical person whom I call myself had not a part in that conversation, my memory is fallacious; it gives a distinct and positive testimony of what is not true. Every man in his senses believes what he distinctly remembers, and everything he remembers convinces him that he existed at the time remembered.

Although memory gives the most irresistible evidence of my being the identical person that did such a thing, at such a time, I may have other good evidence of things which befell me, and which I do not remember: I know who bare me, and suckled me, but I do not remember these events.

It may here be observed (though the observation would have been unnecessary, if some great philosophers had not contradicted it), that it is not my remembering any action of mine that *makes* me to be the person who did it. This remembrance makes me to *know* assuredly that I did it; *but I might have done it, though I did not remember it*. That relation to me, which is expressed by saying that *I did it*, would be the same, though I had not the least remembrance of it. To say that my remembering that I did such a thing, or, as some choose to express it, my being conscious that I did it, makes me to have done it, appears to me as great an absurdity as it would be to say, that my belief that the world was created made it to be created.

When we pass judgment on the identity of other persons than ourselves, we proceed upon other grounds, and determine from a variety of circumstances, which sometimes produce the firmest assurance, and sometimes leave room for doubt. The identity of persons has often furnished matter of serious litigation before tribunals of justice. But no man of a sound mind ever doubted of his own identity, as far as he distinctly remembered.

The identity of a person is a perfect identity: wherever it is real, it admits of no degrees; and it is impossible that a person should be in part the same, and in part different; because a person is a *monad*, and is not divisible into parts. The evidence of identity in other persons than ourselves does indeed admit of all degrees, from what we account certainty, to the least degree of probability. But still it is true, that the same person is perfectly the same, and cannot be so in part or in some degree only.

For this cause, I have first considered personal identity, as that which is perfect in its kind, and the natural measure of that which is imperfect.

We probably at first derive our notion of identity from that natural conviction which every man has from the dawn of reason of *his own* identity and continued existence. The operations of our minds, are all successive, and have no continued existence. But the thinking being has a continued existence, and we have an invincible belief, that it remains the same when all its thoughts and operations change.

Our judgments of the identity of objects of sense seem to be formed much upon the same grounds as our judgments of the identity of *other persons* than ourselves. Wherever we observe great *similarity*, we are apt to presume identity, if no reason appears to the contrary. Two objects ever so like, when they are perceived at the same time, cannot be the same; but if they are presented to our senses at different times, we are apt to think them the same, merely from their similarity.

Whether this be a natural prejudice, or from whatever cause it proceeds, it certainly appears in children from infancy; and when we grow up, it is confirmed in most instances by experience: for we rarely find two individuals of the same species that are not distinguishable by obvious differences. A man challenges a thief whom he finds in possession of his horse or his watch, only on similarity. When the watchmaker swears that he sold this watch to such a person, his testimony is grounded on similarity. The testimony of witnesses to the identity of a person is commonly grounded on no other evidence.

Thus it appears, that the evidence we have of our own identity, as far back as we remember, is totally of a different kind from the evidence we have of the identity of other persons, or of objects of sense. The first is grounded on *memory*, and gives undoubted certainty. The last is grounded on *similarity*, and on other circumstances, which in many cases are not so decisive as to leave no room for doubt. It may likewise be observed, that the identity of *objects of sense* is never perfect. All bodies, as they consist of innumerable parts that may be disjoined from them by a great variety of causes, are subject to continual changes of their own substance, increasing, diminishing, changing insensibly. When such alterations are gradual, because language could not afford a different name for every different state of such a changeable being, it retains the same name, and is considered as the same thing. Thus we say of an old regiment, that it did such a thing a century ago, though there now is not a man alive who then belonged to it. We say a tree is the same in the seed-bed and in the forest. A ship of war, which has successively changed her anchors, her tackle, her sails, her masts, her planks, and her timbers, while she keeps the same name, is the same.

The identity, therefore, which we ascribe to bodies, whether natural or artificial, is not perfect identity; it is rather something which, for the convenience of speech, we call identity. It admits of a great change of the subject, providing the change be *gradual*; sometimes, even of a total change. And the changes which in common language are made consistent with identity differ from those that are thought to destroy it, not in *kind*, but in *number* and *degree*. It has no fixed nature when applied to bodies; and questions about the identity of a body are very often questions about words. But identity, when applied to persons, has no ambiguity, and admits not of degrees, or of more and less. It is the foundation of all rights and obligations, and of all accountableness; and the notion of it is fixed and precise.

Thought Requires a Thinker

The thoughts of which I am conscious are the thoughts of a being which I call MYSELF, my MIND, my PERSON.

The thoughts and feelings of which we are conscious are continually changing, and the thought of this moment is not the thought of the last; but something which I call *myself* remains under this change of thought. This self has the same relation to all the successive thoughts I am conscious of; they are all *my* thoughts; and every thought which is not my thought must be the thought of some other person.

If any man asks a proof of this, I confess I can give none; there is an evidence in the proposition itself which I am unable to resist. Shall I think, that thought can stand by itself without a thinking being? or that ideas can feel pleasure or pain? My nature dictates to me that it is impossible. And that nature has dictated the same to all men appears from the structure of all languages: for in all languages men have expressed thinking, reasoning, willing, loving, hating, by *personal* verbs, which from their nature require a person who thinks, reasons, wills, loves, or hates. From which it appears, that men have been taught by nature to believe that thought requires a thinker, reason a reasoner, and love a lover.

Here we must leave Mr. Hume, who conceives it to be a vulgar error, that, besides the thoughts we are conscious of, there is a mind which is the subject of those thoughts. If the mind be anything else than impressions and ideas, it must be a word without a meaning. The mind, therefore, according to this philosopher, is a word which signifies a bundle of perceptions; or, when he defines it more accurately, "it is that succession of related ideas and impressions, of which we have an intimate memory and consciousness."

I am, therefore, that succession of related ideas and impressions of which I have the intimate memory and consciousness. But who is the *I* that has this memory and consciousness of a succession of ideas and impressions? Why, it is nothing but that succession itself. Hence I learn, that this succession of ideas and impressions intimately remembers, and is conscious of itself. I would wish to be further instructed, whether the impressions remember and are conscious of the ideas, or the ideas remember and are conscious of the impressions, or if both remember and are conscious of both? and whether the ideas remember those that come after them, as well as those that were before them? These are questions naturally arising from this system, that have not yet been explained.

This, however, is clear, that this succession of ideas and impressions not only remembers and is conscious, but that it judges, reasons, affirms, denies; nay, that it eats and drinks, and is sometimes merry and sometimes sad. If these things can be ascribed to a succession of ideas and impressions, in a consistency with common sense, I should be very glad to know what is nonsense.

The scholastic philosophers have been wittily ridiculed, by representing them as disputing upon this question, *Num chimaera bombinans in vacuo possit comedere secundas intentiones?** And I believe the wit of man cannot invent a more ridiculous question. But, if Mr. Hume's philosophy be admitted, this question deserves to be treated more gravely; for if, as we learn from this philosophy, a succession of ideas and impressions may eat, and drink, and be merry, I see no good reason why a chimera, which, if not the same, is of kin to an idea, may not chew the cud upon that kind of food which the schoolmen call *second intentions*.

Some Strange Consequences of Locke's Account of Personal Identity

Mr. Locke tells us "that personal identity, that is, the sameness of a rational being, *consists in consciousness alone*, and, as far as this consciousness can be extended backwards to any past action or thought, so far reaches the identity of that person. So that whatever has the consciousness of present and past actions is the same person to whom they belong."

---

*This quotation is part of a passage in *Gargantua and Pantagruel* in which Rabelais is poking fun at the "choice books of the Library of St. Victor," one of which, we are told, is entitled *Quaestio Subtilissima, utrum Chimaera in vacuo bombinans possit comedere secundas intentiones: et fuit debatuata per decem hebdomadas in Consilio Constatiensi.* Father Allan B. Wolter of the Catholic University of America, to whom I am indebted for this information, has suggested the following idiomatic translation: *On the most subtle question: Could a creature of fantasy buzzing in a perfect vacuum feed upon ideas of ideas, debated over a period of ten weeks by the Council of Constance.* [Ed.]

This doctrine has some strange consequences, which the author was aware of. (1) . . . that if the same consciousness can be transferred from one intelligent being to another, which he thinks we cannot show to be impossible, *then two or twenty intelligent beings may be the same person.* (2) And if the intelligent being may lose the consciousness of the actions done by him, which surely is possible, then he is not the person that did those actions; so that *one intelligent being may be two or twenty different persons,* if he shall so often lose the consciousness of his former actions.

(3) There is another consequence of this doctrine, which follows no less necessarily, though Mr. Locke probably did not see it. It is, *that a man may be, and at the same time not be, the person that did a particular action.* Suppose a brave officer to have been flogged when a boy at school for robbing an orchard, to have taken a standard from the enemy in his first campaign, and to have been made a general in advanced life; suppose, also, which must be admitted to be possible, that, when he took the standard, he was conscious of his having been flogged at school, and that, when made a general, he was conscious of his taking the standard, but had absolutely lost the consciousness of his flogging. These things being supposed, it follows, from Mr. Locke's doctrine, that he who was flogged at school is the same person who took the standard, and that he who took the standard is the same person who was made a general. Whence it follows, if there be any truth in logic, that the general is the same person with him who was flogged at school. But the general's consciousness does not reach so far back as his flogging; therefore, according to Mr. Locke's doctrine, he is not the person who was flogged. Therefore the general is, and at the same time is not, the same person with him who was flogged at school. . . .

12

IMMANUEL KANT

⤲

Refutation of Mendelssohn's Proof of the Permanence of the Soul

⤳

THIS ACUTE PHILOSOPHER [Moses Mendelssohn] perceived very quickly how the usual argument that the soul (if it is once admitted to be a simple being) cannot cease to exist by *decomposition*, was insufficient to prove its necessary continuance, because it might cease to exist by simply *vanishing*. He therefore tried, in his *Phaedon*, to prove that the soul was not liable to that kind of perishing which would be a real annihilation, by endeavouring to show that a simple being cannot cease to exist. Since the soul could not be diminished, and thus gradually lose something of its existence, and be changed, little by little, into nothing (it having no parts, and therefore no multiplicity in itself), there could be no time between the one moment in which it exists, and the other in which it exists no longer; and this would be impossible.

He did not consider, however, that, though we might allow to the soul this simple nature, namely, that it contains no manifold of elements external to one another, and therefore no extensive quantity, yet we

This selection is a subsection of the section entitled "Paralogisms of Pure Reason," in the second edition of the *Critique of Pure Reason* (1787). The translation by Max Müller was published in London in 1896. It has here been slightly revised by the editor.

Mendelssohn died in 1786 and hence did not live to see Kant's criticism of his position. Although he was on friendly terms with Kant and read the first edition of the *Critique*, he continued to accept the ontological as well as the design argument for the existence of God in his *Morgenstunden oder Vorlesungen über das Daseyn Gottes* (*Morning Hours or Lectures on the Existence of God* [1785]). The views criticized by Kant in the present selection appeared in *Phädon* (1767), a dialogue modeled on Plato's *Phaedo*.

could not deny to it, as little as to any other existing thing, intensive quantity, i.e., a degree of reality with respect to all its faculties, nay, to all which constitutes its existence. Such a degree of reality might diminish by an infinite number of smaller degrees, and thus the supposed substance (the thing, the permanence of which has not yet been established), might be changed into nothing, not indeed through decomposition, but through a gradual remission of its powers, or, if I may use this term, by elanguescence. For even consciousness has always a degree, which admits of being diminished, and therefore also the faculty of being conscious of oneself, as well as of all other faculties.

The permanence of the soul, therefore, considered merely as an object of the internal sense, remains undemonstrated and undemonstrable. Its permanence during life, however, is self-evident while the thinking being (as man) is likewise an object of the external senses. But this does not satisfy the rational psychologist, who undertakes to prove, from mere concepts, the absolute permanence of the soul, even beyond this life.

13

JOSEPH PRIESTLEY

⤷

Materialism, Personal Identity and Life After Death

⤶

Preface

IT MAY APPEAR something extraordinary, but it is strictly true, that but a very few years ago, I was so far from having any thoughts of writing on the subject of this publication, that I had not even adopted the opinion contended for in it. Like the generality of Christians in the present age, I had always taken it for granted, that man had a soul distinct from his body, though with many modern divines, I supposed it to be incapable of exerting any of its faculties, independently upon the body; and I believed this soul to be a substance so entirely distinct from matter, as to have no property in common with it. . . .

Not but that I very well remember that many doubts occurred to me on the subject of the intimate union of two substances so entirely heterogeneous as the soul and the body were represented to be. And even when I first entered upon metaphysical inquiries, I thought that either the material, or immaterial part of the universal system was superfluous. But not giving any very particular attention to a subject on which I could get no light, I relapsed into the general hypothesis of two entirely distinct and independent principles in man, connected in some unknown and incomprehensible manner; and I acquiesced in it as well as I could. . . .

This selection consists of parts of the preface, section 3, and parts of sections 4, 5, 13, and 18 of Priestley's *Disquisitions Relating to Matter and Spirit*, which was published in 1777.

It was upon resuming some of my metaphysical speculations, to which (like most other persons of a studious turn) I had been exceedingly attached in the early period of my literary life (when I published my *Examination of the Principles of Common Sense,* as maintained by Dr. Beattie, &c. and when I republished Dr. Hartley's *Theory of the Human Mind*) that I first entertained a serious doubt of the truth of the vulgar hypothesis; and writing, as I always do, with great frankness, I freely expressed that doubt, exactly as it then stood in my mind; and I think it is hardly possible to express any thing with more hesitation and diffidence. The paragraph I allude to is the following:

> I am rather inclined to think, though the subject is beyond our comprehension at present, that man does not consist of two principles so essentially different from one another as matter and spirit, which are always described as having no one common property, by means of which they can affect, or act upon, each other; the one occupying space, and the other not only not occupying the least imaginable portion of space, but incapable of bearing any relation to it; insomuch that, properly speaking, my mind is no more in my body, than it is in the moon. I rather think that the whole man is of some uniform composition; and that the property of perception, as well as the other powers that are termed mental, is the result (whether necessary, or not) of such an organical structure as that of the brain: consequently, that the whole man becomes extinct at death, and that we have no hope of surviving the grave, but what is derived from the scheme of revelation.

I little imagined that such a paragraph as this could have given the alarm that I presently found it had done. My doubts were instantly converted into a full persuasion, and the cry against me as an unbeliever, and a favourer of atheism, was exceedingly general and loud; and was echoed from quarters where more candor and better discernment might have been expected. With what intention this was done, is best known to the authors of such gross defamation. I shall proceed to relate the consequences of it, for which they are, in some measure, answerable.

This odium, which I had thus unexpectedly drawn upon myself, served to engage my more particular attention to the subject of it; and this at length terminated in a full conviction, that the doubt I had expressed was well founded. Continuing to reflect upon the subject, I became satisfied that, if we suffer ourselves to be guided in our inquiries by the universally acknowledged rules of philosophizing, we shall find ourselves entirely unauthorized to admit any thing in man besides that body which is the object of our senses; and my own observations, and my collection of opinions on the subject, presently swelled to the bulk that is now before the Public.

Of the Seat of the Soul

I now proceed to inquire whether, when the nature of matter is rightly understood, there be any reason to think that there is in man any substance essentially different from it; that is, anything possessed of other properties besides such as may be superadded to those of attraction and repulsion which we have found to belong to matter or that may be consistent with those properties. For if this be the case true philosophy, which will not authorize us to multiply causes or kinds of substance without necessity, will forbid us to admit of any such substance. If one kind of substance be capable of supporting all the known properties of man; that is, if those properties have nothing in them that is absolutely incompatible with one another, we shall be obliged to conclude (unless we openly violate the rules of philosophizing) that no other kind of substance enters into his composition—the supposition being manifestly unnecessary in order to account for any appearance whatever.

All the properties that have hitherto been attributed to matter may be comprized under those of attraction and repulsion (all the effects of which have been shown to be produced by powers independent of all solidity) and of extension by means of which matter occupies a certain portion of space. Besides these properties man is possessed of the powers of sensation or perception and thought. But if, without giving the reins to our imaginations, we suffer ourselves to be guided in our inquiries by the simple rules of philosophising abovementioned, we must necessarily conclude, as it appears to me, that these powers also may belong to the same substance that has also the properties of attraction, repulsion and extension which I, as well as others, call by the name of matter; though I have been obliged to divest it of one property which has hitherto been thought essential to it, as well as to give it others which have not been thought essential to it; and consequently my idea of this substance is not, in all respects, the same with that of other metaphysicians.

The reason of the conclusion abovementioned is simply this, that the powers of sensation or perception and thought, as belonging to man, have never been found but in conjunction with a certain organized system of matter; and therefore, that those powers necessarily exist in, and depend upon, such a system. This, at least, must be our conclusion, till it can be shown that these powers are incompatible with other known properties of the same substance; and for this I see no sort of pretence.

It is true that we have a very imperfect idea of what the power of perception is, and it may be as naturally impossible that we should have a clear idea of it as that the eye should see itself. But this very ignorance ought to make us cautious in asserting with what other properties it may, or may not, exist. Nothing but a precise and definite knowledge of the nature of perception and thought can authorize any person to affirm whether they may not belong to an extended substance which has also the properties of attraction and repulsion. Seeing, therefore, no sort of reason to imagine that these different properties are really inconsistent, any more than the different properties of resistance and extension, I am, of course, under the necessity of being guided by the phenomena in my conclusions concerning the proper seat of the powers of perception and thought. These phenomena I shall now briefly represent.

Had we formed a judgment concerning the necessary seat of thought by the circumstances that universally accompany it which is our rule in all other cases, we could not but have concluded that in man it is a property of the nervous system or rather of the brain. Because, as far as we can judge, the faculty of thinking, and a certain state of the brain, always accompany and correspond to one another; which is the very reason why we believe that any property is inherent in any substance whatever. There is no instance of any man retaining the faculty of thinking when his brain was destroyed; and whenever that faculty is impeded, or injured, there is sufficient reason to believe that the brain is disordered in proportion; and therefore we are necessarily led to consider the latter as the seat of the former.

Moreover, as the faculty of thinking in general ripens, and comes to maturity with the body, it is also observed to decay with it; and if, in some cases, the mental faculties continue vigorous when the body in general is enfeebled, it is evidently because, in those particular cases, the brain is not much affected by the general cause of weakness. But, on the other hand, if the brain alone be affected as by a blow on the head, by actual pressure within the skull, by sleep or by inflammation the mental faculties are universally affected in proportion.

Likewise, as the mind is affected in consequence of the affections of the body and brain, so the body is liable to be reciprocally affected by the affections of the mind, as is evident in the visible effects of all strong passions, hope or fear, love or anger, joy or sorrow, exultation or despair. These are certainly irrefragable arguments that it is properly no other than one and the same thing that is subject to these affections, and that they are necessarily dependent upon one another. In fact, there is just the same reason to conclude, that the powers of sensation and thought are the necessary result of a particular organization, as that sound is the necessary result of a particular concussion of the air. For in both cases equally the one constantly accompanies the other, and there is not in nature a stronger argument for a necessary connection of any cause and any effect.

To adopt an opinion different from this, is to form an hypothesis without a single fact to support it. And to conclude, as some have done, that a material system is so far from being a necessary pre-requisite to the faculty of thinking, that it is an obstruction to it, is to adopt a method of argumentation the very reverse of everything that has hitherto been followed in philosophy. It is to conclude, not only without, but directly contrary to all appearances whatsoever.

That the perfection of thinking should depend on the sound state of the body and brain in this life, insomuch that a man has no power of thinking without it, and to suppose him capable of thinking better when the body and brain are destroyed, seems to be the most unphilosophical and absurd of all conclusions. If death be an advantage with respect to thinking, disease ought to be a proportional advantage likewise; and universally, the nearer the body approaches to a state of dissolution, the freer and less embarrassed might the faculties of the mind be expected to be found. But this is the very reverse of what really happens. . . .

It is still more unaccountable in Mr. Locke to suppose, as he did, and as he largely contends, that for anything that we know to the contrary, the faculty of thinking may be a property of the body and yet to think it more probable that this faculty inhered in a different substance, viz. an immaterial soul. A philosopher ought to have been apprized that we are to suppose no more causes than are necessary to produce the effects; and therefore that we ought to conclude that the whole man is material unless it should appear that he has some powers or properties that are absolutely incompatible with matter.

Since then Mr. Locke did not apprehend that there was any real inconsistency between the known properties of body, and those that have generally been referred to mind, he ought, as became a philosopher, to have concluded that the whole substance of man, that which supports all his powers and properties, was one uniform substance and by no means that he consisted of two substances, and those so very different from one another as body and spirit are usually represented to be; so much so, that they have been generally thought incapable of having one common property. Accordingly, the best writers upon this subject always consider the union of these two very different substances as a most stupendous and wonderful thing.

The Materiality of the Soul

. . . The only reason why it has been so earnestly contended for that there is some principle in man that is not material, is that it might subsist and be capable of sensation and action when the body was dead. But if the mind was naturally so independent of the body, as to be capable of subsisting by itself and even of appearing to more advantage after the death of the body, it might be expected to discover some signs of its independence before death and especially when the organs of the body were obstructed so as to leave the soul more at liberty to exert itself, as in a state of sleep or swooning which most resemble the state of death in which it is pretended that the soul is most of all alive, most active, and vigorous.

But, judging by appearances, the reverse of all this is the case. That a man does not think during sleep, except in that imperfect manner which we call dreaming, and which is nothing more than an approach to a state of vigilance, I shall not here dispute, but take for granted; referring my readers to Mr. Locke, and other writers upon that subject; and that all power of thinking is suspended during a swoon I conclude with certainty, because no appearance whatever can possibly lead us to suspect the contrary.

If the mental principle was, in its own nature, immaterial and immortal, all its particular faculties would be so too; whereas we see that every faculty of the mind, without exception, is liable to be impaired and even to become wholly extinct before death. Since, therefore, all the faculties of the mind, separately taken, appear to be mortal, the substance or principle in which they exist must be pronounced to be mortal too. Thus we might conclude that the body was mortal from observing that all the separate senses and limbs were liable to decay and perish.

If the sentient principle in man be immaterial it can have no extension, it can neither have length, breadth, nor thickness, and consequently everything within it, or properly belonging to it, must be simple and indivisible. Besides, it is universally acknowledged that if the substance of the soul was not simple and indivisible, it would be liable to corruption and death, and therefore that no advantage would be gained by supposing the power of thinking to belong to any substance distinct from the body. Let us now consider how this notion agrees with the phenomena of sensation and ideas which are the proper subject of thought.

It will not be denied but that sensations or ideas properly exist *in the soul* because it could not otherwise retain them, so as to continue to perceive and think after its separation from the body. Now whatever ideas are in themselves, they are evidently produced by external objects, and must therefore correspond to them; and since many of the objects or archetypes of ideas are divisible, it necessarily follows that the ideas themselves are divisible also. The idea of a man, for instance, could in no sense correspond to a man which is the archetype of it, and therefore could not be the idea of a man if it did not consist of the ideas of his head, arms, trunk, legs etc. It therefore consists of parts and consequently is divisible. And how is it possible that a thing (be the nature of it what it may) that is divisible should be contained in a substance, be the nature of it likewise what it may, that is indivisible?

If the archetypes of ideas have extension, the ideas which are expressive of them and are actually produced by them according to certain mechanical laws, must have extension likewise; and therefore the mind in which they exist, whether it be material or immaterial, must have extension also. But how anything can have extension and yet be immaterial without coinciding with our idea of mere empty space, I know not. I am therefore obliged to conclude that the sentient principle in man, containing ideas which certainly have parts and are divisible and consequently must have extension, cannot be that simple, indivisible and immaterial substance that some have imagined it to be; but something that has real extension and therefore may have the other properties of matter.

Objections to the System of Materialism Considered

OBJECTION FROM THE INFLUENCE OF REASONS.

Mr. Wollaston argues that the mind cannot be material because it is influenced by reasons. "When I begin to move myself," says he, "I do it for some reason and with respect to some end. But who can imagine matter to be moved by arguments, or ever ranked syllogisms and demonstrations among levers and pullies? Do we not see, in conversation, how a pleasant thing will make people break out into laughter, a rude thing into a passion, and so on. These affections cannot be the physical effects of the words spoken because then they would have the same effect, whether they were understood or not. It is therefore the sense of the words which is an immaterial thing, that by passing through the understanding and causing that which is the subject of the intellectual faculties to influence the body, produces those motions in the spirits, blood and muscles."*

I answer that since it is a fact that reasons, whatever they may be, do ultimately move matter, there is certainly much less difficulty in conceiving that they may do this in consequence of their being the affection of some material substance, than upon the hypothesis of their belonging to a substance that has no common property with matter.

OBJECTION FROM THE EXPRESSION "MY BODY", ETC.

"As a man considers his own body, does it not appear to be something different from the considerer, and when he uses this expression my body, or the body of me, may it not properly be demanded who is meant by *me*, or what *my* relates to? Man being supposed a person consisting of two parts, soul and body, the whole person may say of this,

*This passage is quoted from the seventh edition of William Wollaston's *Religion of Nature* (1750).

or that part of him, *the soul of me* or the *body of me*. But if he were either all soul, or all body, and nothing else, he could not speak in this manner."

According to this merely verbal argument, there ought to be something in man besides all the parts of which he consists. When a man says I devote my soul and body, what is it that makes the devotement? It cannot be the things devoted. Besides, in Mr. Wollaston's own phrase, it ought, in strictness to be the body only that says *my soul*. Nothing surely can be inferred from such phraseology as this, which, after all, is only derived from vulgar apprehensions.

OBJECTION FROM THE CORRUPTIBILITY OF MATTER.

The greatest cause of that aversion which we feel to the supposition of the soul being material, is our apprehension that it will then be liable to corruption, which we imagine it cannot be if it be immaterial. But, for anything that we know, neither of these inferences are just, and therefore no advantage whatever is, in fact, gained by the modern hypothesis. All things material are not liable to corruption, if by corruption be meant dissolution, except in circumstances to which they are not naturally exposed. It is only very compound bodies that are properly liable to corruption, and only vegetable and animal substances ever become properly putrid, and offensive, which is the real source of the objection.

It is possible, however, that even a human body may be wholly exempt from corruption, though those we have at present are not, as is evident from the account that the apostle Paul gives of the bodies with which we shall rise from the dead; when from earthly they will become spiritual; from corruptible, incorruptible; and from mortal, immortal.

Besides, how does it follow that an immaterial substance cannot be liable to decay or dissolution as well as a material one? In fact, all the reason that any person could ever have for imagining this, must have been that an immaterial substance, being, in all respects, the reverse of a material one, must be incorruptible, because the former is corruptible. But till we know something positive concerning this supposed immaterial substance, and not merely its not being matter, it is impossible to pronounce whether it may not be liable to change, and be dissolved, as well as a material substance. . . .

Personal Identity and Bodily Resurrection

The opinion of the mortality of the thinking part of man is thought by some to be unfavorable to mortality and religion, but without the least reason, as they who urge this objection at present must be unacquainted with the sentiments of Christian divines upon the subject in ancient and present times. The excellent bishop of Carlisle has sufficiently proved the insensibility of the soul from death to the resurrection (which has the same practical consequences) to be the doctrine of the scriptures. . . . In fact, the common opinion of the soul of man surviving the body was (as will be shown) introduced here into Christianity from the Oriental and Greek philosophy, which in many respects exceedingly altered and debased the true Christian system. This notion is one of the main bulwarks of popery; it was discarded by Luther, and many other reformers in England and abroad; and it was wisely left out in the last correction of the articles of the Church of England, though incautiously retained in the burial service. Now, can it be supposed that the Apostles, the primitive Fathers, and modern reformers, should all adopt an opinion unfavourable to morality?

It was objected to the primitive Christians, as it may be at present, that if all our hopes of a future life rest upon the doctrine of a resurrection, we place it upon a foundation that is very precarious. It is even said, that a proper resurrection is not only, in the highest degree, improbable, but even actually impossible; since, after death, the body putrefies, and the parts that composed it are dispersed, and form other bodies, which have an equal claim to the same resurrection. And where, they say, can be the propriety of rewards and punishments, if the man that rises again be not identically the same with the man that acted and died?

Now, though it is my own opinion that we shall be identically the same beings after the resurrection that we are at present, I shall, for the sake of those who may entertain a different opinion, speculate a little upon their hypothesis; to show that it is not inconsistent with a state of future rewards and punishments, and that it supplies motives sufficient for the regulation of our conduct here, with a view to it. And, metaphysical as the subject necessarily is, I do not despair of satisfying those who will give a due attention to it, that the propriety of rewards and punishments, with our hopes and fears derived from them, do not at all depend upon such a kind of identity as the objection that I have stated supposes.

If I may be allowed, for the sake of distinction, to introduce a new term, I would say that the "identity of the man," is different from the "identity of the person"; and it is the latter, and not the former, that we ought to consider in a disquisition of this kind. The distinction I have mentioned may appear a paradox, but in fact similar distinctions are not uncommon, and they may illustrate one another.

Ask any person to show you the river Thames, and he will point to water flowing in a certain channel, and you will find that he does not consider the banks, or the bed of the river, to be any part of it. And yet though the water be continually and visibly changing, so as not to be the same any one day with the preceding, the use of language proves that there is a sense in which it may be called, to every real purpose, the same river that it was a thousand years ago. So also the Nile, the Euphrates, and the Tiber have an identity as rivers, independently of the water, of which alone they consist. In the same manner forests, which consist of trees growing in certain places, preserve their identity, though all the trees of which they consist decay, and others grow up in their places.

In like manner, though every person should be satisfied of what I believe is not true, that, in the course of nutrition, digestion and egestion, every particle of the body, and even of the brain (and it should be taken for granted that the whole man consisted of nothing else) was entirely changed, and that this change, though gradual and insensible, could be demonstrated to take place completely in the course of a year, we should, I doubt not, still retain the idea of a real identity, and such a one as would be the proper foundation for approbation, or self reproach, with respect to the past, and for hope and fear with respect to the future. A man would claim his wife, and a woman her husband, after more than a year's absence, debts of a year's standing would not be considered as cancelled, and the villain who had absconded for a year would not escape punishment.

In fact, the universal and firm belief of this hypothesis would make no change whatever in our present conduct, or in our sense of obligation, respecting the duties of life, and the propriety of rewards and punishments; and consequently all hopes and fears, and expectations of every kind, would operate exactly as before. For notwithstanding the complete change of the *man*, there would be no change of what I should call the *person*.

Now if the water of a river, the trees of a forest, or the particles that constitute the man, should change every moment, and we were all acquainted with it, it would make no more difference in our conduct than if the same change had been considered as taking place more slowly. Supposing that this change should constantly take place during sleep, our behaviour to each other in the morning would still be regulated by a regard to the transactions of the preceding day. In this case, were any person fully persuaded, that every particle of which he consisted should be changed, he would nevertheless consider himself as being the same person to-morrow, that he was yesterday, and the same twenty years hence, that he was twenty years ago; and, I doubt not, he would feel himself concerned as for a future self, and regulate his conduct accordingly.

As far as the idea of identity is requisite as a foundation for rewards and punishments, the sameness and continuity of consciousness seems to be the only circumstance attended to by us. If we knew that a person had by disease, or old age, lost all remembrance of his past actions, we should, in most cases, immediately see that there would be an impropriety in punishing him for his previous offences, as it would answer no end of punishment, to himself or others. In the case, however, of notorious criminality, the association of a man's crime, with everything belonging to him, is so strong, and so extensive, that we wreak our vengeance upon the dead body, the children, the habitation, and every thing that had been connected with the criminal; and likewise in the case of distinguished merit, we extend our gratitude and benevolence to all the remains and connections of the hero and the friend. But as men habituate themselves to reflection, they lay aside this indiscriminate vengeance, and confine it to the person of the criminal, and to the state in which he retains the remembrance of his crimes. Every thing farther is deemed barbarous and useless.

Admitting, therefore, that the man consists wholly of matter, as much as the river does of water, or the forest of trees, and that this matter should be wholly changed in the interval between death and the resurrection; yet, if, after this state, we shall all know one another again, and converse together as before, we shall be, to all intents and purposes, the same persons. Our personal identity will be sufficiently preserved, and the expectation of it at present will have a proper influence on our conduct.

To consider the matter philosophically, what peculiar excellence is there in those particles of matter which compose my body, more than those which compose the table on which I write; and consequently what rational motive can I have for preferring, or attaching myself to the one more than to the other. If I knew that they were instantly, and without any painful sensation to myself, to change places, I do not think that it would give me any concern. As to those who are incapable of reflecting in this manner, as they cannot understand the objection, there is no occasion to make them understand the answer.

However, notwithstanding I give this solution of the difficulty, for the satisfaction of sceptical and metaphysical persons, I myself believe the doctrine of the resurrection of the dead in another and more literal sense. Death, with its concomitant putrefaction, and dispersion of parts, is only a decomposition; and whatever is decomposed, may be recomposed by the being who first composed it; and I doubt not but that, in the proper sense of the word, the same body that dies shall rise again, not with every thing that is adventitious and extraneous (as all that we receive by nutrition) but with the same stamina, or those particles that really belonged to the germ of the organical body. And there can be no proof that these particles are ever properly destroyed, or interchanged. This opinion was advanced by Dr. Watts, and no man can say that it is unphilosophical.

That excellent philosopher Mr. Bonnet* supposes and advances a variety of arguments from new and curious experiments on the repro-

---

*Charles Bonnet (1720–1793) was a Swiss naturalist and philosopher who gained fame through his discovery of the parthenogenesis in plant life.

duction of the parts of animals to prove that all the germs of future plants, organical bodies of all kinds, and the reproducible parts of them, were really contained in the first germ; and though the consideration confounds us when we contemplate it, we are not more confounded than in the contemplation of other views of the system of which we make a part; and the thing is no more incompatible with our idea of the omnipotence of its author. Those who laugh at the mere mention of such a thing have certainly a small share of natural science, which indeed generally accompanies conceit and dogmatism.

This idea of the doctrine of the resurrection is perfectly agreeable to the light in which St. Paul represents it (though I should not condemn his comparison, if it should be found not to be so complete) when he compares it to the revival of a seed that has been sown in the earth, and become seemingly dead. For the germ does not die, and in our future transformation we may be as different from what we are in our present state, as the plant is from the seed, or the butterfly from the egg, and yet be essentially the same.

Dr. Hartley* also, and others, suppose that, strictly speaking, there will be nothing more miraculous in our resurrection to a future life, than there was in our birth, to the present; for that, in the circumstances in which the world will be at the general consummation of all things, these germs, as we may call them, may naturally and necessarily revive, according to some fixed, but to us unknown laws of nature. . . .

I shall close this section with some observations respecting a term I made use of when I gave to the public the first hint of the sentiment maintained in this treatise, which was in my edition of Dr. Hartley's theory. It was that, according to appearances, the whole man becomes extinct at death. This was thought to be rather incautious by some of my friends, and my enemies eagerly catched at it, as thinking I had given them a great advantage over me; and yet I still think the term very proper, and that to object to this application betrays an ignorance even of the real meaning of that English word.

Some of them seem to have supposed that by the extinction of the whole man, I mean the absolute annihilation of him, so that when a man dies, whatever it was that constituted him, ceases to exist. But then I must have supposed that the moment a man is dead, he absolutely vanishes away, so that his friends can find nothing of him left to carry to the grave. . . .

Nor does the word "extinction," as it is generally understood, imply any such thing as annihilation. When we say that a candle is extin-

*David Hartley (1705–1757) an English psychologist and philosopher, is known primarily as the founder of associationism in psychology. Hartley also advanced a materialistic theory about the nature of thinking. Priestley, who was an ardent admirer of Hartley, published an abridged version of his *Observations on Man, His Frame, His Duty and His Expectations*.

guished, which is using the word in its primary and most proper sense, we surely do not mean that it is annihilated, and therefore that there is nothing left to light again. Even the particles of light which it has emitted we only suppose to be dispersed, and therefore capable of being collected again. As, therefore, a candle, though extinguished, is capable of being lighted again, so, though a man may be said, figuratively speaking, to become extinct at death, and his capacity for thinking cease, it may only be for a time: for no particle of that which ever constituted the man is lost. And, as I observed before, whatever is decomposed may certainly be recomposed, by the same Almighty Power that first composed it, with whatever change in its constitution, advantageous or disadvantageous, he shall think proper; and then the powers of thinking, and whatever depended upon them, will return of course, and the man will be, in the proper sense, the same being that he was before.

This is precisely the apostle Paul's idea of the resurrection of the dead, as the only foundation for a future life; and it is to this to which I mean to adhere, exclusive of all the additional vain supports which either the Oriental, or Platonic philosophy has been thought to afford to this great doctrine of pure revelation. I have, however, been represented as having, by this view of the subject, furnished a stronger argument against revelation than any that infidelity has hitherto discovered, and the atheists of the age have been described as triumphing in my concessions; when, whatever triumph atheists may derive from my concessions, and my writings, the very same they may derive from the writings of St. Paul himself, which is certainly much more to their purpose. . . .

The Souls of Brutes

The souls of brutes, which have very much embarrassed the modern systems, occasioned no difficulty whatever in that of the ancients. They considered all souls as originally the same, in whatever bodies they might happen to be confined. Today it might be that of a man, tomorrow that of a horse, then that of a man again, and lastly be absorbed into the universal soul, from which it proceeded.

But Christianity made a great difference between men and brutes. To the former a happy immortality was promised, and in such a manner as made it impossible to think that brutes could have any title to it. It was absolutely necessary, therefore, to make a change in the former uniform and comprehensive system; and though some philosophical Christians still retained the doctrine of transmigration, it was generally given up. . . .

To account for the great difference which Christianity made between the future state of men and brutes, and yet retain the separate state of the soul, it was necessary to find some specific difference between them. But a most unhappy one was pitched upon, one that is contradicted by every appearance. It has, however, been so necessary to the rest of the now disjointed system, that notwithstanding this circumstance, it has maintained its ground, in some sort, to this day. It is that, though the soul of a man is immortal, that of a brute is not; and yet it is evident that brutes have the rudiments of all our faculties, without exception; so that they differ from us in degree only, and not in kind. But the consequence of supposing the soul of a man and that of a brute to be of the same nature, was absolutely inadmissible; for they must then, it was thought, have been provided for in a future state as well as our own. . . .

I am most surprised to find Mr. Locke among those who maintain, that, though the souls of men are, in part, at least, immaterial, those of brutes, which resemble men so much, are wholly material. It is evident, however, from the manner in which he expresses himself on the subject, not only that this was his own opinion, but that it was the general opinion of his time. He says

> "Though to me sensation be comprehended under thinking in general, yet I have spoke of sense in brutes as distinct from thinking; — and to say that flies and mites have immortal souls will probably be looked on as going a great way to serve an hypothesis. Many, however, have been compelled by the analogy between men and brutes to go thus far. I do not see how they can stop short of it."

It would be endless to recite all the hypotheses that have been framed to explain the difference between brutes and men, with respect to their intellects here, and their fate hereafter. I shall, however, mention that of Mr. Locke, who says,

> "This, I think, I may be positive in, that the power of abstraction is not at all in them, and that the having of general ideas is that which puts a perfect distinction between men and brutes. For it is evident we observe no footsteps in them of making use of general signs for universal ideas, from which we have reason to imagine that they have not the faculty of abstracting, or making general ideas, since they have no use of words, or any general signs."

In fact, however, as brutes have the same external senses that we have, they have, of course, all the same inlets to ideas that we have; and though, on account of their wanting a sufficient quantity of brain, perhaps, chiefly, the combination and association of their ideas cannot be so complex as ours, and therefore they cannot make so great a progress in intellectual improvements, they must necessarily have, in kind, every faculty that we are possessed of. Also since they evidently have memory, passions, will, and judgment too, as their actions demonstrate, they must, of course, have the faculty that we call abstraction as well as the rest; though, not having the use of words, they cannot communicate their ideas to us. They must, at least, have a natural capacity for what is called abstraction, it being nothing more than a particular case of the appreciation of ideas, of which, in general, they are certainly possessed as well as ourselves.

Besides, if dogs had no general or abstract ideas, but only such as were appropriated to particular individual objects, they could never be taught to distinguish a man, as such, a hare, as such, or a partridge, as such, &c. But their actions show that they may be trained to catch hares, set partridges, or birds in general, and even attack men, as well as to distinguish their own master, and the servants of the family in which they live.

Whether brutes will survive the grave we cannot tell. This depends upon other considerations than their being capable of reason and reflection. If the resurrection be properly miraculous, and entirely out of all the established laws of nature, it will appear probable that brutes have no share in it; since we know of no declaration that God has made to that purpose, and they can have no expectation of any such thing. But if the resurrection be, in fact, within the proper course of nature, extensively considered, and consequently there be something remaining of every organized body that death does not destroy, there will be reason to conclude that they will be benefited by it as well as ourselves. And the great misery to which some of them are exposed in this life, may incline us to think, that a merciful and just God will make them some recompence for it hereafter. He is their maker and father as well as ours. But with respect to this question, we have no sufficient data from which to argue; and therefore must acquiesce in our utter ignorance; satisfied that the Maker and Judge of all will do what is right.

14

JOHN STUART MILL

ce&

Immortality

&

THE INDICATIONS OF immortality may be considered in two divisions: those which are independent of any theory respecting the Creator and his intentions, and those which depend upon an antecedent belief on that subject.

Of the former class of arguments speculative men have in different ages put forward a considerable variety, of which those in the Phaedon of Plato are an example; but they are for the most part such as have no adherents, and need not be seriously refuted, now. They are generally founded upon preconceived theories as to the nature of the thinking principle in man, considered as distinct and separable from the body, and on other preconceived theories respecting death. As, for example, that death, or dissolution, is always a separation of parts; and the soul being without parts, being simple and indivisible, is not susceptible of this separation. Curiously enough, one of the interlocutors in the Phaedon anticipates the answer by which an objector of the present day would meet this argument: namely, that thought and consciousness, though mentally distinguishable from the body, may not be a substance separable from it, but a result of it, standing in a relation to it (the illustration is Plato's) like that of a tune to the musical instrument on which it is played; and that the arguments used to prove that the soul does not die with the body, would equally prove that the tune does not

This selection consists of the major portions of part 3 of "Theism," which originally appeared in Mill's posthumously published *Three Essays on Religion* (1874).

die with the instrument, but survives its destruction and continues to exist apart. In fact, those moderns who dispute the evidences of the immortality of the soul, do not, in general, believe the soul to be a substance *per se*, but regard it as the name of a bundle of attributes, the attributes of feeling, thinking, reasoning, believing, willing, &c., and these attributes they regard as a consequence of the bodily organization, which therefore, they argue, it is as unreasonable to suppose surviving when that organization is dispersed, as to suppose the colour or odour of a rose surviving when the rose itself has perished. . . .

. . . The evidence is well nigh complete that all thought and feeling has some action of the bodily organism for its immediate antecedent or accompaniment; that the specific variations and especially the different degrees of complication of the nervous and cerebral organization, correspond to differences in the development of the mental faculties; and though we have no evidence, except negative, that the mental consciousness ceases for ever when the functions of the brain are at an end, we do know that diseases of the brain disturb the mental functions and that decay or weakness of the brain enfeebles them. We have therefore sufficient evidence that cerebral action is, if not the cause, at least, in our present state of existence, a condition *sine quá non* of mental operations; and that assuming the mind to be a distinct substance, its separation from the body would not be, as some have vainly flattered themselves, a liberation from trammels and restoration to freedom, but would simply put a stop to its functions and remand it to unconsciousness, unless and until some other set of conditions supervenes, capable of recalling it into activity, but of the existence of which experience does not give us the smallest indication.

At the same time it is of importance to remark that these considerations only amount to defect of evidence; they afford no positive argument against immortality. . . . Experience furnishes us with no example of any series of states of consciousness, without this group of contingent sensations attached to it; but it is as easy to imagine such a series of states without, as with, this accompaniment, and we know of no reason in the nature of things against the possibility of its being thus disjoined. We may suppose that the same thoughts, emotions, volitions and even sensations which we have here, may persist or recommence somewhere else under other conditions, just as we may suppose that other thoughts and sensations may exist under other conditions in other parts of the universe. . . .

There is, therefore, in science, no evidence against the immortality of the soul but that negative evidence, which consists in the absence of evidence in its favour. And even the negative evidence is not so strong as negative evidence often is. In the case of witchcraft, for instance, the fact that there is no proof which will stand examination of its having ever existed, is as conclusive as the most positive evidence of its nonexistence would be; for it exists, if it does exist, on this earth, where if it had existed the evidence of fact would certainly have been available to prove it. But it is not so as to the soul's existence after death. That it does not remain on earth and go about visibly or interfere in the events of life, is proved by the same weight of evidence which disproves witchcraft. But that it does not exist elsewhere, there is absolutely no proof. A very faint, if any, presumption, is all that is afforded by its disappearance from the surface of this planet. . . .

The belief, however, in human immortality, in the minds of mankind generally, is probably not grounded on any scientific arguments either physical or metaphysical, but on foundations with most minds much stronger, namely on one hand the disagreeableness of giving up existence, (to those at least to whom it has hitherto been pleasant) and on the other the general traditions of mankind. The natural tendency of belief to follow these two inducements, our own wishes and the general assent of other people, has been in this instance reinforced by the utmost exertion of the power of public and private teaching; rulers and instructors having at all times, with the view of giving greater effect to their mandates whether from selfish or from public motives, encouraged to the utmost of their power the belief that there is a life after death, in which pleasures and sufferings far greater than on earth, depend on our doing or leaving undone while alive, what we are commanded to do in the name of the unseen powers. As causes of belief these various circumstances are most powerful. As rational grounds of it they carry no weight at all.

That what is called the consoling nature of an opinion, that is, the pleasure we should have in believing it to be true, can be a ground for believing it, is a doctrine irrational in itself and which would sanction half the mischievous illusions recorded in history or which mislead individual life. It is sometimes, in the case now under consideration, wrapped up in a quasi-scientific language. We are told that the desire of immortality is one of our instincts, and that there is no instinct which has not corresponding to it a real object fitted to satisfy it. Where there is hunger there is somewhere food, where there is sexual feeling there is somewhere sex, where there is love there is somewhere something to be loved, and so forth: in like manner since there is the instinctive desire of eternal life, eternal life there must be. The answer to this is patent on the very surface of the subject. It is unnecessary to go into any recondite considerations concerning instincts, or to discuss whether the desire in question is an instinct or not. Granting that wherever there is an instinct there exists something such as that instinct demands, can it be affirmed that this something exists in boundless quantity, or sufficient to satisfy the infinite craving of human desires? What is called the desire of eternal life is simply the desire of life; and does there not exist that which this desire calls for? Is there not life?

And is not the instinct, if it be an instinct, gratified by the possession and preservation of life? To suppose that the desire of life guarantees to us personally the reality of life through all eternity, is like supposing that the desire of food assures us that we shall always have as much as we can eat through our whole lives and as much longer as we can conceive our lives to be protracted to. . . .

. . . It remains to consider what arguments are supplied by such lights, or such grounds of conjecture, as natural theology affords, on those great questions.

We have seen that these lights are but faint; that of the existence of a Creator they afford no more than a preponderance of probability; of his benevolence a considerably less preponderance; that there is, however, some reason to think that he cares for the pleasures of his creatures, but by no means that this is his sole care, or that other purposes do not often take precedence of it. His intelligence must be adequate to the contrivances apparent in the universe, but need not be more than adequate to them, and his power is not only not proved to be infinite, but the only real evidences in natural theology tend to show that it is limited, contrivance being a mode of overcoming difficulties, and always supposing difficulties to be overcome.

We have now to consider what inference can legitimately be drawn from these premises, in favour of a future life. It seems to me, apart from express revelation, none at all.

The common arguments are, the goodness of God; the improbability that he would ordain the annihilation of his noblest and richest work, after the greater part of its few years of life had been spent in the acquisition of faculties which time is not allowed him to turn to fruit; and the special improbability that he would have implanted in us an instinctive desire of eternal life, and doomed that desire to complete disappointment.

These might be arguments in a world the constitution of which made it possible without contradiction to hold it for the work of a Being at once omnipotent and benevolent. But they are not arguments in a world like that in which we live. The benevolence of the divine Being may be perfect, but his power being subject to unknown limitations, we know not that he could have given us what we so confidently assert that he must have given; *could* (that is) without sacrificing something more important. Even his benevolence, however justly inferred, is by no means indicated as the interpretation of his whole purpose, and since we cannot tell how far other purposes may have interfered with the exercise of his benevolence, we know not that he *would*, even if he could have granted us eternal life. With regard to the supposed improbability of his having given the wish without its gratification, the same answer may be made; the scheme which either limitation of power, or conflict of purposes, compelled him to adopt, may have *required* that we should have the wish although it were not destined to be gratified. One thing, however, is quite certain in respect to God's government of the world; that he either could not, or would not, grant to us every thing we wish. We wish for life, and he has granted some life: that we wish (or some of us wish) for a boundless extent of life and that it is not granted, is no exception to the ordinary modes of his government. Many a man would like to be a Croesus or an Augustus Caesar, but has his wishes gratified only to the moderate extent of a pound a week or the Secretaryship of his Trades Union. There is, therefore, no assurance whatever of a life after death, on grounds of natural religion. But to any one who feels it conducive either to his satisfaction or to his usefulness to hope for a future state as a possibility, there is no hindrance to his indulging that hope. Appearances point to the existence of a Being who has great power over us—all the power implied in the creation of the cosmos, or of its organized beings at least—and of whose goodness we have evidence though not of its being his predominant attribute: and as we do not know the limits either of his power or of his goodness, there is room to hope that both the one and the other may extend to granting us this gift provided that it would really be beneficial to us. The same ground which permits the hope warrants us in expecting that if there be a future life it will be at least as good as the present, and will not be wanting in the best feature of the present life, improvability by our own efforts. Nothing can be more opposed to every estimate we can form of probability, than the common idea of the future life as a state of rewards and punishments in any other sense than that the consequences of our actions upon our own character and susceptibilities will follow us in the future as they have done in the past and present. Whatever be the probabilities *of* a future life, all the probabilities *in case of* a future life are that such as we have been made or have made ourselves before the change, such we shall enter into the life hereafter; and that the fact of death will make no sudden break in our spiritual life, nor influence our character any otherwise than as any important change in our mode of existence may always be expected to modify it. Our thinking principle has its laws which in this life are invariable, and any analogies drawn from this life must assume that the same laws will continue. To imagine that a miracle will be wrought at death by the act of God making perfect every one whom it is his will to include among his elect, might be justified by an express revelation duly authenticated, but is utterly opposed to every presumption that can be deduced from the light of Nature.

15

WILLIAM JAMES

The Theory of the Soul

THE THEORY OF the Soul is the theory of popular philosophy and of scholasticism, which is only popular philosophy made systematic. It declares that the principle of individuality within us must be *substantial*, for psychic phenomena are activities, and there can be no activity without a concrete agent. This substantial agent cannot be the brain but must be something *immaterial*; for its activity, thought, is both immaterial, and takes cognizance of immaterial things, and of material things in general and intelligible, as well as in particular and sensible ways, — all which powers are incompatible with the nature of matter, of which the brain is composed. Thought moreover is simple, whilst the activities of the brain are compounded of the elementary activities of each of its parts. Furthermore, thought is spontaneous or free, whilst all material activity is determined *ab extra*; and the will can turn itself against all corporeal goods and appetites, which would be impossible were it a corporeal function. For these objective reasons the principle of psychic life must be both immaterial and simple as well as substantial, must be what is called *a Soul*. The same consequence follows from subjective reasons. Our consciousness of personal identity assures us of our essential simplicity: the owner of the various constituents of the self, as we have seen them, the hypothetical Arch-Ego whom we provisionally conceived as possible, is a real entity of whose existence self-consciousness makes us directly aware. No material agent could thus turn round

This selection is part of volume 1, chapter 10, of *The Principles of Psychology* (1890).

and grasp *itself*—material activities always grasp something else than the agent. And if a brain *could* grasp itself and be self-conscious, it would be conscious of itself *as* a brain and not as something of an altogether different kind. The Soul then exists as a simple spiritual substance in which the various psychic faculties, operations, and affections inhere.

If we ask what a Substance is, the only answer is that it is a self-existent being, or one which needs no other subject in which to inhere. At bottom its only positive determination is Being, and this is something whose meaning we all realize even though we find it hard to explain. The Soul is moreover an *individual* being, and if we ask what that is, we are told to look in upon our Self, and we shall learn by direct intuition better than through any abstract reply. Our direct perception of our own inward being is in fact by many deemed to be the original prototype out of which our notion of simple active substance in general is fashioned. The *consequences* of the simplicity and substantiality of the Soul are its incorruptibility and natural *immortality*—nothing but God's direct *fiat* can annihilate it—and its *responsibility* at all times for whatever it may have ever done.

This substantialist view of the soul was essentially the view of Plato and of Aristotle. It received its completely formal elaboration in the middle ages. It was believed in by Hobbes, Descartes, Locke, Leibnitz, Wolf, Berkeley, and is now defended by the entire modern dualistic or spiritualistic or common-sense school. Kant held to it while denying its fruitfulness as a premise for deducing consequences verifiable here below. Kant's successors, the absolute idealists, profess to have discarded it,—how that may be we shall inquire ere long. Let us make up our minds what to think of it ourselves.

It is at all events needless for expressing the actual subjective phenomena of consciousness as they appear. We have formulated them all without its aid, by the supposition of a stream of thoughts, each substantially different from the rest, but cognitive of the rest and "appropriative" of each other's content. At least, if I have not already succeeded in making this plausible to the reader, I am hopeless of convincing him by anything I could add now. The unity, the identity, the individuality, and the immateriality that appear in the psychic life are thus accounted for as phenomenal and temporal facts exclusively, and with no need of reference to any more simple or substantial agent than the present Thought or "section" of the stream. We have seen it to be single and unique in the sense of having no *separable* parts...—perhaps that is the only kind of simplicity meant to be predicated of the soul. The present Thought also has being,—at least all believers in the Soul believe so—and if there be no other Being in which it "inheres," it ought itself to be a "substance." If *this* kind of simplicity and substantiality were all that is predicated of the Soul, then it might appear that we had been talking of the soul all along, without knowing it, when we treated the present Thought as an agent, an owner, and the like. But the Thought is a perishing and not an immortal or incorruptible thing. Its successors may continuously succeed to it, resemble it, and appropriate it, but they *are* not it, whereas the Soul-Substance is supposed to be a fixed unchanging thing. By the Soul is always meant something *behind* the present Thought, another kind of substance, existing on a non-phenomenal plane.

When we brought in the Soul as an entity which the various brain-processes were supposed to affect simultaneously, and which responded to their combined influence by single pulses of its thought, it was to escape integrated mind-stuff on the one hand, and an improbable cerebral monad on the other. But when (as now, after all we have been through since that earlier passage) we take the two formulations, first of a brain to whose processes pulses of thought *simply* correspond, and second, of one to whose processes pulses of thought *in a Soul* correspond, and compare them together, we see that at bottom the second formulation is only a more roundabout way than the first, of expressing the same bald fact. That bald fact is that *when the brain acts, a thought occurs*. The spiritualistic formulation says that the brain-processes knock the thought, so to speak, out of a Soul which stands there to receive their influence. The simpler formulation says that the thought simply *comes*. But what positive meaning has the Soul, when scrutinized, but the *ground of possibility* of the thought? And what is the "knocking" but the *determining of the possibility to actuality*? And what is this after all but giving a sort of concreted form to one's belief that the coming of the thought, when the brain-processes occur, has *some* sort of ground in the nature of things? If the word Soul be understood merely to express that claim, it is a good word to use. But if it be held to do more, to gratify the claim, — for instance, to connect rationally the thought which comes, with the processes which occur, and to mediate intelligibly between their two disparate natures, — then it is an illusory term. It is, in fact, with the word Soul as with the word Substance in general. To say that phenomena inhere in a Substance is at bottom only to record one's protest against the notion that the bare existence of the phenomena is the total truth. A phenomenon would not itself be, we insist, unless there were something *more* than the phenomenon. To the more we give the provisional name of Substance. So, in the present instance, we ought certainly to admit that there is more than the bare fact of coexistence of a passing thought with a passing brain-state. But we do not answer the question "What is that more?" when we say that it is a "Soul" which the brain-state affects. This kind of more *explains* nothing; and when we are once trying metaphysical explanations we are foolish not to go as far as we can. For my own part I confess that the moment I become metaphysical and try to define the more, I find the notion of some sort of an *anima mundi* thinking in all of us to be a more promising hypothesis, in spite of all its difficulties, than that of a lot of absolutely individual souls. Meanwhile, as *psychologists*, we need not be metaphysical at all. The phenomena are enough, the passing Thought itself is the only *verifiable* thinker, and its empirical connection with the brain-process is the ultimate known law.

To the other arguments which would prove the need of a soul, we may also turn a deaf ear. The argument from free-will can convince only those who believe in free-will; and even they will have to admit that spontaneity is just as possible, to say the least, in a temporary spiritual agent like our "Thought" as in a permanent one like the supposed Soul. The same is true of the argument from the kinds of things cognized. Even if the brain could not cognize universals, immaterials, or its "Self," still the "Thought" which we have relied upon in our account *is* not the brain, closely as it seems connected with it; and after all, if the brain could cognize at all, one does not well see why it might not cognize one sort of thing as well as another. The great difficulty is in seeing how a thing can cognize *anything*. This difficulty is not in the least removed by giving to the thing that cognizes the name of Soul. The Spiritualists do not deduce any of the properties of the mental life from otherwise known properties of the soul. They simply find various characters ready-made in the mental life, and these they clap into the Soul, saying, "Lo! behold the source from whence they flow!" The merely verbal character of this "explanation" is obvious. The Soul invoked, far from making the phenomena more intelligible, can only be made intelligible itself by borrowing their form, — it must be represented, if at all, as a transcendent stream of consciousness duplicating the one we know.

Altogether, the Soul is an outbirth of that sort of philosophizing whose great maxim, according to Dr. Hodgson, is: "Whatever you are *totally* ignorant of, assert to be the explanation of everything else."

Locke and Kant, whilst still believing in the soul, began the work of undermining the notion that we know anything about it. Most modern writers of the mitigated, spiritualistic, or dualistic philosophy — the Scotch school, as it is often called among us — are forward to proclaim this ignorance, and to attend exclusively to the verifiable phenomena of self-consciousness, as we have laid them down. Dr. Wayland, for example, begins his *Elements of Intellectual Philosophy* with the phrase "Of the essence of Mind we know nothing," and goes on: "All that we are able to affirm of it is that it is *something* which perceives, reflects, remembers, imagines, and wills; but what that something *is* which exerts these energies we know not. It is only as we are conscious of the action of these energies that we are conscious of the existence of mind.

It is only by the exertion of its own powers that the mind becomes cognizant of their existence. The cognizance of its powers, however, gives us no knowledge of that essence of which they are predicated. In these respects our knowledge of mind is precisely analogous to our knowledge of matter." This analogy of our two ignorances is a favorite remark in the Scotch school. It is but a step to lump them together into a single ignorance, that of the "Unknowable" to which any one fond of superfluities in philosophy may accord the hospitality of his belief, if it so please him, but which any one else may as freely ignore and reject.

The Soul-theory is, then, a complete superfluity, so far as accounting for the actually verified facts of conscious experience goes. So far, no one can be compelled to subscribe to it for definite scientific reasons. The case would rest here, and the reader be left free to make his choice, were it not for other demands of a more practical kind.

The first of these is *Immortality*, for which the simplicity and substantiality of the Soul seem to offer a solid guarantee. A "stream" of thought, for aught that we see to be contained in its essence, may come to a full stop at any moment; but a simple substance is incorruptible and will, by its own inertia, persist in Being so long as the Creator does not by a direct miracle snuff it out. Unquestionably this is the stronghold of the spiritualistic belief, — as indeed the popular touchstone for all philosophies is the question, "What is their bearing on a future life?"

The Soul, however, when closely scrutinized, guarantees no immortality of a sort *we care for*. The enjoyment of the atom-like simplicity of their substance *in sœcula sœculorum* would not be most people seem a consummation devoutly to be wished. The substance must give rise to a stream of consciousness continuous with the present stream, in order to arouse our hope, but of this the mere persistence of the substance *per se* offers no guarantee. Moreover, in the general advance of our moral ideas, there has come to be something ridiculous in the way our forefathers had of grounding their hopes of immortality on the simplicity of their substance. The demand for immortality is nowadays essentially teleological. We believe ourselves immortal because we believe ourselves *fit* for immortality. A "substance" ought surely to perish, we think, if not worthy to survive, and an insubstantial "stream" to prolong itself, provided it be worthy, if the nature of Things is organized in the rational way in which we trust it is. Substance or no substance, soul or "stream," what Lotze says of immortality is about all that human wisdom can say:

> "We have no other principle for deciding it than this general idealistic belief: that every created thing will continue whose continuance belongs to the meaning of the world, and so long as it does so belong; whilst every one will pass away whose reality is justified only in a transitory phase of the world's course. That this principle admits of no further application in human hands need hardly be said. *We* surely

know not the merits which may give to one being a claim on eternity, nor the defects which would cut others off."*

A second alleged necessity for a soul-substance is our forensic responsibility before God. Locke caused an uproar when he said that the unity of *consciousness* made a man the same *person*, whether supported by the same *substance* or no, and that God would not, in the great day, make a person answer for what he remembered nothing of. It was supposed scandalous that our forgetfulness might thus deprive God of the chance of certain retributions, which otherwise would have enhanced his "glory." This is certainly a good speculative ground for retaining the Soul—at least for those who demand a plenitude of retribution. The mere stream of consciousness, with its lapses of memory, cannot possibly be as "responsible" as a soul which *is* at the judgment day all that it ever was. To modern readers, however, who are less insatiate for retribution than their grandfathers, this argument will hardly be as convincing as it seems once to have been.

One great use of the Soul has always been to account for, and at the same time to guarantee, the closed individuality of each personal consciousness. The thoughts of one soul must unite into one self, it was supposed, and must be eternally insulated from those of every other soul. But we have already begun to see that, although unity is the rule of each man's consciousness, yet in some individuals, at least, thoughts may split away from the others and form separate selves. As for insulation, it would be rash, in view of the phenomena of thought-transference, mesmeric influence and spirit-control, which are being alleged nowadays on better authority than ever before, to be too sure about that point either. The definitively closed nature of our personal consciousness is probably an average statistical resultant of many conditions, but not an elementary force or fact; so that, if one wishes to preserve the Soul, the less he draws his arguments from *that* quarter the better. So long as our self, on the whole, makes itself good and practically maintains itself as a closed individual, why, as Lotze says, is not that enough? And why is the *being*-an-individual in some inaccessible metaphysical way so much prouder an achievement?

My final conclusion, then, about the substantial Soul is that it explains nothing and guarantees nothing. Its successive thoughts are the only intelligible and verifiable things about it, and definitely to ascertain the correlations of these with brain-processes is as much as psychology can empirically do. From the metaphysical point of view, it is true that one may claim that the correlations have a rational ground; and if the word

---

*Metaphysik, §245 *fin.* This writer, who in his early work, the *Medizinische Psychologie*, was (to my reading) a strong defender of the Soul-Substance theory, has written in §§243–5 of his *Metaphysik* the most beautiful criticism of this theory which exists.

Soul could be taken to mean merely some such vague problematic ground, it would be unobjectionable. But the trouble is that it professes to give the ground in positive terms of a very dubiously credible sort. I therefore feel entirely free to discard the word Soul from the rest of this book. If I ever use it, it will be in the vaguest and most popular way. The reader who finds any comfort in the idea of the Soul, is, however, perfectly free to continue to believe in it; for our reasonings have not established the non-existence of the Soul; they have only proved its superfluity for scientific purposes.

16

HUGH ELLIOT

Tantalus

THE ESSENCE OF the automaton theory is that all the actions of men are explicable as purely material and mechanical sequences, without invoking the assistance of mind or consciousness, or anything but matter and energy working under their ordinary laws. Consciousness appears only as an inert accompaniment of material cerebral changes. This is the theory to which Huxley gave the name of epiphenomenalism.

It is attacked mainly on the grounds of introspection. If I desire to raise my arm, I can do so. The desire is a fact of consciousness: and the movement is a fact of matter. It seems therefore that consciousness has broken into the course of physical and chemical sequences. But it is not really so. For the desire exists not only as consciousness, but as a particular state of the brain; and the precedent to the motion of the arm is not the mental desire, but the cerebral substratum underlying the state of consciousness called desire. Until educated, we are quite unaware that any cerebral condition does underlie consciousness. We therefore inevitably assume that consciousness does what in reality is only done by its physical concomitant. An illustration will elucidate the difficulty.

Suppose there existed a Tantalus who was condemned for evermore to strike with a hammer upon an anvil. Suppose that Tantalus, his hammer, and his anvil were concealed from the observer's view by a

This selection is reprinted from chapter 5 of Elliot's *Modern Science and the Illusions of Professor Bergson*, published in 1912.

screen or otherwise, and that a light, carefully arranged, threw the shadow of the hammer and anvil upon a wall where it could easily be seen. Suppose an observer, whose mind was *tabula rasa* were set to watch the shadow. Every time the shadow of the hammer descended upon the shadow of the anvil, the sound of the percussion is heard. The sound is only heard when the two shadows meet. The hammer's shadow occasionally beats fast, occasionally slow: the succession of sounds exactly corresponds. Perhaps the hammer raps out a tune on the anvil; every note heard follows upon a blow visible in the shadows. The two series correspond invariably and absolutely; what is the inevitable effect upon the observer's mind? He knows nothing of the true cause of sound behind the screen: his whole experience is an experience of shadows and sounds. He cannot escape the conclusion that the cause of each sound is the blow which the shadow of the hammer strikes upon the shadow of the anvil.

The observer is in the position of an introspective philosopher. Introspection teaches us nothing about nerve currents or cerebral activity: it speaks in terms of mind and sensation alone. To the introspective philosopher, it is plain that some mental or psychical process is the condition of action. He thinks, he feels, he wills, and then he acts. Therefore the thinking and feeling and willing are the cause of the acting. Introspection *can* get no farther. But now the physiologist intervenes. He skilfully dissects away the screen, and behold! there is a real hammer and a real anvil, of which nothing but the shadow was formerly believed to exist. He proves that states of consciousness are shadows accompanying cerebral functioning; he shows that the cause of action lies in the cerebral functioning and not in the shadows which accompany it. For all men up to a certain age, and for the vast majority of men of all ages, that screen is never removed; they never learn that physical processes are invariable concomitants of mental processes. They are only aware of the mental processes and of the outward result. Necessarily they are bound to attribute the one to the other. The case is, indeed, far stronger than is indicated by the analogy. For the analogy deals with only one kind of action; whereas psychical processes are of innumerable kinds and the connection between particular feelings and particular motions is welded by years of experience. Need we wonder that men hesitate to recognise the illusory nature of the causal sequence?

17

JOHN FOSTER

The Objections to Epiphenomenalism

LIKE MOST OTHER current philosophers, I regard epiphenomenalism as unnatural and implausible. In the first place, it is in radical conflict with our conception of ourselves as agents. If mental states have no causal influence on behavior, then behavior cannot be thought of as intentional in any decent sense, even if the subject happens to have certain intentions which it fulfills. And if behavior is not intentional, it does not qualify as action in a sense which distinguishes it from mere bodily movement. The epiphenomenalist might reply that the general conformity of our behavior to our intentions is not merely accidental; it is ensured by the very structure of our brains and their muscular extensions in the framework of physical and psychophysical law. But even so, the behavior would not be intentional in the requisite sense, since the intentions and the psychophysical laws that control their occurrence would be irrelevant to its production. Second, human behavior exhibits certain complex regularities that call for explanation and that, at present, we explain (at least partly) in psychological terms. These psychological explanations, though typically of a rational rather than a mechanistic kind, attribute a causal efficacy to the mental; they represent behavior as falling under the control of the subject's beliefs and desires, or under the control of the subject's decisions, which are

This discussion is part of John Foster's "A Defence of Dualism," originally published in J. R. Smythies and J. Beloff (eds.), *The Case for Dualism* (1989). It is reprinted with the permission of the University Press of Virginia.

responsive to (if not determined by) his beliefs and desires. And these explanations gain credence from the fact that, as well as being, in their own terms, successful, they cannot, at present, be replaced by nonpsychological explanations that cover the same ground. Third, it is difficult to see how, if epiphenomenalism were true, the mind could form a subject matter for overt discussion. Certainly, if mental states have no causal access to our speech centers, the notion of an introspective report collapses: even if the subject retains an introspective knowledge of his mental states, his utterances would not count as expressing that knowledge if it contributes nothing to their production. But it is not even clear how, on the epiphenomenalistic view, our language, as a medium for our utterances, makes semantic contact with the mind at all. In what sense, for example, could the word "pain," as overtly used, be said to signify a certain type of sensation, if neither the occurrence of the sensations nor our introspective conception of their type affects the overt use? Quite generally, it seems that if the mental contributes nothing to the way in which the linguistic practices involving "mental" terms are developed and sustained in the speech community and in no other way affects the production of utterances employing these terms, then, in respect of their overt use, the terms should be analyzed in a purely behaviorist or functionalist fashion—which would deprive the epiphenomenalist of the linguistic resources to enunciate his thesis. It is true, of course, that each language user may mentally interpret each term as signifying a certain kind of (dualistically conceived) mental state. But how could such interpretations have any bearing on the objective meaning of the terms, as employed in speech and writing, if they are causally idle?

None of these points shows that epiphenomenalism is logically untenable, in the sense of being incoherent or self-contradictory. Even the third point, if correct, only shows that when overtly expressed, epiphenomenalism is self-refuting—that the very attempt to provide an audible or visible formulation of the thesis presupposes its falsity. Nonetheless, we have, I think, very strong, and perhaps even conclusive, reasons for rejecting it. And, because of this, I should not want my defense of dualism to involve my acceptance of anything but an interactionist position. . . .

18

RAYNOR JOHNSON

Preexistence, Reincarnation and Karma

IT IS PROBABLY true to say that a number of my readers have already reacted to the title of this chapter with some measure of emotional interest or aversion. Some people seem curiously and almost instinctively interested in these topics, others, frequently religious-minded people, feel antagonistic, as though some strange pagan faith was subtly menacing their cherished beliefs. The average thoughtful Western man has in general given little consideration to these matters, although his reticence does not always match his knowledge. In any attempt to formulate a philosophy of life and endeavour to see meaning in our pilgrimage, these ancient beliefs cannot be lightly set aside. It is our duty to weigh them carefully, and without prejudice, in order to see if they illuminate for us tracts of experience which would otherwise remain dark and mysterious. . . .

I. The Case for Pre-Existence

(a) We start from indisputable ground. Here we are on earth, going through a set of experiences in physical form along with millions of others. We were born into these conditions, into a particular nation and a particular family, without, so far as we are aware, having had any

The extracts forming this selection are reprinted from chapter 18 of *The Imprisoned Splendor*, published in 1953 by Hodder and Stoughton, with whose permission they are reprinted.

opportunity of choice in these matters. Let us look particularly at the tragic side of life, because this presents the thoughtful person with doubts and problems far more than does the attractive and happy side of life. We see children born into the world under the greatest variety of conditions. Some have sound, healthy bodies with good brains, keen, alert and capable, when fully matured, of sustaining great thoughts. Others are handicapped from the beginning with unhealthy bodies, blindness, deafness, disease and defective intelligence. For some the environment is one of security and affection, encouragement, culture and aesthetic interest; for others it is depravity, squalor and ugliness, and one of indifference or gross cruelty by the parents. For some, opportunity stands knocking at the door waiting to welcome and assist; for others it passes by, or knocks too late. Are these things just chance, or are they "planned by God"? If neither of these alternatives is acceptable, what explanation have we to offer which carries with it the reasonable assurance that we live in a just world? If God is just, and good and all-loving, the person who supposes each soul born into the world to be a new creation of God is faced with a real dilemma. There is no doubt that the conditions into which some souls are born preclude their proper development in this life. In some cases the physical body is a wretched tenement: consider the imbecile and the Mongolian idiot. In other cases the environment of fear, cruelty and brutality is calculated to crush and brutalise before the child's personality can possibly resist it. Is it conceivable that God is capable of doing something which any ordinary decent person would do all in his power to prevent or mitigate? The Christian, at least, should remember the words of Jesus, "If ye then, being evil, know how to give good gifts unto your children, *how much more* shall your Father which is in heaven give good things to them that ask Him?" The commonplace orthodox answer to this dilemma is quite frankly an evasion. It runs something like this. "Certainly there is inequality, but in the light of a future state there is justice too. Life, we must remember, is a handicap race. To whom much was given, from him much will be required. Shakespeares and Newtons must make good use of their talents. The idiots, the suffering and crushed must do their best, realising that God is just and merciful, that He only expects achievement commensurate with their talents, and that in the end all will have been found to be worth while." However true these affirmations may be, they do not face the problem, which is concerned not with compensations in a future state, but with an explanation of the present state. There is an obvious way out of the difficulty — namely, to abandon the idea that each soul born into this world is in some mysterious way a fresh creation of God. If we do so we need not assume that chance or accident is an alternative "explanation" of the gross inequalities at birth. We can take our stand on the Law of Cause and Effect, and say that all these grossly unequal conditions of birth and childhood are the results of prior causes. Since these causes are not by any means apparent in the present lives, this involves as a logical necessity the pre-existence of souls. It is then possible to affirm that we are the product of our past, that present circumstances arise as the result of self-generated forces in states of prior existence.

It is curious that in the West we have come to accept the Law of Cause and Effect without question in the scientific domain, but seem reluctant to recognise its sway on other levels of significance. Yet every great religion teaches this as part of its ethical code. "Whatsoever a man sows that shall he also reap." In Oriental philosophy this is the great Law of Karma. Whatsoever a man sows, whether in the field of action or thought, sometime and somewhere the fruits of it will be reaped by him. As a boomerang thrown by a skilled person will move rapidly away to a great distance on a circular path, but finally returns to the hand of the thrower, so there is an inexorable law of justice which runs through the world on all these levels. There is no question of rewards and punishments at all: it is simply a question of inevitable consequence, and applies equally to good things and evil things. We must, moreover, remember that we are none of us isolated beings. We manifest in a web of relationships and are interlinked with persons both in this world and others, whose thoughts and actions affect ours, and whom we in our turn affect. We reap effects which others have sown, and we sow causes which influence others; but a justice which inheres in the ultimate nature of things—the Law of Karma—governs all.

Such a viewpoint is logical, and avoids the incredible supposition that God places one newly created soul in a position of advantage and another in a position of extreme disadvantage, and in effect tells them both to make the best of it. If we suppose that a man is born an idiot because of his activity in previous lives it may seem brutal, but let us be clear that it is not the explanation which is brutal, but the facts. Heredity, of course, is operative: no one denies this. It must, however, be seen as an effect as well as a cause. Looking behind the heredity, we infer, on this view, that the Law of Karma operates so as to direct or draw a person to be born to certain parents under certain conditions.

(b) The pre-existence of the human soul is also supported by the widely different degrees of spiritual achievement we find around us. There is a vast gulf between the spiritual quality of the best person we know and the worst, between the saint or sage on the one hand and a degenerate wretch on the other. It is so great a gulf that many consider it cannot be accounted for in terms of failure or achievement in one life-span of seventy years. It seems to me to represent a gulf quite as enormous as that which on the physical evolutionary level separates primitive and advanced forms of life. It suggests the probability that the two spiritual states are the culmination of very varying moral and spiritual struggle through a long past.

The same remarks apply equally to the chasms found in intellectual and artistic capacity. We have on the one hand a Plato, an Einstein, a Michael Angelo or a Leonardo da Vinci, and on the other we have the primitive tribesmen of equatorial Africa. It is well-nigh impossible to believe that the difference between the highest men of our race and the lowest is accountable in terms of one life-time of effort in newly created beings. It suggests rather that these differences represent the result of ages of past achievement, striving and discipline in lives prior to the present.

(c) A special form of the previous argument concerns the appearance from time to time of infant prodigies. We have a Mozart or a Chopin composing symphonies of great musical maturity or playing an instrument with outstanding skill at an early age, which the teaching or environment are completely inadequate as explanations. We occasionally come across mathematical prodigies — mere boys who can perform elaborate mathematical operations without any adequate teaching or training. We are told of Sir William Hamilton, who started to learn Hebrew at the age of three, and

> "at the age of seven he was pronounced by one of the Fellows of Trinity College, Dublin, to have shown a greater knowledge of the language than many candidates for a fellowship. At the age of thirteen he had acquired considerable knowledge of at least thirteen languages. Among these, beside the classical and the modern European languages, were included Persian, Arabic, Sanskrit, Hindustani and even Malay. . . . He wrote at the age of fourteen, a complimentary letter to the Persian ambassador who happened to visit Dublin; and the latter said he had not thought there was man in Britain who could have written such a document in the Persian language.
> "A relative of his says, 'I remember him a little boy of six, when he would answer a difficult mathematical question, and run off gaily to his little cart.' Dr. Brinkley (Astronomer Royal of Ireland) said of him at the age of eighteen, 'This young man, I do not say *will be*, but *is*, the first mathematician of his age.'"*

Genius at an early age cannot be conveniently ignored because of its rarity. It calls for an explanation. By recognising pre-existence, we may reasonably suppose that such outstanding gifts represent an overflow into the present life of great prior achievement in particular fields. In this connection we may recall Plato's theory of Reminiscence: the view that knowledge we acquire easily is "old" knowledge with which our enduring self has in a previous state of being been acquainted. On the other hand, knowledge which we find difficult to assimilate, or in which we lack interest, may be that which we meet for the first time. So, too, Intuition is possibly to be regarded as based on wisdom assimilated through the experience of past lives.

*Quoted in "The Ancient Wisdom" by A. Besant, from *North British Review*, September 1866.

(*d*) The commonplace matter of family differences is one which must frequently create speculation. Physical differences and likenesses are doubtless covered by genetical laws, but differences of a profound kind in mental, moral and artistic characteristics sometimes occur, and remain quite inexplicable on biological grounds. This would not be unreasonable if we assume that each soul has a long past behind it, and was drawn to incarnate according to karmic laws in a family whose parents could provide him with the physical vehicle and environment most suited to his further development. It has been remarked that Johann Sebastian Bach was born into a family with a long musical tradition, but we need not infer from this that his genius could be accounted for by his heredity. Rather the view would be that his musical genius needed a special quality of physical vehicle and a certain environment for its satisfactory expression and further progress, and his soul chose, or was directed towards, parents capable of providing that opportunity. The soul determines the heredity, not the heredity the soul.

(*e*) In the field of personal relationships there are occasionally friendships and antipathies of a very marked kind where no psychological explanation seems to fit the facts. Cases of love at first sight, though necessarily suspect through being so much the stock-in-trade of the romantic novelist, may find an explanation on the lines indicated. They may represent the reaction to relationships which have pre-existed the present lives. . . .

(*f*) Finally, I think we should consider a viewpoint expressed by Plato in the *Phaedo*, that if souls be only supposed to come into existence at birth, their survival of death would seem to a philosopher improbable. We may express it positively thus: that if the nature of the soul is immortal (as Plato believed), an immortality which implies an infinite future also implies an infinite past. To accept the one without the other, as some appear to do, is a strange feat of mental gymnastics, the grounds for which are difficult to discover.

Such, I think, is the case for our pre-existence of this life.

2. *The Idea of Reincarnation*

If the case for pre-existence is considered a strong one, then the idea of re-incarnation presents no logical difficulties, whatever be the emotional reaction to it. What the soul has done once by the process of incarnation in a physical body, it can presumably do again. (By the term "soul" we mean that individualised aspect of the Self, including buddhi—the Intuitive self—and Higher Mind, all of which are regarded as immortal.) We should of course bear in mind that what is meant by the phrase "have lived before" is not that the physical form Raynor Johnson has lived on earth previously, but rather that Raynor Johnson is only a particular and temporary expression of an underlying immortal soul which has adopted previous and quite possibly different appearances. . . .

3. Some Objections to Reincarnation

There is a number of questions which inevitably arise in the mind of anyone who seriously considers this subject.

Why do persons not remember their past lives? It is, I think, a reasonable reply to say that when we know how memory works we may hope to have an answer. The memory of events in our present life gets more and more sparse and uncertain as we go back to early years. Few people can recall much of the third year of their life, and almost certainly nothing of the second year of life. This datum of observation suggests that we ought not *normally* to expect to recover memories of pre-existent life, and their absence should not be taken as evidence against pre-existence. It may be remarked that under hypnosis extremely early memories have been recovered from the deeper mind, which must clearly store them somehow. All that we may deduce from this is that if the memories of pre-existent lives are in fact recoverable, we should only expect it to be possible in unusual circumstances or with a special technique.

The fact is that some persons have claimed to possess *memories* for which they cannot account in terms of their present life. . . .

There are some persons who feel antipathetic to the conception of Karma on the ground that it leads to fatalism. By fatalism we understand a philosophy of life which assumes that all that we experience arises from a destiny or powers outside ourselves which we can in no way influence or control. It makes human life the sport of destiny, and necessarily leads to resigned indifference or cynicism. Such a philosophy is not a legitimate deduction from the idea of Karma, which says, rather, that there is no fate or destiny which we have not made and do not make for ourselves. We are today the product of our long past, and we shall be tomorrow what we make of ourselves today. Karma may be inescapable, but it is not unchangeable. The fatalist who stands on the river-bank and, seeing a person who cannot swim struggling in the water, says to his friend, a swimmer, "Let him alone: it is his Karma," is misunderstanding Karma. It may have been the man's Karma to tumble into the river, but it was equally a part of his Karma to do so when there was a man on the river-bank who could help him. . . .

19

C. J. DUCASSE

Survival as Transmigration

The Popularity of the Transmigration Hypothesis

THE HYPOTHESIS OF survival as rebirth (whether immediate or delayed) in a material world (whether the earth or some other planet) is of course not novel. It has been variously called reincarnation, transmigration, metempsychosis, or palingenesis; and, as W. R. Alger declares, "No other doctrine has exerted so extensive, controlling, and permanent an influence upon mankind as that of the metempsychosis—the notion that when the soul leaves the body it is born anew in another body, its rank, character, circumstances, and experience in each successive existence depending on its qualities, deeds, and attainments in its preceding lives."[1]

Not only has it had wide popular acceptance, but it has also commended itself to some of the most eminent thinkers not only in the East but also in the West.[2] Among these have been Pythagoras, Plato, and Plotinus; and Origen and some others of the early Christian fathers. Indeed, the statement twice reported of Jesus that John the Baptist was the prophet Elijah who was to come, suggests that Jesus himself perhaps held the doctrine. In more recent times, David Hume, although

[1]W. R. Alger, *A Critical History of the Doctrine of a Future Life*, p. 475.
[2]Cf. E. D. Walker, *Reincarnation, a Study of Forgotten Truth*, London, 1988.

This selection consists of extracts from chapter 21 of *Nature, Mind and Death*, published in 1951 by The Open Court Co., with whose permission they are reprinted.

not himself professing it, asserts that it is the only conception of survival that philosophy can hearken to.[3] Schopenhauer's contention that death of the body is not death of the will, and that so long as the will-to-live persists it will gain bodily objectification, amounts to acceptance of the idea of rebirth. McTaggart regards earthly rebirth as "the most probable form of the doctrine of immortality."[4] And Alger, who in spite of the merits he finds in the doctrine apparently does not himself hold it, nevertheless declares—somewhat optimistically— that its "sole difficulty is a lack of positive proof."[5]

This difficulty, however, is one which attaches equally to rival conceptions of survival, and indeed, as we concluded in the preceding chapter, to the hypothesis of survival itself, irrespective of kind. But since, in respect of practical significance for us now, the transmigration hypothesis apparently would have in addition to concreteness the merits Alger describes, it will be worth while now to inquire in some detail whether it really is theoretically tenable, or on the contrary faces insuperable difficulties. . . .

The hypothesis of survival as rebirth—let us say, on this earth—at once raises the question whether one's present life is not itself a rebirth; for logically, even if not in point of practical interest, the hypothesis of earlier lives is exactly on a par with that of later lives. Hence, assuming transmigration, to suppose that one's present life is the first of one's series of lives would be as arbitrary as to suppose that it is going to be the last, i.e.., that one will not survive the death of it although it is a survival of earlier deaths.

Now, the supposition that one's present life not only will have successors but also has had predecessors, immediately brings up the objection that we have no recollection of having lived before. But, as we have already several times had occasion to remark, if absence of memory of having existed at a certain time proved that we did not exist at that time, it would then prove far too much; for it would prove that we did not exist during the first few years of the life of our present body, nor on most of the days since then, for we have no memories whatever of the great majority of them, nor of those first few years. Lack of memory of lives earlier than our present one is therefore no evidence at all that we did not live before.

Moreover, there is occasional testimony of recollection of a previous life, where the recollection is quite circumstantial and even alleged to have been verified. One such case may be cited here without any claim that it establishes preexistence, but only to substantiate the assertion that specific testimony of this kind exists. . . .

[3]Hume, *Essay on Immortality*. [See this volume, p. 139].
[4]McTaggart, *Some Dogmas of Religion*, p. xiii, and Chap. IV.
[5]Alger, *op cit.*, p. 482.

It is that of "The Rebirth of Katsugoro," recorded in detail and with many affidavits respecting the facts, in an old Japanese document translated by Lafcadio Hearn.[6] The story is, in brief, that a young boy called Katsugoro, son of a man called Genzo in the village of Nakanomura, declared that in his preceding life a few years before he had been called Tozo; that he was then the son of a farmer called Kyubei and his wife Shidzu in a village called Hodokubo; that his father had died and had been replaced in the household by a man called Hanshiro; and that he himself, Tozo, had died of smallpox at the age of six, a year after his father. He described his burial, the appearance of his former parents, and their house. He eventually was taken to their village, where such persons were found. He himself led the way to their house and recognized them; and they confirmed the facts he had related. Further, he pointed to a shop and a tree, saying that they had not been there before; and this was true.

Testimony of this kind is directly relevant to the question of rebirth. The recollections related in this case are much too circumstantial to be dismissed as instances of the familiar and psychologically well-understood illusion of *déja vu*, and although the testimony that they were verified is not proof that they were, it cannot be rejected *a priori*. Its reliability has to be evaluated in terms of the same standards by which the validity of testimonial evidence concerning anything else is appraised.

A second objection to the transmigration hypothesis is that the native peculiarities of a person's mind as well as the characteristics of his body appear to be derived from his forebears in accordance with the laws of heredity. McTaggart, whose opinion that earthly rebirth is the most probable form of survival we have already mentioned, considers that objection and makes clear that "there is no impossibility in supposing that the characteristics in which we resemble the ancestors of our bodies may be to some degree characteristics due to our previous lives." He points out that "hats in general fit their wearers with far greater accuracy than they would if each man's hat were assigned to him by lot. And yet there is very seldom any causal connexion between the shape of the head and the shape of the hat. A man's head is never made to fit his hat, and, in the great majority of cases, his hat is not made to fit his head. The adaptation comes about by each man selecting, from hats made without any special reference to his particular head, the hat which will suit his particular head best." And, McTaggart goes on to say: "This may help us to see that it would be possible to hold that a man whose nature had certain characteristics when he was about to be reborn, would be reborn in a body descended from ancestors of a similar character. His character when reborn would, in this

[6]L. Hearn, *Gleanings in Buddha Fields*, Chap. X.

case, be decided, as far as the points in question went, by his character in his previous life, and not by the character of the ancestors of his new body. But it would be the character of the ancestors of the new body, and its similarity to his character, which determined the fact that he was reborn in that body rather than another."[7]

McTaggart's use of the analogy of the head and the hats if taken literally would mean, as a correspondent of mine suggests, that, like a man looking for a hat to wear, a temporarily bodiless soul would shop around, trying on one human foetus after another until it finds one which in some unexplained manner it discovers will develop into an appropriate body. McTaggart, however, has in mind nothing so far fetched, but rather an entirely automatic process. He refers to the analogy of chemical affinities in answer to the question how each person might be brought into connection with the new body most appropriate to him.

But although McTaggart's supposition is adequate to dispose of the difficulty which the facts of heredity otherwise constitute, the rebirth his supposition allows is nevertheless not personal rebirth if, by a man's personality, one means what we have meant in which precedes, namely, the habits, the skills, the knowledge, character, and memories, which he gradually acquires during life on earth. These, we have said, may conceivably persist for a longer or shorter time after death, but, if our present birth is indeed a rebirth, they certainly are not brought to a new earth life; for we know very well that we are not born with the knowledge, habits, and memories we now have, but gained them little by little as a result of the experiences and efforts of our present lifetime.

But this brings up another difficulty, namely, what then is there left which could be supposed to be reborn? A possible solution of it, which at the same time would provide empirical content for Broad's postulated but undescribed "psychic factor," is definable in terms of the difference familiar in psychology between, on the one hand, *acquired* skills, habits, and memories, and on the other *native* aptitudes, instincts, and proclivities; that is, in what a human being is at a given time we may distinguish two parts, one deeper and more permanent, and an other more superficial and transient. The latter consists of everything he has acquired since birth: habits, skills, memories, and so on. This is his personality. The other part, which, somewhat arbitrarily for lack of a better name we may here agree to call his individuality, comprises the aptitudes and dispositions which are native in him. These include not only the simple ones, such as aptitude for tweezer dexterity, which have been studied in laboratories because they so readily lend themselves to it, but also others more elusive: intellectual, social, and es-

[7]McTaggart, *Some Dogmas of Religion*, p. 125.

thetic aptitudes, dispositions, and types of interest or of taste. Here the task of discriminating what is innate from what is acquired is much more difficult, for it is complicated by the fact that some existent aptitudes may only become manifest after years have passed, or perhaps never, simply because not until then, or never, did the external occasion present itself for them to be exercised—just as aptitude for tweezer dexterity, for instance, in those who have it, must remain latent so long as they are not called upon to employ tweezers.

There can be no doubt that each of us, on the basis of his same individuality—that is, of his same stock of innate latent capacities and incapacities—would have developed a more or less different empirical mind and personality if, for instance, he had been put at birth in a different family, or had later been thrust by some external accident into a radically different sort of environment, or had had a different kind of education, or had met and married a very different type of person, and so on. Reflection on this fact should cause one to take his present personality with a large grain of salt, viewing it no longer humorlessly as his absolute self, but rather, in imaginative perspective, as but one of the various personalities which his individuality was equally capable of generating had it happened to enter phenomenal history through birth in a different environment. Thus, to the question: What is it that could be supposed to be reborn? an intelligible answer may be returned by saying that it might be the core of positive and negative aptitudes and tendencies which we have called a man's individuality, as distinguished from his personality. And the fact might further be that, perhaps as a result of persistent striving to acquire a skill or trait he desires, but for which he now has but little gift, aptitude for it in future births would be generated and incorporated into his individuality. . . .

Another objection which has been advanced against the transmigration hypothesis is that without the awareness of identity which memory provides, rebirth would not be discernibly different from the death of one person followed by the birth of another. In this connection, Lamont quotes Leibniz's question: "Of what use would it be to you, sir, to become king of China, on condition that you forgot what you have been? Would it not be the same as if God, at the same time he destroyed you, created a king in China?"[8]

But continuousness of memory, rather than preservation of a comprehensive span of memories, is what is significant for consciousness of one's identity. Thus, for example, none of us finds his sense of identity impaired by the fact that he has no memories of the earliest years of his present life. And if, on each day, he had a stock of memories relating to, let us say, only the then preceding ten years, or some other perhaps

---

[8]Corliss Lamont, *The Illusion of Immortality*, p. 22; Leibniz, *Philosophische Schriften*, ed. Gerhardt, IV, 300.

even shorter period, this would provide all that would be needed for a continuous sense of identity. The knowledge he would have of his personal history would, it is true, comprise a shorter span than it now does, but the span in either case would have an earliest term, and in either case the personality known would have a substantial amount of historical dimension. That the sense of identity depends on *gradualness of change* in ourselves, rather than on preservation unchanged of any specific part of ourselves, strikes one forcibly when he chances to find letters, perhaps, which he wrote thirty or forty years before. Many of them may awaken no recollections whatever, even of the existence of the persons to whom they were addressed or whom they mentioned, and it sometimes seems incredible also that the person who wrote the things they contain should be the same as his present self. In truth, it is not the same in any strict sense, but only continuous with the former person. The fact, as the Buddha insisted, is that one's personality, like everything else that exists in time, changes as time passes—some constituents of it remaining for shorter or longer periods, while others are being lost and others acquired. Yet, because of the gradualness and diverse speeds of the changes between one's earlier and one's present personality, the sense of identity is at no time lacking.

In conclusion, . . . let it be emphasized again that no claim is made that this conception of survival is known to be true, or even known to be more probably true than not; but only (1) that it is possible in the threefold sense stated earlier; (2) that belief or disbelief of it has implications for conduct; (3) that, if true, it would satisfy pretty well most of the demands which make the desire for survival so widespread; and (4) that, notwithstanding some gaps in that conception due to our ignorance of mechanisms such as certain of those it postulates, it is yet clear and definite enough to refute the allegation it was designed to refute, namely, that no life after death both possible and significant can be imagined.

20

PAUL EDWARDS

Karmic Tribulations

"Whatever is, is just"

THE LAW OF Karma asserts that the world is *wholly* just, where justice is equated with retribution or, more accurately, with appropriate rewards and punishments for all morally significant acts. Believers in Karma are fond of quoting St. Paul's statement in his letter to the Galatian churches that "whatever a man sows, that he shall also reap."[1] Professor Joseph Prabhu, an Indian Buddhist currently teaching philosophy at California State University in Los Angeles, explains that the "reaping" may but need not occur in the present life. If the reaping does not come in the present life, it will surely happen "in some later one."[2] Not infrequently disasters occur in a person's life which cannot reasonably be regarded as the appropriate punishment for anything he has done. This is particularly obvious in the case of "children and infants stricken with illnesses or handicaps." It would be quite wrong to blame God or fate for such disasters. For they are the fully deserved punishment of "some crime committed in a previous life."[3] The same line of reasoning is found in the writings of Christmas Humphreys, a distinguished En-

---

[1] *Galatians*, 6:7.
[2] "The Idea of Reincarnation," in S. T. Davis (ed.), *Death and Afterlife* (London: Macmillan, 1989), p. 73.
[3] Ibid.

This article is a revised version of the opening section of part 2 of "The Case Against Reincarnation," which appeared in the Winter 1986–1987 issue of *Free Inquiry*.

glish prosecutor who in 1926 founded the British Buddhist Society and who until his much lamented recent death was one of the leading figures in Anglo-Saxon Buddhism. Humphreys illustrates the Karmic teaching by considering the "Biblical inquiry" into the responsibility for the blindness of men born blind. To the question "who did sin, this man or his parents, that he was born blind?" the believer in Karma answers that it must have been the blind man himself who had sinned. In a previous life he had behaved so "as to cause . . . the effect of blindness." In this way the Karmic doctrine supplies a "natural and therefore reasonable answer to the apparent injustice of the daily round."[4] Like Prabhu and Humphreys, the late Dr. Raynor Johnson, a Christian reincarnationist who was for many years Master of Queens College of the University of Melbourne, asserted that "whether in the field of action or thought, some time and somewhere a man will reap the fruits of whatever he has sown," adding that we have here a "reasonable law of justice which runs through the world on all levels" and applies "equally to good and evil things."[5]

The Karmic picture of the universe has excited much admiration even in people who do not accept it. Thus Martin Gardner, a noted author of numerous books on scientific topics who is a believer in personal immortality but not in either reincarnation or Karma, maintains that the "Karmic model" possesses "singular beauty" and adds a special "grandeur to the spectacle of evolution."[6] The most enthusiastic encomiums are found in A Critical History of the Doctrine of a Future Life, a huge and immensely learned work which was published in 1870 and went through no less than ten editions. Its author, the Reverend William Rounseville Alger, was a Unitarian minister who explicitly disavowed belief in either reincarnation or Karma. These doctrines are "destitute of any substantial evidence" and quite unable to "face the severity of science."[7] However, if they were true, then they would offer a "striking" explanation of "the principal physical and moral phenomena of life." If we could "gaze around the world" with the eyes of a believer in Karma, we would see how "its material conditions and spiritual elements combine in one vast scheme of unrivaled order" and how "the total experience of humanity forms a magnificent picture of perfect poetic justice."[8] When writing his rhapsodies, Alger completely forgets that the "marvelous" theory under discussion is "destitute of any substantial evidence" and unlike its more cautious

---

[4]Buddhism (London: Penguin Books, 1951), pp. 100–101.
[5]The Imprisoned Splendor (London: Hodder and Stoughton, 1954), p. 377. [see this volume, p. 190.]
[6]The Whys of a Philosophical Scrivener (New York: Quill, 1983), p. 255.
[7]Volume 2, p. 484.
[8]Op. cit., p. 482.

supporters, he is quite prepared to extend its application to all living things:

> Every flower blighted or diseased,—every shrub gnarled, awry, and blasted,—every brute ugly and maimed—every man deformed, wretched, or despised,—is reaping in these hard conditions of being, as contrasted with the fate of the favored and perfect specimens of the kind, the fruit of sin in a foregone existence.[9]

Aside from presenting us with a magnificent picture of the universe, the doctrine of Karma supplies its devotees with a uniquely powerful stimulus for self-improvement. Alger points out that in the Western world the hope of attaining great wealth or a position of power has not infrequently stimulated enormous efforts "of labor and endurance." He then reasons that if, as in the case of the believer in reincarnation, the prize is ever so much grander—the nature of one's conditions and experiences "in life after life"—the exertions of the individual will be incomparably greater. Here, writes Alger, we meet "the secret fountain of that irresistible force which enables the devotees" to endure the most hideous tortures and to perform "superhuman deeds." Alger thought that the Karmic theory would explain even the activities of the lowliest animals. At least that is what he seemed to mean when he wrote that "crawling as an almost invisible bug in a heap of carrion, he (i.e., the individual who has become a bug) can still think within himself, holding fast to the law of righteousness and love," and thus he may "ascend, through births innumerable, to the 'topmost summit of the universe.'"[10]

The passages quoted in preceding paragraphs have a distinctly Panglossian flavor. They remind one of the famous verse in Alexander Pope's *Essay on Man* which was ridiculed in the article "Tout est bien" in Voltaire's *Philosophical Dictionary*:

> All Nature is but Art, unknown to thee;
> All Chance, Direction which thou canst not see;
> All Discord, Harmony not understood;
> All partial Evil, universal Good;
> And, spite of Pride, in erring Reason's spite,
> One truth is clear, "Whatever is, is RIGHT."

The believer in Karma would endorse the first part of this stanza, but he is not committed to the view that "whatever is, is right." He maintains that whatever is is just, and this is not the same thing. He can quite consistently admit that a world in which human beings will not commit as many morally wrong acts as they actually do is entirely conceivable. Belief in Karma is also compatible with an admission that ours is far

[9]Ibid.
[10]Op. cit., p. 487.

from being the best of all possible worlds. Although all the suffering in it is deserved we can conceive of a world in which people are better and hence not subject to the terrible punishments which so many of them have to endure in the actual world.

I cannot share the sentiments of Martin Gardner and the Rev. Alger concerning the "singular beauty" and "moral grandeur" of the Karmic scheme. It has always seemed to me cruel and inhuman to blame people for their genetic defects or to tell them that disasters which wrecked their lives are fully deserved. It should be emphasized that the Karmic believer does not have the slightest evidence for the actual guilt of any of these individuals; and to blame people in the absence of concrete evidence offends not only elementary decency but also all canons of civilized law. However, I do not wish to dwell on these issues. My main concern in this article is to show that, when it is carefully examined, the law of Karma is seen to have no content at all and that no moral directives of any kind can be logically derived from it. I shall also try to show that, contrary to the claims of numerous supporters of Karma, they cannot dispense with theological assumptions. In conclusion I will briefly discuss the claim that all scientific laws can be regarded as exemplifications of Karma.

The Pseudo-empirical Nature of the Law of Karma

The Law of Karma appears to be an empirical claim. It asserts a causal connection in both directions between two classes of observable phenomena—suffering and happiness are, at least in a broad sense, observable, and so are sinful and meritorious actions. There is admittedly some difficulty about getting a consensus as to what counts as sinful and meritorious behavior, but we may here ignore all problems of this kind. Except for its vastly greater significance, the Law of Karma is regarded by its proponents as entirely comparable to "natural" or scientific laws. Karma, writes Annie Besant, is a "natural law" and as such it "is no more sacred than any other natural law."[11] "The sins of the previous life of the Ego," to quote Madame Blavatsky, are punished by "this mysterious, inexorable, but in the equity and wisdom of its decrees infallible law."[12]

Now a little reflection shows that the Law of Karma is not an empirical statement and that it is wholly unlike "natural" laws. To begin with, the Law of Karma has no predictive value whatsoever. A simple example will make this clear. Let us suppose that a plane takes off in which all the crew and passengers are, as far as we can tell, thoroughly decent

---

[11]A Study in Karma (Krotona, 1918), pp. 5–6.
[12]Quoted in R. W. Neufeldt, Karma and Rebirth (Albany: State University of New York Press, 1986), p. 243.

people. The believer in Karma cannot predict any more or less confidently than the unbeliever that the plane will not crash. The best he can do is offer a statistical prediction based not on Karma but on data concerning the safety of airplanes or, perhaps more specifically, of the kind of plane in which these people are flying. Let us now suppose that a madman or a terrorist planted a time-bomb on the plane and, furthermore, that it is a very efficiently constructed time-bomb. The lunatic, because of his empirical information, can predict with high probability that the plane is going to crash.

It may be argued that the lack of predictive content of Karma is not a serious matter since some scientific laws, notably Darwin's theory of natural selection, also lack predictive content. I do not think that this comparison is sound, but I will not press the point and will concentrate on a more basic consideration that incorporates whatever is significant in the observation that the Karmic law is devoid of predictive value. Scientific laws and indeed all statements that are not empty are *not* compatible with anything that may happen. All of them exclude some conceivable state of affairs: If such an excluded state of affairs were to obtain, the statement would be false. Just like Boyle's law or the second law of thermodynamics, Darwin's theory of natural selection is *not* compatible with anything.

The Law of Karma on the other hand *is* compatible with anything. The emptiness of the Karmic theory can be seen most clearly if we compare it to another pseudoscientific theory that on analysis turns out to be completely empty. I am thinking of social Darwinism as advocated, for example, by the American sociologist William Graham Sumner. Sumner was a militant opponent of any kind of social legislation that might help the poor, the sick, or even the unemployed, and he justified his stand by reference to the principle that those who are successful have thereby proven their fitness while those who are downtrodden have thereby proven their unfitness and inferiority. The following is a report provided by one of Sumner's admirers of a conversation between Sumner and a student dissenter:

> "Professor, don't you believe in any government aid to industries?"
> "No! it's root, hog, or die."
> "Yes, but hasn't the hog got a right to root?"
> "There are no rights. The world owes nobody a living."
> "You believe then, Professor, in only one system, the contract-competitive system?"
> "That's the only sound economic system. All others are fallacies."
> "Well, suppose some professor of political economy came along and took your job away from you. Wouldn't you be sore?"
> "Any other professor is welcome to try. If he gets my job, it is my fault. My business is to teach the subject so well that no one can take the job away from me."[13] . . .

---

[13]Quoted in R. Hofstadter, *Social Darwinism in American Thought* (Boston: Beacon Press, 1955), p. 54.

There is some evasion in the last statement, in which Sumner talks about his teaching the subject so well that no one else can take the job away from him. Many people who, by all usual standards, are inferior teachers might take his job away from him — by intrigues, by spreading rumors about his private life, or perhaps by such drastic measures as poisoning him. However, what is relevant for our purposes is that Sumner does not know who is fittest until the outcome, until the competition has been resolved. He, Sumner, is the fittest if he keeps his job. If somebody else, X, gets the job in his place, then X has turned out to be the fittest in virtue of his success. It should be remarked parenthetically that in Darwinism or neo-Darwinian theory, as contrasted with social Darwinism, "fit" can be defined in such a way that it is *not* synonymous with "surviving" or "winning out," so that the statement "the fittest tend to win out in the competition for the means of survival" is a synthetic statement and not a tautology. In social Darwinism, at least in Sumner's version, the statement that the fittest succeed *is* a tautology. Sumner does not define "fittest" or "fit" independently of succeeding. We do *not* have a statement about the connection between two characteristics but two words for the same characteristic. The theory is empty and totally *post hoc*. We know who is fittest only after the issue has been resolved. Sumner's claim is consistent with anything whatever. Sumner himself had no doubt that socialist revolutionaries would never win out; but, if they had, they would automatically have shown themselves to be the fittest.

It is easy to see that the Law of Karma, too, is compatible with anything and hence totally empty. Let us suppose that a horrible criminal like Hitler is finally brought to justice. This of course confirms the principle since the criminal's suffering was the result of his evil deeds. Suppose, however, that a person who, according to all the best available information, is decent and kind comes to a bad end, as the result of being run over by a drunken driver, a judicial frameup, or perhaps because of some dreadful illness. Would this disconfirm the principle? Not at all. It only shows that in a previous life he committed evil deeds of which his present suffering is the just punishment. Let us suppose that we know that the next incarnation of this individual is going to be one long horrendous nightmare of torture and persecution. Would this show that the Law of Karma is not true? Not at all: It would only show that his sins in past lives were so enormous that the disasters of his present life were insufficient punishment.

In 1965 there was an instructive exchange in the *Philosophical Quarterly*, an Indian publication not to be confused with the Scottish journal of the same name, between Professor Warren E. Steinkraus, a liberal Christian with an interest in Oriental philosophy, and Professor G. R. Malkani, a Hindu believer in Karma. Professor Steinkraus expressed his consternation as to how the Law of Karma can be reconciled with the staggering sufferings experienced by a great many people:

The punishments do not fit the crime. Some of the miseries of disease and the excruciating pains of injuries suffered by human beings would not be inflicted by the most vindictive of human judges for the most heinous crimes . . . [14]

Steinkraus concludes by raising the question:

Can the defender of *Karma* admit that some suffering is outrageously severe or must he say that all suffering is *a priori* just and necessarily deserved merely because it occurs . . . [15]

Professor Steinkraus was firmly put in his place by Professor Malkani, who, as the editor of the *Philosophical Quarterly*, saw to it that he had the last word. After remarking, quite irrelevantly, that any explanation of evil and injustice in the world must leave God "blameless," Malkani insisted that there are certain ultimate mysteries that we must "not seek to probe any further." One of these is the question of "what punishment is appropriate for what sin or accumulation of sins." We are not gods and cannot know the answer to the question of why there is "so much punishment and for what." This unavoidable human ignorance is not, it appears, incompatible with total assurance that the world is just and that what may appear to be excessive punishment is not in fact excessive at all:

It should suffice to console us that there is no limit to the enormity of the errors of omission and commission which an individual might have committed in his countless past lives. . . . [16]

It should be emphasized that, when the partisans of Karma "explain" the misfortunes that befall apparently decent human beings by telling us that they sinned in a previous life, their pronouncements are just like Sumner's claims about who is fittest, *totally post hoc*. Sumner cold not identify an individual as "the fittest" until he was sure that he had won out, and the Karmic theorists cannot say anything about past misdeeds until suffering and misfortune have befallen a human being. To this it must be added that the "wisdom after the event" possessed by Sumner and by the Karmic believer is radically different from the real wisdom after the event that we often possess as the result of causal investigations. All of us are often wise only after the event, but we are really "wise" if we can offer a retrodictive explanation that is supported by adequate evidence. A plane crashes on takeoff at the Miami airport. It was not predicted, but we find evidence that a certain defect in the engine caused the crash. The Karmic procedure is also *post hoc* but it does not provide any genuine wisdom after the event. After a person who was a fine human being is run over by a drunken driver the Karmic

[14]*Philosophical Quarterly*, 1965, p. 151.
[15]Ibid.
[16]*Philosophical Quarterly*, 1966, p. 45.

theorist tells us that this happened because of his sin in a previous life. Unlike the investigators of the plane crash, he is *not* wise after the event. For he cannot tell us how and where the person had sinned. He does not have any information corresponding to the information obtained by the crash investigators about the engine defect. He makes a retrodictive claim; but, unlike the retrodictive statement about the cause of the crash, his claim is pure dogmatism.

To avoid unfairness to certain reincarnationists, the above remarks require one qualification. Some Karmic theorists who also believe in Nirvana or a superhuman Absolute Mind maintain that after his last incarnation the individual will be able to review in one glance the infinite number of lives he has lived. Reincarnationists holding this view could consistently allow that *their* Karmic theory is falsifiable by a review that showed the absence of any dependable moral pattern. Their position is thus not compatible with any conceivable state of affairs and hence it is not open to the charge that it is empty. However, one cannot help wondering how a human being could "in one glance" or for that matter in more than one glance survey an infinite number of past lives; and, furthermore, all the pronouncements about misdeeds in past lives are just as *post hoc* and just as much pure *ipse dixits* as those of Karmic believers who do not allow a final review.

Karmic Administration Problems

Anybody not intimidated by the virulence with which the champions of Karma brush off objections to their theory will want to raise a very simple and, as it seems to me, utterly devastating question about the execution and more generally the "administration" of Karmic ordinances. It should here be emphasized that many of the believers in Karma do not believe in a god and that those who do nevertheless maintain that the Law of Karma operates autonomously. Professor Malkani combines belief in the Karmic law with "the best form of theism," but he does not maintain that God is in any way involved in the administration of Karma. On the inexorable and autonomous operation of Karma, Malkani, who here fairly represents the Hindu position, is in complete agreement with the atheist and agnostic supporters of Karma. Karma, he writes, "automatically produces the appropriate results like any other law in the natural domain. Nobody can cheat the law. It is as inexorable as any natural law."

The claim that Karma operates autonomously invites the following questions: How, to begin with, are good and bad deeds registered? Is there some cosmic repository like a huge central social security office in which the relevant information is recorded and translated into some kind of "balance"? Next, how and where is it decided what will happen to a person in his next incarnation as a result of the balance of his acts in a given life? How and where, for example, is it decided that in the next life he will become a human being rather than a roach, a man rather than a woman, an American rather than an Indian, white rather than black or yellow, physically well formed rather than crippled, intelligent rather than retarded, sane rather than insane? Finally, there is still the problem of how such decisions are translated into reality. As an illustration I will use a natural disaster, the famous Lisbon earthquake of 1755. A large number of people perished as a result of it. An even larger number were injured and also lost their possessions; and a number of people indirectly benefited because of the death and injury of others. Somebody who does not believe in Karma and who also does not believe that the earthquake was a special intervention on the part of the Deity would of course regard it as a purely natural phenomenon that is entirely explicable in terms of natural, in this instance, geological, causes. The believer in Karma, by contrast, must be prepared to claim that the earthquake was brought about in order to punish or reward the various people who suffered or benefited from the earthquake. How and where were the bad deeds of those killed and injured and the good deeds of those spared registered? How and where were the penalties and rewards decided? And just how did Karma determine the geological conditions whose existence is not disputed as the "natural" or at least the "immediate" cause of the disaster? Surely, if ever intelligent planning was needed, this is a case in point. Let us assume that the chief of a terrorist organization is about to send his forces into a town in which there are 5,000 houses. His instructions are to burn down all but the hundred that belong to secret supporters of his cause. Let us also suppose that these hundred houses are spread all over the town. Such an operation obviously requires a great deal of careful planning and a high level of intelligence on the part of the planners. Even then it is entirely possible that mistakes will be made so that some houses of the sympathizers will be destroyed while some belonging to the enemy will be spared. The Law of Karma by contrast is infallible. It never punishes the innocent and never spares the guilty; and it does so although it is not an intelligent person or principle. To rephrase our earlier question: Just how did this nonintelligent principle set up the geological forces in the present case so as to achieve the desired results with complete precision?

In this connection even the otherwise so confident Professor Malkani is almost reduced to silence. All he can offer is the following lame response:

> Does the law of Karma act upon the forces of nature and bring about cyclones, earthquakes, floods, etc., which in their turn cause widespread havoc and destruction of both life and property affecting millions? But if a metaphysical law, like the law of Karma, cannot do that,

can it do anything whatsoever? Is it a law only in name? A powerless law is as good as no law. . . . [17]

This bluff and bluster answers nothing. If defenders of Karma cannot do better they should surely adopt the alternative mentioned in a tone of horror at the end of Malkani's outburst and admit that Karma "is as good as no law."

Unlike the more sophisticated champions of Karma, Mrs. Besant saw the need for introducing divine Karmic administrators. In *The Ancient Wisdom*, her best-known work, she first insists that "in no case can a man suffer that which he has not deserved."[18] . . . She then speaks of the "Lords of Karma" who are "great spiritual intelligences" keeping "the karmic records" and adjusting "the complicated workings of karmic law." They know the Karmic record of every man and with their 'omniscient wisdom" they "select and combine portions of that record to form a plan of a single life."[19] . . . This means primarily that they select the race, the country, and the parents of the soul or Ego in its next incarnation. Thus an Ego with highly developed musical faculties will be "guided to take its physical body in a musical family"; an Ego of "very evil type" will be guided "to a coarse and vicious family, whose bodies were built of the coarsest combination"; while an Ego who yields to drunkenness will be led to a "family whose nervous systems were weakened by excess," and he will be born from "drunken parents who would supply diseased materials for his physical envelope."[20] . . . It is in this way that the Lords of Karma "adjust means to ends," ensure the doing of justice, and see to it that the Ego can carry his "karmic possessions and faculties" into his next life.

This solution of the "administration" problem calls for two comments. In the first place, the lords of Karma have not been seen by anybody recently and, even during the decades when Mrs. Besant flourished, they were, as far as I know, not perceived by anybody other than Mrs. Besant, not even by Madame Blavatsky. Secondly, Mrs. Besant did not have an adequate grasp of the scope of the problem. To solve it we not only need an explanation of how the lords of Karma secure appropriate bodies for Egos in subsequent incarnations. We also need to be told how they affect natural objects and forces so as to bring about events like the Lisbon earthquake that in one swoop punish thousands of the wicked and reward large numbers of the good. To this question Mrs. Besant totally failed to address herself.

---

[17]Op. cit., p. 43.
[18]*The Ancient Wisdom* (London: Theosophical Publishing Society, 1897), p. 293.
[19]Op. cit., pp. 293–294.
[20]Op. cit., p. 295.

The Emptiness of Karmic Directives

So, far from providing moral guidance, the doctrine of Karma is bound to lead to perplexity, and it is hence apt to paralyze action. The ordinary person who does not believe in Karma usually has no difficulty in deciding whether it is right to help people who are ill, who have become the victims of accidents, or who are in various other kinds of difficulties. Things are not so easy for the believer in Karma. The suffering individual on his view *deserves* to suffer because he committed evil acts in this or else in a previous life. It is not only not our duty to help him but it would seem on Karmic principles that it is our duty *not* to help him. "It would be impossible," wrote Madame Blavatsky, "either to delay or to hasten the Karma in the fulfillment of justice," and in order to expiate one's sins fully it is necessary "to suffer all the consequences to the bitter end, to exhaust all the defects until they have reached their plenitude."[21] Mrs. Besant, who started her career as a radical, apparently had not lost all her humanity after she succeeded Madame Blavatsky as leader of the theosophists. She reports "some members saying: I cannot help this man since what he is suffering is his karma." She thought them cruel and wrong-headed and compared them to somebody who says, "I cannot pick up this child who just fell, since the law of gravitation is opposed to it." . . . [22]

I do not think that this is a fair analogy and it does not answer the members who refuse to help people in need. The law of gravitation is not a moral law and the fact that the child fell down does not, without bringing in Karmic morality, imply that it is now being punished for an earlier sin. As far as I can see, no prescription of any kind can be derived from the Law of Karma for this situation or for any other; and, if this is so, Karma is completely vacuous as a principle of moral guidance. No matter what we do, whether we help the individual or whether we refuse to help him, we will be doing the right thing. If we help him and cut short his suffering, this means that his earlier deed did not require more severe punishment than what he suffered until we brought relief. If on the other hand we ignore him and let him continue in his misery, this shows that his sin was so great as to deserve the total amount of his suffering—what he suffered before we could have intervened as well as what he suffered afterward when we failed to come to his assistance. Believers in Karma constantly and emphatically insist that their theory does not imply fatalism, that, quite on the contrary, it is entirely compatible with belief in human freedom, understood as our

---

[21]Quoted in P. Siwek, *The Enigma of the Hereafter* (New York: Philosophical Library, 1952), p. 122.
[22]*Popular Lectures on Theosophy* (Chicago, 1910).

ability to shape our lives, within limits, in accordance with our desires and choices, and that our efforts frequently do make a great deal of difference to what happens. I see no reason to dispute this claim, but it in no way answers the challenge of vacuousness. The vacuousness, as far as moral prescriptions are concerned, follows from the Karmic doctrine that the world is just. A Karmic believer's commitment to this proposition is unqualified — it is categorical and not merely hypothetical. He does not maintain that the world *would* be just if we did certain things: He maintains that the world *is* just regardless of what in fact we do. No matter what happens, whether we help the underdog or not, whether our efforts at making lives less full of suffering and sorrow succeed or not, the ultimate outcome will be just, in the sense that every human being will be getting exactly — no more and no less — what he deserves.

This is as good a place as any to point out that believers in Karma, especially those in the West, are careful not to spell out certain of the implications of their theory that would strike most people as appalling. It follows from their principle that Abraham Lincoln, Jean Jaurès, the two Kennedy brothers, and Martin Luther King got no more than they deserved when they were assassinated. It equally follows that the six million Jews exterminated by the Nazis deserved their fate. I will add one more of the morally outrageous consequences of Karma. Contrary to what almost everybody believed and believes, the seven astronauts who perished in the *Challenger* space shuttle in 1986 were entirely responsible for their deaths, and the grief felt by millions of people all over the world was quite out of place. The reckless NASA officials whom the Rogers Commission found to be responsible for the *Challenger* explosion were in fact (not consciously, of course) only executing the ordinances of Karma. The case of the astronauts illustrates particularly well the completely *post hoc* procedure of the Karmic theorists. Is there the slightest empirical evidence that the seven astronauts who died were morally any worse than the astronauts who did not participate in the mission and were thus spared? Of course there is no such evidence. The only reason a Karmic theorist would or could give is that they in fact died while the others are alive. Returning to the Jews and their Nazi exterminators, it would seem that, since the Jews deserved extinction, the Nazis were not really criminals and should not have been prosecuted. I assume that Eichmann deserved to be hanged since he *was* hanged, but the many Nazis who escaped deserved to escape. Speaking of executions, the main argument against the death penalty evidently collapses if the Law of Karma is true. For in that case no innocent man can ever be executed. People may indeed be innocent of the crime with which they are charged, but if they are executed this is what they deserved. It makes one dizzy.

"Cosmic" Claims

My discussion of Karma would be incomplete without saying a few words about certain "cosmic" claims found in the writings of reincarnationists. It is commonly asserted that all lawful connections in the universe are really "nothing more" than instances of Karma. Dr. Raynor Johnson, the Christian reincarnationist mentioned earlier, writes that "the Law of Cause and Effect, as we know it in the material world," is really "nothing more than a special case" of the Law of Karma.[23] Again, it has been claimed—and perhaps this is what Dr. Johnson had in mind—that the same tendency to restore balance or equilibrium that appropriate punishments and rewards exemplify is found throughout the universe. Thus in a rather haughty note in the *Aryan Review* of October 1936, in which the editor offers advice to the author of the preceding article, the author being none other than A. J. Ayer, we are assured that "Karma is an undeviating and unerring tendency in the universe to restore equilibrium." It "operates incessantly" and, what is more, "it operates on all things and beings from the minutest conceivable atom to the highest of human souls." All such claims are open to the criticism that, if they are interpreted in a fairly straightforward way, they are simply absurd and, if they are interpreted in such a way as to avoid absurdity, they say absolutely nothing. If it is maintained that the lawful behavior of molecules or mountains or planets are instances of rewards and punishments, this is plainly absurd, since molecules, planets, and mountains cannot perform good and evil deeds. If, to avoid this absurdity, "Karma" is taken in a broader sense in which it is simply a synonym for "lawfulness" or "regularity," then calling the various laws of nature instances of Karma is saying nothing at all. It is plain that we do not understand the regularities of the world any better and nothing whatever has been added to the content of any known law. Calling natural regularities instances of Karma is about as enlightening as describing them as manifestations of the Absolute Mind or as instances of the dialectical interplay of Being and Non-Being.

[23]*The Imprisoned Splendor*, p. 388.

21

H. H. PRICE

What Kind of Next World?

IF WE ARE to discuss the problem of survival intelligently, we must try to form some idea of what the life after death might conceivably be like. If we cannot form such an idea, however rough and provisional, it is pointless to discuss the factual evidence for or against the "survival hypothesis." A critic may object that there *is* no such hypothesis, on the ground that the phrase "survival of human personality after death" has no intelligible meaning at all.

When we speak of the after-life or of life after death, the "life" we have in mind is not life in the physiological sense (by definition this ceases at death). "Life" here means consciousness or experience. And consciousness has to be consciousness *of* something. Experiences must have objects of some sort. In this way, the idea of life after death is closely bound up with the idea of "The Next World" or "The Other World." This Other World is what the surviving person is supposed to be conscious *of*. It provides the objects of his after-death experiences. The idea of life after death is indeed a completely empty one unless we can form at any rate some rough conception of what "The Other World" might be like.

On the face of it, there are two different ways of conceiving of the Next World. They correspond to two different conceptions of survival itself, and something must first be said about these. On the one hand,

This article first appeared in *Tomorrow* (1956). It is reprinted with the kind permission of Katherine Price.

there is what I shall call the "embodied" conception of survival. On this view personality cannot exist at all without a body of some kind. At death one loses one's physical body. So after death one must have a body of another sort, an etheric body or an astral body, composed of a "higher" kind of matter. It is generally held, by those who accept this view, that each of us does in fact possess such a "higher" body even in this present life, and that this is the explanation of what are called "out-of-the-body" experiences (experiences of being out of the *physical* body).

It is interesting to notice that this conception of survival is compatible with a new version of materialism. According to the classical version of the materialist theory, the one which philosophers call epiphenomenalism, consciousness is unilaterally dependent on processes in the physical body and could not continue once the physical body has disintegrated. But suppose it was suggested, instead, that consciousness is unilaterally dependent on processes in the "higher" body. This would be a new version of the materialist theory of human personality, and it would be compatible with survival, as the old version is not. Similarly there might be a new version of behaviourism. Instead of saying that consciousness is reducible in one way or another to the behaviour of the physical organism (a view which excludes the possibility of survival) someone might suggest that it is reducible to the behaviour of the "higher" organism. Perhaps some view of this kind — "higher body" materialism as one might call it — will be the prevailing one among the tough-minded naturalistic thinkers of the 21st century. Perhaps it is already the prevailing view among the tough-minded thinkers of the Next World, if there is one.

I turn now to the "disembodied" conception of survival. On this view what survives death is just the soul or spirit, and it is a wholly immaterial entity. Its essential attributes are consciousness, thought, memory, desire and the capacity of having emotions. In this present life the immaterial soul interacts continually with the physical organism, especially with the brain. At death, this interaction ceases; or rather, death just *is* the permanent cessation of this interaction. And thereafter the immaterial soul continues to exist in a disembodied state. Most of the thinkers who have conceived of survival in this way, Plato and Descartes for instance, have also accepted the doctrine of a substantial soul. But the disembodied conception of survival is equally compatible with the "Serial Analysis" of personality advocated by David Hume* the philosopher, William James** the psychologist, and in the east, by the Buddhists. We should merely have to say that the series of mental events which constitutes a person can be divided into two parts, an *ante*

*See selection 8 of this volume. [Ed.]
**See selection 15 of this volume. [Ed.]

mortem part and a *post mortem* part; and that those in the first part are closely associated with physical events in a certain brain, whereas those in the second part are not associated with physical events of any kind. (This serial conception of personal identity is also, of course, compatible with the "Embodied" conception of survival; and Buddhism, at least according to some Western interpretations of it, appears to accept both.)

The Next World — Two Views

Corresponding to these two different conceptions of survival, there are two different conceptions of the Next World; a quasi-physical conception of it on the one hand, and a psychological conception of it on the other.

If we accept the "embodied" conception of survival, we think of the Next World as a kind of material world. It would be the environment of the etheric or astral body, and composed of the same sort of "higher" matter. Presumably this body would have sense organs of some kind, though they might be very different from our present ones, and by means of them we should be aware of our after-death environment. In this way we should be provided with objects to be conscious of, and could have desires and emotions concerning them. Among such objects there would be the "higher" bodies of other surviving human beings; and possibly we might also encounter some personalities embodied in the same manner who had never had *physical* bodies at all.

The Other World, thus conceived, must of course be a spatial one. Both the "higher" body and the objects which constitute its environment would have to have properties which are at any rate analogous to shape, size, location and mobility as we know them in this present life. But if the Other World is a spatial one, *where* is it? Is it "above the bright blue sky" perhaps (that is, in or beyond the stratosphere)? Or is it somewhere in the bowels of the earth? Could we reach it by means of a rocket, or by digging a deep enough tunnel? Anyone who accepts this conception of the Other World must hold that such questions arise from a misunderstanding. We have no *a priori* reason for assuming that the physical space with which we are now familiar is the only space there is. There might perfectly well be two worlds, each standing in no spatial relation to the other, or indeed there might be more than two. Suppose that in the Next World there is a New Jerusalem, and that it is quite literally a spatial entity, with a shape and a size and complex spatial relations between its parts, as the traditional descriptions of it imply. It does not follow the New Jerusalem stands in any spatial relation at all to the old Jerusalem in Palestine. The Next World and all that is in it might just be in a space of its own, different from the space of the physical universe. Moreover, it might be a different *sort* of space as well. Its geometry need not be even approximately Euclidian. It might have more than three dimensions. When I say that the space of the Next World "might" have some queer features, I mean that its possession of them is compatible with the "embodied" conception of survival from which this whole line of thought starts. And similarly the causal laws which prevail in it might be very different from the laws of physics. Indeed, they *must* differ to some extent from the laws of physics if such phrases as "higher" body and "higher kind of matter" are to have any meaning.

A Kind of Dream World

But now suppose we start from what I called the disembodied conception of survival. If the after-death personality is something wholly immaterial, can there be any sort of other world at all? It seems to me that there can. We could think of it as a kind of dream-world. To put it in another way, we could suppose that in the next life mental imagery will play the part which sense-perception plays in this one. People sometimes ask what is "the purpose" or "the point" of our present life in this world, or whether it has any. Perhaps this question is not so utterly senseless as most contemporary philosophers suppose. We might even be able to suggest an answer to it. The point of life in this present world, we might say, is to provide us with a stock of memories out of which an image world may be constructed when we are dead.

It might be objected, however, that in this present life we know — or claim to know — where dream-images are. We are inclined to say that a person's dream-images are "in his head," that is, in some region or other of his brain; and obviously they cannot occur there after the brain itself has disintegrated. But what exactly do we mean by the word "in" when we say (of a living and physically-embodied person) that his dream-images are in his head? I think we can only mean that some cerebral processes or other, which do quite literally occur in his head, are *causes* or part-causes of the dream-images he has in this present life. But the images themselves are not located in physical space at all. Suppose I dream of a wolf emerging from a dark forest. Then the wolf-image is indeed located in relation to the images of the trees. But does it make any sense at all to ask whereabouts this wolf-image is in the space of the physical world? Is it, for instance, two and a half inches to the north-west of the dreamer's left ear? So far as I can see, there is no meaning in such a question. (It is rather like asking how far away Fairyland is from London.) Dream-images are in a space of their own. They do have spatial relations to other dream-images. But so far as physical space is concerned they are not anywhere; or rather the question "where they are" does not arise.

We are also liable to think that there is something "unreal" about mental images in general and about dream-images in particular. This too seems to me to be a confusion. Mental images are non-physical, certainly, but they are as real as anything can be. They do actually exist or occur. Moreover, some mental images (visual and tactile ones) are spatial entities, though they are not in physical space. But perhaps when people say that mental images are "unreal" they are using the word in a kind of evaluative sense. Perhaps they mean that mental images make no appeal to our feelings, that they are uninteresting or unexciting, that they "cut no ice" with us from the emotional point of view. But surely this is false, as anyone who has ever had a nightmare knows. Both for good and for ill, our dream experiences may be as vividly felt as any of our waking ones, or more so. And for some people, indeed for many people on some occasions, the mental images they experience when awake are more interesting — more attention-absorbing — than the physical objects they perceive. Moreover, waking mental images may be interesting in an alarming or horrifying way, as dream images can. They may force themselves on our attention when we would much rather be without them.

It is worth while to emphasise these points, because this way of conceiving life after death does enable us to answer a logically irrelevant but emotionally powerful objection to the whole idea of survival, the objection that it is "too good to be true." On the contrary, such a dream-like next world, composed of mental images, might be a very unpleasant world for some people and a rather unpleasant one for almost all of us some of the time.

It would of course be a psychological world and not a physical one. It might indeed *seem* to be physical to those who experience it. The image-objects which compose it might appear very like physical objects, as dream objects often do now; so much so that we might find it difficult at first to realise that we were dead (a point often mentioned in mediumistic communications). Nevertheless, the causal laws obeyed by these image-objects would not be the laws of physics, but something more like the laws of depth psychology which such investigators as Sigmund Freud and C. G. Jung began to explore. It is of course sometimes said that dreams are "incoherent," and this again may be part of what is meant by calling dream objects unreal. But dreams (or waking fantasies) are only incoherent if judged by the irrelevant standard of the laws of physics; and this is only another way of saying that dream objects are not physical objects, and that an image-world, as we are conceiving of it, would indeed be an "other" world, which is just what it ought to be.

To put it rather differently, the other world, according to this conception of it, would be the manifestation in image form of the memories and desires of its inhabitants, including their repressed or unconscious memories and desires. It might be every bit as detailed, as vivid and as complex as this present perceptible world which we experience now. We may note that it might well contain a vivid and persistent image of one's own body. The surviving personality, according to this conception of survival, is in actual fact an immaterial entity. But if one habitually *thinks* of oneself as embodied (as one well might, at least for a considerable time) an image of one's own body might be as it were the persistent centre of one's image world, much as the perceived physical body is the persistent centre of one's perceptible world in this present life.

It may be thought that such a Next World would be a purely private and subjective one, that each discarnate personality would experience a Next World of his own, with no access to anyone else's. But suppose we bring telepathy into the picture. It may well be that in this present life the physical brain inhibits the operation of our telepathic powers, or at any rate tends to prevent the results of their operations from reaching consciousness. In the after-life, if there is one, telepathy might well be much more extensive and continuous than it is now. If so, we might expect that A's images would manifest not only his own desires and memories, but also the desires and memories of other personalities B, C, D, etc. if these were sufficiently similar to his own. In this way there might be a common image world for each group of sufficiently "like-minded" personalities, common to all the members of the group though private to the group as a whole. There would still be many Next Worlds and not one (a suggestion which most religious traditions would, I think, support) but none of them would be wholly private and subjective.

Physical and Psychological Conceptions

Let us now compare these two conceptions of the other world, the quasi-physical conception of it which goes with the "embodied" conception of survival, and the psychological conception of it which goes with the "disembodied" conception of survival. At first sight these two ways of thinking of the other world appear entirely different and indeed incompatible. If one is right, surely the other must be wrong? But perhaps they are not quite so different as they look. They do agree on several important points. In both, the Next World is a spatial one (I would remind the reader that visual and tactical images are spatial entities). In both, the space of the Next World is different from physical space. In both, the causal laws are other than the laws of physics. In the first, the discarnate personality has a body, but it is not an ordinary physical body. In the second he has a dream body or image body.

What we have really done in this discussion of the Other World is to start from two different analogies and work out their consequences.

The first analogy which we considered was a physical one, suggested by our experience of the material world. The second was a psychological one, suggested by our experience of dreams and other forms of mental imagery. Some people will feel more at home with the physical analogy; others will be more attracted by the psychological one. But perhaps the choice between them is only a choice between starting points. Both analogies have to be stretched in one way or another if we are to achieve our aim, which is to give some intelligible content to the notion of the "next life" or the "next world."

It may well be that the two lines of thought, if pushed far enough, would meet in the middle. It is at any rate an attractive speculation that there may be realities in the universe which are intermediate between the physical and the psychological realms as these are ordinarily conceived. The contents of the other world, if there is one, may be in this intermediate position, more material than ordinary dream-images, more image-like or dream-like than ordinary material objects; like material objects in possessing spatial properties of some sort, and some degree at any rate of permanence; like mental images in that the causal laws they obey are the laws of psychology rather than the laws of physics.

22

ANTONY FLEW

❦

The Cartesian Assumption

❦

. . . PLATO AND ARISTOTLE can be regarded as the archetypical protag-
onists of two opposing views of man. Plato is the original spokesman for
a dualistic view, and it seems that it is upon dualism that a doctrine of
personal immortality must be grounded if it is to possess any initial
plausibility. As a defender of a monistic view, Aristotle was neither so
consistent nor so wholehearted. Yet it is still fair to see him at his most
characteristic as the philosophical founding father of the view that the
person is the living human organism, a view that apparently leaves no
room whatsoever for belief in personal immortality. Aquinas, who generally followed Aristotle on this point, characteristically attempted a
synthesis that would have opened, had it been successful, the doors to
heaven and to hell. In the present perspective Descartes must be
placed squarely in the Platonic tradition. Thus, in the final paragraph of
Part V of the *Discourse on Method*, after remarking that "next to the
error of those who deny God . . . there is none which is more effec-
tual in leading feeble spirits from the straight path of virtue, than to
imagine that . . . after this life we having nothing to fear or to hope
for, any more than the flies or the ants," Descartes concluded that "our
soul is in its nature entirely independent of the body, and in consequence that it is not liable to die with it. And then, inasmuch as we

This discussion is a section of Antony Flew's "Immortality" in volume 4 of *The
Encyclopedia of Philosophy* (1967). It is reprinted with the permission of the Macmillan
Publishing Co.

observe no other causes capable of destroying it, we are naturally inclined to judge that it is immortal."

Soul as a Thinking Substance

. . . Although his conclusions were thoroughly traditional, Descartes was nevertheless a revolutionary thinker. Unlike Plato, his chief intellectual interests were science, in particular physiology. Like Hobbes, the other great metaphysician of his period, Descartes quickly grasped the wider significance of the work of Harvey and Galileo. Harvey's discovery of the circulation of the blood suggested to Descartes that both animals and human bodies might be regarded as machines. Descartes then asked himself how the creatures that we know might be distinguished from living machines. His answer was that with respect to animals there simply was no distinction in principle but that an automaton in human shape, however brilliantly constructed, could always be distinguished from a true human being in two ways. There were two sorts of test which were bound to reveal the absence of the vital rational soul: without a rational soul such an automaton would not be able "to reply appropriately to everything . . . said in its presence, as even the lowest type of man can do," and their lack of versatility would always reveal that the automata "did not act from knowledge, but only from the disposition of their organs" (*Discourse on Method*, Part V).

One fundamental distinction, often overlooked in discussing these questions, is that between logical and technical impossibility. In Part V of the *Discourse*, his first published treatment, Descartes seems to have been making a purely factual claim "that it is morally impossible that there should be sufficient diversity in any machine to allow it to act in all the events of life in the same way as our reason causes us to act." To make any such would-be factual claim must be both rashly premature and scientifically defeatist. Elsewhere and later, it becomes clear that what Descartes, like so many successors, really wanted to say is that it is inconceivable that any material mechanism could be responsible for certain sorts of things. Thus, in the *Passions of the Soul* he laid down the principle "that all that which is in us and which we cannot in any way conceive as possibly pertaining to a body, must be attributed to our soul" (I, iv). And in his view what has to be thus attributed is thought, in his own rather broad sense of "thought," which seems to include all actions and passions considered to involve consciousness (*ibid.*, I, xvii ff.). "By the word thought I understand all that of which we are conscious as operating in us. And that is why not only understanding, willing, imaging, but feeling also here count as thought" (*Principles of Philosophy*, I, ix).

Descartes was thus insisting that it is inconceivable that matter, however disposed, could in this sense think. This is a notion of the same sort as the idea that purposive and rational beings could not, without benefit of control by some Higher Purpose, have evolved first from creatures of a lower order and, ultimately, from inanimate matter, an idea found in both some objections to evolutionary theory and some versions of the Argument to Design. Presumably, Descartes would have accepted both contentions and many others like them because they fall under the generic principle, which he formulated as the fourth of his "axioms or common notions"; "All the reality of perfection which is in a thing is found formally or eminently in its first and total cause" (Addendum to the Replies to the Second Set of Objections to the *Meditations*).

It has since Kant become the custom to dignify such principles with the title "synthetic a priori propositions." But the one with which we are here concerned, though certainly synthetic, can be described as a priori only in the quite artificial sense that it is wholly arbitrary and unwarranted. Descartes's more specific idea had been forcibly challenged long before by the Epicureans (see, for instance, Lucretius, *De Rerum Natura* II. 865–870 and 875–882). The challenge was later repeated by both Spinoza and Locke even before Hume launched his decisive onslaught on the generic notion that it is possible to know a priori that some thing or sort of thing must be or cannot be the cause of some other thing or sort of thing. The points made, in their different ways, by both Spinoza and Locke were that there is no contradiction in the idea of something material being endowed with thought and that we are in no position to deny dogmatically that there are material creatures so endowed.

Subjectivism

. . . Thus far, Descartes's originality, as against the Platonic tradition, has chiefly been in his positive scientific interests and in his mechanistic ideas about the body. His achievement was to form a new framework of discussion and to provide a metaphysical foundation for the further development of physiology. He was also revolutionary on a second count, for it was he who developed with compelling dramatic power a new approach to questions of mind and matter. For three full centuries this remained part of the accepted philosophical orthodoxy, an orthodoxy which even Hume seems never to have thought to question. This approach can be characterized, though with no intended moral overtones, as self-centered.

Whereas Plato generally—and Descartes, too, when he suggested tests of humanity—approached people from our common public world, Descartes at his most characteristic tried to approach the world from inside the closed circle of his logically private consciousness. Thus, in Part IV of the *Discourse*, having reached his rock bottom certainty in the proposition *cogito ergo sum*, he asked what he was. "I saw that I could conceive that I had no body, and there was no world nor place where I might be; but yet that I could not for all that conceive that I was not." He concluded that he "was a substance the whole essence or nature of which is to think, and that for its existence there is no need of any place, nor does it depend on any material thing; so that this 'me,' that is to say, the soul by which I am what I am, is entirely distinct from body, . . . and even if the body were not, the soul would not cease to be what it is" (compare, especially, *Meditations*, II).

Much of the power of the Cartesian argument lies in the use of the first-person personal pronoun and in the idiosyncratic choice of tenses and moods. For there is surely no difficulty at all, even for Descartes, in supposing that Descartes may one day be annihilated or that Descartes might never have been born. The most fundamental objections are founded upon a rejection of his unstated general assumption that (his) words obtain their meaning by reference to (his) logically private experiences. In particular, Descartes mistakenly assumed that all the words for all the things that he comprehended under the term "thinking" are words for such private experiences. Only on this assumption is it possible to assert that there could be — much less that we are — essentially incorporeal beings and, as such, fully capable of every sort of thinking. To insist that this assumption is wrong is not necessarily to adopt either a complete logical behaviorism — saying that all terms of this type refer only to public performances — or Wittgenstein's extreme later position — apparently denying the very possibility of a language's containing words defined in terms of one man's logically private experience. It is sufficient to commit oneself only to the more modest claim that most think words refer wholly or partly to various actual or possible proceedings that are necessarily corporeal. To recognize that this is true and could scarcely be otherwise, it is sufficient to reflect for a moment upon the whole context in which we learn to use these terms; consider how we should teach the meaning of "He argued with her" or "She drew her own conclusions." In this perspective it becomes no wonder that, as Wittgenstein said, "The human face is the best picture of the human soul."

Personal Identity and Parapsychology

. . . The appeal of the Cartesian approach and its influence can be appreciated by considering two examples, both relevant to the question of immortality — first, the discussion of personal identity initiated by Locke and continued by Butler, Hume, and Reid and, second, the investigation of the question of human survival by modern parapsychologists through the study of the possible relevance of the evidence furnished by all types of mediumistic performances.

Both investigations have started from the self-centered Cartesian standpoint and have taken for granted that, essentially, people are bodiless. Thus, the problem of personal identity was generally taken to be one of the identity of an incorporeal thinking thing. Locke tried to provide an analysis of personal identity, so construed, in terms of consciousness (memory). The decisive objection to any such analysis was sharply put by Butler: "And one should really think it self-evident that consciousness of personal identity presupposes, and therefore cannot constitute, personal identity" (Dissertation 1, "Personal Identity," appended to the *Analogy of Religion*).

But most of Locke's critics, Butler included, seem to have failed to appreciate just how difficult—even, perhaps, impossible—the problems of the nature of the identity and of the principle of the individuation of such putative incorporeal beings must be. If people are thought of as incorporeal substances having sorts of thinking, in the wide Cartesian sense, as their qualities (the substance, or "pure ego," theory of the self), then the question is how such substances are to be identified, what sense can be given to the expression "pure ego." If, with Hume, one is unable to provide any satisfactory answer to this question, the only alternative seems to be thinking of people as collections of experiences (the serial, or "bundle," theory of the self). Theories of this sort face two difficulties. First, it does not seem to make sense to speak of thoughts or experiences as "loose and separate" without anyone's having them, and, second, there seems to be no string capable of tying the bundles of experiences together while keeping one bundle distinct from another. The first difficulty may or may not be merely grammatical. The second, once the impossibility of using memory as the string is fully realized, appears very formidable. It was the second difficulty in a slightly different form that Hume had to confess to be "too hard for my understanding" (Appendix to *Treatise of Human Nature*).

In parapsychology it seems to have been almost universally assumed that mediumistic material, insofar as it cannot be either satisfactorily explained away in terms of fraud and delusion or conveniently redescribed in terms of telepathic and clairvoyant transactions among the living, can and must be interpreted as evidence for human survival. Yet to interpret such material in this way is not to provide support for, but rather to presuppose, a Platonic-Cartesian view of man. For it is only insofar as a person is essentially incorporeal that it can even make sense to suggest that someone years ago dead, buried, and dissolved is even now communicating with us through a medium.

23

PETER GEACH

Immortality

EVERYBODY KNOWS THAT men die, and though most of us have read the advertisement "Millions now living will never die," it is commonly believed that every man born will some day die; yet historically many men have believed that there is a life after death, and indeed that this after-life will never end. That is: there has been a common belief both in *survival* of bodily death and in *immortality*. Now a philosopher might interest himself specially in immortality, as opposed to survival; conceding survival for the sake of argument, he might raise and examine conceptual difficulties about *endless* survival. But the question of immortality cannot even arise unless men do survive bodily death; and, as we shall see, there are formidable difficulties even about survival. It is these difficulties I shall be discussing, not the special ones about endless survival.

There are various views as to the character of the after-life. One view is that man has a subtle, ordinarily invisible, body which survives the death of the ordinary gross body. This view has a long history, and seems to be quite popular in England at the moment. So far as I can see, the view is open to no philosophical objection, but likewise wholly devoid of philosophical interest; the mind-body problem must after all be just the same for an ethereal body as for a gross one. There could clearly be no philosophical reasons for belief in such subtle bodies, but

This selection is chapter 2 of Geach's *God and the Soul,* published in 1969 by Routledge and Kegan Paul, with whose permission it is reprinted.

only empirical ones; such reasons are in fact alleged, and we are urged to study the evidence.

Philosophy can at this point say something: about what sort of evidence would be required. The existence of subtle bodies is a matter within the purview of physical science; evidence for it should satisfy such criteria of existence as physicists use, and should refer not only to what people say they have seen, heard, and felt, but also to effects produced by subtle bodies on physicists' apparatus. The believer in "subtle bodies" must, I think, accept the physicist's criteria of existence; there would surely be a conceptual muddle in speaking of "bodies" but saying they might be incapable of affecting any physical apparatus. For what distinguishes real physical objects from hallucinations, even collective hallucinations, is that physical objects act on one another, and do so in just the same way whether they are being observed or not; this is the point, I think, at which a phenomenalist account of physical objects breaks down. If, therefore, "subtle bodies" produce no physical effects, they are not bodies at all.

How is it, then, that "subtle bodies" have never forced themselves upon the attention of physicists, as X-rays did, by spontaneous interference with physical apparatus? There are supposed to be a lot of "subtle bodies" around, and physicists have a lot of delicate apparatus; yet physicists not engaged in psychical research are never bothered by the interference of "subtle bodies." In the circumstances I think it wholly irrational to believe in "subtle bodies." Moreover, when I who am no physicist am invited to study the evidence for "subtle bodies," I find that very fact suspicious. The discoverers of X-rays and electrons did not appeal to the lay public, but to physicists, to study the evidence; and so long as physicists (at least in general) refuse to take "subtle bodies" seriously, a study of evidence for them by a layman like myself would be a waste of time.

When *philosophers* talk of life after death, what they mostly have in mind is a doctrine that may be called Platonic—it is found in its essentials in the *Phaedo*. It may be briefly stated thus: "Each man's make-up includes a wholly immaterial thing, his mind and soul. It is the mind that sees and hears and feels and thinks and chooses—in a word, is conscious. The mind is the person; the body is extrinsic to the person, like a suit of clothes. Though body and mind affect one another, the mind's existence is quite independent of the body's; and there is thus no reason why the mind should not go on being conscious indefinitely after the death of the body, and even if it never again has with any body that sort of connexion which it now has."

This Platonic doctrine has a strong appeal, and there are plausible arguments in its favour. It appears a clearly intelligible supposition that I should go on after death having the same sorts of experience as I now have, even if I then have no body at all. For although these experiences are connected with processes in the body — sight, for example, with processes in the eyes, optic nerves, and brain — nevertheless there is no necessity of thought about the connexion — it is easy to conceive of someone who has no eyes having the experience called sight. He would be having the same experiences as I who have eyes do, and I know what sort of experience that is because I have the experience.

Let us now examine these arguments. When a word can be used to stand for a private experience, like the words "seeing" or "pain," it is certainly tempting to suppose that the giving these words a meaning is itself a private experience — indeed that they get their meaning just from the experiences they stand for. But this is really nonsense: if a sentence I hear or utter contains the word "pain," do I help myself to grasp its sense by giving myself a pain? Might not this be, on the contrary, rather distracting? As Wittgenstein said, to think you get the concept of pain by having a pain is like thinking you get the concept of a minus quantity by running up an overdraft. Our concepts of seeing, hearing, pain, anger, etc., apply in the first instance to human beings; we willingly extend them (say) to cats, dogs, and horses, but we rightly feel uncomfortable about extending them to very alien creatures and speaking of a slug's hearing or an angry ant. Do we know at all what it would be to apply such concepts to an immaterial being? I think not.

One may indeed be tempted to evade difficulties by saying: "An immaterial spirit is angry or in pain if it feels *the same way* as I do when I am angry or in pain." But, as Wittgenstein remarked, this is just like saying: "Of course I know what it is for the time on the Sun to be five o'clock: it's five o'clock on the Sun at the very moment when it's five o'clock here!" — which plainly gets us no further. If there is a difficulty in passing from "I am in pain" or "Smith is in pain" to "an immaterial spirit is in pain," there is equally a difficulty in passing from "Smith feels the same way as I do" to "an immaterial spirit feels the same way I do."

In fact, the question is, whether a private experience does suffice, as is here supposed, to a give a meaning to a psychological verb like "to see." I am not trying to throw doubt on there being private experiences; of course men have thoughts they do not utter and pains they do not show; of course I may see something without any behaviour to show I see it; nor do I mean to emasculate these propositions with neo-behaviourist dialectics. But it is not a question of whether seeing is (sometimes) a private experience, but whether one can attach meaning to the verb "to see" by a private uncheckable performance; and this is what I maintain one cannot do to any word at all.

One way to show that a word's being given a meaning cannot be a private uncheckable performance is the following: We can take a man's word for it that a linguistic expression has given him some private experience — e.g. has revived a painful memory, evoked a visual image, or given him a thrill in the pit of the stomach. But we cannot take his word for it that he attached a sense to the expression, even if we accept his *bona fides*; for later events may convince us that in fact he attached no sense to the expression. Attaching sense to an expression is thus not to be identified with any private experience that accompanies the expression; and I have argued this, not by attacking the idea of private experiences, but by contrasting the attaching of sense to an expression with some typical private experiences that may be connected with the expression.

We give words a sense — whether they are psychological words like "seeing" and "pain," or other words — by getting into a way of using them; and though a man can invent for himself a way of using a word, it must be a way that other people *could* follow — otherwise we are back to the idea of conferring meaning by a private uncheckable performance. Well, how do we eventually use such words as "see," "hear," "feel," when we have got into the way of using them? We do not exercise these concepts only so as to pick our cases of seeing and the rest in our separate worlds of sense-experience; on the contrary, these concepts are used in association with a host of other concepts relating, e.g., to the physical characteristics of what is seen and the behaviour of those who do see. In saying this I am not putting forward a theory, but just reminding you of very familiar features in the everyday use of the verb "to see" and related expressions; our ordinary talk about seeing would cease to be intelligible if there were cut out of it such expressions as "I can't see, it's too far off," "I caught his eye," "Don't look round," etc. Do not let the bogy of behaviourism scare you off observing these features; I am not asking you to believe that "to see" is itself a word for a kind of behaviour. But the concept of seeing can be maintained only because it has threads of connexion with these other non-psychological concepts; break enough threads, and the concept of seeing collapses.

We can now see the sort of difficulties that arise if we try to apply concepts like *seeing* and *feeling* to disembodied spirits. Let me give an actual case of a psychological concept's collapsing when its connexions were broken. Certain hysterics claimed to have a magnetic sense; it was discovered, however, that their claim to be having magnetic sensations did not go with the actual presence of a magnet in their environment, but only with their belief that a magnet was present. Psychologists did not now take the line: We may take the patients' word for it that they have peculiar sensations — only the term "magnetic sensations" has proved inappropriate, as having been based on a wrong causal hypothesis. On the contrary, patients' reports of magnetic sensations were thenceforward written off as being among the odd things that hysterical patients sometimes say. Now far fewer of the ordinary connexions of a sensation-concept were broken here than would be broken if we tried to apply a sensation-concept like seeing to a disembodied spirit.

If we conclude that the ascription of sensations and feelings to a disembodied spirit does not make sense, it does not obviously follow, as you might think, that we must deny the possibility of disembodied spirits altogether. Aquinas for example was convinced that there are disembodied spirits but ones that cannot see or hear or feel pain or fear or anger; he allowed them no mental operations except those of thought and will. Damned spirits would suffer from frustration of their evil will, but not from aches and pains or foul odours or the like. It would take me too far to discuss whether his reasons for thinking this were good; I want to show what follows from this view. In our human life thinking and choosing are intricately bound up with a play of sensations and mental images and emotions; if after a lifetime of thinking and choosing in this human way there is left only a disembodied mind whose thought is wholly nonsensuous and whose rational choices are unaccompanied by any human feelings—can we still say there remains the same person? Surely not: such a soul is not the person who died but a mere remnant of him. And this is just what Aquinas says (in his commentary on I Corinthians 15): *anima mea non est ego*, my soul is not I; and if only souls are saved, *I* am not saved, nor is any man. If some time after Peter Geach's death there is again a man identifiable as Peter Geach, then Peter Geach again, or still, lives: otherwise not.

Though a surviving mental remnant of a person, preserving some sort of physical continuity with the man you knew, would not be Peter Geach, this does not show that such a measure of survival is not possible; but its possibility does raise serious difficulties, even if such dehumanized thinking and willing is really conceivable at all. For *whose* thinking would this be? Could we tell whether *one* or *many* disembodied spirits thought the thoughts in question? We touch here on the old problem: what constitutes there being two disembodied minds (at the same time, that is)? Well, what constitutes there being two pennies? It may happen that one penny is bent and corroded while another is in mint condition; but such differences cannot be what make the two pennies to be two—the two pennies could not have these varied fortunes if they were not already distinct. In the same way, differences of memories or of aims could not constitute the difference between two disembodied minds, but could only supervene upon a difference already existing. What does constitute the difference between two disembodied human minds? If we could find no ground of differentiation, then not only would that which survived be a mere remnant of a person—there would not even be a surviving individuality.

Could we say that souls are different because in the first instance they were souls of different bodies, and then remain different on that account when they are no longer embodied? I do not think this solution would do at all if differentiation by reference to different bodies were merely retrospective. It might be otherwise if we held, with Aquinas, that the relation to a body was not merely retrospective—that each disembodied human soul permanently retained a capacity for reunion to such a body as would reconstitute a man identifiable with the man who died. This might satisfactorily account for the individuation of disembodied human souls; they would differ by being fitted for reunion to different bodies; but it would entail that the possibility of disembodied human souls stood or fell with the *possibility* of a dead man's living again *as a man*.

Some Scholastics held that just as two pennies or two cats differ by being different bits of matter, so human souls differ by containing different "spiritual matter." Aquinas regarded this idea as self-contradictory; it is at any rate much too obscure to count as establishing a possibility of distinct disembodied souls. Now this recourse to "spiritual matter" might well strike us merely as the filling of a conceptual lacuna with a nonsensical piece of jargon. But it is not only Scholastic philosophers who assimilate mental processes to physical ones, only thinking of mental processes as taking place in an *immaterial* medium; and many people think it easy to conceive of distinct disembodied souls because they are illegitimately ascribing to souls a sort of differentiation—say, by existing *side by side*—that can be significantly ascribed only to bodies. The same goes for people who talk about souls as being "fused" or "merged" in a Great Soul; they are imagining some such change in the world of souls as occurs to a drop of water falling into a pool or to a small lump of wax that is rubbed into a big one. Now if only people *talked* about "spiritual matter," instead of just thinking in terms of it unawares, their muddle could be more easily detected and treated.

To sum up what I have said so far: The possibility of life after death for Peter Geach appears to stand or fall with the possibility of there being once again a man identifiable as Peter Geach. The existence of a disembodied soul would not be a survival of the person Peter Geach; and even in such a truncated form, individual existence seems to require at least a persistent possibility of the soul's again entering into the make-up of a man who is identifiably Peter Geach.

This suggests a form of belief in survival that seems to have become quite popular of late in the West—at any rate as a half-belief—namely, the belief in reincarnation. Could it in fact have a clear sense to say that a baby born in Oxford this year is Hitler living again?

How could it be shown that the Oxford baby was Hitler? Presumably by memories and similarities of character. I maintain that no amount of such evidence would make it reasonable to identify the baby as Hitler. Similarities of character are of themselves obviously insufficient. As regards memories: If on growing up the Oxford baby reveals knowledge of what we should ordinarily say only Hitler can have known, does this establish a presumption that the child is Hitler? Not at all. In normal circumstances we know when to say "only he can have known that"; when queer things start happening, we have no right to stick to our ordinary assumptions as to what can be known. And suppose that for some time the child "is" Hitler by our criteria, and later on "is" Goering? or might not several children simultaneously satisfy the criteria for "being" Hitler?

These are not merely captious theoretical objections. Spirit-mediums, we are told, will in trance convincingly enact the part of various people: sometimes of fictitious characters, like Martians, or Red Indians ignorant of Red Indian languages, or the departed "spirits" of Johnny Walker and John Jamieson; there are even stories of mediums' giving convincing "messages" from people who were alive and normally conscious at the time of the "message." Now a medium giving messages from the dead is not said to be the dead man, but rather to be controlled by his spirit. What then can show whether the Oxford child "is" Hitler or is merely "controlled" by Hitler's spirit? For all these reasons the appearance that there might be good evidence for reincarnation dissolves on a closer view.

Nor do I see, for that matter, how the mental phenomena of mediumship could ever make it reasonable to believe that a human soul survived and communicated. For someone to carry on in a dramatic way quite out of his normal character is a common hysterical symptom; so if a medium does this in a trance, it is no evidence of anything except an abnormal condition of the medium's own mind. As for the medium's telling us things that "only the dead can have known," I repeat that in these queer cases we have no right to stick to our ordinary assumptions about what can be known. Moreover, as I said, there are cases, as well-authenticated as any, in which the medium convincingly enacted the part of X and told things that "Only X could have known" when X was in fact alive and normally conscious, so that his soul was certainly not trying to communicate by way of the medium! Even if we accept all the queer stories of spirit-messages, the result is only to open up a vast field of queer possibilities — not in the least to force us to say that mediums were possessed by such-and-such souls. This was argued by Bradley long ago in his essay "The Evidences of Spiritualism," and he has never been answered.

How could a living man be rightly identifiable with a man who previously died? Let us first consider our normal criteria of personal identity. When we say an old man is the same person as the baby born seventy years before, we believe that the old man has material continuity with the baby. Of course this is not a criterion in the sense of being what we judge identity by; for the old man will not have been watched for seventy years continuously, even by rota! But something we regarded as disproving the material continuity (e.g. absence of a birthmark, different fingerprints) would disprove personal identity. Further, we believe that material continuity establishes a one – one relation: one baby grows up into an old man, and one old man has grown out of one baby. (Otherwise there would have to be at some stage a drastic change, a fusion or fission, which we should regard as destroying personal identity.) Moreover, the baby-body never coexists with the aged body, but develops into it.

Now it seems to me that we cannot rightly identify a man living "again" with a man who died unless *material* conditions of identity are fulfilled. There must be some one–one relation of material continuity between the old body and the new. I am not saying that the new body need be even in part materially *identical* with the old; this, unlike material continuity, is not required for personal identity, for the old man need not have kept even a grain of matter from the baby of seventy years ago.

We must here notice an important fallacy. I was indicating just now that I favour Aquinas's doctrine that two coexisting souls differ by being related to two different bodies and that two coexisting human bodies, like two pennies or two cats, differ by being different bits of matter. Well, if it is difference of matter that makes two bodies different, it may seem to follow that a body can maintain its identity only if at least some identifiable matter remains in it all the time; otherwise it is no more the same body than the wine in a cask that is continuously emptied and refilled is the same wine. But just this is the fallacy: it does not follow, if difference in a certain respect at a certain time suffices to show non-identity, that sameness in that respect over a period of time is necessary to identity. Thus, Sir John Cutler's famous pair of stockings were the same pair all the time, although they started as silk and by much mending ended as worsted; people have found it hard to see this, because if at a given time there is a silk pair and also a worsted pair then there are two pairs. Again, it is clear that the same man may be in Birmingham at noon and in Oxford at 7 p.m., even though a man in Birmingham and a man in Oxford at a given time must be two different men. Once formulated, the fallacy is obvious, but it might be deceptive if not formulated.

"Why worry even about material continuity? Would not mental continuity be both necessary and sufficient?" Necessary, but not sufficient. Imagine a new "Tichborne" trial.* The claimant knows all the things he ought to know, and talks convincingly to the long-lost heir's friends.

---

*Roger Tichborne, an English aristocrat, was lost at sea in 1854. His mother, Lady Tichborne, refused to accept his death and advertised for information concerning his whereabouts. In 1865 a man in Australia claimed to be Roger Tichborne and was acknowledged by Lady Tichborne as her son. He thereupon brought an ejection suit against Roger's nephew who had inherited the Tichborne baronetcy and estates. The jury declared that he was an imposter. His real name was Arthur Orton. He was tried for perjury and sentenced to imprisonment for fourteen years. Orton later published a confession. [Ed.]

But medical evidence about scars and old fractures and so on indicates that he cannot be the man; moreover, the long-lost heir's corpse is decisively identified at an exhumation. Such a case would bewilder us, particularly if the claimant's *bona fides* were manifest. (He might, for example, voluntarily take a lie-detecting test.) But we should certainly not allow the evidence of mental connexions with the long-lost heir to settle the matter in the claimant's favour: the claimant cannot be the long-lost heir, whose body we know lies buried in Australia, and if he honestly thinks he is then we must try to cure him of a delusion.

"But if I went on being conscious, why should I worry which body I have?" To use the repeated "I" prejudges the issue; a fairer way of putting the point would be: If there is going to be a consciousness that includes ostensible memories of my life, why should I worry about which body this consciousness goes with? When we put it that way, it is quite easy to imagine circumstances in which one would worry— particularly if the ostensible memories of my life were to be produced by processes that can produce entirely spurious memories.

If, however, memory is not enough for personal identity; if man's living again does involve some bodily as well as mental continuity with the man who lived formerly; then we might fairly call his new bodily life a resurrection. So the upshot of our whole argument is that unless a man comes to life again by resurrection, he does not live again after death. At best some mental remnant of him would survive death; and I should hold that the possibility even of such survival involves at least a permanent *capacity* for renewed human life; if reincarnation is excluded, this means: a capacity for resurrection. It may be hard to believe in the resurrection of the body: but Aquinas argued in his commentary on I Corinthians 15, which I have already cited, that it is much harder to believe in an immortal but permanently disembodied human soul; for that would mean believing that a soul, whose very identity depends on the capacity for reunion with one human body rather than another, will continue to exist for ever with this capacity unrealized.

Speaking of the resurrection, St. Paul used the simile of a seed that is planted and grows into an ear of corn, to show the relation between the corpse and the body that rises again from the dead. This simile fits in well enough with our discussion. In this life, the bodily aspect of personal identity requires a one–one relationship and material continuity; one baby body grows into one old man's body by a continuous process. Now similarly there is a one–one relationship between the buried seed and the ear that grows out of it; one seed grows into one ear, one ear comes from one seed; and the ear of corn is materially continuous with the seed but need not have any material identity with it.

There is of course no philosophical reason to expect that from a human corpse there will arise at some future date a new human body, continuous in some way with the corpse; and in some particular cases there appear strong empirical objections. But apart from the *possibility* of resurrection, it seems to me a mere illusion to have any hope for life after death. I am of the mind of Judas Maccabeus: if there is no resurrection, it is superfluous and vain to pray for the dead.

The traditional faith of Christianity, inherited from Judaism, is that at the end of this age Messiah will come and men rise from their graves to die no more. That faith is not going to be shaken by inquiries about bodies burned to ashes or eaten by beasts; those who might well suffer just such death in martyrdom were those who were most confident of a glorious reward in the resurrection. One who shares that hope will hardly wish to take out an occultistic or philosophical insurance policy, to guarantee some sort of survival as an annuity, in case God's promise of resurrection should fail.

24

JOHN HICK

⤛⤜

The Recreation of the Psycho-Physical Person

⤛⤜

The Immortality of the Soul

SOME KIND OF distinction between physical body and immaterial or semimaterial soul seems to be as old as human culture; the existence of such a distinction has been indicated by the manner of burial of the earliest human skeletons yet discovered. Anthropologists offer various conjectures about the origin of the distinction: perhaps it was first suggested by memories of dead persons; by dreams of them; by the sight of reflections of oneself in water and on other bright surfaces; or by meditation upon the significance of religious rites which grew up spontaneously in face of the fact of death.

It was Plato (428/7 – 348/7 B.C.), the philosopher who has most deeply and lastingly influenced Western culture, who systematically developed the body – mind dichotomy and first attempted to prove the immortality of the soul.[1]

Plato argues that although the body belongs to the sensible world,[2] and shares its changing and impermanent nature, the intellect is related to the unchanging realities of which we are aware when we think not of particular good things but of Goodness itself, not of specific just acts

---

[1]*Phaedo*. [See selection 1 in this book.]
[2]The world known to us through our physical senses.

This selection consists of the first two sections of chapter 7 of *Philosophy of Religion* (2nd ed. 1973). It is reprinted with the permission of Prentice Hall.

but of Justice itself, and of the other "universals" or eternal Ideas in virtue of which physical things and events have their own specific characteristics. Being related to this higher and abiding realm, rather than to the evanescent world of sense, reason or the soul is immortal. Hence, one who devotes his life to the contemplation of eternal realities rather than to the gratification of the fleeting desires of the body will find at death that whereas his body turns to dust, his soul gravitates to the realm of the unchanging, there to live forever. Plato painted an awe-inspiring picture, of haunting beauty and persuasiveness, which has moved and elevated the minds of men in many different centuries and lands. Nevertheless, it is not today (as it was during the first centuries of the Christian era) the common philosophy of the West; and a demonstration of immortality which presupposes Plato's metaphysical system cannot claim to constitute a proof for the twentieth-century disbeliever.

Plato used the further argument that the only things that can suffer destruction are those that are composite, since to destroy something means to disintegrate it into its constituent parts. All material bodies are composite; the soul, however, is simple and therefore imperishable. This argument was adopted by Aquinas and has become standard in Roman Catholic theology, as in the following passage from the modern Catholic philosopher, Jacques Maritain:

> A spiritual soul cannot be corrupted, since it possesses no matter; it cannot be disintegrated, since it has no substantial parts; it cannot lose its individual unity, since it is self-subsisting, nor its internal energy, since it contains within itself all the sources of its energies. The human soul cannot die. Once it exists, it cannot disappear; it will necessarily exist for ever, endure without end. Thus, philosophic reason, put to work by a great metaphysician like Thomas Aquinas, is able to prove the immortality of the human soul in a demonstrative manner.[3]

This type of reasoning has been criticized on several grounds. Kant pointed out that although it is true that a simple substance cannot disintegrate, consciousness may nevertheless cease to exist through the diminution of its intensity to zero.[4] Modern psychology has also questioned the basic premise that the mind is a simple entity. It seems instead to be a structure of only relative unity, normally fairly stable and tightly integrated but capable under stress of various degrees of division and dissolution. This comment from psychology makes it clear that the assumption that the soul is a simple substance is not an empirical observation but a metaphysical theory. As such, it cannot provide the basis for a general proof of immortality.

[3]Jacques Maritain, *The Range of Reason* (London: Geoffrey Bles Ltd. and New York: Charles Scribner's Sons, 1953), p. 60.
[4]Kant, *Critique of Pure Reason, Transcendental Dialectic,* "Refutation of Mendeles-sohn's Proof of the Permanence of the Soul." [See selection 12.]

The body–soul distinction, first formulated as a philosophical doctrine in ancient Greece, was baptized into Christianity, ran through the medieval period, and entered the modern world with the public status of a self-evident truth when it was redefined in the seventeenth century by Descartes. Since World War II, however, the Cartesian mind–matter dualism, having been taken for granted for many centuries, has been strongly criticized by philosophers of the contemporary analytical school.[5] It is argued that the words that describe mental characteristics and operations—such as "intelligent," "thoughtful," "carefree," "happy," "calculating" and the like—apply in practice to types of human behavior and to behavioral dispositions. They refer to the empirical individual, the observable human being who is born and grows and acts and feels and dies, and not to the shadowy proceedings of a mysterious "ghost in the machine." Man is thus very much what he appears to be—a creature of flesh and blood, who behaves and is capable of behaving in a characteristic range of ways—rather than a nonphysical soul incomprehensibly interacting with a physical body.

As a result of this development much mid-twentieth-century philosophy has come to see man in the way he is seen in the biblical writings, not as an eternal soul temporarily attached to a mortal body, but as a form of finite, mortal, psychophysical life. Thus, the Old Testament scholar, J. Pedersen, says of the Hebrews that for them ". . . the body is the soul in its outward form."[6] This way of thinking has led to quite a different conception of death from that found in Plato and the neo-Platonic strand in European thought.

The Recreation of the Psycho-Physical Person

Only toward the end of the Old Testament period did after-life beliefs come to have any real importance in Judaism. Previously, Hebrew religious insight had focused so fully upon God's covenant with the nation, as an organism that continued through the centuries while successive generations lived and died, that the thought of a divine purpose for the individual, a purpose that transcended this present life, developed only when the breakdown of the nation as a political entity threw into prominence the individual and the problem of his personal destiny.

When a positive conviction arose of God's purpose holding the individual in being beyond the crisis of death, this conviction took the non-Platonic form of belief in the resurrection of the body. By the turn of the eras, this had become an article of faith for one Jewish sect, the

[5]Gilbert Ryle's *The Concept of Mind* (London: Hutchinson & Co., Ltd., 1949) is a classic statement of this critique.
[6]*Israel* (London: Oxford University Press, 1926), I, 170.

Pharisees, although it was still rejected as an innovation by the more conservative Sadducees.

The religious difference between the Platonic belief in the immortality of the soul, and the Judaic-Christian belief in the resurrection of the body is that the latter postulates a special divine act of re-creation. This produces a sense of utter dependence upon God in the hour of death, a feeling that is in accordance with the biblical understanding of man as having been formed out of "the dust of the earth,"[7] a product (as we say today) of the slow evolution of life from its lowly beginnings in the primeval slime. Hence, in the Jewish and Christian conception, death is something real and fearful. It is not thought to be like walking from one room to another, or taking off an old coat and putting on a new one. It means sheer unqualified extinction — passing out from the lighted circle of life into "death's dateless night." Only through the sovereign creative love of God can there be a new existence beyond the grave.

What does "the resurrection of the dead" mean? Saint Paul's discussion provides the basic Christian answer to this question.[8] His conception of the general resurrection (distinguished from the unique resurrection of Jesus) has nothing to do with the resuscitation of corpses in a cemetery. It concerns God's re-creation or reconstitution of the human psychophysical individual, not as the organism that has died but as a *soma pneumatikon*, a "spiritual body," inhabiting a spiritual world as the physical body inhabits our present physical world.

A major problem confronting any such doctrine is that of providing criteria of personal identity to link the earthly life and the resurrection life. Paul does not specifically consider this question, but one may, perhaps, develop this thought along lines such as the following.[9]

Suppose, first, that someone — John Smith — living in the USA were suddenly and inexplicably to disappear from before the eyes of his friends, and that at the same moment an exact replica of him were inexplicably to appear in India. The person who appears in India is exactly similar in both physical and mental characteristics to the person who disappeared in America. There is continuity of memory, complete similarity of bodily features including fingerprints, hair and eye coloration, and stomach contents, and also of beliefs, habits, emotions, and mental dispositions. Further, the "John Smith" replica thinks of himself as being the John Smith who disappeared in the USA. After all possible tests have been made and have proved positive, the factors leading his friends to accept "John Smith" as John Smith would surely prevail and would cause them to overlook even his mysterious transference from

[7]Genesis, 2:7; Psalm 103:14.

[8]I Corinthians 15.

[9]The following paragraphs are adapted, with permission, from a section of my article, "Theology and Verification," published in *Theology Today* (April, 1960) and reprinted in *The Existence of God* (New York: The Macmillan Company, 1964).

one continent to another, rather than treat "John Smith," with all John Smith's memories and other characteristics, as someone other than John Smith.

Suppose, second, that our John Smith, instead if inexplicably disappearing, dies, but that at the moment of his death a "John Smith" replica, again complete with memories and all other characteristics, appears in India. Even with the corpse on our hands we would, I think, still have to accept this "John Smith" as the John Smith who died. We would have to say that he had been miraculously re-created in another place.

Now suppose, third, that on John Smith's death the "John Smith" replica appears, not in India, but as a resurrection replica in a different world altogether, a resurrection world inhabited only by resurrected persons. This world occupies its own space distinct from that with which we are now familiar. That is to say, an object in the resurrection world is not situated at any distance or in any direction from the objects in our present world, although each object in either world is spatially related to every other object in the same world.

This supposition provides a model by which one may conceive of the divine re-creation of the embodied human personality. In this model, the element of the strange and the mysterious has been reduced to a minimum by following the view of some of the early Church Fathers that the resurrection body has the same shape as the physical body,[10] and ignoring Paul's own hint it may be as unlike the physical body as a full grain of wheat differs from the wheat seed.[11]

What is the basis for this Judaic-Christian belief in the divine re-creation or reconstitution of the human personality after death? There is, of course, an argument from authority, in that life after death is taught throughout the New Testament (although very rarely in the Old Testament). But, more basically, belief in the resurrection arises as a corollary of faith in the sovereign purpose of God, which is not restricted by death and which holds man in being beyond his natural mortality. In the words of Martin Luther, "Anyone with whom God speaks, whether in wrath or in mercy, the same is certainly immortal. The Person of God who speaks, and the Word, show that we are creatures with whom God wills to speak, right into eternity, and in an immortal manner."[12] In a similar vein it is argued that if it be God's plan to create finite persons to exist in fellowship with himself, then it contradicts both his own intention and his love for the creatures made in his image if he allows men to pass out of existence when his purpose for them remains largely unfulfilled.

---

[10]For example, Irenaeus, *Against Heresies*, Book II, Chap. 34, para. 1.
[11]I Corinthians, 15:37.
[12]Quoted by Emil Brunner, *Dogmatics*, II, 69.

It is this promised fulfillment of God's purpose for man, in which the full possibilities of human nature will be realized, that constitutes the "heaven" symbolized in the New Testament as a joyous banquet in which all and sundry rejoice together. As we saw when discussing the problem of evil, no theodicy can succeed without drawing into itself this eschatological[13] faith in an eternal, and therefore infinite, good which thus outweighs all the pains and sorrows that have been endured on the way to it.

Balancing the idea of heaven in Christian tradition is the idea of hell. This, too, is relevant to the problem of theodicy. For just as the reconciling of God's goodness and power with the fact of evil requires that out of the travail of history there shall come in the end an eternal good for man, so likewise it would seem to preclude man's eternal misery. The only kind of evil that is finally incompatible with God's unlimited power and love would be utterly pointless and wasted suffering, pain which is never redeemed and worked into the fulfilling of God's good purpose. Unending torment would constitute precisely such suffering; for being eternal, it could never lead to a good end beyond itself. Thus, hell as conceived by its enthusiasts, such as Augustine or Calvin, is a major part of the problem of evil! If hell is construed as eternal torment, the theological motive behind the idea is directly at variance with the urge to seek a theodicy. However, it is by no means clear that the doctrine of eternal punishment can claim a secure New Testament basis.[14] If, on the other hand, "hell" means a continuation of the purgatorial suffering often experienced in this life, and leading eventually to the high good of heaven, it no longer stands in conflict with the needs of theodicy. Again, the idea of hell may be deliteralized and valued as a *mythos*, as a powerful and pregnant symbol of the grave responsibility inherent in man's freedom in relation to his Maker.

Postscript (1988)

Terence Penelhum has discussed this concept of resurrection and suggests that although the identification of resurrection-world Mr X with the former earthly Mr X is possible it is not mandatory. He argues that in my cases number two and three (and probably number one also) it would be a matter for decision whether or not to make the identification. The general principle on which he is working is that there can only be an automatic and unquestionable identification when there is bodily continuity. As soon as this is lost, identity becomes a matter for decision, with arguments arising both for and against. He concludes

[13]From the Greek *eschaton*, end.
[14]The Greek word *aionios*, which is used in the New Testament and which is usually translated as "eternal" or "everlasting," can bear either this meaning or the more limited meaning of "for the aeon, or age."

that although "the identification of the former and the later persons in each of the three pictures is not absurd," yet "in situations like these it is a matter of decision whether to say that physical tests of identity reveal personal identity or very close similarity. We can, reasonably, decide for identity, but we do not have to. And this seems to leave the description of the future life in a state of chronic ambiguity." (*Survival and Disembodied Existence*, New York: Humanities Press, 1970, pp. 100–1).

I agree with Penelhum that these are indeed cases for decision. It is possible to rule that the John Smith in the resurrection world is the same person as the earthly John Smith, or that he is a different person. But that such a question is a matter for decision is not peculiar to this case. Ordinary straightforward everyday identity provides the paradigm that is, by definition, unproblematic; but all cases that diverge from it call for decision. This has recently been made very clear by Derek Parfit in his *Reasons and Persons*, Part III. Suppose, for example, that the cells of my brain are surgically replaced one by one, under local anaesthetic, with physically identical cells. My consciousness and other characteristics continue essentially unchanged throughout the operation. When only 1% of the cells have been replaced we shall probably all agree that I am the same person. But what do we say when 50% have been replaced? And what when 99% have been replaced? And what when they have all been replaced? Is this still me, or do I no longer exist and this is now a replica of me? Or again, consider the teletransporter (somewhat as in *Star Trek*) which scans my body, including the brain, records its state in complete detail, and then destroys it, the next moment forming an exact replica on Mars. The Mars replica's consciousness is continuous with that of the earthly me; but nevertheless is it *me* on Mars? Have I been teletransported, or has someone different been created in place of me? This is a question for decision. My contention is that the best decision, the one that best satisfies our intuitions and that gives rise to the fewest practical problems, is that the replica on Mars *is* me; and also that the John Smith "replica" in the resurrection world is John Smith.

25

PETER VAN INWAGEN

The Possibility of Resurrection

. . . SUPPOSE A CERTAIN monastery claims to have in its possession a manuscript written in St. Augustine's own hand. And suppose the monks of this monastery further claim that this manuscript was burned by Arians in the year 457. It would immediately occur to me to ask how *this* manuscript, the one I can touch, could be the very manuscript that was burned in 457. Suppose their answer to this question is that God miraculously recreated Augustine's manuscript in 458. I should respond to this answer as follows: the deed it describes seems quite impossible, even as an accomplishment of omnipotence. God certainly might have created a perfect duplicate of the original manuscript, but it would not be *that* one; its earliest moment of existence would have been after Augustine's death; it would never have known the impress of his hand; it would not have been a part of the furniture of the world when he was alive; and so on.

Now suppose our monks were to reply by simply asserting that the manuscript now in their possesion *did* know the impress of Augustine's hand; that it *was* a part of the furniture of the world when the Saint was alive; that when God recreated or restored it, He (as an indispensable component of accomplishing this task) saw to it that the object He produced had all these properties.

I confess I should not know what to make of this. I should have to tell

This article is reprinted from volume 9 (1978) of the *International Journal for Philosophy of Religion* by permission of the author and Kluwer Academic Publishers.

:he monks that I did not see how what they believed could *possibly* be true. They might of course reply that their belief is a mystery, that God had *some* way of restoring the lost manuscript, but that the procedure surpasses human understanding. Now I am sometimes willing to accept such answers; for example, in the case of the doctrine of the Trinity. But there are cases in which I would never accept such an answer. For example, if there were a religion that claimed that God had created two adjacent mountains without thereby bringing into existence an intermediate valley, I should regard any attempt to defend this doctrine as a "mystery" as so much whistle-talk. After all, I can hardly expect to be able to understand the Divine Nature; but I do understand mountains and valleys. And I understand manuscripts, too. I understand them sufficiently well to be quite confident that the monks' story is impossible. Still, I wish to be reasonable. I admit that one can be mistaken about conceptual truth and falsehood. I know from experience that a proposition that *seems* to force itself irresistibly upon the mind as a conceptual truth can turn out to be false. (If I had been alive in 1890, I should doubtless have regarded the Galilean Law of the Addition of Velocities and the Unrestricted Comprehension Principle in set theory as obvious conceptual truths.) Being reasonable, therefore, I am willing to listen to any *argument* the monks might have for the conclusion that what they believe is possible. Most arguments for the conclusion that a certain proposition is possibly true take the form of a story that (the arguer hopes) the person to whom the argument is addressed will accept as possible, and which (the arguer attempts to show) entails the proposition whose modal status is in question.

Can such a story be told about the manuscript of Augustine? Suppose one of the monks is, in a very loose sense, an Aristotelian. He tells the following story (a version of a very popular tale): "Augustine's manuscript consisted of a certain 'parcel' of matter upon which a certain form had been impressed. It ceased to exist when this parcel of matter was radically deformed. To recreate it, God needed only to collect the matter (in modern terms, the atoms) that once composed it and reimpress that form upon it (in modern terms, cause these atoms to stand to one another in the same spatial and chemical relationships they previously stood in)."

This story is defective. The manuscript God creates in the story is not the manuscript that was destroyed, since the various atoms that compose the tracings of ink on its surface occupy their present positions not as a result of Augustine's activity but of God's. Thus what we have is not a manuscript in Augustine's hand. (Strictly speaking, it is not even a *manuscript*.) (Compare the following conversation: "Is that the house of blocks your daughter built this morning?" "No, I built this one after I accidentally knocked hers down. I put all the blocks just where she did, though. Don't tell her.")

I think the philosophical problems that arise in connection with the burned manuscript of St. Augustine are very like the problems that arise in connection with the doctrine of the Resurrection. If a man should be totally destroyed, then it is very hard to see how any man who comes into existence thereafter could be the *same* man. And I say this not because I have no criterion of identity I can employ in such cases, but because I have a criterion of identity for men and it is, or *seems* to be, violated. And the popular quasi-Aristotelian story which is often supposed to establish the conceptual possibility of God's restoring to existence a man who has been totally destroyed does not lead me to think that I have got the wrong criterion or that I am misapplying the right one. The popular story, of course, is the story according to which God collects the atoms that once composed a certain man and restores them to the positions they occupied relative to one another when that man was alive; thereby (the story-teller contends) God restores the man himself. But this story, it seems to me, does not "work." The atoms of which I am composed occupy at each instant the positions they do because of the operations of certain processes within me (those processes that, taken collectively, constitute my being alive). Even when I become a corpse—provided I decay slowly, and am not, say, cremated—the atoms that compose me will occupy the positions relative to one another that they do occupy, *largely* because of the processes of life that *used* to go on within me: or this will be the case for at least some short period. Thus a former corpse in which the processes of life have been "started up again" may well be the very man who was once before alive, provided the processes of dissolution did not progress too far while he was a corpse. But if a man does not simply die but is totally destroyed (as in the case of cremation), then *he* can never be reconstituted, for the causal chain has been irrevocably broken. If God collects the atoms that used to constitute that man and "reassembles" them, they will occupy the positions relative to one another they occupy because of God's miracle and not because of the operation of the natural processes that, taken collectively, were the life of that man. (I should also be willing to defend the following theses: the thing such an action of God's would produce would not be a member of our species and would not speak a language or have memories of any sort, though, of course, he—or it—would *appear* to have these features.)

This much is analogous to the case of the burned manuscript. Possibly no one will find what I have said very convincing unless he thinks very much like me. Let me offer three arguments against an "Aristotelian" account of the Resurrection that have no analogues in the case of the manuscript, and which will perhaps be more convincing to the generality of philosophers. Arguments (a) and (b) are *ad homines,* directed against Christians who might be inclined towards the "Aristotelian" theory. Argument (c) attempts to show that the "Aristotelian" theory has an impossible consequence.

a. The atoms of which I am composed cannot be destroyed by burning or the natural processes of decay; but they *can* be destroyed, as can atomic nuclei and even subatomic particles. (Or so it would seem: the principles for identity through time for subatomic particles are very hazy; physical theory has little if anything to say on the subject.) If, in order to raise a man on the Day of Judgment, God had to collect the "building blocks"—atoms, neutrons, or what have you—of which that man had once been composed, then a wicked man could hope to escape God's wrath by seeing to it that all his "building blocks" were destroyed. But according to Christian theology, such a hope is senseless. Thus, unless the nature of the ultimate constituents of matter is different from what it appears to be, the "Aristotelian" theory is inimical to a central point of Christian theology.

b. The atoms (or what have you) of which I am composed may very well have been parts of other people at some time in the past. Thus, if the "Aristotelian" theory is true, there could be a problem on the day of resurrection about *who* is resurrected. In fact, if that theory were true, a wicked man who had read his Aquinas might hope to escape punishment in the age to come by becoming a lifelong cannibal. But again, the possibility of such a hope cannot be admitted by any Christian.

c. It is possible that none of the atoms that are now parts of me were parts of me when I was ten years old. It is therefore possible that God could collect all the atoms that were parts of me when I was ten, without destroying me, and restore them to the positions they occupied relative to one another in 1952. If the "Aristotelian" theory were correct, this action would be sufficient for the creation of a boy who could truly say, "I am Peter van Inwagen." In fact, he and I could stand facing one another and each say truly to the other, "I am you." But this is conceptually impossible, and, therefore, the "Aristotelian" theory is *not* correct.

No story other than our "Aristotelian" story about how it might be that a man who was totally destroyed could live again seems even superficially plausible. I conclude that my initial judgment is correct and that it is absolutely impossible, even as an accomplishment of God, that a man who has been burned to ashes or been eaten by worms should ever live again. What follows from this about the Christian hope of resurrection? Very little of any interest, I think. All that follows is that if Christianity is true, then what I earlier called "certain facts about the present age" are not facts.

It is part of the Christian faith that all men who share in the sin of Adam must die. What does it mean to say that I must die? Just this: that one day I shall be composed entirely of non-living matter; that is, I shall be a corpse. It is not part of the Christian faith that I must at any time be totally annihilated or disintegrate. (One might note that Christ, whose story is supposed to provide the archetype for the story of each man's resurrection, became a corpse but did not, even in His human nature, cease to exist.) It is of course true that men apparently cease to exist: those who are cremated, for example. But it contradicts nothing in the creeds to suppose that this is not what really happens, and that God preserves our corpses contrary to all appearance. . . . Perhaps at the moment of each man's death, God removes his corpse and replaces it with a simulacrum which is what is burned or rots. Or perhaps God is not quite so wholesale as this: perhaps He removes for "safekeeping" only the "core person" — the brain and central nervous system — or even some special part of it. These are details.

I take it that this story shows that the resurrection is a feat an almighty being *could* accomplish. I think this is the *only* way such a being could accomplish it. Perhaps I'm wrong, but that's of little importance. What *is* important is that God can accomplish it this way or some other. Of course one might wonder *why* God would go such lengths to make it look as if most people not only die but pass into complete nothingness. This is a difficult question. I think it can be given a plausible answer, but not apart from a discussion of the nature of religious belief. I will say just this. If corpses inexplicably disappeared no matter how carefully they were guarded, or inexplicably refused to decay and were miraculously resistant to the most persistent and ingenious attempts to destroy them, then we should be living in a world in which observable events that were *obviously* miraculous, *obviously* due to the intervention of a power beyond Nature, happened with monotonous regularity. In such a world we should all believe in the supernatural: its existence would be the best explanation for the observed phenomena. If Christianity is true, God wants us to believe in the supernatural. But experience shows us that, if there is a God, He does not do what He very well *could* do: provide us with a ceaseless torrent of public, undeniable evidence of a power outside the natural order. And perhaps it is not hard to think of good reasons for such a policy.

Author's Note (added in 1990)

If I were writing a paper on this topic today, I should not make the definite statement, "I think this is the *only* way such a being could accomplish it." I am now inclined to think that there may well be other ways, ways that I am unable even to form an idea of because I lack the conceptual resources to do so. An analogy would be this: a medieval philosopher, or even a nineteenth-century physicist, could have formed no idea of the mechanisms by which the sun shines, not because these mechanisms are a mystery that surpasses human understanding, but simply because some of the concepts needed to describe them were not available before the twentieth century.

26

DONALD MACKAY

✏

Computer Software and Life After Death

✏

MECHANISTIC BRAIN SCIENCE proceeds on the working assumption that every bodily event has a physical cause in the prior state of the central nervous system. Traditional moral and religious thought, on the other hand, has always presupposed that some at least of our behaviour is determined by our thinking and deciding. This apparent conflict has given rise to suggestions that unless some parts of our nervous system are found to be open to non-physical influences, brain science will effectively debunk all talk of man as a spiritual being, and oblige us to accept a purely materialistic view of our nature. Many people seem to expect a battle to be fought between religion and the neurosciences like that waged by some theologians in the nineteenth century against evolutionary biology.

How justified is this impression? It is true that the seventeenth-century French philosopher – mathematician René Descartes held that the mind or soul would be powerless to influence bodily action unless some part of the brain could act as a transmitter – receiver for its controlling signals. He considered that the pineal gland, in the middle of the head, was ideally suited to the purpose. "In man," he says,

> the brain is also acted on by the soul which has some power to change cerebral impressions just as those impressions in their turn have the power to arouse thoughts which do not depend on the will. . . . Only

This article originally appeared in the *Oxford Companion to the Mind* (ed. Richard Gregory, 1987) and is reprinted with the permission of Oxford University Press.

[figures of excitation] traced in spirits on the surface of [the pineal] gland, where the seat of imagination and common sense [the coming together of the senses] is . . . should be taken to be . . . the forms or images that the rational soul will consider directly when, being united to this machine, it will imagine or will sense any object.

In recent years the neurophysiologist Sir John Eccles and the philosopher Sir Karl Popper have advanced theories of the "interaction" of mind and brain, which, though they differ in important respects from that of Descartes, agree with him that the brain must be open to non-physical influences if mental activity is to be effective.

At first sight this might indeed seem obvious common sense; but a simple counter-example throws some doubt on the logic of the argument. We are nowadays accustomed to the idea that a computer can be set up to solve a mathematical equation. The mathematician means by this that the behaviour of the computer is *determined* by the equation he wants to solve; were it not so, it would be of no interest to him. On the other hand, if we were to ask a computer engineer to explain what is happening in the computer, he could easily demonstrate that every physical event in it was fully *determined* (same word) by the laws of physics as applied to the physical components. Any appearance of conflict here would be quite illusory. There is no need for a computer to be "open to non-physical influences" in order that its behaviour may be determined by a (non-physical) equation *as well as* by the laws of physics. The two "claims to determination" here are not mutually exclusive; rather they are *complementary*.

The analogy is of course a limited one. We (unlike our computing machines) are conscious agents. The data of our conscious experience have first priority among the facts about our world, since it is only through our conscious experience that we learn about anything else. Our consciousness is thus not a matter of convention (like the mathematical significance of the computer's activity) but a matter of fact which we would be lying to deny. Nevertheless the logical point still holds. If we think of our mental activity as "embodied" in our brain activity, in the sense in which the solving of an equation can be embodied in the workings of a computer, then there is a clear parallel sense in which our behaviour can be determined by that mental activity, regardless of the extent to which our brain activity is determined by physical laws. The two explanations, in mental and in physical terms, are not rivals but complementary.

Note that we are here thinking of mental activity as *embodied in* brain activity rather than *identical with* brain activity. The latter is a notion favoured by what is called "materialist monism," at the opposite extreme from the "interactionism" of Eccles and Popper. This would simply identify "mind" and "brain," and would go so far as to attribute "thinking" and other mental activities to the matter of which the brain is composed. The objection to this extreme view can be understood by once again considering the example of a computer. It is true that the solving of an equation is not a separate series of events, running in parallel with the physical happenings in the machine. It is rather the mathematical significance of one and the same series of events, whose physical aspect is well explained by the engineer. On the other hand it would be nonsensical on these grounds to identify equations with computers as physical objects, or to attribute mathematical properties (such as "convergence" or "being quadratic") to the physical matter in which the equation is embodied.

By the same token, even if we regard our thinking and deciding as a "mental" or "inner" aspect of one and the same (mysterious) activity that the neuroscientist can study from the outside as brain activity, this gives no rational grounds for taking the material aspect as more "real" than the mental, still less for identifying the two and speaking of thinking and deciding as attributes of matter. This would be a confusion of categories belonging to different logical levels, for which nothing in brain science offers any justification.

It might appear that thinking of our conscious experience as "embodied" in our brains would still be incompatible with the Christian concept of "life after death." What we have seen in the case of the computer, however, shows that there need be no conflict. The physical destruction of a computer is certainly the end of *that particular embodiment* of the equation it was solving. But it leaves entirely open the possibility that the same equation could be re-embodied, perhaps in a quite different medium, if the mathematician so desires. By the same logic, mechanistic brain science would seem to raise equally little objection to the hope of eternal life expressed in biblical Christian doctrine, with its characteristic emphasis on the "resurrection" (not to be confused with resuscitation) of the body. The destruction of our present embodiment sets no logical barrier to *our* being re-embodied, perhaps in a quite different medium, if our Creator so wishes.

27

PAUL AND LINDA BADHAM

∽

The Evidence From Psychical Research

∽

THE SIGNIFICANCE OF psychical research is that it appears to provide a substantial body of evidence which calls into question some of the presuppositions, or as C. D. Broad calls them, "the basic limiting principles"[1] of the naturalistic world-view normally taken for granted in modern societies. Broad gives four examples of such presuppositions, namely: that thoughts cannot pass from one person to another without some of the sensory equipment of both being called into play at some stage; that a person cannot have any non-inferential knowledge of the future; that our volitions can only *directly* influence the movements of our own bodies; and that when a person's body dies, his consciousness either ceases altogether, or at any rate, ceases to be able to manifest itself in any way to those still living on earth.[2] Our present concern is primarily with the first and last of these presuppositions, but in fact the validation of any claim to extra-sensory perception or influence would serve to undermine the authority of all such limiting principles.

In an earlier work I argued that there was now abundant evidence for believing both that telepathy is a reality, and that it cannot be incorporated into a materialist world-view.[3] I shall not rehearse the case here

1. C. D. Broad, *Religion, Philosophy and Psychical Research* (RKP, 1953) p. 1.
2. C. D. Broad, *Lectures on Psychical Research* (RKP, 1962) pp. 3–4.
3. Cf. P. Badham, *Christian Beliefs about Life after Death* (Macmillan, 1976) pp-113–24.

This selection is chapter 6 of *Immortality or Extinction?* (1982). It is reprinted with the permission of Macmillan (London).

except to say that, in the years since I completed the research for that book, the case for extra-sensory perception has grown much stronger.

First, Professor C. E. M. Hansel's "hatchet-job" on ESP (*ESP: A Scientific Evaluation*) has itself been demolished. Hansel's case depended on showing that the key experimenters might have rigged their results. To do this he relied on an analysis of their work made by Dr. G. R. Price for the journal *Science* in 1955.[4] But in January 1972 Dr. Price wrote a letter to that journal confessing that his earlier work had been based on inadequate information, was "highly unfair" to the experimenters he had falsely accused, and after seventeen years he wished to put the record straight.[5] So the work of Drs. Rhine and Soal has been "re-habilitated" and the rug pulled from under Hansel's feet.

Moreover in recent years a "consistent scorer" has at last been found who can be tested repeatedly in laboratory trials for ESP ability. For twelve years Pavel Stepanek delighted parapsychologists by choosing correctly between two targets approximately 55 per cent of the time instead of the 50 per cent success rate chance would have predicted.[6] This most utterly boring and, in a sense, trivial "ability" has the advantage of lending itself to statistical evaluation under controlled conditions in endlessly repeated experiments in research laboratories. And statisticians believe that this marginal improvement on chance when sustained over tens of thousands of tests during more than a decade demonstrates ESP beyond dispute.[7] So although in one sense the Stepanek experiments seem banal and pointless, and demonstrate no worthwhile or usable ESP qualities, they nevertheless are sufficient to call in question the naturalistic world-view under which such an inexplicable variation from chance ought not to happen.

However for the purposes of our present discussion earlier ESP research which concentrated on the phenomenon of telepathy is of greater significance. In my former book I discussed the evidence for telepathy emphasising Professor L. L. Vasiliev's *Experiments in Mental Suggestion* which involved the telepathic transmission of simple commands to hypnotised subjects.[8] I also stressed the number of eminent persons and societies who have participated in telepathic experiments.[9] Both the quality and quantity of evidence for this phenomenon now

4. C. E. M. Hansel, *ESP: A Scientific Evaluation* (Macgibbon and Kee, 1966) pp. 114–6, 234–5; cf. Badham, *Christian Beliefs*, p. 115.
5. Cited in E. D. Mitchell, *Psychic Exploration* (Putnam, 1974) p. 47.
6. J. G. Pratt, "In search of the consistent scorer," in J. Beloff, *New Directions in Parapsychology* (Elek, 1974) chapter 5.
7. C. Honorton and S. Krippner, "Hypnosis and ESP performance" in R. A. White, *Surveys in Parapsychology* (Scarecrow Press, 1976) p. 255. (Note Hansel, p. 173, for early criticism of Stepanek and compare with p. 257 of Honorton and Krippner and with Beloff's introduction to Pratt, "In search of the consistent scorer").
8. Badham, *Christian Beliefs*, p. 116; cf. L. L. Vasiliev, *Experiments in Mental Suggestion* (Galley Hull Press, 1963).
9. Badham, *Christian Beliefs*, pp. 114–15.

force its opponents into desperate straits to deny its reality. As Dr Welman comments: "If the only answer to the vast amount of solid experimental evidence is incompetence or fraud on a global scale by men with credentials equal to those of their scientific peers, working in academic surroundings, and whose work extends historically in time over at least three generations, then the adherents of this position would seem to have adopted a stance that is even more difficult to defend than the psi hypothesis."[10]

Yet to accept the reality of psychical phenomena requires a very considerable break with the prevailing monistic naturalism. Keith Campbell offered a large hostage to fortune when he declared, "if even a single example of para-normal phenomena is genuine, central state materialism is false";[11] for it seems that not one, but many examples are now available. And though at some stage in the future men may re-frame their naturalism to embrace psychic phenomena, this in no way alters the fact that such data are incompatible with present day materialism, and strongly favour a dualist account of man's being. Since the discrediting of a dualist doctrine of man makes most theories of a future life unthinkable,[12] the *prima facie* support for dualism which psychical phenomena provide is of great importance.[13]

But any vindication of psychical research in general and of telepathy in particular has an even greater potential significance for life after death research than just the support it gives to dualism. For if the evidence for telepathy shows that thoughts can, on occasion, pass from one mind to another without the use of the neural pathways of the brain, it provides a possible channel for communication between the living and the dead. For if mental life continues in being after bodily death the only way it could manifest itself to an embodied person would be through a telepathically communicated message. R. H. Thouless writes, "no other person can know directly whether x's consciousness has or has not continued after the death of x. It may however be verified indirectly in communications ostensibly from him, received after death. Such identification may be taken as indirect evidence that x's stream of consciousness is going on after his death."[14]

10. M. Welman in introduction to E. D. Mitchell, *Psychic Exploration* (Putnam's, 1974) p. 47.

11. K. Campbell, *Body and Mind* (Macmillan, 1970) p. 91.

12. For discussion of this point, cf. H. D. Lewis, *Persons and Life after Death* (Macmillan, 1978).

13. There are difficulties with this position. Identical twins appear to have the strongest sense of telepathic rapport which suggests that a material basis for telepathy might yet be found. And alleged evidence for telepathic rapport between man and animals (e.g. horses, dogs and dolphins) reminds us of the problem that even on a dualist account of mentality, it is hard to draw an absolute line between man and other animals. For evidence of animal ESP see J. Randall, "Biological Aspects of Psi," in J. Beloff, *New Directions in Parapsychology*, and in G. N. M. Tyrrell, *Apparitions* (Duckworth, 1953) pp. 76-7.

14. R. H. Thouless, "Theories about survival," *Journal of the Society for Psychical Research*, vol. 50, no. 779 (March 1979) p. 2.

But do the dead ever communicate with the living? Osis and Haraldsson write, "Spontaneous experiences of contact with the dead are surprisingly widespread. In a national opinion poll . . . twenty-seven per cent of the American population said that they had . . . Widows and widowers . . . reported encounters with their dead spouses twice as often—51 per cent."[15] Moreover such surveys have not been confined to the USA. Similar results have been obtained in mid-Wales, south-east London, Tokyo,[16] and also in Iceland.[17]

Nor can all claims to have had contact with a lost loved-one be written off as illusory, an hallucinatory consolation prize conjured up by the grieving mind to soothe its hurt. For there have been studies to show that in some cases, there are features of the hallucination which warrant its being counted as "veridical" rather than "delusionary" or "subjective." The classic survey is G. N. M. Tyrrell's analysis of an SPR "Census of Hallucinations," in which he was particularly interested in cases where "a person had a waking hallucination of a recognised friend at precisely the time when that friend died."[18] He builds up a case to show that the chances of having such an hallucination, if there were no direct link between its occurrence and the friend's death, is very much more remote than is the *de facto* incidence of such reports.[19] Moreover where details of the hallucination can be verified independently we have even stronger grounds for supposing that the hallucination is not solely the product of the percipient's mind. Myers, for example cites the case of "Archdeacon Farler, who twice during one night saw the dripping figure of a friend who, as it turned out, had drowned during the previous day."[20]

An even stronger case could be made if it could be shown that an apparition had communicated veridical information to the percipient which only the dead person had known. Cases like this have been cited since at least the time of St Augustine in the fourth century.[21] The classic modern case is that of James L. Chaffin who died in North Carolina in 1921, apparently leaving his farm and all his property to his third son under a will dated 1905. His wife and three other children received nothing. However four years after Chaffin's death, the inheriting son also died leaving the property to his widow and son. At this point Chaffin senior appeared to his second son, and told him where a later will could be found dividing the property equally between his four children. The will was found where indicated, proved in the law courts, and implemented. The son to whom the father appeared de-

15. K. Osis and E. Haraldsson, *At the Hour of Death* (Avon, 1977) pp. 13–14.
16. W. D. Rees, "The Hallucinations of Widowhood," BMJ, 4, (1971) pp. 37–41.
17. Osis and Haraldsson, *At the Hour of Death*, pp. 13–14.
18. G. N. M. Tyrrell, *Apparitions*, p. 19.
19. Ibid., p. 21.
20. F. W. H. Myers, *Human Personality* (Longmans, Green, 1909) p. 227.
21. Augustine's story may be read in Michael Perry, *The Resurrection of Man* (Mowbrays, 1975) pp. 21–2.

clared, "We never heard of the existence of the [later] will till the visitation from my father's spirit."[22] This case is often cited, partly because all the details of it were thoroughly investigated and recorded in a court of law, and partly because the importance of the matter to those concerned in it lends credibility to the second son's testimony of his earlier ignorance. In other circumstances one would have been more ready to interpret the apparition as a vivid calling to mind of a forgotten memory of the father in his life-time telling his son where his will could be found. But where what was at stake was the inheritance of the entire family estate it is hard to think of any son forgetting so vital a piece of information! This consideration lends support to the view that his apparition was verdical.

Some people believe that direct contact with the dead can be achieved through mediums who allegedly have the ability, while in a state of trance, to transmit messages between the dead and the living. Belief in the reality of such communications is the life-blood of the Spiritualist Churches, and mourners who consult mediums are often impressed by the convincing descriptions of departed loved-ones which the mediums give. On occasion a medium may also show knowledge of the deceased's former life. However, there are serious grounds for questioning the evidential value of these descriptions for detailed examination of these cases shows that acute observation, and intelligent guesswork would explain much of their success. Mrs. Leonard was one of the most famous mediums of all time, and her work brought great comfort to many sorrowing relatives of persons killed in the First World War, who believed that she was genuinely in touch with their lost sons, whom she described in detail. However although Mrs. Leonard's descriptions were thought to be so accurate, a research officer of the Society for Psychical Research found that at the first fourteen seances he listened in to, bereaved relatives were all given essentially the same description. Evidently Mrs. Leonard had "developed a model of the average young British officer as remembered by the average mother."[23] It transpired from further seances that equally stock descriptions of elderly ladies were available for those who disclaimed all personal knowledge of deceased soldiers. This investigation brings home just how little descriptive accuracy is needed to convince mourning relatives that the medium is indeed in touch with their dead.

The presentation of accurate knowledge of events in the life of the deceased cannot always be accounted for by intelligent guesswork cued by the responses of the inquiring relative. In some cases telepathic ability must be presumed to exist in order for this knowledge to be

22. For a full account of this case see, C. D. Broad, *Lectures on Physical Research*, pp. 137–9.
23. C. E. M. Hansel, *ESP: A Scientific Evaluation*, pp. 228–9.

acquired by the medium. But any knowledge of the deceased which the sitter found impressive would normally be present in the sitter's memory, albeit the unconscious memory, and telepathy from the sitter to the medium would seem to explain almost all cases.[24] Such an explanation would seem confirmed by the experience of Rosalind Heywood: "Soon after the Second World War I decided to test a medium by having an anonymous sitting with her and mentally asking the fate of a German friend, of whom I had heard nothing since 1938 . . . I feared he must have been killed. He soon appeared to turn up at the sitting, gave his Christian name and spoke through the medium in character and reminded me of various pleasant experiences which he had shared with my family . . . He then said he had been killed in grim circumstances. *After* the sitting I made inquiries about his fate . . . He was eventually traced to a neutral country . . . where he was happily living . . . Here, then it looks as if the medium . . . was building a picture of the German from my subconscious memories and my fears as to his fate."[25]

I suggest that an explanation of this sort would cover at least the vast majority of cases of alleged communication with the dead through mediums. The mode of contact between the living and the dead would have to have a channel at least akin to telepathy and virtually all cases of spontaneous telepathy or of spontaneous apparitions of the departed occur between people who are very close to each other either through family relationship or friendship. It must therefore always seem intrinsically improbable that a medium could on demand establish telepathic rapport with a deceased stranger, at least in comparison with the likelihood of the medium making such a contact with the person sitting with her. In almost all cases therefore the sitter, rather than the deceased, would seem the more likely source of the apparent information. It is therefore very hard to see how any reports arising from mediumship could ever be decisively established as coming from the dead rather than the living.

All the pioneers of psychical research came to realise this problem. For decades F. W. H. Myers, Henry Sidgwick and Edmund Gurney gathered data on apparitions and investigated the claims of mediums. Yet their findings seemed distinctly unsatisfying. It became clear to them that most mediums were charlatans and that even though some evidence from genuine mediums seemed quite strong one could never rule out the possibility of alternative explanations of how the mediums acquired their knowledge. Consequently all three of them died aware of the fact that their work had failed in its purpose of demonstrating the

24. Cf. M. Perry, *The Resurrection of Man*, pp. 28–9.
25. R. Heywood, "Death and Psychical Research," in A. Toynbee, *Man's Concern with Death* (Hodder, 1968) p. 233.

truth of the survival hypothesis to which they were committed. Myers
died in 1901 leaving the unfinished manuscript of his two-volume work
Human Personality and Its Survival of Bodily Death still awaiting the
key evidence. His son published the work in 1903 but Myers died
conscious that it did not answer his purpose.

At this point however the most dramatic evidence for life after death
begins to emerge. For Myers had resolved in advance that if he discovered that he *had* survived death after all, he would do all in his power to
provide his successors in the Society for Psychical Research with the
sort of evidence that would prove it. Mrs. A. W. Verrall, a lecturer in
Classics at Newnham College, Cambridge, decided to try and enable
Myers to demonstrate his survival of death through automatic writing
done by herself. Her daughter Helen also began automatic writing and
it was noticed that before she had seen her mother's scripts she was
referring to the same subjects. Almost simultaneously Mrs. Piper, a
medium in America began to "receive" messages purporting to come
from Myers and it was resolved that they would each send their scripts
independently to the Society for Psychical Research. A few years later,
Mrs. Fleming in India began to undertake automatic writing and she
too sent her scripts to the SPR. From 1905 onwards Gurney and Sidgwick supposedly began to join Myers in attempting to "prove" their
survival, and in due course about a dozen people were involved in
automatic writing which seemed to show that all three were attempting
to send messages. Later, it seemed that Dr. A. W. Verrall (d. 1912) and
Professor Henry Butcher (d. 1910) had also joined in the attempts to
send messages back to the living.[26]

To ease exposition, I will describe what happened as if Myers *et al.*
really were sending messages back, since to preface every remark with
"it seems as if" would be extremely tedious. I do not intend any
question-begging here—the case must be judged on its merits.

The way Myers and the others attempted to prove their survival was
to send incomplete and partial messages to a variety of respondents.
Taken in isolation each individual script does not make much sense, but
when scripts are related to one another they are discovered to fit
together like parts of a jigsaw, forming a coherent whole. According to
Tyrrell, "These communicators gave clearly and candidly the reason
for the cross-correspondences which they claimed to be producing.
They said that they were doing it because a single theme distributed
between various automatists none of whom knew what the others were
writing, would prove that a single independent mind or group of minds
was at the back of the whole phenomenon."[27]

26. This description of the cross-correspondences owes much to R. Heywood, *The
Sixth Sense* (Chatto and Windus, 1959) chapters 8 and 9.
27. G. N. M. Tyrrell, *The Personality of Man* (Penguin, 1948) pp. 145–6.

Most of the allusions were to recondite and obscure points of classical literature known to the alleged respondents who were all scholars in the forefront of classical study, while the medium (Mrs. Piper) and most of the automatists through whom they were working, knew no Latin or Greek and yet were writing out sentences in these languages derived from exceedingly rare and obscure authors they could never have known about. (It has been suggested that Mrs. Verrall, herself a classicist and the leading automatist, was the source of the messages. But they continued after her death in 1916, and none of the other automatists had anywhere near the requisite classical background.)

One of the more simple cross-correspondences may be given as an example. In April 1907 Mrs. Piper in three successive trances uttered words recorded as *Sanatos, Tanatos,* and then *Thanatos.* This final word was repeated four times. Meanwhile Mrs. Fleming[28] in India wrote automatically "Maurice, Morris, *Mors.* And with that the shadow of death fell upon him and his soul departed out of his limbs." Mrs. Verrall wrote automatically, "Warmed both hands before the fire of life. it fails and I am ready to depart . . . Come away come away . . . *Pallida mors aequo pede pauperum tabernas regumque turres [pulsat].*"[29]

"Thanatos," written by Mrs. Piper who knew no Greek, is the Greek for "death"; "mors," written by Mrs. Fleming who knew no Latin, is the Latin for "death"; and of the quotations cited by Mrs. Verrall, "Come away, come away *death*" is part of a song by Shakespeare, and the Latin sentence means "Pale death with equal foot strikes the huts of the poor and the towers of the rich." When the three scripts arrived at the SPR it became apparent that a single theme united the three messages received from Myers by the three different people, two of whom could not have understood what they wrote.

Most of the scripts are vastly more complex and require not only a profound knowledge of the classics but also an ability to solve crossword puzzles and to spot allusions and quotations. The obscurity of the messages is part of the scheme. After all, if a person writing automatically simple wrote, "this is from Myers, please tell everyone I have survived" the script would have no evidential value whatever. If however two uneducated people separately write half of an obscure Greek poem which after much research is tracked down to a very obscure book, and if it is later discovered that one of the alleged correspondents had lectured on this book, then the case begins to be evidential.

Thousands of scripts were received by the SPR over a thirty year period and the Second Earl Balfour and Mr. J. E. Piddington devoted most of their lives to working out the correspondences between

28. Mrs. Fleming is known in the earlier literature as Mrs. Holland, a pseudonym which she used because her relatives did not approve of her involvement with this research.

29. Cf. Tyrrell, *The Personality of Man,* p. 146.

them.[30] Almost all who have made a detailed study of the scripts find them convincing.

However, the fact that the correspondences need "working out" raises the possibility that the source of the interconnections between the script is the ingenuity of the living collator, rather than the mind of the departed respondent. The complexity, the allusive character and the sheer number of scripts raise this question. On the other hand, the principal scripts are available for investigation in the *Proceedings of the Society for Psychical Research*. Those who have studied them most clearly believe with W. H. Salter that "the scheme is really there, and not an invention of the perfervid ingenuity of the interpreters, for it rests on careful documentation, painstaking research into facts, and commonsense handling of symbols and allusions."[31] Moreover, those who actually knew the deceased, argue that the scripts are powerfully suggestive of the specific person whom they used to know. In some of the scripts they see the stamp of the alleged author's individuality all over them. For example, concerning one of Dr. Verrall's scripts, his "oldest and dearest friend," the Rev. M. A. Bayfield wrote, "All this is Verrall's manner to the life in animated conversation . . . when I first read the words . . . I received a series of little shocks, for the turns of speech are Verrall's . . . I could hear the very tones in which he would have spoken each sentence."[32]

Professor Gardner Murphy writes, "The initiative seems to come from the deceased . . . there seems to be a will to communicate . . . the autonomy, the purposiveness, the cogency and above all the individuality, of the source of the messages cannot be bypassed. This looks like communion with the deceased . . ." for the "messages were completely characteristic of themselves and of no others."[33] For Gardner Murphy, the cross-correspondences pose an insuperable problem. Committed as he himself is to the view that "the theoretical objections" to life after death "are so enormous that no empirical evidence could stand against them," yet he affirms belief that the cross-correspondences do actually supply solid empirical evidence for this impossibility! There seems to him to be no way around this impasse.[34] From such a quarter, this is no insubstantial endorsement of the quality of this material. And one is tempted to wonder whether Myers in death did indeed succeed in providing what Myers in life had been searching for—evidence for the human personality's survival of bodily death. . . .

30. Heywood, *The Sixth Sense*, p. 73.
31. W. H. Salter, *Zoar: The Evidence of Psychical Research Concerning Survival* (Sidgwick and Jackson, 1961), p. 207.
32. Cited in F. H. Saltmarsh, *The Evidence of Personal Survival from Cross-correspondences* (Bell, 1938) p. 141.
33. G. Murphy, *The Challenge of Psychical Research* (Harpers, 1961) p. 271.
34. Ibid., p. 273.

28

JOHN BELOFF

∽ℰ∽

Is There Anything Beyond Death?
A Parapsychologist's Summation

∽ℰ∽

BELIEF IN SOME form of an afterlife can be found in every society known to us and, from the evidence of ceremonial burial practices, appears to go back to remote prehistoric times. Various psychological explanations for this fact have been advanced. We are the only species that understands that we are doomed to die and the idea of a life beyond the grave may be our way of compensating for the menace of our mortality. Such an idea could derive substance from our dream life, because in our dreams we engage in diverse activities while our body lies prone on the bed. The fact, moreover, that it is impossible to *imagine* one's own total annihilation, because something must be left over to do the imagining, would reinforce such a belief. At a more sophisticated level, we have a tenacious belief in a just world. But, because the world we know contradicts this belief so flagrantly, it becomes necessary to invent a world where we do all ultimately receive our just deserts.

At present, however, belief in an afterlife has been severely eroded by the advance of science, which reveals that the mind is so intimately dependent on the proper functioning of the brain that the very idea that we could, in some form, survive the destruction of our brain now strikes many educated people as so farfetched as to be no longer worth considering. Where such belief remains strong is among religious fundamentalists. All three main monotheistic religions, Judaism, Christian-

*This essay was specially written for the present volume.

259

ity, and Islam, teach the immortality of the soul. This is especially the case with Christianity because of the central position of the Resurrection in Christian doctrine. The faithful are promised a share in Jesus' own triumph over death or, as Paul puts it, "For, as in Adam all die, so also in Christ shall all be made alive."[1]

It is not surprising, therefore, that where religion is still strong, belief in some form of survival is still prevalent. Thus, for the United States, Gallup[2] puts the figure at around 70 percent as compared with Western Europe where it is a mere 43 percent, while within Europe itself it is strongest in countries like Ireland, where religion still counts (64 percent) and weakest in a nonreligious country like Denmark (26 percent). It is true that some modern Christian theologians, influenced by certain trends in modern philosophy, have discarded the notion of survival as they have discarded the miraculous element in religion generally. The basic argument here is that personal identity becomes meaningless without the body as one's point of reference.[3] But the argument is questionable and, in my view, unsound. At all events, the reason so many people still cling to a belief in an afterlife is that this is what their religion teaches them.

In what follows, however, I want to discuss not *why* people believe in an afterlife, but, rather, what *empirical evidence* there is that would justify such a belief. This brings us into the domain of psychical research.

The Evidence

I shall start by listing four broad categories of evidence. The first and oldest type of evidence involves the alleged manifestations of deceased individuals or what, in common parlance, would be called "ghosts." The second, and by far the most important evidentially, consists of communications, ostensibly from deceased entities, as purveyed by a medium. The third, which only recently has become a target for serious research, consists of evidence that persons now alive have had a previous life on earth. And the fourth, which is even more recent as a topic for research, involves the so-called near-death experience. This means that someone, after being pronounced clinically dead, is resuscitated and is then able to recall some special kind of experience during this critical interval, usually of an otherworldly kind.

Let us now consider each of these in turn.

1. There can be no doubt that people do see apparitions and, in some instances, the apparition is so lifelike that it is only after it has disap-

---

1. I Corinthians, 15–22.
2. G. Gallup with W. Proctor, *Adventures in Immortality* (New York: McGraw-Hill, 1982).
3. Cf. Antony Flew, *Body, Mind and Death* (London: Macmillan, 1964).

peared that the observer realizes that it was not an actual person. There is also evidence of apparitions being seen collectively by more than one observer at the same time or by several observers independently on successive occasions. However, apart from the so-called crisis apparitions where it transpires that the person whose apparition was seen had just died, such manifestations rarely communicate any important information, contrary to what one might infer from fictional accounts of hauntings. It is more as if the places in question retain a sort of memory of their past inhabitants. One of the best attested ghost stories in the literature is that of the so-called Cheltenham ghost of 1885 in which the figure of a woman in black, thought to be a previous owner, was seen on many occasions by various witnesses. What makes that case more trustworthy than most is that the principal witness, Rosina Despard, the daughter of the current owner (known in the literature as Rose Morton), was then studying medicine and shortly afterwards become a practising doctor, a rare accomplishment for any woman of that period.[4]

2. The mediumistic evidence is the legacy of the spiritualist movement, which erupted quite suddenly in 1848, in Upper New York State, but then within the course of just a few years spread to almost every country in the world and penetrated almost every stratum of society, although, in England at least, it was strongest among the upper working class which had turned its back on the established churches.

The most common form of communication is a verbal message delivered by the medium in her own person. In the case of a so-called "trance medium," however, the supposed communicator or some "spirit control" would speak in the first person using the vocal mechanisms of the medium or, in the case of a written communication, the medium's hand. In the early part of this century there were a number of remarkable women who practised such "automatic writing." They were not mediums in the professional sense, but were educated women who happened to be devotees of psychical research.

If we go back to the early days of spiritualism we find that the phenomena were far more bizarre than anything we would nowadays associate with mediumship. The furniture and objects of the seance room would be moved about or even levitated, musical instruments would appear to play of their own accord, the spirit might speak directly from some point in the room rather than through the medium's mouth, or might inscribe a message direct onto a pad or slate without using the medium's hand. Most spectacular of all was the phenomenon

---

4. A good summary of this case may be found in Andrew MacKenzie, *The Unexplained* (London: Arthur Barker, 1966; New York: Abelard-Schuman, 1970). A curious aspect of the case is that her father, Captain Despard, was never able to see the apparition even when in a position where this would be expected.

of materialization in which the spirit would seek to manifest temporarily as a quasi-physical phantom, usually, it was thought, by extracting matter, or "ectoplasm," from the medium's body. A "full form materialization" was always a rarity but partial materializations of a hand or a face were common enough. I need hardly add that these florid physical phenomena were always the focus of intense suspicion and controversy. However, the whole fraught topic of physical mediumship, although of obvious interest to the student of the paranormal, is of dubious relevance to the question of survival; it was, in the end, the great trance mediums, such as Leonora Piper of Boston (whose career began in 1884 and who died in 1950), who provided the most telling evidence we have for the reality of survival. We shall come back to her later.

3. But now let us turn to the evidence from past lives. Here we are no longer concerned with existence in some other world but, rather, with another life in this world. It has, of course, always been a feature of Hindu and Buddhist teachings that we are destined to be repeatedly reborn in this world unless we can escape eventually from this cycle of rebirths and enter Nirvana. No doubt belief in reincarnation in the West derives originally from this source. When we turn to the evidence, however, we find that it is of two kinds: (a) the ostensible memories of a past life that can be elicited under hypnosis, and (b) memories of a previous life that are occasionally reported spontaneously by young children.

Hypnosis was already being used to elicit memories of past lives in the late nineteenth century and was part of a late flowering of the once powerful mesmeric movement. What gave it impetus in recent times, however, was the publication of the book by Morey Bernstein called *The Search for Bridey Murphy*.[5] It tells of a housewife in Colorado, known in the book as Ruth Simmons, who, under hypnosis, recalls her life in nineteenth-century Belfast. No one, however, has been able to trace the identity of this "Bridey Murphy" who, nevertheless, it must be said, showed a surprising knowledge of that place and period. In general, I would say that in all the cases reported so far that have been elicited under hypnosis, either there was no such person as the one described or the character in question could have been known to the informant who, in all innocence, might consciously be quite unaware of the source of this knowledge—a case of what psychologists call "cryptomnesia."

The evidence based on the ostensible memories of the very young is on a much sounder footing, thanks entirely to the heroic labors of one individual, Ian Stevenson, a professor of psychiatry at the University of Virginia who has made it his life's mission to investigate such cases. The

5. Morey Bernstein, *The Search for Bridey Murphy* (London: Hutchinson 1956).

University of Virginia Press has now brought out five volumes of his case studies, drawn mainly from Middle East, India, and Sri Lanka, plus a further volume written for the general reader.[6] Yet another volume in the offing deals with the so-called birthmark cases. In such cases the child's verbal account is reinforced by a physical sign. Thus, if the previous personality had died a violent death (and violence figures prominently in the reincarnation literature), the mortal wounds of the previous personality are reflected by birthmarks on the body of the child.

In an ideal Stevensonian case, events might proceed somewhat as follows. Almost as soon as the child learns to speak it would start talking about another family elsewhere to which it rightfully belonged. Its parents would, understandably, discourage such talk but, if the child persisted and could furnish enough particulars, attempts would be made to contact this other family, wherever they might be. If the case attracted enough attention it would come to the notice of one of Stevenson's informants in those parts and Stevenson himself would visit the family and try to be present when the two families first met. Then, acting through an interpreter, he would devise tests to see whether the child would duly recognize certain people, objects, or places connected with its previous personality. As the child grew up its memories of a former life would fade but certain traits of personality or certain habits or strong likes or dislikes would persist.

4. The final category we shall consider, the so-called near-death experience, is essentially a peculiarly vivid hallucination. That there should be any mental experiences whatsoever when a patient is presumed to be in a deep coma is itself an anomaly but it is the form it takes that makes it relevant to the survival problem. Typically, individuals report passing through the following four stages: (a) hovering some distance above their body while watching attempts being made to induce resuscitation; (b) entering a long dark tunnel from which they emerge into a dazzling and glorious pool of light; (c) finding themselves in some kind of paradise where they meet lost loved ones and beg to be allowed to stay but are told to go back as there is still important work to be done on earth; and (d) finding themselves back in their physical body gasping for breath.

Many who report such experiences say that they are no longer afraid of death. Sometimes the effect is like a religious conversion where the convert thereafter tries to be a better and more loving person. Estimates of the proportion of those who have reported such an experience

6. See *Twenty Cases Suggestive of Reincarnation 1966/1974; Cases of the Reincarnation Type:* vol. 1, *India 1975;* vol. 2, *Sri Lanka 1977;* vol. 3, *Lebanon and Turkey 1980;* vol. 4, *Thailand and Burma 1983.* For the general reader, see his *Children Who Remember Previous Lives: A Question of Reincarnation,* 1987. All these books are published by the University Press of Virginia in Charlottesville.

after being resuscitated vary from one researcher to another but some medical authorities have put it as high as 50 percent. Unlike the other categories we have mentioned, it is only quite recently that the near-death experience has attracted the attention of psychical researchers. An American medical man, Raymond Moody, published a short collection of such cases in 1975.[7] Much to his own and his publishers' astonishment, the book soon became a best-seller. Today a whole new field of near-death studies has developed, replete with its own professional organization, The International Association of Near Death Studies; its own specialist journal, *Anabiosis*; and many volumes of research findings by doctors, psychologists, and others.[8]

A related phenomenon is the so-called death-bed vision. In this case we are dealing with someone who is actually dying and who is aware of the situation and surroundings. But, here again, we find references to celestial visions and to seeing the figures of those who had gone before and have now come to take the dying one away. Sometimes a revered religious figure, such as Jesus, acts as the guide to the next world. In 1926, William Barrett, a physicist and pioneer psychical researcher, published a book called *Death-Bed Visions*, but current interest in the topic stems from a monograph, published in 1961 by the Parapsychology Foundation of New York, by their then research officer, Karlis Osis, called *Deathbed Observations by Physicians and Nurses*. Osis went on collecting death-bed visions but, eventually, he wanted to find out how far they were influenced by the subject's cultural background. He therefore collaborated with a doctor in India, working with a predominantly Hindu population, so as to be able to compare findings. The outcome was published in 1977.[9] Although there were some clear cultural differences in the kinds of visions described, there was also much in common. Thus, according to the authors: "When the dying see apparitions, they are nearly always experienced as messengers from a post-mortem mode of existence" whose function, in both cultures, is "to take the patient to the other world."

Evaluation

So what, you may ask, are we to conclude? It would be nice if one could say that those who had studied the evidence were convinced of survival whereas those who were ignorant dismissed it. But such is not the case. From the outset, psychical researchers have been deeply divided on this issue. This lack of consensus among the authorities is

7. Raymond Moody, *Life After Life* (New York: Bantam, 1975).

8. For the recent literature see G. Roberts and J. Owen, "The Near-Death Experience," *British Journal of Psychiatry* 153 (1988), 607–617, or K. Ring *Heading towards Omega: In Search of the Meaning of the Near-Death Experience* (New York: W. Morrow, 1984).

9. K. Osis and E. Haraldsson, *At the Hour of Death* (New York: Avon Books, 1977).

not surprising. The fact is that we can set no limit on the psychic powers of the living. Hence, if a medium makes statements purporting to come from the deceased, how can we be sure that she is not merely personifying information she has gleaned using her telepathic or clairvoyant powers? It is true that such a medium would be unlikely to succeed on any standard test for ESP but we know that paranormal phenomena are highly sensitive to situational factors and it may be that only the conditions of the seance suffice to bring out her special gifts.

A point on which nearly all the experts would agree is that the information supplied by a medium such as Mrs. Piper cannot be explained away along the lines we would use to dismiss the claims of some inferior medium, such as relying on generalities, fishing for hints from the sitter's reactions, trading on items of inside knowledge about the case in question, and so forth. The precautions which Richard Hodgson, her chief investigator, took with Mrs. Piper border on the paranoid. Not only were sitters always introduced anonymously and after she had gone into her trance but they even took up a position behind her where she could not have seen them had she had her eyes open. Furthermore, Hodgson had her tailed by private detectives who even opened her mail, yet nothing suspicious ever turned up. Yet Mrs. Piper continued to pour forth a profusion of pertinent statements, not only when she was on her home turf in Boston but when she traveled to England and was tested in Liverpool, Cambridge, and London. As she was paid a retaining fee throughout her career by the Society for Psychical Research in London, she was able to devote herself full time to research instead of giving private sittings.

Probably the person for whose postmortem existence we have the best evidence is a George Pellew. He was a Bostonian gentleman, a member of the newly founded American S.P.R., and, although he did not himself believe in survival, he once told his friend Hodgson that, should he die in the not too distant future and then discover that he *had* survived, he would earnestly attempt to communicate the fact through Mrs. Piper. In the event, he did die soon afterward in an accident at the early age of 33 and, lo and behold, a spirit-control calling itself George Pellew (in the literature, for the sake of anonymity, he is referred to as George Pelham, or just G. P.) duly began communicating through Mrs. Piper. Whenever she held a sitting at which any of his friends were present, he never failed to greet them whereas, conversely, he never greeted anyone he had not known during his lifetime. In this way he correctly recognized 30 out of a possible 150 individuals without making a single error.[10]

---

10. See Richard Hodgson, "A further Record of Observations of Certain Phenomena of Trance," *Proceedings of the Society for Psychical Research* 13 (1898), 284–588, esp. sect. 3, "History of the G.P. Communications," 295–335. Both the strengths and weaknesses of this case are considered at length by the author.

Then, after some years, he stopped communicating. It appears to be a general rule that it is the recent dead who communicate through mediums, especially when they have died prematurely, leaving unfinished business. This raises the question as to what happens to us eventually, assuming we do survive. Do we, in due course, progress to some higher spiritual sphere where we lose all interest in earthly matters? Does our private ego merge with some universal cosmic mind? We can but speculate. However, a case like that of G. P. reminds us that, perhaps, some people are better *able* to communicate than others, just as some are more psychically gifted than others. It also reminds us that survival does not necessarily imply eternal life.

Hodgson, himself, died soon afterward, also somewhat prematurely at the age of 50 while playing squash. He likewise soon began communicating through Mrs. Piper, and it then fell to his friend William James to study and evaluate the R.H. control. James, the great pioneer of psychology in America and a Harvard professor, was the one who had originally discovered Mrs. Piper. As befits an academic, he was very cautious about coming to a definite conclusion about anything, but he had no doubt whatever that the entranced Mrs. Piper knew more about Richard Hodgson than she could possibly have known in her waking life.[11]

Perhaps, the most sophisticated attempts to demonstrate survival that has ever been undertaken is one that began in 1901 with the death of Frederic Myers, perhaps the most important pioneer of psychical research and the author of *Human Personality and Its Survival of Bodily Death*. Messages purporting to come from the deceased Myers began being picked up in the automatic scripts of Margaret Verrall. Margaret Verrall was a lecturer in classics at Newnham College, Cambridge, the wife of Arthur Verrall, who was likewise a classicist at Cambridge. The plan the postmortem Myers had concocted was to involve a number of mediums who practised automatic writing. He would select themes from Greek and Latin literature and convey these piecemeal through different mediums so that only when pieced together would the complete story emerge. Hence the expression "cross-correspondences" for this whole episode. The mediums were widely scattered and were kept in ignorance of what was going on.[12]

There can be no doubt that the cross-correspondences remain one of the priceless treasures and enigmas of psychical research but they demand so much application, knowledge, and subtlety of interpretation

11. See William James, "Report on Mrs Piper's Hodgson-control," *Proceedings of the Society for Psychical Research* 23 (1909), 2–121. The *Proceedings* are the primary source for most of the Piper investigations. In this same issue, see Oliver Lodge, "Report on Some Trance Communications Received Chiefly through Mrs Piper," 127–285.
12. For a fuller discussion of the cross-correspondences, see selection 27 by Paul and Linda Badham in this volume.

that, considered as a proof of survival, they are surely misconceived. If only Myers could have given us a convincing picture of what it was like to survive the death of one's body, instead of playing these involved and erudite literary games, we might now be in a better position to solve this great mystery!

What of our other three categories? I do not think that the spontaneous cases can compare with the best of the mediumistic as evidence for survival, whatever intrinsic interest they may have. As regards reincarnation, the evidence from childhood memories, which Stevenson has so painstakingly amassed, presents a formidable puzzle but, although I do not doubt that something paranormal is going on, I have yet to be convinced that the survival of the previous personality is the only interpretation. It could be that, in some obscure way, the child tunes in to the life of this deceased person with whom it then inevitably identifies. It is, surely, significant that nearly all such cases occur in societies where belief in reincarnation is part of the ethos. In any case, from the fact that the occasional child remembers a past life it would not follow that we are all destined to be reborn.

As regards my fourth category, the near-death experience, to which survivalists nowadays pay so much attention, again, although I would concede that paranormal elements may be involved, it remains open to a wide variety of psychological and physiological interpretations — such as cerebral anoxia, or oxygen starvation of the brain, a self-defensive strategy in the face of imminent extinction, and so forth. At all events, it would be premature to interpret it at face value as affording a vision of the next world. All the same, there is no denying the effect such an experience has on those who have it. It may be worth mentioning in this context that the late Sir Alfred Ayer, a lifelong rationalist and sceptic, had a near-death experience while in the hospital when his heart stopped beating for all of four minutes. His experience was not typical or particularly blissful, nor did it convert him to a belief in survival. However, he was sufficiently impressed to write about it at length afterward in the press, where he admitted that it had made him rethink his attitude to survival, which, like so many modern philosophers, he had refused to take seriously.[13]

Conclusion

On the positive side we have a great many pointers to the possibility of there being something beyond death. On the negative side, there are too many unanswered questions for such indications to be entirely convincing. In particular, we have no very coherent account of what this other world would be like if that is where we go. Moreover, if *we*

13. Ayer's description of his experience is reprinted in selection 29 of this book.

survive death, what about animals? To make an exception for ourselves seems to fly in the face of evolutionary thinking, at the same time to suppose that animals, too, have souls capable of transcending the dissolution of their organism becomes ever more preposterous the further down we go on the phylogenetic scale. The best evidence, as I have indicated, derives from the practice of mediumship, yet most of that evidence is now very old. Today there simply are no mediums of the caliber of a Mrs. Piper and, even if there were, it would be most unlikely, given our mercenary society, that they would devote themselves to research rather than, like Doris Stokes, amass a fortune from public performances and popular books. Of course, evidence does not lose its cogency just because it is old but we are handicapped if we can only fall back on bygone examples.

Not being a materialist, I think it is foolish to underestimate the power of mind. Accordingly, I remain open to persuasion about the possibility of the self surviving in a form other than its present embodiment. I regret only that my conclusions should have to be so guarded and that I cannot offer the reader greater hope or consolation.

29

A. J. AYER

What I Saw When I Was Dead

MY FIRST ATTACK of pneumonia occurred in the United States. I was in hospital for ten days in New York, after which the doctors said that I was well enough to leave. A final X-ray, however, which I underwent on the last morning, revealed that one of my lungs was not yet free from infection. This caused the most sympathetic of my doctors to suggest that it would be good for me to spend a few more days in hospital. I respected his opinion but since I was already dressed and psychologically disposed to put my illness behind me, I decided to take the risk. I spent the next few days in my stepdaughter's apartment, and then made arrangements to fly back to England.

When I arrived I believed myself to be cured and incontinently plunged into an even more hectic social round than that to which I had become habituated before I went to America. Retribution struck me on Sunday, May 30. I had gone out to lunch, had a great deal to eat and drink and chattered incessantly. That evening I had a relapse. I could eat almost none of the food which a friend had brought to cook in my house.

On the next day, which was a bank holiday, I had a longstanding engagement to lunch at the Savoy with a friend who was very anxious for me to meet her son. I would have put them off if I could, but my friend lives in Exeter and I had no idea how to reach her in London. So I

*This article appeared in the August 28, 1988, issue of the *Sunday Telegraph*. It is reprinted with the permission of the Sunday Telegraph Ltd.

took a taxi to the Savoy and just managed to stagger into the lobby. I could eat hardly any of the delicious grilled sole that I ordered, but forced myself to keep up my end of the conversation. I left early and took a taxi home.

That evening I felt still worse. Once more I could eat almost none of the dinner another friend had brought me. Indeed she was so alarmed by my weakness that she stayed overnight. When I was no better the next morning, she telephoned to my general practitioner and to my elder son Julian. The doctor did little more than promise to try to get in touch with the specialist, but Julian, who is unobtrusively very efficient, immediately rang for an ambulance. The ambulance came quickly with two strong attendants, and yet another friend, who had called opportunely to pick up a key, accompanied it and me to University College Hospital.

I remember very little of what happened from then on. I was taken to a room in the private wing, which had been reserved for me by a specialist, who had a consulting room on the same floor. After being X-rayed and subjected to a number of tests which proved beyond question that I was suffering from pneumonia, I was moved into intensive care in the main wing of the hospital.

Fortunately for me, the young doctor who was primarily responsible for me had been an undergraduate at New College, Oxford, while I was a Fellow. This made him extremely anxious to see that I recovered; almost too much so, in fact he was so much in awe of me that he forbade me to be disturbed at night, even when the experienced sister and nurse believed it to be necessary.

Under his care and theirs I made such good progress that I expected to be moved out of intensive care and back into the private wing within a week. My disappointment was my own fault. I did not attempt to eat the hospital food. My family and friends supplied all the food I needed. I am particularly fond of smoked salmon, and one evening I carelessly tossed a slice of it into my throat. It went down the wrong way and almost immediately the graph recording my heart beats plummeted. The ward sister rushed to the rescue, but she was unable to prevent my heart from stopping. She and the doctor subsequently told me that I died in this sense for four minutes, and I have no reason to disbelieve them.

The doctor alarmed my son Nicholas, who had flown from New York to be at my bedside, by saying it was not probable that I should recover and, moreover, that if I did recover physically it was not probable that my mental powers would be restored. The nurses were more optimistic and Nicholas sensibly chose to believe them.

I have no recollection of anything that was done to me at that time. Friends have told me that I was festooned with tubes but I have never learned how many of them there were or, with one exception, what purpose they served. I do not remember having a tube inserted in my throat to bring up the quantity of phlegm which had lodged in my lungs. I was not even aware of my numerous visitors, so many of them, in fact, that the sister had to set a quota. I know that the doctors and nurses were surprised by the speed of my recovery and that when I started speaking, the specialist expressed astonishment that anyone with so little oxygen in his lungs should be so lucid.

My first recorded utterance, which convinced those who heard it that I had not lost my wits, was the exclamation: "You are all mad." I am not sure how this should be interpreted. It is possible that I took my audience to be Christians and was telling them that I had not discovered anything "on the other side." It is also possible that I took them to be sceptics and was implying that I had discovered something. I think the former is more probable as in the latter case I should properly have exclaimed "We are all mad." All the same, I cannot be sure.

The earliest remarks of which I have any cognisance, apart from my first exclamation, were made several hours after my return to life. They were addressed to a French woman with whom I had been friends for over fifteen years. I woke to find her seated by my bedside and starting talking to her in French as soon as I recognised her. My French is fluent and I spoke rapidly, approximately as follows: "Did you know that I was dead? The first time that I tried to cross the river I was frustrated, but my second attempt succeeded. It was most extraordinary, my thoughts became persons."

The content of those remarks suggests that I have not wholly put my classical education behind me. In Greek mythology the souls of the dead, now only shadowly embodied, were obliged to cross the river Styx in order to reach Hades, after paying an obol to the ferryman, Charon. I may also have been reminded of my favourite philosopher, David Hume, who during his last illness, a "disorder of the bowels," imagined that Charon, growing impatient, was calling him "a lazy loitering rogue." With his usual politeness, Hume replied that he saw without regret his death approaching and that he was making no effort to postpone it. This is one of the rare occasions on which I have failed to follow Hume. Clearly I had made an effort to prolong my life.

The only memory that I have of an experience closely encompassing my death, is very vivid. I was confronted by a red light, exceedingly bright, and also very painful even when I turned away from it. I was aware that this light was responsible for the government of the universe. Among its ministers were two creatures who had been put in charge of space. These ministers periodically inspected space and had recently carried out such an inspection. They had, however, failed to do their work properly, with the result that space, like a badly fitted jigsaw puzzle, was slightly out of joint.

A further consequence was that the laws of nature had ceased to function as they should. I felt that it was up to me to put things right. I also had the motive of finding a way to extinguish the painful light. I assumed that it was signalling that space was awry and that it would switch itself off when order was restored. Unfortunately, I had no idea where the guardians of space had gone and feared that even if I found them I should not be allowed to communicate with them. It then occurred to me that whereas, until the present century, physicists accepted the Newtonian severance of space and time, it had become customary, since the vindication of Einstein's general theory of relativity, to treat space-time as a single whole. Accordingly I thought that I could cure space by operating upon time.

I was vaguely aware that the ministers who had been given charge of time were in my neighbourbood and I proceeded to hail them. I was again frustrated. Either they did not hear me, or they chose to ignore me, or they did not understand me. I then hit upon the expedient of walking up and down, waving my watch, in the hope of drawing their attention not to my watch itself but to the time which it measured. This elicited no response. I became more and more desperate, until the experience suddenly came to an end.

This experience could well have been delusive. A slight indication that it might have been veridical has been supplied by my French friend, or rather by her mother, who also underwent a heart arrest many years ago. When her daughter asked her what it had been like, she replied that all that she remembered was that she must stay close to the red light.

On the face of it, these experiences, on the assumption that the last one was veridical, are rather strong evidence that death does not put an end to consciousness. Does it follow that there is a future life? Not necessarily. The trouble is that there are different criteria for being dead, which are indeed logically compatible, but may not always be satisfied together.

In this instance, I am given to understand that the arrest of the heart does not entail, either logically or causally, the arrest of the brain. In view of the very strong evidence in favour of the dependence of thoughts upon the brain, the most probable hypothesis is that my brain continued to function although my heart had stopped.

If I had acquired good reason to believe in a future life, it would have applied not only to myself. Admittedly, the philosophical problems of justifying one's confident belief in the existence and contents of other minds has not yet been satisfactorily solved. Even so, with the possible exception of Fichte—who complained that the world was his idea but may not have meant it literally—no philosopher has acquiesced in solipsism, no philosopher has seriously asserted that of all the objects in the universe, he alone was conscious. Moreover it is commonly taken for granted, not only by philosophers, that the minds of others bear a sufficiently close analogy to one's own. Consequently, if I had been vouchsafed a reasonable expectation of a future life, other human beings could expect one too.

Let us grant, for the sake of argument, that we could have future lives. What form could they take? The easiest answer would consist in the prolongation of our experiences, without any physical attachment. This is the theory that should appeal to radical empiricists. It is, indeed, consistent with the concept of personal identity which was adopted both by Hume and by William James, according to which one's identity consists, not in the possession of an enduring soul but in the sequence of one's experiences, guaranteed by memory. They did not apply their theory to a future life, in which Hume at any rate disbelieved.

For those who are attracted by this theory, as I am, the main problem, which Hume admitted that he was unable to solve, is to discover the relation, or relations, which have to be held between experiences for them to belong to one and the same self. William James thought that he had found the answers with his relations of the felt togetherness and continuity of our thoughts and sensations, coupled with memory, in order to unite experiences that are separated in time. But while memory is undoubtedly necessary, it can be shown that it is not wholly sufficient.

I myself carried out a thorough examination and development of the theory in my book *The Origins of Pragmatism*. I was reluctantly forced to conclude that I could not account for personal identity without falling back on the identity, through time, of one or more bodies that the person might successively occupy. Even then, I was unable to give a satisfactory account of the way in which a series of experiences is tied to a particular body at any given time.

The admission that personal identity through time requires the identity of a body is a surprising feature of Christianity. I call it surprising because it seems to me that Christians are apt to forget that the resurrection of the body is an element in their creed. The question of how bodily identity is sustained over intervals of time is not so difficult. The answer might consist in postulating a reunion of the same atoms, perhaps in there being no more than a strong physical resemblance, possibly fortified by a similarity of behaviour.

A prevalent fallacy is the assumption that a proof of an afterlife would also be a proof of the existence of a deity. This is far from being the case. If, as I hold, there is no good reason to believe that a god either created or presides over this world, there is equally no good reason to believe that a god created or presides over the next world, on the unlikely supposition that such a thing exists. It is conceivable that one's experiences in the next world, if there are any, will supply evidence of god's existence, but we have no right to presume on such evidence, when we have not had the relevant experiences.

It is worth remarking, in this connection, that the two most important

Cambridge philosophers in this century, J. E. McTaggart and C. D. Broad, who have believed, in McTaggart's case that he would certainly survive his death, in Broad's that there was about a fifty-per-cent probability that he would, were both of them atheists. McTaggart derived his certainty from his metaphysics, which implied that what we confusedly perceive as material objects, in some case housing minds, are really souls, eternally viewing one another with something of the order of love.

The less fanciful Broad was impressed by the findings of psychical research. He was certainly too intelligent to think that the superior performances of a few persons in the game of guessing unseen cards, which he painstakingly proved to be statistically significant, has any bearing on the likelihood of a future life. He must therefore have been persuaded by the testimony of mediums. He was surely aware that most mediums have been shown to be frauds, but he was convinced that some have not been. Not that this made him optimistic. He took the view that this world was very nasty and that there was a fair chance that the next world, if it existed, was even nastier. Consequently, he had no compelling desire to survive. He just thought that there was an even chance of his doing so. One of his better epigrams was that if one went by the reports of mediums, life in the next world was like a perpetual bump supper at a Welsh university.

If Broad was an atheist, my friend Dr Alfred Ewing was not. Ewing, who considered Broad to be a better philosopher than Wittgenstein, was naif, unworldly even by academic standards, intellectually shrewd, unswervingly honest and a devout Christian. Once, to tease him, I said: "Tell me, Alfred, what do you most look forward to in the next world?" He replied immediately: "God will tell me whether there are *a priori* propositions." It is a wry comment on the strange character of our subject that this answer should be so funny.

My excuse for repeating this story is that such philosophical problems as the question whether the propositions of logic and pure mathematics are deductively analytic or factually synthetic, and, if they are analytic, whether they are true by convention, are not to be solved by acquiring more information. What is needed is that we succeed in obtaining a clearer view of what the problems involve. One might hope to achieve this in a future life, but really we have no good reason to believe that our intellects will be any sharper in the next world, if there is one, than they are in this. A god, if one exists, might make them so, but this is not something that even the most enthusiastic deist can count on.

The only philosophical problem that our finding ourselves landed on a future life might clarify would be that of the relation between mind and body, if our future lives consisted, not in the resurrection of our bodies, but in the prolongation of the series of our present experiences.

We should then be witnessing the triumph of dualism, which Descartes thought that he had established. If our lives consisted in an extended series of experiences, we should still have no good reason to regard ourselves as spiritual substances.

So there it is. My recent experiences have slightly weakened my conviction that my genuine death, which is due fairly soon, will be the end of me, though I continue to hope that it will be. They have not weakened my conviction that there is no god. I trust that my remaining an atheist will allay the anxieties of my fellow supporters of the British Humanist Association, the Rationalist Press Association and the South Place Ethical Society.

Later Developments

Ayer's article was published in the United States by the National Review *on October 14, 1988. It was featured on the cover as "A. J. Ayer's Intimations of Immortality." Its subtitle — "What Happens When the World's Most Eminent Atheist Dies" — was no more misleading than the title chosen by the* Sunday Telegraph. *Scientists interviewed by the* Manchester Guardian *were skeptical about any "intimations of immortality." According to Colin Blakemore, professor of physiology at Cambridge, "What happened to Freddie Ayer was that lack of oxygen disordered the interpretative methods of his cortex, which led to hallucinations." Sir Herman Bondi, a distinguished physicist who is master of Churchill College, Cambridge, and president of the Rationalist Press Association, is quoted as "totally unimpressed," adding that "it is difficult enough to be wise when one is well." Ayer himself published what amounted to a retraction in the* Spectator *of October 15, 1988, entitled "Postscript to a Postmortem." He now asserted that his experience had not weakened and "never did weaken" his conviction that death means annihilation. "I said in my article," he went on, "that the most probable explanation of my experiences was that my brain had not ceased to function during the four minutes of my heart arrest. I have since been told, rightly or wrongly, that it would not have functioned on its own for any longer period without being damaged. I thought it so obvious that the persistence of my brain was the most probable explanation that I did not bother to stress it. I stress it now. No other hypothesis comes anywhere near to superseding it."*

30

C. D. BROAD

On Survival Without a Body

AS REGARDS UNEMBODIED survival, I would make the following remarks. The few Western philosophers in modern times who have troubled to discuss the question of survival seem generally to have taken for granted that the survival of a human personality would be equivalent to its persistence without any kind of physical organism. Some of them have proceeded to argue that the attempt to conceive a personal stream of experience, without a body as organ and centre of perception and action and as the source of a persistent background of bodily feeling, is an attempt to suppose something self-contradictory in principle or inconceivable when one comes down to detail. They have concluded that it is simply meaningless to talk of a human personality surviving the death of its body. Their opponents in this matter have striven to show that the supposition of a personal stream of experience, in the absence of any kind of associated organism, is self-consistent in principle and conceivable in detail. They have concluded that it is possible, at any rate in the sense of conceivable without inconsistency, that a human personality should survive the death of the body with which it has been associated.

Now I have two comments to make on this. One concerns both parties, and the other concerns the second group of them.

(a) Of all the hundreds of millions of human beings, in every age and clime, who have believed (or have talked or acted as if they believed) in

*This selection is from the epilogue of Broad's *Lectures on Psychical Research* (1962). It is reprinted with the permission of Routledge Publishers.

human survival, hardly any have believed in *unembodied* survival. Hindus and Buddhists, e.g., believe in reincarnation in an ordinary human or animal body or occasionally in the non-physical body of some non-human rational being, such as a god or a demon. Christians (if they know their own business, which is not too common nowadays) believe in some kind of (unembodied?) persistence up to the General Resurrection, and in survival thereafter with a peculiar kind of supernatural body (St Paul's πνευματικὸν σῶμα) correlated in some intimate and unique way with the animal body (ψυχικὸν σῶμα), which has died and rotted away. Nor are such views confined to babes and sucklings. Spinoza, e.g., certainly believed in human immortality; and he cannot possibly have believed, on his general principles, in the existence of a mind without some kind of correlated bodily organism. Leibniz said explicitly that, if *per impossibile* a surviving mind were to be without an organism, it would be a "deserter from the general order." It seems to me rather futile for a modern philosopher to discuss the possibility of human survival on an assumption which would have been unhesitatingly rejected by almost everyone, lay or learned, who has ever claimed seriously to believe in it.

(*b*) Suppose it could be shown that it is not inconceivable, either in principle or in detail, that there should be a personal stream of experience not associated with any kind of bodily organism. That would by no means be equivalent to showing that it is not inconceivable that the personality of a human being should survive, in an unembodied state, the death of his physical body. For such survival would require that a certain one such *unembodied* personal stream of experience stands to a certain one *embodied* personal stream of experience, associated with a human body now dead, in those peculiar and intimate relations which must hold if both are to count as successive segments of the stream of experience of one and the same person. Is it conceivable that the requisite continuity and similarity should hold between two successive strands of personal experience so radically different in nature as those two would seem *prima facie* to be? Granted that there might conceivably be unembodied persons, and that there certainly have been embodied persons who have died, it might still be quite inconceivable or overwhelmingly improbable that any of the former should be personally identical with any of the latter.

Speaking for myself, I find it more and more difficult, the more I try to go into concrete detail, to conceive of a person so unlike the only ones that I know anything about, and from whom my whole notion of personality is necessarily derived, as an unembodied person would inevitably be. He would have to perceive foreign things and events (if he did so at all) in some kind of clairvoyant way, without using special sense-organs, such as eyes and ears, and experiencing special sensations through their being stimulated from without. He would have to act upon foreign things and persons (if he did so at all) in some kind of telekinetic way, without using limbs and without the characteristic feelings of stress, strain, etc., that come from the skin, the joints, and the muscles, when we use our limbs. He would have to communicate with other persons (if he did so at all) in some kind of telepathic way, without using vocal organs and emitting articulate sounds; and his conversations with himself (if he had any) would have to be conducted purely in imagery, without any help from incipient movements in the vocal organs and the sensations to which they give rise in persons like ourselves.

All this is "conceivable," so long as one keeps it in the abstract; but, when I try to think "what it would be like" in concrete detail, I find that I have no clear and definite ideas. That incapacity of mine, even if it should be shared by most others, does not of course set any limit to what may in fact exist and happen in nature. But it does set a very definite limit to profitable speculation on these matters. And, if I cannot clearly conceive what it would be like to be an unembodied person, I find it almost incredible that the experiences of such a person (if such there could be) could be sufficiently continuous with those had in his lifetime by any deceased human being as to constitute together the experiences of *one and the same person.*

31

JOHN HOSPERS

⤳

Is the Notion of Disembodied Existence Intelligible?

⤳

. . . HUME ALLEGED THAT if two things, or qualities, A and B, always occur together, they can be imagined to occur separately (the one without the other), and it is a matter of empirical inquiry whether they do. As a general principle one could question this; can color occur without extension? can color occur without shape? But let us ask, in the present context, whether consciousness can occur without a body, even though all the instances of consciousness we are familiar with are related (causally or otherwise) to bodies.

Try to imagine yourself without a body. Imagine thinking thoughts, having feelings and memories, and even having experiences of seeing, hearing, and so on *without* the sense organs that in this life are the empirically necessary conditions of having these experiences. Having eyes is one thing; seeing colors is another. Isn't it conceivable — whether or not it occurs in fact — to see colors even though you lack the sense organs which in your present life are the *means* by which you see colors?

You go to bed one night and go to sleep, then awaken some hours later and see the sunlight streaming in the window, the clock pointing to eight, the mirror at the other side of the room; and you wonder what you will do today. Still in the bed, you look down where your body should be, but you do not see your body — the bedsheets and blankets

*This selection is a section of chapter 6 of *An Introduction to Philosophical Analysis* (3d ed., 1988). It is reprinted with the permission of Prentice-Hall.

are there, but there is no body under them. Startled, you look in the mirror, and see the reflection of the bed, the pillows, and blankets, and so on—but no *you*; at least there is no reflection of your face or body in the mirror. "Have I become invisible?" you ask yourself. Thinking of H. G. Wells' invisible man, who could be touched but not seen, you try to touch yourself; but there is nothing there to be touched. A person coming into the room would be unable to see or touch you, or to hear you either; a person could run his hands over the entire bed without ever coming in contact with a body. You are now thoroughly alarmed at the idea that no one will know you exist. You try to walk forward to the mirror, but you have no feet. You might find the objects near the mirror increasing in apparent size, just *as if* you were walking toward the mirror. These experiences might occur as before, the only difference being that there is no body that can move or be seen or touched.

Now, have we succeeded in at least imagining existence without a body? Not quite. There are implicit references to body even in the above description. You see—with eyes?—*no*, you have no eyes, since you have no body. But let that pass for the moment; you have experiences similar to what you *would* have if you had eyes to see with. But how can you *look* toward the foot of the bed or toward the mirror? Isn't looking an activity that requires having a body? How can you look in one direction or another if you have no head to turn? And this isn't all; we said that you can't touch your body because there is no body there; how did you discover this? Did you reach out with your fingers to touch the bed? But you have no fingers, since you have no body. What would you touch (or try to touch) *with*? You move, or seem to move, toward the mirror—but what is it that moves or seems to move? Not your body, for again you have none. All the same, things seem to get larger in front of you and smaller behind you, just as if you were moving. In front of and behind what? Your body? Your body seems to be involved in every activity we try to describe even though we have tried to imagine existing without it.

Every step along the way is riddled with difficulties. It is not just that we are accustomed to think of people as having bodies and can't get out of the habit. This makes things more difficult, but it is only part of the problem. The fact is that you can't imagine doing things like looking in a different direction without turning your head, which is usually the result of a decision to do this—and of course you can't turn your head if you have no head to turn. If you *decide* to turn your head, you can't carry out this decision in the absence of a head, and so on. There seems to be a whole nest of difficulties—not merely technical but logical—constantly embedded in the attempted description.

> There is no necessary, conceptual, connection between the experience we call "seeing" and the processes that physiologists tell us happen in the eye and brain; the statement "James can still see,

although his optic centers are destroyed," is very unlikely in inductive grounds but perfectly intelligible—after all, people used the word "see" long before they had any idea of things happening in the optic centers of the brain. It therefore appears to be clearly conceivable that seeing and other "sensuous" experiences might go on continuously even after death of the organism with which they are now associated, and that the inductive reasons for doubting whether this ever happens might be outweighed by the evidence of Psychical Research.

I think it is an important conceptual inquiry to consider whether *really* disembodied seeing, hearing, pain, hunger, emotion, etc., are so clearly intelligible as is supposed in this common philosophical point of view. . . .

"The verb 'to see' has its meaning for me because I *do* see—I have that experience!" Nonsense. As well suppose that I can come to know what a minus quantity is by setting out to lose weight. What shows a man to have the concept *seeing* is not merely that he sees, but that he can take an intelligent part in our everyday use of the word "seeing." Our concept of sight has its life only in connection with a whole set of other concepts, some of them relating to the behavior of people who see things. (I express exercise of this concept in such utterances as, "I can't see, it's too far off—now it's coming into view!" "He couldn't see me, he didn't look round," "I caught his eye," etc.

. . . [T]he exercise of one concept is intertwined with the exercise of others; as with a spider's web, some connections may be broken with impunity; but if you break enough the whole web collapses—the concept becomes unusable. Just such a collapse happens, I believe, when we try to think of seeing, hearing, pain, emotion, etc., going on independently of a body.*

There is a whole web of meaning-connections between perceiving and having a body; when we try to break all the connections we appear to be reduced to unintelligibility. But perhaps we used a bad example; perhaps we can imagine thinking, wondering, doubting, and so on (mental operations) taking place without a body. *Where* do these operations occur? They occur, one might say, in a mind; and a mind, unlike a brain, does not exist at any physical *place*. But what do you think about? Surely about a world that is not your mind. And what causes you to have the thoughts you do? Not a brain process, because you have no brain. And once again the description begins to be suspect. What is the *you*? . . .

*P. T. Geach, *Mental Acts: Their Content and Their Objects* (London: Routledge, 1965), pp. 112–113. See also selection 23, pp. 227 ff.

32

WILLIAM JAMES

❧

Consciousness, The Brain, And Immortality

❧

IN 1898, JAMES *gave the annual Ingersoll Lecture at Harvard, entitled "Human Immortality: Two Supposed Objections to the Doctrine." The lecture was later published as a small book. The first of the two objections mentioned in the title is the one derived from the evidence amassed by physiologists that consciousness depends on the brain. The second objection is that consistency would require one to extend immortality to all human beings, including our "half-brutish prehistoric brothers," and even to animals and plants. Most of the lecture is devoted to a response to the first objection. The present selection consists of James's discussion of this objection, omitting his footnotes and a few inessential remarks. James's reply to the second objection is discussed in some detail in the Introduction to this volume (see pp. 67ff.). As a postscript, the selection includes James's preface to the second edition of his book in which he attempts to remove misunderstandings of his remarks in the original lecture.*

. . . The first of these difficulties is relative to the absolute dependence of our spiritual life, as we know it here, upon the brain. One hears not only physiologists, but numbers of laymen who read the popular science books and magazines, saying all about us, How can we believe in life hereafter when Science has once for all attained to proving, beyond possibility of escape, that our inner life is a function of that famous material, the so-called "gray matter" of our cerebral convolutions? How can the function possibly persist after its organ has undergone decay?

Thus physiological psychology is what is supposed to bar the way to the old faith. And it is now as a physiological psychologist that I ask you to look at the question with me a little more closely.

It is indeed true that physiological science has come to the conclusion cited; and we must confess that in so doing she has only carried out a little farther the common belief of mankind. Every one knows that arrests of brain development occasion imbecility, that blows on the head abolish memory or consciousness, and that brain-stimulants and poisons change the quality of our ideas. The anatomists, physiologists, and pathologists have only shown this generally admitted fact of a dependence to be detailed and minute. What the laboratories and hospitals have lately been teaching us is not only that thought in general is one of the brain's functions, but that the various special forms of thinking are functions of special portions of the brain. When we are thinking of things seen, it is our occipital convolutions that are active; when of things heard, it is a certain portion of our temporal lobes; when of things to be spoken, it is one of our frontal convolutions. Professor Flechsig of Leipzig* (who perhaps more than any one may claim to have made the subject his own) considers that in other special convolutions those processes of association go on, which permit the more abstract processes of thought, to take place. I could easily show you these regions if I had a picture of the brain. Moreover, the diminished or exaggerated associations of what this author calls the *Körperfühls-phäre* with the other regions, accounts, according to him, for the complexion of our emotional life, and eventually decides whether one shall be a callous brute or criminal, an unbalanced sentimentalist, or a character accessible to feeling, and yet well poised. Such special opinions may have to be corrected; yet so firmly established do the main positions worked out by the anatomists, physiologists, and pathologists of the brain appear, that the youth of our medical schools are everywhere taught unhesitatingly to believe them. The assurance that observation will go on to establish them ever more and more minutely is the inspirer of all contemporary research. And almost any of our young psychologists will tell you that only a few belated scholastics, or possibly some crack-brained theosophist or psychical researcher, can be found holding back, and still talking as if mental phenomena might exist as independent variables in the world.

For the purposes of my argument, now, I wish to adopt this general doctrine as if it were established absolutely, with no possibility of restriction. During this hour I wish you also to accept it as a postulate, whether you think it incontrovertibly established or not; so I beg you to agree with me to-day in subscribing to the great psycho-physiological formula: *Thought is a function of the brain.*

The question is, then, Does this doctrine logically compel us to disbelieve in immortality? Ought it to force every truly consistent

*Paul Flechsig (1847–1929), German neurologist, pioneer in the evolutionary approach to the study of the nervous system and the brain.

thinker to sacrifice his hopes of an hereafter to what he takes to be his duty of accepting all the consequences of a scientific truth?

Most persons imbued with what one may call the puritanism of science would feel themselves bound to answer this question with a yes. If any medically or psychologically bred young scientists feel otherwise, it is probably in consequence of that incoherency of mind of which the majority of mankind happily enjoy the privilege. At one hour scientists, at another they are Christians or common men, with the will to live burning hot in their breasts; and, holding thus the two ends of the chain, they are careless of the intermediate connection. But the more radical and uncompromising disciple of science makes the sacrifice, and, sorrowfully or not, according to his temperament, submits to giving up his hopes of heaven.

This, then, is the objection to immortality; and the next thing in order for me is to try to make plain to you why I believe that it has in strict logic no deterrent power. I must show you that the fatal consequence is not coercive, as is commonly imagined; and that, even though our soul's life (as here below it is revealed to us) may be in literal strictness the function of a brain that perishes, yet it is not at all impossible, but on the contrary quite possible, that the life may still continue when the brain itself is dead.

The supposed impossibility of its continuing comes from too superficial a look at the admitted fact of functional dependence. The moment we inquire more closely into the notion of functional dependence, and ask ourselves, for example, how many kinds of functional dependence there may be, we immediately perceive that there is one kind at least that does not exclude a life hereafter at all. The fatal conclusion of the physiologist flows from his assuming off-hand another kind of functional dependence, and treating it as the only imaginable kind.

When the physiologist who thinks that his science cuts off all hope of immortality pronounces the phrase, "Thought is a function of the brain," he thinks of the matter just as he thinks when he says, "Steam is a function of the tea-kettle," "Light is a function of the electric circuit," "Power is a function of the moving waterfall." In these latter cases the several material objects have the function of inwardly creating or engendering their effects, and their function must be called *productive* function. Just so, he thinks, it must be with the brain. Engendering consciousness in its interior, much as it engenders cholesterin and creatin and carbonic acid, its relation to our soul's life must also be called productive function. Of course, if such production be the function, then when the organ perishes, since the production can no longer continue, the soul must surely die. Such a conclusion as this is indeed inevitable from that particular conception of the facts.

But in the world of physical nature productive function of this sort is not the only kind of function with which we are familiar. We have also releasing or permissive function; and we have transmissive function.

The trigger of a crossbow has a releasing function: it removes the obstacle that holds the string, and lets the bow fly back to its natural shape. So when the hammer falls upon a detonating compound. By knocking out the inner molecular obstructions, it lets the constituent gases resume their normal bulk, and so permits the explosion to take place.

In the case of a colored glass, a prism, or a refracting lens, we have transmissive function. The energy of light, no matter how produced, is by the glass sifted and limited in color, and by the lens or prism determined to a certain path and shape. Similarly, the keys of an organ have only a transmissive function. They open successively the various pipes and let the wind in the air-chest escape in various ways. The voices of the various pipes are constituted by the columns of air trembling as they emerge. But the air is not engendered in the organ. The organ proper, as distinguished from its air-chest, is only an apparatus for letting portions of it loose upon the world in these peculiarly limited shapes.

My thesis now is this: that, when we think of the law that thought is a function of the brain, we are not required to think of productive function only; *we are entitled also to consider permissive or transmissive function.* And this the ordinary psycho-physiologist leaves out of his account.

Suppose, for example, that the whole universe of material things — the furniture of earth and choir of heaven — should turn out to be a mere surface-veil of phenomena, hiding and keeping back the world of genuine realities. Such a supposition is foreign neither to common sense nor to philosophy. Common sense believes in realities behind the veil even too superstitiously; and idealistic philosophy declares the whole world of natural experience, as we get it, to be but a time-mask, shattering or refracting the one infinite Thought which is the sole reality into those millions of finite streams of consciousness known to us as our private selves.

> "Life, like a dome of many-colored glass,
> Stains the white radiance of eternity."

Suppose, now, that this were really so, and suppose, moreover, that the dome, opaque enough at all times to the full super-solar blaze, could at certain times and places grow less so, and let certain beams pierce through into this sublunary world. These beams would be so many finite rays, so to speak, of consciousness, and they would vary in quantity and quality as the opacity varied in degrees. Only at particular times and places would it seem that, as a matter of fact, the veil of nature can grow thin and rupturable enough for such effects to occur. But in those places gleams, however finite and unsatisfying, of the absolute life of the universe, are from time to time vouchsafed. Glows of feeling, glimpses of insight, and streams of knowledge and perception float into our finite world.

Admit now that *our brains* are such thin and half-transparent places in the veil. What will happen? Why, as the white radiance comes through the dome, with all sorts of straining and distortion imprinted on it by the glass, or as the air now comes through my glottis determined and limited in its force and quality of its vibrations by the peculiarities of those vocal chords which form its gate of egress and shape it into my personal voice, even so the genuine matter of reality, the life of souls as it is in its fullness, will break through our several brains into this world in all sorts of restricted forms, and with all the imperfections and queernesses that characterize our finite individualities here below.

According to the state in which the brain finds itself, the barrier of its obstructiveness may also be supposed to rise or fall. It sinks so low, when the brain is in full activity, that a comparative flood of spiritual energy pours over. At other times, only such occasional waves of thought as heavy sleep permits get by. And when finally a brain stops acting altogether, or decays, that special stream of consciousness which it subserved will vanish entirely from this natural world. But the sphere of being that supplied the consciousness would still be intact; and in that more real world with which, even whilst here, it was continuous, the consciousness might, in ways unknown to us, continue still.

You see that, on all these suppositions, our soul's life, as we here know it, would none the less in literal strictness be the function of the brain. The brain would be the independent variable, the mind would vary dependently on it. But such dependence on the brain for this natural life would in no wise make immortal life impossible, — it might be quite compatible with supernatural life behind the veil hereafter.

As I said, then, the fatal consequence is not coercive, the conclusion which materialism draws being due solely to its one-sided way of taking the word "function." And whether we care or not for immortality in itself, we ought, as mere critics doing police duty among the vagaries of mankind, to insist on the illogicality of a denial based on the flat ignoring of a palpable alternative. How much more ought we to insist, as lovers of truth, when the denial is that of such a vital hope of mankind!

In strict logic, then, the fangs of cerebralistic materialism are drawn. My words ought consequently already to exert a releasing function on your hopes. You *may* believe henceforward, whether you care to profit by the permission or not. But, as this is a very abstract argument, I think it will help its effect to say a word or two about the more concrete conditions of the case.

All abstract hypotheses sound unreal; and the abstract notion that our brains are colored lenses in the wall of nature, admitting light from the super-solar source, but at the same time tingeing and restricting it, has a thoroughly fantastic sound. What is it, you may ask, but a foolish metaphor? And how can such a function be imagined? Isn't the common materialistic notion vastly simpler? Is not consciousness really more comparable to a sort of steam, or perfume, or electricity, or nerveglow, generated on the spot in its own peculiar vessel? Is it not more rigorously scientific to treat the brain's function as function of production?

The immediate reply is, that, if we are talking of science positively understood, function can mean nothing more than bare concomitant variation. When the brain-activities change in one way, consciousness changes in another; when the currents pour through the occipital lobes, consciousness *sees* things; when through the lower frontal region, consciousness *says* things to itself; when they stop, she goes to sleep, etc. In strict science, we can only write down the bare fact of concomitance; and all talk about either production or transmission, as the mode of taking place, is pure superadded hypothesis, and metaphysical hypothesis at that, for we can frame no more notion of the details on the one alternative than on the other. Ask for any indication of the exact process either of transmission or of production, and Science confesses her imagination to be bankrupt. She has, so far, not the least glimmer of a conjecture or suggestion, — not even a bad verbal metaphor or pun to offer. *Ignoramus, ignorabimus,* is what most physiologists, in the words of one of their number, will say here.* The production of such a thing as consciousness in the brain, they will reply with the late Berlin professor of physiology, is the absolute world-enigma, — something so paradoxical and abnormal as to be a stumbling block to Nature, and almost a self-contradiction. Into the mode of production of steam in a tea-kettle we have conjectural insight, for the terms that change are physically homogeneous one with another, and we can easily imagine the case to consist of nothing but alterations of molecular motion. But in the production of consciousness by the brain, the terms are heterogeneous natures altogether; and as far as our understanding goes, it is as great a miracle as if we said, Thought is "spontaneously generated," or "created out of nothing."

The theory of production is therefore not a jot more simple or credible in itself than any other conceivable theory. It is only a little more popular. All that one need do, therefore, if the ordinary materialist should challenge one to explain how the brain *can* be an organ for limiting and determining to a certain form of consciousness elsewhere produced, is to retort with a *tu quoque,* asking him in turn to explain

*James is referring to a famous lecture by the German physiologist Emil DuBois-Reymond (1818–1896) about the seven "riddles of the universe," three of which are said to be forever insoluble. One of the latter is the origin of sensations and consciousness. About these insoluble riddles all we can say is *"ignoramus et ignorabimus"* ("we do not know and we shall not know"). [Ed.]

how it can be an organ for producing consciousness out of whole cloth. For polemic purposes, the two theories are thus exactly on a par.

But if we consider the theory of transmission in a wider way, we see that it has certain positive superiorities, quite apart from its connection with the immortality question.

Just how the process of transmission may be carried on, is indeed unimaginable; but the outer relations, so to speak, of the process, encourage our belief. Consciousness in this process does not have to be generated *de novo* in a vast number of places. It exists already, behind the scenes, coeval with the world. The transmission-theory not only avoids in this way multiplying miracles, but it put itself in touch with general idealistic philosophy better than the production-theory does. It should always be reckoned a good thing when science and philosophy thus meet.

It puts itself also in touch with the conception of a "threshold," —a word with which, since Fechner wrote his book called "Psychophysik," the so-called "new Psychology" has rung.* Fechner imagines as the condition of consciousness a certain kind of psycho-physical movement, as he terms it. Before consciousness can come, a certain degree of activity in the movement must be reached. This requisite degree is called the "threshold"; but the height of the threshold varies under different circumstances: it may rise or fall. When it falls, as in states of great lucidity, we grow conscious of things of which we should be unconscious at other times; when it rises, as in drowsiness, consciousness sinks in amounts. This rising and lowering of a psycho-physical threshold exactly conforms to our notion of a permanent obstruction to the transmission of consciousness, which obstruction may, in our brains, grow alternately greater or less.

The transmission-theory also puts itself in touch with a whole class of experiences that are with difficulty explained by the production-theory. I refer to those obscure and exceptional phenomena reported at all times throughout human history, which the "psychical-researchers," with Mr. Frederic Myers at their head, are doing so much to rehabilitate; such phenomena, namely, as religious conversions, providential leadings in answer to prayer, instantaneous healings, premonitions, apparitions at time of death, clairvoyant visions or impressions, and the whole range of mediumistic capacities, to say nothing of still more exceptional and incomprehensible things. If all our human thought be a function of the brain, then of course, if any of these things are facts, —and to my own mind some of them are facts, —we may not

*James's reference is to *Elemente der Psychophsik* (1860). Fechner was noted for both his pioneering work in experimental psychology and his religious and metaphysical speculations. There is a long footnote about the former in the lecture on immortality which is not reproduced here. James also discusses Fechner in volume 1 of his *Principles of Psychology* and in lecture 4 of *A Pluralistic Universe*. [Ed.]

suppose that they can occur without preliminary brain-action. But the ordinary production-theory of consciousness is knit up with a peculiar notion of how brain-action *can* occur,—that notion being that all brain-action, without exception, is due to a prior action, immediate or remote, of the bodily sense-organs *on* the brain. Such action makes the brain produce sensations and mental images, and out of the sensations and images the higher forms of thought and knowledge in their turn are framed. As transmissionists, we also must admit this to be the condition of all our usual thought. Sense-action is what lowers the brain-barrier. My voice and aspect, for instance, strike upon your ears and eyes; your brain thereupon becomes more pervious, and an awareness on your part of what I say and who I am slips into this world from the world behind the veil. But, in the mysterious phenomena to which I allude, it is often hard to see where the sense-organs can come in. A medium, for example, will show knowledge of his sitter's private affairs which it seems impossible he should have acquired through sight or hearing, or inference therefrom. Or you will have an apparition of some one who is now dying hundreds of miles away. On the production-theory one does not see from what sensations such odd bits of knowledge are produced. On the transmission-theory, they don't have to be "produced,"—they exist ready-made in the transcendental world, and all that is needed is an abnormal lowering of the brain-threshold to let them through. In cases of conversion, in providential leadings, sudden mental healings, etc., it seems to the subjects themselves of the experience as if a power from without, quite different from the ordinary action of the senses or of the sense-led mind, came into their life, as if the latter suddenly opened into that greater life in which it has its source. The word "influx," used in Swedenborgian circles, well describes this impression of new insight, or new willingness, sweeping over us like a tide. All such experiences, quite paradoxical and meaningless on the production-theory, fall very naturally into place on the other theory. We need only suppose the continuity of our consciousness with a mother sea, to allow for exceptional waves occasionally pouring over the dam. Of course the causes of these odd lowerings of the brain's threshold still remain a mystery on any terms. . . .

. . . Add, then, this advantage to the transmission theory—an advantage which I am well aware that some of you will not rate very high—and also add the advantage of not conflicting with a life hereafter, and I hope you will agree with me that it has many points of superiority to the more familiar theory.

Postscript (Preface to Second Edition)

So many critics have made one and the same objection to the doorway to immortality which my lecture claims to be left open by the "transmission theory" of cerebral action, that I feel tempted, as the book is again going to press, to add a word of explanation.

If our finite personality here below, the objectors say, be due to the transmission through the brain of portions of a pre-existing larger consciousness, all that can remain after the brain expires is the larger consciousness itself as such, with which we should thenceforth be perforce reconfounded, the only means of our existence in finite personal form having ceased.

But this, the critics continue, is the pantheistic idea of immortality, survival, namely, in the soul of the world, not the Christian idea of immortality, which means survival in strictly personal form.

In showing the possibility of a mental life after the brain's death, they conclude, the lecture has thus at the same time shown the impossibility of its identity with the personal life, which is the brain's function.

Now I am myself anything but a pantheist of the monistic pattern; yet for simplicity's sake I did in the lecture speak of the "mother-sea" in terms that must have sounded pantheistic, and suggested that I thought of it myself as a unit. . . . I even added that future lecturers might prove the loss of some of our personal limitations after death not to be matter for absolute regret. The interpretation of my critics was therefore not unnatural; and I ought to have been more careful to guard against its being made.

. . . I partially guarded against it by saying that the "mother-sea" from which the finite mind is supposed to be strained by the brain, need not be conceived of in pantheistic terms exclusively. There might be, I said, many minds behind the scenes as well as one. The plain truth is that *one may conceive the mental world behind the veil in as individualistic a form as one pleases, without any detriment to the general scheme by which the brain is represented as a transmissive organ.*

If the extreme individualistic view were taken, one's finite mundane consciousness would be an extract from one's larger, truer personality, the latter having even now some sort of reality behind the scenes. And in transmitting it—to keep to our extremely mechanical metaphor, which confessedly throws no light on the actual *modus operandi*— one's brain would also leave effects upon the part remaining behind the veil, for when a thing is torn, both fragments feel the operation.

And just as (to use a very coarse figure) the stubs remain in a checkbook whenever a check is used, to register the transaction, so these impressions on the transcendent self might constitute so many vouchers of the finite experiences of which the brain had been the mediator; and ultimately they might form that collection within the larger self of memories of our earthly passage, which is all that, since Locke's day, the continuance of our personal identity beyond the grave has by psychology been recognized to mean.

It is true that all this would seem to have affinities rather with pre-existence and with possible reincarnations than with the Christian notion of immortality. But my concern in the lecture was not to discuss immortality in general. It was confined to showing it to be *not incompatible* with the brain-function theory of our present mundane consciousness. I hold that it is so compatible, and compatible moreover in fully individualized form. The reader would be in accord with everything that the text of my lecture intended to say, were he to assert that every memory and affection of his present life is to be preserved, and that he shall never *in saecula saeculorum* cease to be able to say to himself: "I am the same personal being who in old times upon the earth had those experiences."

33

PAUL EDWARDS

౪

The Dependence of Consciousness on the Brain

౪

IN THIS ARTICLE I will discuss the case against survival after death based on what is known about the dependence of consciousness on the brain. This may be called the body–mind dependence argument. I shall try to bring out what a formidable argument it is. Among other things I shall try to show that the various replies to it by philosophers and theologians are unsound.

I will make two assumptions which are favorable to the case for survival. By this I mean that without them one of the major forms of survival-belief would be ruled out from the start. I will assume, first, that some form of dualism is true, i.e., that a person is a body and a mind in a sense in which the mind cannot be identified with any bodily processes or behavior. I will also assume that when we talk about personal identity, bodily continuity is not an essential ingredient in what we mean. The view that bodily continuity is an essential ingredient in personal identity has sometimes been referred to as "corporealism" and I will here assume that corporealism is false.

The Scope of the Argument

In a rudimentary form the argument can already be found in Lucretius and Pomponazzi and, since Bishop Butler expressly argued against it in

Some of the material contained in this article first appeared in "The Case Against Reincarnation, part 3," *Free Inquiry*, Spring 1987.

the first chapter of his *Analogy of Religion*, we may infer that it was current among English free-thinkers in the early years of the eighteenth century. However, the first full statement with which I am familiar occurs in Hume's posthumous essay on immortality:

> Where any two objects are so closely connected that all alterations which we have ever seen in the one are attended with proportionable alterations in the other; we ought to conclude, by all rules of analogy, that, when there are still greater alterations produced in the former, and it is totally dissolved, there follows a total dissolution of the latter. . . . The weakness of the body and that of the mind in infancy are exactly proportioned; their vigour in manhood, their sympathetic disorder in sickness; their common gradual decay in old age. The step further seems unavoidable; their common dissolution in death. The last symptoms which the mind discovers, are disorder, weakness, insensibility, and stupidity; the forerunners of its annihilation. The further progress of the same causes increasing, the same effects totally extinguish it.[1]

Some of Hume's detailed observations are of course quite indefensible. There is surely no "exact" proportionality between physical and mental development or between bodily and mental "decay." Nor is it true that all human beings are "insensible" and "stupid" immediately before their death. Hume was also handicapped by the undeveloped state of brain physiology in the eighteenth century. Nevertheless his statement conveys very vividly the basic idea of the argument.

More recent defenders have placed heavy emphasis on information about the relation between the brain and our mental states and processes. Unlike Hume Professor J. J. C. Smart rejects dualism. As a materialist he maintains that mental states are identical with brain states, but he nevertheless endorses the body – mind dependence argument as valid within a dualistic framework.

> Even if some form of philosophical dualism is accepted and the mind is thought of as something over and above the body, the empirical evidence in favor of an invariable correlation between mental states and brain states is extremely strong: that is, the mind may be thought of as in some sense distinct from the body but also as fundamentally dependent upon physical states. Without oxygen or under the influence of anesthetics or soporific drugs, we rapidly lose consciousness. Moreover, the quality of our consciousness can be influenced in spectacular ways by appropriate drugs or by mechanical stimulation of different areas of the brain. In the face of all the evidence that is being accumulated by modern research in neurology, it is hard to believe that after the dissolution of the brain there could be any thought or conscious experience whatever.[2]

---

[1] "On the Immortality of the Soul." [See this volume, p. 138.]
[2] "Religion and Science," *The Encyclopedia of Philosophy* (New York and London: Macmillan, 1967), volume 7, p. 161.

I will add one other recent formulation which states the argument simply and forcefully and is based on the most recent evidence from neurology. "What we call 'the mind,'" writes Colin McGinn,

> is in fact made up of a great number of sub-capacities, and each of these depends upon the functioning of the brain.

Now, the facts of neurology

> compellingly demonstrate . . . that everything about the mind, from the sensory-motor periphery to the inner sense of self, is minutely controlled by the brain: if your brain lacks certain chemicals or gets locally damaged, your mind is apt to fall apart at the seams. . . . If parts of the mind depend for their existence upon parts of the brain, then the whole of the mind must so depend too. Hence the soul dies with the brain, which is to say it is mortal.[3]

It should be emphasized that the argument does *not* start from the premise that after a person is dead he never again acts in the world. A correspondent in the *London Review* replied to McGinn by observing that we do not need his or the neuropathologist's "assistance to learn that all behavior stops at death." Similarly, John Stuart Mill in his chapter on "Immortality" in *Three Essays on Religion* thought the argument inconclusive on the ground that the absence of any acts by an individual after his death is as consistent with the view that he will "recommence" his existence "elsewhere" as it is with the assumption that he has been extinguished forever. Such remarks are due to a misunderstanding. The absence of any actions by the dead is certainly not irrelevant, but the argument is primarily based on the observed dependence of our mental states and processes on what goes on in the brain.

At first sight it may seem that, if valid, the argument merely rules out the survival of the disembodied mind and leaves other forms of survival untouched. In fact, however, it equally rules out reincarnation and the more sophisticated or replica-version of resurrectionism. This is so because the conclusion of the argument is that my mind depends on *my* brain. It does not merely support the less specific conclusion that my mind needs *some* brain as its foundation. If my mind is finished when my brain dies, then it cannot transmigrate to any other body. Similarly, if God created a duplicate of my body containing a duplicate of my brain, *my* mind would not be able to make use of it since it stopped existing with the death of my original body. The argument does not refute belief in the literal resurrection of the body. For on this view God will reconstitute our *original* bodies and hence also our original brains on the Day of Judgment. There are indeed vast numbers of fundamentalists and also a few pious philosophers who believe or say that they believe in resurrection in this literal sense, but to the great

majority of scientists and philosophers and of educated persons generally it seems totally incredible. However, if anybody does believe in
survival in *this* sense our argument has no bearing on his view.

Alzheimer's Disease and Comas

The literature on survival contains a number of standard rejoinders to
the body–mind dependence argument. Before turning to them, I will
consider two concrete instances of body–mind dependence which will
help to bring out the full force of the argument. The first is Alzheimer's
disease, a dreadful affliction that ruins the last years of a sizable percentage of the world's population. Almost everybody above the age of
thirty has known some elderly relative or friend afflicted with this
illness. I can therefore be brief in my description of what happens to
Alzheimer patients. In the early stages the person misses appointments,
he constantly loses and mislays objects, and he frequently cannot recall
events in the recent past. As the illness progresses he can no longer
read or write and his speech tends to be incoherent. In nursing homes
Alzheimer patients commonly watch television, but there is no evidence that they understand what is happening on the screen. The
decline in intellectual function is generally accompanied by severe
emotional symptoms, such as extreme irritability and violent reactions
to persons in the environment, as well as hallucinations and paranoid
fears. In the final stages the patient is totally confused, frequently
incontinent, and quite unable to recognize anybody, including the
closest relatives and friends. At present Alzheimer's is incurable and,
unlike in the case of Parkinson's disease, there are no known means of
slowing down the deterioration. It is also as yet a mystery why Alzheimer's strikes certain individuals while sparing the majority of old
people. However, a great deal is known about what goes on in the
brains of Alzheimer patients. Alois Alzheimer, the neurologist after
whom the disease is named, found in 1906 that the cerebral cortex and
the hippocampus of his patients contained twisted tangles and filaments
as well as abnormal neurites known as "neuritic" or "senile plaques." It
has since been determined that the density of these abnormal components is directly proportional to the severity of the disorder. Autopsies
have shown that Alzheimer victims have a vastly reduced level of an
enzyme called "choline acetyltransferase," which is needed for producing the neurotransmitter acetylcholine. Although the reduced level
of the enzyme and the neurotransmitter appear in the cortex, the origin
of the trouble lies in another region of the brain, the nucleus basalis,
which is situated just above the place where the optic nerves meet and
cross. Autopsies have revealed a dramatic loss of neurons from the
nucleus basalis in Alzheimer victims, and this explains why so little of
the enzyme is manufactured in their brains.

The information just summarized has been culled from articles about

Alzheimer's that have appeared in magazines and popular science monthlies in recent years. The authors of these articles are evidently not concerned with the question of survival after death, but they invariably use such phrases as "destruction of the mind" in describing what happens to the victims. In an article in *Science 84* entitled "The Clouded Mind," the author, Michael Shodell, speaks of Alzheimer's as "an illness that destroys the mind, leaving the body behind as a grim reminder of the person who once was there." Similarly, the cover story in *Newsweek* of December 3, 1984, which contained many heart-rending illustrations and listed some of the famous men and women who are suffering from Alzheimer's, was entitled "A Slow Death of the Mind." I think that these descriptions are entirely appropriate: A person who can no longer read or write, whose memory has largely disappeared, whose speech is incoherent, and who is totally indifferent to his environment has in effect lost all or most of what we normally call his mind. The relevance of this to our discussion is obvious. While still alive, an Alzheimer patient's brain is severely damaged and most of his mind has disappeared. After his death his brain is not merely damaged but completely destroyed. It is surely logical to conclude that now his mind is also gone. It seems preposterous to assert that, when the brain is completely destroyed, the mind suddenly returns intact, with its emotional and intellectual capacities, including its memory, restored. How does the *complete* destruction of the brain bring about a cure that has so far totally eluded medical science?

The same obviously applies to people in irreversible comas. Karen Ann Quinlan lay in a coma for over ten years before she finally died. The damage to her brain had made her, in the phrase used by the newspapers, nothing more than a "vegetable." Her E.E.G. was flat; she was unable to speak or write; visits by her foster parents did not register the slightest response. A more recent widely publicized case was that of the great American tenor Jan Peerce. Peerce had amazed the musical public by singing right into his seventies with only a slight decline in his vocal powers. In the end, however, he was felled by two severe strokes, and he spent the last year of his life in an irreversible coma. Relatives and friends could get no response of any kind. Peerce died in December 1984, and Karen Ann Quinlan in June 1985. Did the total destruction of the bodies of these individuals suddenly bring back their emotional and intellectual capacities? If so, where were these during the intervening periods?

The Body as the Instrument of the Mind

The first of the rejoinders I will consider does not dispute the manifold dependence of mental functions on brain processes. It is claimed, however, that these facts are not inconsistent with survival. They are indeed compatible with the view that the mind is annihilated at death, but they are also compatible with the very different position that the mind continues to exist but has lost its "instrument" for acting in the world, and more specifically, for communicating with people who are still alive. An excellent illustration of what the supporters of this rejoinder have in mind is supplied by Father John A. O'Brien in his pamphlet: *The Soul — What Is It?*[4] In order to carve a statue, Father O'Brien writes, a sculptor needs his tools, his hammer and chisel. If the tools are seriously damaged, the quality of his work will be correspondingly impaired, but this does not mean that the sculptor cannot exist if the tools are completely destroyed.

Variants of this argument are found in numerous Protestant theologians, in Catholic philosophers who have frequently relied on the distinction between what they call "extrinsic" and "intrinsic" dependence, and in several secular philosophers, including Descartes, Kant, James, Schiller and McTaggart. "I do not agree with you," writes Descartes to Gassendi in his "Reply to the Fifth Objection" to his *Meditations*,

> that the mind waxes and wanes with the body; for from the fact that it does not work equally well in the body of a child and in that of a grown man, and that its actions are often impeded by wine and other bodily things, it follows merely that while it is united to the body is uses the body as an instrument in its normal operations.[5]

Have we any reason, asks McTaggart, to suppose that "a body is essential to a self"? Not at all. The facts support the very different proposition that "while a self has a body, that body is essentially connected with the self's mental life." A self needs "sufficient data" for its mental activity. In this life the material is given in the form of sensations, and these can only be obtained by means of a body. It does not follow, however, that "it would be impossible for a self without a body to get data in some other way." McTaggart then offers an analogy which has frequently been quoted by believers in survival:

> If a man is shut up in a house, the transparency of the windows is an essential condition of his seeing the sky. But it would not be prudent to infer that, if he walked out of the house, he could not see the sky because there was no longer any glass through which he might see it.[6]

McTaggart is totally unimpressed by the evidence from brain physiology which, it is safe to say, he did not study in detail and which was very extensive even in 1906 when his book was published. He does not dispute that "diseases or mutilations of the brain affect the course of

---

[4]New York: The Paulist Press, 1946.

[5]My attention to this passage was called by Jonathan Bennett who quotes it on p. 132 of *A Study of Spinoza's Ethics* (Indianapolis: Hackett, 1984).

[6]*Some Dogmas of Religion* (London: Edward Arnold, 1906), p. 105.

thought," but "the fact that an abnormal state of the brain may affect our thought does not prove that the normal states of the brain are necessary for thought."[7]

It may be instructive at this stage to consider some of the exchanges between Professor Ian Stevenson, the well-known champion of reincarnation, and two of his skeptical interrogators in the course of a BBC program that took place in the spring of 1976. The program dealt with the claims of Edward Ryall, an elderly Englishman who in May 1970 had written a letter to the *Daily Express* in which he mentioned his clear and extensive memories of a life in the seventeenth century as a West Country farmer by the name of John Fletcher. Stevenson corresponded with Ryall and became convinced of the authenticity of his recollections. He encouraged Ryall to write a book about his previous life. *Second Time Around* appeared in 1974, with an introduction and supplementary notes by Stevenson. Besides Stevenson and Ryall, the participants in the BBC program were John Taylor, professor of mathematics at London University, and John Cohen, professor of psychology at Manchester. Here are some of the exchanges that are relevant to our discussion.

> Cohen: . . . memories are tied to a particular brain tissue. If you take away the brain, there is no memory.
>
> Stevenson: I think that's an assumption. Memories may exist in the brain and exist elsewhere also.
>
> Cohen: But we have not the slightest evidence, even a single case, of a memory existing without a brain. We have plenty of slight damage to a brain which destroys memory, but not the other way around.
>
> Stevenson: I feel that's one of the issues here—whether memories can, in fact, survive the destruction of the brain.
>
> Taylor: Professor Stevenson, do you have any evidence, other than these reincarnation cases, that memories can survive the destruction of physical tissue?
>
> Stevenson: No. I think the best evidence comes from the reincarnation cases.[8]

Taylor then brought up the well-known case of people who lose all or most of their memories as a result of brain injuries. Stevenson was not fazed.

> Stevenson: Well, it's possible that what is affected is his ability to express memories that he may still have.
>
> Taylor: But are you suggesting, in fact, that memories themselves are in some way nonphysically bound up, and can be stored in a nonphysical manner?
>
> Stevenson: Yes, I'm suggesting that there might be a nonphysical process of storage.
>
> Taylor: What does that mean? Nonphysical storage of what?

[7]Ibid.
[8]*The Listener*, June 3, 1976, p. 698.

Stevenson: The potentiality for the reproduction of an image memory.

Taylor: But information itself involves energy. Is there such a thing as nonphysical energy?

Stevenson: I think there may be, yes.

Taylor: How can you define it? Nonphysical energy, to me, is a complete contradiction in terms. I can't conceive how on earth you could ever conceive of such a quantity. . . .

Stevenson: Well, it might be in some dimension of which we are just beginning to form crude ideas, through the study of what we parapsychologists call paranormal phenomena. We are making an assumption of some kind of process that is not, and maybe cannot be, understood in terms of current physical concepts. That is a jump, a gap, I freely admit.[9]

These exchanges bring out very clearly what is at issue between those who accept the body–mind dependence argument and the supporters of the instrument theory.

It has on occasion been suggested that we have no way of deciding between these two rival explanations of the relevant facts. I see no reason to accept such an agnostic conclusion. It seems to me that by retrodictive extrapolation to cases like Alzheimer patients or people in comas we can see that the alternative to annihilation proposed by the instrument theory is absurd. Let us consider the behavior of Alzheimer patients in the later stages of their affliction. The more specific the case, the clearer the implications of the rival views will appear. The mother of a close friend of mine, Mrs. D., recently died from Alzheimer's after suffering from the disease for about eight years. Mrs. D. was a prosperous lady from Virginia, the widow of a banker. In her pre-Alzheimer days she was a courteous and well-behaved person, and she had of course no difficulty recognizing her daughter or any of her other relatives or friends. I do not know what her feelings were about paralyzed people, but my guess is that she pitied them and certainly had no wish to beat them up. As her illness progressed she was put into a nursing home run by nuns who were renowned for their gentle and compassionate ways. She shared a room with an older lady who was paralyzed. For the first year or so Mrs. D. did not become violent. Then she started hitting the nurses. At about the time when she could no longer recognize her daughter, she beat up the paralyzed lady on two or three occasions. From then on she had to be confined to the "seventh floor," which was reserved for violent and exceptionally difficult patients.

Let us now see what the survival theorists would have to say about Mrs. D.'s behavior. It should be remembered that on this view Mrs. D., after her death, will exist with her mind intact and will only lack the means of communicating with people on earth. This view implies that

[9]Ibid.

throughout her affliction with Alzheimer's Mrs. D.'s mind *was* intact. She recognized her daughter but had lost her ability to express this recognition. She had no wish to beat up an inoffensive paralyzed old woman. On the contrary, "inside" she was the same considerate person as before the onset of the illness. It is simply that her brain disease prevented her from acting in accordance with her true emotions. I must insist that these *are* the implications of the theory that the mind survives the death of the brain and that the brain is only an instrument for communication. Surely these consequences are absurd: The facts are that Mrs. D. no longer recognized her daughter and that she no longer had any compassionate feelings about paralyzed old women. At any rate, we have the same grounds for saying this as we do in any number of undisputed cases in which people do not suffer from Alzheimer's and fail to recognize other human beings or fail to feel compassion.

The guards in Argentine dungeons who tortured and killed liberals had no compassion for their victims, and neither of course did the Nazis who rounded up and then shot Jews in Poland and elsewhere. We have exactly the same kind of evidence for concluding that Mrs. D., who probably did feel compassion for paralyzed people before she suffered from Alzheimer's, no longer felt compassion when beating up her paralyzed roommate. As for memories, all of us sometimes cannot place a familiar tune or remember the name of a person we know well; and in such cases it makes good sense to say that the memories are still there. Even when the name never comes back there is a suspicion that the memory may not have been lost: it is entirely possible that one could bring it back under hypnosis. However, the memory loss in Alzheimer's is totally different, and the same of course applies to people in irreversible comas. It is surely fantastic to maintain that during his last months Jan Peerce did recognize his wife and children and simply could not express his recognition. If anybody makes such a claim it can only be for ulterior metaphysical reasons and not because it is supported by the slightest evidence.

Mill, Butler, Ewing — The Absense of Direct Negative Evidence

Mill's posthumously published essay on "Theism" contains a chapter on immortality in which he surveys and evaluates all the major arguments on both sides that were known to him. Mill finds all of them defective and concludes on a note of complete agnosticism. We have here, he writes, "one of those very rare cases in which there is really a total absence of evidence on either side" and "in which the absence of evidence for the affirmative does not, as in so many other cases, create a strong presumption in favor of the negative."[10]

[10]*Three Essays on Religion* (London: Longman's Green, Reader and Dyer, 1876), p. 203.

Mill discusses in some detail the evidence from brain physiology. It supplies us with "sufficient evidence that cerebral action is, if not the cause, at least, in our present state of existence, a condition *sine qua non* of mental operations." We are entitled to conclude that the death of the brain would put a stop to all mental function and "remand it [the mind] to unconsciousness unless and until some other set of conditions supervenes, capable of recalling it into activity." The facts of brain physiology most emphatically do not prove that the mind cannot exist after death. "The same thoughts, emotions, volitions, and even sensations which we have here" may, for all we can tell, "persist or recommence somewhere else under other conditions." This is no less possible than that "other thoughts and sensations may exist under other conditions in other parts of the universe."[11] What Mill evidently seems to require in order to establish the negative case is that we observe the nonexistence of the thoughts, volitions, and sensations of the dead person; and this the body–mind dependence argument does not give us.

Independently of this argument, Bishop Butler insists on the same requirement and regards its nonfulfillment as a fatal flaw in the unbeliever's position. Not only do we never directly observe the nonexistence of human minds, but the same is also true of animals. We never "find anything throughout the whole analogy of nature" that could afford us "even the slightest presumption, that animals ever lose their living powers." This is so because we have "no faculties wherewith to trace any beyond or through death to see what becomes of them."[12] In the case of human beings and animals alike death only destroys "the sensible proof which we had before their death of their being possessed of living powers," but it does not "afford the least reason" for supposing that death causes the extinction of their minds.

A much more recent philosopher, the late A. C. Ewing, used the same kind of reasoning to rebut the unbeliever's argument. Ewing first observes that there is no logically necessary connection between bodily and mental events, something that all dualists would endorse. This means that no deductive argument is available to the unbeliever. At the same time he is also unable to mount an inductive argument. He cannot do this because "we have never observed a mind being annihilated at death."[13] The only one who could do this is the person himself. "No one could observe this," Ewing writes, "but the mind in question itself, and even that could not because it was annihilated, so, if a phenomenon, it is certainly an unobservable one."[14] Ewing is happy to note that once we have disposed of the argument from the connection between body and mind the field is left open "for any empirical evidence drawn

---

[11]Op. cit., p. 200. [See this volume, p. 173.]
[12]*The Analogy of Nature*, Chapter 1. [See this volume, p. 123.]
[13]*Non-Linguistic Philosophy* (London: Allen and Unwin, 1968), p. 173.
[14]Ibid.

from psychical research and any arguments for survival there may be based on ethics and religion."[15]

Butler deserves credit for realizing that his reasoning applies to animals and not only to human beings. It is not clear that either Mill or Ewing saw this. However, not even Butler carried the argument far enough. What reason do we have for denying that purely inanimate objects have an "inner" psychic life? What evidence do I have that the chocolate cream puff I am about to eat does not bitterly resent this murderous activity on my part and how do I know that a tennis ball I am about to serve does not acutely suffer as a result of being hit? For that matter how do I know that the tennis ball does not enjoy the experience of being hit? Since we have no access to the inner life of tennis balls, if they have any, we cannot know either that the tennis ball does or does not like being hit. Not only cannot we know that tennis balls do not have an inner life. We also cannot know that they, or any other inanimate objects, do not continue to have an inner, psychical life after the death of their bodies, whether as disembodied minds or in conjunction with replicas that will be produced in a resurrection world. It is true that we have no evidence that such an inner life will continue after the death of their bodies, but we equally have none that it will not. A complete suspense of judgment is the only defensible attitude.

All who regard panpsychism as either false or meaningless will surely regard the fact that the rejoinder here under discussion can be extended to inanimate objects as its *reductio ad absurdum*. Others will go further and treat the entire rejoinder as a *reductio ad absurdum* of dualism. For clearly we do know that tennis balls and cream puffs do not have an inner life and we can and do know that human beings and animals have certain feelings or sensations. However, we have agreed to accept dualism throughout this article, and it can be shown that the rejoinder is invalid even within a dualistic framework. After all, dualists allow that although we cannot inspect the minds of others we can frequently know that they have certain experiences. We can know that another person is in pain or that he is angry, and we can at least have strong evidence that he has certain thoughts. Now, the same *kind* of evidence is available to us that other people do *not* have these experiences. We can know that somebody has ceased to be in pain, that his anger is gone, or that he no longer thinks about a certain subject. I do not have to *be* the other person to know that he is no longer in pain or angry. By the same token I do not have to be Mrs. D., the Alzheimer patient herself, to know that her memory is gone and I equally do not have to be Jan Peerce in his coma to know that he no longer recognizes his family. In such cases we surely have the right to assert more than that the memories and thoughts have been "remanded to unconscious-

[15]Ibid.

ness." This description fits a person under general anesthesia or during dreamless sleep who may very well return to full consciousness, but it is highly misleading about people in a coma or with advanced Alzheimer's. The only description that is fitting in such cases is that the thoughts and memories have been destroyed; and if they have been destroyed then they cannot be "recalled into activity" when a "different set of conditions supervenes."

Ducasse's Rejoinder

Perhaps the ablest defender of belief in survival in recent decades, at least among those who attempt to judge the issue in terms of evidence and do not simply appeal to faith, was Professor C. J. Ducasse. In almost all of his many discussions of the subject he took note of the argument with which we are concerned in this article. He invariably rejects it on the ground that it logically presupposes epiphenomenalism and that epiphenomenalism is plainly false. As Ducasse states it quite fairly, epiphenomenalism asserts that mental events are by-products or automatic accompaniments of cerebral activity but do not in turn "cause or affect the latter."[16] Such a theory implies that "mental states and activities cannot possibly continue after the life of the brain has ceased." Ducasse does not dispute that many mental events are physically caused. This is particularly obvious in the case of "the several kinds of sensations" which "can, at will, be caused by appropriate stimulation of the body."[17] But although it cannot be denied that "sensations and some other mental states can be so caused," we have "equally good and abundant evidence that mental states can cause various bodily events." Ducasse quotes John Laird who offers a long list of illustrations including "the fact that merely willing to raise one's arm normally suffices to cause it to rise and . . . that certain thoughts cause tears, pallor, blushing, or fainting." The evidence we have that in such cases mental states have bodily effects "is exactly the same here as where bodily processes cause mental states."[18] To the extent to which it constitutes a search for the physical causes of mental phenomena, epiphenomenalism may be a "legitimate research program," but the philosophers who support it have "arbitrarily transmuted it into a materialistic metaphysical dogma."[19] Ducasse concludes that the body – mind – dependence argument fails. "So far as anything that epi-

[16]A *Critical Examination of the Belief in Life After Death* (Springfield, Ill.: Charles C. Thomas, 1961), p. 75.
[17]*Nature, Mind and Death* (La Salle, Ill.: Open Court, 1951), p. 455.
[18]Ibid.
[19]"Life After Death Conceived as Reincarnation," The 1960 Garvin Lecture, printed in the collection of Garvin Lectures, *In Search of God and Immortality* (Boston: Beacon Press, 1961), p. 148.

phenomenalists have shown to the contrary," he writes, "after-death mental life — at least of certain kinds — remains both a theoretical and an empirical possibility."[20]

The answer to Ducasse is that somebody who maintains that consciousness cannot exist without an intact brain *may* advocate epiphenomenalism but is in no way committed to it. He maintains that the brain is a *necessary* condition for the existence of all conscious states and processes, but this does not imply that conscious states and processes are incapable of influencing behavior. Ducasse mentions the standard example supporting mind–body interaction, namely "the fact that merely willing to raise one's arm normally suffices to cause it to rise." This is a very incomplete account of the facts of the case even if one accepts interactionism. If at the moment when the individual decided to raise his arm he had suffered a stroke, or if the brain had been damaged in certain other ways, the arm would not have gone up. This is all that the defender of the indispensability of an intact brain is committed to. He need not in the least deny that willing to raise the arm is causally relevant, i.e., that it is part of what in the context is the sufficient condition of the arm's movement. The scholastic philosophers distinguished between what they called a *"causa in fieri"* which literally means "cause in becoming" but is more accurately rendered as "productive cause" and *"causa in esse"* or sustaining cause. My parents are my *causa in fieri* or at least a major part of it. The air I breathe and the food I eat are a part of my *causa in esse*: they keep me alive but they did not produce me. Using this terminology we may express Ducasse's confusion by saying that his opponent is committed to the assertion that an intact brain is a *causa in esse* of all conscious states and not to the much stronger claim that it is their *causa in fieri*.

The preceding remarks are quite sufficient as an answer to Ducasse's objection. It should be added for the record, however, that various of his statements obscure the situation concerning the causal relations between the body and the mind. It may in fact be the case that the mind affects the body just as much as the body affects the mind, but there is an important asymmetry. If a mental state like a desire precedes a certain action of which it is taken to be the cause, it is always accompanied by a physical fact, namely a state of the brain. We already noted that the brain state is a necessary condition of the action, but it is at least conceivable that it, or it in conjunction with other bodily states, is the sufficient condition as well; and if this is so then the desire, if it is interpreted as a purely mental fact, is causally irrelevant. On the other hand, the physical antecedents of mental states which are regarded as their causes are *not* accompanied by mental antecedents corresponding to the brain states which are present in the putative mind–body inter-

---

[20]*A Critical Examination of the Belief in Life After Death*, op. cit., p. 80.

actions. Here therefore there is no alternative to the physical antecedent as cause of the mental state. If the situation were really as symmet-
rical as Ducasse maintains, there surely would never have been any
epiphenomenalists. Epiphenomenalism may be false, but it is not *obviously* false, and epiphenomenalists are not simply deluded fools.

"Extra-Cerebral" Memories

It will be recalled that in the exchanges in the BBC discussion of the
Ryall case the question came up whether memories can exist without
the brain. Professors Cohen and Taylor regarded the notion of extra-cerebral memories as totally absurd. Professor Stevenson vehemently
disagreed. "Memories may exist in the brain," he said, and "exist
elsewhere also." The best evidence that they may exist elsewhere,
Stevenson continued, comes from his own reincarnation research. On
the question of the "storage" of memories he remarked that there
"might be a non-physical process of storage." The memories "might be
in some dimension . . . which cannot be understood in terms of current physical concepts."[21]

Unlike Stevenson the late Professor H. H. Price did not believe in
reincarnation but he took communications from or through mediums
very seriously. As far as I know he remained an agnostic on the subject
of survival, but he insisted that if brain physiology supplies us with
evidence against the existence of extra-cerebral memories, certain of
the data assembled by parapsychologists provide evidence in its favor.
"It will, of course, be objected," Price wrote, "that memories cannot
exist in the absence of a physical brain, nor yet desires, nor images
either." Against this it must be emphasized that "any evidence which
directly supports the Survival Hypothesis (and there is quite a lot of
evidence which does) . . . is *pro tanto* evidence against the Materialistic conception of human personality,"[22] by which Price here simply
means the view that consciousness depends on the brain for its
existence.

I will confine myself to two brief comments. First, Price is quite right
in maintaining that the issue is one of weighing the evidence from brain
physiology against that from parapsychology. For my own part I do not
see how any rational person can hesitate in regarding the former evidence as *vastly* more impressive. I spent the better part of two years
studying Stevenson's evidence and found it exceedingly weak if not
indeed utterly worthless. I hesitate to speak about mediumistic communications but most of these, by the almost common consent of the more

---

[21]*The Listener*, op. cit., p. 686.
[22]"Survival and the Idea of 'Another World,' " in J. R. Smythies, Ed., *Brain and Mind*
(London: Routledge, 1965), p. 18.

respectable students of the subject, have a tendency to break down on close examination. Some impressive cases remain but even they do not compare in solidity with the careful, controlled studies of brain physiologists. Next, it should be pointed out that many parapsychologists are not supporters of belief in any kind of survival and, what is perhaps more the the point, rejection of extra-cerebral memories has no logical bearing on the "this-worldly" phenomena studied in parapsychology. Telepathic communications, to take one example, are between persons who have brains; and if these communications really occur they do not have the slightest tendency to support the existence of any extra-cerebral mental processes. As for Stevenson's nonphysical storage depot of extra-cerebral memories—"the dimension which cannot be understood in terms of current physical concepts"—it must surely be dismissed as nothing but a vague picture which is of no scientific value whatsoever.

The Mind and the Soul

The last rejoinder to be considered involves a distinction between the mind, which is identical with the phenomenal or empirical self whose existence is not disputed by Hume and other empiricists, and another nonphysical entity to which various labels have been applied. It is the immaterial or spiritual substance of Clarke, Butler, and Reid and numerous other philosophers, past and present, it is the Atman of the Hindu version of reincarnation, the noumenal self of Kant, and the soul (in one of its senses) of the Christian and Jewish traditions. It is argued that, although the mind may indeed so closely depend on the body that it must cease with the body's death, the same is not true of the soul. The soul is the "I" that "owns" both the body and the mind. I am five feet seven inches tall, I weigh one hundred and fifty pounds, I have blue eyes and brown hair; but I also have certain sensations and feelings and thoughts. I have various physical skills and I also possess certain emotional and intellectual dispositions. It is this underlying "I"—the subject of both the body and the mind—that has not been shown to require a body for its existence.

There are two objections to this rejoinder, each of them fatal. In the first place, although the way we speak in certain contexts suggests an underlying subject of both body and mind, there is no reason to suppose that it exists. Hume's theory that human beings are nothing but "bundles of impressions and ideas" is seriously inadequate. Each of us, at least while he is sane, has a sense of himself, more specifically, a sense of himself as continuing the same person from moment to moment. However, what this consists in is not the totally unchanging metaphysical entity that Hume rightly rebelled against. It is a sense of continuity in certain bodily sensations (especially of our limbs and certain muscle groups) and of our various tastes, opinions, and hab-its—more generally of our emotional and intellectual dispositions. These, together with our bodies, make us the kinds of persons we are. Although our emotional and intellectual dispositions are subject to change, unlike our moods and sensations, they are relatively stable. If this is what is meant by "soul," there is no reason to deny that we have a soul; but the soul in this sense is just as dependent on the body and the brain as any particular sensations, feelings, and thoughts.

The second objection to this rejoinder is that if there were such a thing as the spiritual substance or the metaphysical soul, it would not be what anybody means by "I." Human beings who are afraid of death dread the annihilation of their *empirical* selves and it is these empirical selves which they would like to survive. This is true of Western and Eastern believers alike. The great seventeenth-century philosopher Pierre Gassendi, who was both a Catholic priest and an atomistic mate-rialist, professed belief in the metaphysical soul. He also believed that insanity was a brain disease. Since the soul or reason (Gassendi pre-ferred the latter word) did not depend on the body, he concluded quite consistently that the soul or reason remained sane even when the individual had become insane. Gassendi's consistency led to a *reductio ad absurdum* of his position. If I go mad and if at the same time my soul remains sane then I and my soul are not the same thing.

34

DEREK PARFIT

Divided Minds and the Nature of Persons

IT WAS THE split-brain cases which drew me into philosophy. Our knowledge of these cases depends on the results of various psychological tests, as described by Donald MacKay.[1] These tests made use of two facts. We control each of our arms, and see what is in each half of our visual fields, with only one of our hemispheres. When someone's hemispheres have been disconnected, psychologists can thus present to this person two different written questions in the two halves of his visual field, and can receive two different answers written by this person's two hands.

Here is a simplified imaginary version of the kind of evidence that such tests provide. One of these people looks fixedly at the centre of a wide screen, whose left half is red and right half is blue. On each half in a darker shade are the words, "How many colours can you see?" With both hands the person writes, "Only one." The words are now changed to read, "Which is the only colour that you can see?" With one of his hands the person writes "Red," with the other he writes "Blue."

If this is how such a person responds, I would conclude that he is having two visual sensations—that he does, as he claims, see both red and blue. But in seeing each colour he is not aware of seeing the other. He has two streams of consciousness, in each of which he can see only

---

This essay appeared in C. Blakemore and S. Greenfield (eds.), *Mindwaves*, published in 1987 by Basil Blackwell. It is reprinted with the permission of Derek Parfit and the publisher.

[1]See MacKay's "Divided Brains—Divided Minds?" also in *Mindwaves*.

one colour. In one stream he sees red, and at the same time, in his other stream, he sees blue. More generally, he could be having at the same time two series of thoughts and sensations, in having each of which he is unaware of having the other.

This conclusion has been questioned. It has been claimed by some that there are not *two* streams of consciousness, on the ground that the sub-dominant hemisphere is a part of the brain whose functioning involves no consciousness. If this were true, these cases would lose most of their interest. I believe that it is not true, chiefly because, if a person's dominant hemisphere is destroyed, this person is able to react in the way in which, in the split-brain cases, the sub-dominant hemisphere reacts, and we do not believe that such a person is just an automaton, without consciousness. The sub-dominant hemisphere is, of course, much less developed in certain ways, typically having the linguistic abilities of a three-year-old. But three-year-olds are conscious. This supports the view that, in split-brain cases, there *are* two streams of consciousness.

Another view is that, in these cases, there are two persons involved, sharing the same body. Like Professor MacKay, I believe that we should reject this view. My reason for believing this is, however, different. Professor MacKay denies that there are two persons involved because he believes that there is only one person involved. I believe that, in a sense, the number of persons involved is none.

The Ego Theory and the Bundle Theory

To explain this sense I must, for a while, turn away from the split-brain cases. There are two theories about what persons are, and what is involved in a person's continued existence over time. On the *Ego Theory*, a person's continued existence cannot be explained except as the continued existence of a particular *Ego*, or *subject of experiences*. An Ego Theorist claims that, if we ask what unifies someone's consciousness at any time — what makes it true, for example, that I can now both see what I am typing and hear the wind outside my window — the answer is that these are both experiences which are being had by me, this person, at this time. Similarly, what explains the unity of a person's whole life is the fact that all of the experiences in this life are had by the same person, or subject of experiences. In its best-known form, the *Cartesian view*, each person is a persisting purely mental thing — a soul, or spiritual substance.

The rival view is the *Bundle Theory*. Like most styles in art — Gothic, baroque, rococo, etc. — this theory owes its name to its critics. But the name is good enough. According to the Bundle Theory, we can't explain either the unity of consciousness at any time, or the unity of a whole life, by referring to a person. Instead we must claim that there are long series of different mental states and events—thoughts, sensations, and the like—each series being what we call one life. Each series is unified by various kinds of causal relation, such as the relations that hold between experiences and later memories of them. Each series is thus like a bundle tied up with string.

In a sense, a Bundle Theorist denies the existence of persons. An outright denial is of course absurd. As Reid protested in the eighteenth century, "I am not thought, I am not action, I am not feeling; I am something which thinks and acts and feels." I am not a series of events, but a person. A Bundle Theorist admits this fact, but claims it to be only a fact about our grammar, or our language. There are persons or subjects in this language-dependent way. If, however, persons are believed to be more than this—to be separately existing things, distinct from our brains and bodies, and the various kinds of mental states and events—the Bundle Theorist denies that there are such things.

The first Bundle Theorist was Buddha, who taught "anatta," or the *No Self view*. Buddhists condede that selves or persons have "nominal existence," by which they mean that persons are merely combinations of other elements. Only what exists by itself, as a separate element, has instead what Buddhists call "actual existence." Here are some quotations from Buddhist texts:

> At the beginning of their conversation the king politely asks the monk his name, and receives the following reply: "Sir, I am known as 'Nagasena'; my fellows in the religious life address me as 'Nagasena'. Although my parents gave me the name . . . it is just an appellation, a form of speech, a description, a conventional usage. 'Nagasena' is only a name, for no person is found here."
> A sentient being does exist, you think, O Mara? You are misled by a false conception. This bundle of elements is void of Self, In it there is no sentient being. Just as a set of wooden parts Receives the name of carriage, So do we give to elements The name of fancied being.
> Buddha has spoken thus: "O Brethren, actions do exist, and also their consequences, but the person that acts does not. There is no one to cast away this set of elements, and no one to assume a new set of them. There exists no Individual, it is only a conventional name given to a set of elements."[2]

Buddha's claims are strikingly similar to the claims advanced by several Western writers. Since these writers knew nothing of Buddha, the similarity of these claims suggests that they are not merely part of one cultural tradition, in one period. They may be, as I believe they are, true.

[2]For the sources of these and similar quotations, see my *Reasons and Persons* (1984) pp. 502–3, 532. Oxford: Oxford Univ. Press.

What We Believe Ourselves to Be

Given the advances in psychology and neurophysiology, the Bundle Theory may now seem to be obviously true. It may seem uninteresting to deny that there are separately existing Egos, which are distinct from brains and bodies and the various kinds of mental states and events. But this is not the only issue. We may be convinced that the Ego Theory is false, or even senseless. Most of us, however, even if we are not aware of this, also have certain beliefs about what is involved in our continued existence over time. And these beliefs would only be justified if something like the Ego Theory was true. Most of us therefore have false beliefs about what persons are, and about ourselves.

These beliefs are best revealed when we consider certain imaginary cases, often drawn from science fiction. One such case is *teletransportation*. Suppose that you enter a cubicle in which, when you press a button, a scanner records the states of all of the cells in your brain and body, destroying both while doing so. This information is then transmitted at the speed of light to some other planet, where a replicator produces a perfect organic copy of you. Since the brain of your Replica is exactly like yours, it will seem to remember living your life up to the moment when you pressed the button, its character will be just like yours, and it will be in every other way psychologically continuous with you. This psychological continuity will not have its normal cause, the continued existence of your brain, since the causal chain will run through the transmission by radio of your "blueprint."

Several writers claim that, if you chose to be teletransported, believing this to be the fastest way of travelling, you would be making a terrible mistake. This would not be a way of travelling, but a way of dying. It may not, they concede, be quite as bad as ordinary death. It might be some consolation to you that, after your death, you will have this Replica, which can finish the book that you are writing, act as parent to your children, and so on. But, they insist, this Replica won't be you. It will merely be someone else, who is exactly like you. This is why this prospect is nearly as bad as ordinary death.

Imagine next a whole range of cases, in each of which, in a single operation, a different proportion of the cells in your brain and body would be replaced with exact duplicates. At the near end of this range, only 1 or 2 per cent would be replaced; in the middle, 40 or 60 per cent; near the far end, 98 or 99 per cent. At the far end of this range is pure teletransportation, the case in which all of your cells would be "replaced."

When you imagine that some proportion of your cells will be replaced with exact duplicates, it is natural to have the following beliefs. First, if you ask, "Will I survive? Will the resulting person be me?," there must be an answer to this question. Either you will survive, or you are about to die. Second, the answer to this question must be either a simple "Yes" or a simple "No." The person who wakes up either will or will not be you. There cannot be a third answer, such as that the person waking up will be half you. You can imagine yourself later being half-conscious. But if the resulting person will be fully conscious, he cannot be half you. To state these beliefs together: to the question, "Will the resulting person be me?," there must always *be* an answer, which must be all-or-nothing.

There seem good grounds for believing that, in the case of teletransportation, your Replica would not be you. In a slight variant of this case, your Replica might be created while you were still alive, so that you could talk to one another. This seems to show that, if 100 per cent of your cells were replaced, the result would merely be a Replica of you. At the other end of my range of cases, where only 1 per cent would be replaced, the resulting person clearly *would* be you. It therefore seems that, in the cases in between, the resulting person must be either you, or merely a Replica. It seems that one of these must be true, and that it makes a great difference which is true.

How We Are Not What We Believe

If these beliefs were correct, there must be some critical percentage, somewhere in this range of cases, up to which the resulting person would be you, and beyond which he would merely be your Replica. Perhaps, for example, it would be you who would wake up if the proportion of cells replaced were 49 per cent, but if just a few more cells were also replaced, this would make all the difference, causing it to be someone else who would wake up.

That there must be some such critical percentage follows from our natural beliefs. But this conclusion is most implausible. How could a few cells make such a difference? Moreover, if there is such a critical percentage, no one could ever discover where it came. Since in all these cases the resulting person would believe that he was you, there could never be any evidence about where, in this range of cases, he would suddenly cease to be you.

On the Bundle Theory, we should reject these natural beliefs. Since you, the person, are not a separately existing entity, we can know exactly what would happen without answering the question of what will happen to you. Moreover, in the cases in the middle of my range, it is an empty question whether the resulting person would be you, or would merely be someone else who is exactly like you. These are not here two different possibilities, one of which must be true. These are merely two different descriptions of the very same course of events. If 50 per cent of your cells were replaced with exact duplicates, we could call the resulting person you, or we could call him merely your Replica.

But since these are not here different possibilities, this is a mere choice of words.

As Buddha claimed, the Bundle Theory is hard to believe. It is hard to accept that it could be an empty question whether one is about to die, or will instead live for many years.

What we are being asked to accept may be made clearer with this analogy. Suppose that a certain club exists for some time, holding regular meetings. The meetings then cease. Some years later, several people form a club with the same name, and the same rules. We can ask, "Did these people revive the very same club? Or did they merely start up another club which is exactly similar?" Given certain further details, this would be another empty question. We could know just what happened without answering this question. Suppose that someone said: "But there must be an answer. The club meeting later must either be, or not be, the very same club." This would show that this person didn't understand the nature of clubs.

In the same way, if we have any worries about my imagined cases, we don't understand the nature of persons. In each of my cases, you would know that the resulting person would be both psychologically and physically exactly like you, and that he would have some particular proportion of the cells in your brain and body — 90 per cent, or 10 per cent, or, in the case of teletransportation, 0 per cent. Knowing this, you know everything. How could it be a real question what would happen to you, unless you are a separately existing Ego, distinct from a brain and body, and the various kinds of mental state and event? If there are no such Egos, there is nothing else to ask a real question about.

Accepting the Bundle Theory is not only hard; it may also affect our emotions. As Buddha claimed, it may undermine our concern about our own futures. This effect can be suggested by redescribing this change of view. Suppose that you are about to be destroyed, but will later have a Replica on Mars. You would naturally believe that this prospect is about as bad as ordinary death, since your Replica won't be you. On the Bundle Theory, the fact that your Replica won't be you just consists in the fact that, though it will be fully psychologically continuous with you, this continuity won't have its normal cause. But when you object to teletransportation you are not objecting merely to the abnormality of this cause. You are objecting that this cause won't get *you* to Mars. You fear that the abnormal cause will fail to produce a further and all-important fact, which is different from the fact that your Replica will be psychologically continuous with you. You do not merely want there to be psychological continuity between you and some future person. You want to *be* this future person. On the Bundle Theory, there is no such special further fact. What you fear will not happen, in this imagined case, *never* happens. You want the person on Mars to be you in a specially intimate way in which no future person will ever be you. This means that, judged from the standpoint of your natural beliefs, even ordinary survival is about as bad as teletransportation. *Ordinary survival is about as bad as being destroyed and having a Replica.*

How the Split-Brain Cases Support the Bundle Theory

The truth of the Bundle Theory seems to me, in the widest sense, as much a scientific as a philosophical conclusion. I can imagine kinds of evidence which would have justified believing in the existence of separately existing Egos, and believing that the continued existence of these Egos is what explains the continuity of each mental life. But there is in fact very little evidence in favour of this Ego Theory, and much for the alternative Bundle Theory.

Some of this evidence is provided by the split-brain cases. On the Ego Theory, to explain what unifies our experiences at any one time, we should simply claim that these are all experiences which are being had by the same person. Bundle Theorists reject this explanation. This disagreement is hard to resolve in ordinary cases. But consider the simplified split-brain case that I described. We show to my imagined patient a placard whose left half is blue and right half is red. In one of this person's two streams of consciousness, he is aware of seeing only blue, while at the same time, in his other stream, he is aware of seeing only red. Each of these two visual experiences is combined with other experiences, like that of being aware of moving one of his hands. What unifies the experiences, at any time, in each of this person's two streams of consciousness? What unifies his awareness of seeing only red with his awareness of moving one hand? The answer cannot be that these experiences are being had by the same person. This answer cannot explain the unity of each of this person's two streams of consciousness, since it ignores the disunity between these streams. This person is now having all of the experiences in both of his two streams. If this fact was what unified these experiences, this would make the two streams one.

These cases do not, I have claimed, involve two people sharing a single body. Since there is only one person involved, who has two streams of consciousness, the Ego Theorist's explanation would have to take the following form. He would have to distinguish between persons and subjects of experiences, and claim that, in split-brain cases, there are *two* of the latter. What unifies the experiences in one of the person's two streams would have to be the fact that these experiences are all being had by the same subject of experiences. What unifies the experiences in this person's other stream would have to be the fact that they are being had by another subject of experiences. When this explanation takes this form, it becomes much less plausible. While we could assume that "subject of experiences," or "Ego," simply meant "person," it was easy to believe that there are subjects of experiences. But if there can be subjects of experiences that are not persons, and if in the life of a split-brain patient there are at any time two different subjects of experiences—two different Egos—why should we believe that there really are such things? This does not amount to a refutation. But it seems to me a strong argument against the Ego Theory.

As a Bundle Theorist, I believe that these two Egos are idle cogs. There is another explanation of the unity of consciousness, both in ordinary cases and in split-brain cases. It is simply a fact that ordinary people are, at any time, aware of having several different experiences. This awareness of several different experiences can be helpfully compared with one's awareness, in short-term memory, of several different experiences. Just as there can be a single memory of just having had several experiences, such as hearing a bell strike three times, there can be a single state of awareness both of hearing the fourth striking of this bell, and of seeing, at the same time, ravens flying past the bell-tower.

Unlike the Ego Theorist's explanation, this explanation can easily be extended to cover split-brain cases. In such cases there is, at any time, not one state of awareness of several different experiences, but two such states. In the case I described, there is one state of awareness of both seeing only red and of moving one hand, and there is another state of awareness of both seeing only blue and moving the other hand. In claiming that there are two such states of awareness, we are not postulating the existence of unfamiliar entities, two separately existing Egos which are not the same as the single person whom the case involves. This explanation appeals to a pair of mental states which would have to be described anyway in a full description of this case.

I have suggested how the split-brain cases provide one argument for one view about the nature of persons. I should mention another such argument, provided by an imagined extension of these cases, first discussed at length by David Wiggins.[3]

In this imagined case a person's brain is divided, and the two halves are transplanted into a pair of different bodies. The two resulting people live quite separate lives. This imagined case shows that personal identity is not what matters. If I was about to divide, I should conclude that neither of the resulting people will be me. I will have ceased to exist. But this way of ceasing to exist is about as good—or as bad—as ordinary survival.

Some of the features of Wiggins's imagined case are likely to remain technically impossible. But the case cannot be dismissed, since its most striking feature, the division of one stream of consciousness into separate streams, has already happened. This is a second way in which the actual split-brain cases have great theoretical importance. They challenge some of our deepest assumptions about ourselves.[4]

---

[3]At the end of his *Identity and Spatio-temporal Continuity* (1967). Oxford: Blackwell.
[4]I discuss these assumptions further in part 3 of my *Reasons and Persons*.

Bibliographical Essay

⁓

This bibliography covers all the topics discussed in the selections and the Introduction. The sequence of topics is roughly the same as in the Introduction.

Two recent books provide a good idea of the major contemporary disputes about immortality. S. T. Davis (ed.), *Death and Afterlife* (London 1989) contains a collection of papers delivered at a conference in Claremont, California, in 1987. The editor, John Hick, and Paul Badham defend the Christian position; J. Prabhu supports reincarnation; K. Nielsen represents the unbeliever's viewpoint. P. and L. Badham (eds.), *Death and Immortality in the Religions of the World* (New York 1987) contains essays expounding the views of different religions as well as those of unbelievers. A critical survey of the major philosophical positions is found in A. Flew's article, "Immortality," in the *Encyclopedia of Philosophy* (vol. 4, pp. 139–150). The history of different forms of belief in survival as well as of unbelief is recounted in great detail in W. R. Alger, *The Destiny of the Soul — A Critical History of the Doctrine of a Future Life*, a huge book, which first appeared in 1860 and went through ten editions by 1878 (It was reprinted by Greenwood Publishers of New York in 1968). In addition to being extremely informative, the book's vivid and wonderfully absurd metaphors make it delightful reading. Reincarnation and Karma are praised in glowing language, but in the end Alger comes down in favor of survival in the next world. Man, he reasoned, is "the guest of God in the universe." We may assume that the "infinite Housekeeper" will not be so ungracious as to "blow out the lights and quench the guests." Given the nature of some of these guests one can only conclude that the patience of the infinite Housekeeper is inexhaustible.

There are informative articles on reincarnation in the *Encyclopedia of Religion* (vol. 12, pp. 265–269) and the *Encyclopedia of Philosophy* (vol. 7, pp. 122–125). The former is by J. Bruce Lone, the latter by Ninian Smart. J. Head and S. L. Cranston (eds.), *Reincarnation in World Thought* (New York 1967) is a compilation of writings on reincarnation by past and present believers. J. M. E. McTaggart's defense of reincarnation is found in chapter 4 of *Some Dogmas of Religion* (London 1906). C. J. Ducasse, the author of our selection 19, provides a fuller defense as well as much historical information in *A Critical Examination of the Belief in Life After Death* (Springfield, Ill. 1961). Apologists for reincarnation have a tendency to claim many famous men as fellow believers (Hume and Voltaire, for example) who did not in fact accept such a position. However, Plato (selection 1) did believe in some form of preexistence and Schopenhauer defended an idiosyncratic version of the theory in vol. 3 of *The World as Will and Idea* (1818; first English trans. London 1833). In *Reincarnation As a Christian Hope* (London 1982) G. MacGregor, Emeritus Distinguished Professor of Philosophy at the University of Southern California, argues, in opposition to the position of most Christian theologians, that reincarnation is perfectly compatible with Christianity. Ian Stevenson, the psychiatrist who supports reincarnation on the basis of the recollections of earlier lives by certain children, has summarized his research and theoretical conclusions in *Children Who Remember Previous Lives* (Charlottesville 1987). In chapter 1 of *Beyond Death — Evidence for Life After Death* (Springfield, Ill. 1987), R. Almeder takes the view that Stevenson's research for which he has tremendous admiration supports a stronger conclusion than the one urged by Stevenson himself. In some of his earlier discus-sions, Stevenson allowed the possibility that theories other than reincarnation might account for his data. According to Almeder no other theory could possibly do this. Stevenson is also defended against various objections by the well-known parapsychologist A. Gauld in chapter 12 of *Mediumship and Survival* (London 1982). G. C. Nayak seems to be the only reincarnationist to show some understanding of the objection, based on the widely held view that bodily continuity is an essential ingredient of personal identity, that an individual who is said to be the incarnation of one living at another time cannot be identical with him and that hence we cannot have incarnations of the same person. He attempts to answer this objection in "Survival, Reincarnation and the Problem of Personal Identity," which is available in J. M. O. Wheatley and H. L. Edge (eds.), *Philosophical Dimensions of Parapsychology* (Springfield, Il. 1976).

The following three papers support the view that hypnotic past regressions, however factually accurate, can be explained as cryptomnesia: G. L. Dickinson, "A Case of Emergence of a Latent Memory Under Hypnosis," *Proceedings of the Society for Psychical Research*, 1911; E. S. Zolik, "An Experimental Investigation of the Psychodynamic Implications of the Hypnotic 'Previous Existence' Fantasy," *Journal of Clinical Psychology*, 1958; and Melvin Harris, "Are Past-Life Regressions Evidence for Reincarnation?", *Free Inquiry*, 1986. The coherence of the reincarnation theory is questioned by T. Geach in chapter 1 of *God and the Soul* (London 1969) and in chapter 2 of A. Flew, *The Logic of Mortality* (Oxford 1987). The coherence but not the truth of reincarnationism is defended by R. W. Perrett in chapter 8 of *Death and Immortality* (Dordrecht 1987). A very detailed study of Karma (both critical and sympathetic) is B. R. Reichenbach, *The Law of Karma—A Philosophical Study* (Honolulu 1990). The Buddhist notion of Karma is criticized in P. J. Griffiths, "Notes Towards a Critique of Buddhist Karmic Theory," *Religious Studies*, 1982–83. P. Siwek, S. J., *The Enigma of the Hereafter* (New York 1952) attacks reincarnation and Karma on philosophical as well as empirical grounds. It is written from a conservative Catholic standpoint. In chapter 3 of *Eternal Life* (New York 1984) the liberal Catholic theologian Hans Küng provides a scholarly and sympathetic treatment. Four chapters of J. Hick, *Death and Eternal Life* (New York 1976) are devoted to a restatement of the key ideas of reincarnationists in empirically meaningful language. One of the best-known critiques of Stevenson is found in chapter 3 of Ian Wilson, *Mind Out of Time?* (London 1981). Paul Edwards, "The Case Against Reincarnation," *Free Inquiry*, 1986–1987, is a four-part series attacking reincarnation on both philosophical and empirical grounds. The last of the four pieces in this series deals with the work of Stevenson.

Dr. Stanislav Grof, a Czech psychiatrist now residing in the United States, who has specialized in the treatment of mental disorders by administering high doses of LSD, is an ardent believer in reincarnation, offering the experiences of some of his patients as irrefutable evidence. In *Realms of the Human Unconscious—Observations from LSD Research* (New York 1975), which is the most systematic of his works, he presents the case of a psychotic woman who remembers her life as a snake. Her knowledge of the biology of snakes (which, according to Grof, she could not have obtained in any more familiar fashion) convinced him that she had indeed had an earlier life as a snake. In *Beyond Death* (London 1980), a beautifully illustrated book written with Christina Grof, he reaches the conclusion that "there now exists extensive clinical evidence to support the claims of religion and mythology that biological death is the beginning of an adventure in consciousness." *The Human Encounter with Death* (New York 1977), written by Grof with Joan Halifax and supplied with a foreword by Dr. Kübler-

Ross, deals primarily with dying patients who were given LSD both to make their pains more tolerable and to produce mystical experiences. Grof and Halifax interpret these as reliable premonitions of the next incarnation. Kübler-Ross was probably the ideal person to write the introduction to this last book since she regards reincarnation as a "fact" and since moreover she herself lived in Palestine two thousand years ago as one of the "most important teachers" of Jesus. Who she was in between has not been disclosed.

There is an immense literature on the astral body, much of it completely insane, but some of it also extremely amusing. Astral theorists have a pre-scientific cast of mind, not realizing that their claims require to be supported by evidence. One of the most informative brief statements of the astral philosophy is an article, "Out-of-the Body Experiences and Survival," by Robert Crookall in J. D. Pearce-Higgins and G. S. Whitby (eds.), *Life, Death and Psychical Research* (London 1973). If this piece is of doubtful sanity no such reservations apply to the numerous, full-length books by the same author, such as *The Study and Practice of Astral Projection* (London 1960) and *The Mechanisms of Astral Projection* (London 1968). The most enjoyable of Crookall's vast number of works is *The Next World — And the Next* (London 1966). Several sections of this treatise are devoted to the problem of "ghostly garments" — the question, that is, of what clothes (if any) astral bodies wear. One of the saner presentations of the astral theory is R. Shirley, *The Mystery of the Human Double* (London 1938). The phenomenon of "bilocation" is discussed in detail in chapter 4 of Ernesto Bozzano, *Discarnate Influence in Human Life* (London 1938), a book regarded as a classic by occultists. The passage from William Gerhardi quoted in the introduction in which he tells how his astral double was "neatly folded" inside his physical body comes from his autobiographical novel *Resurrection* (London 1930). One of the best-known presentations of the astral theory in recent years is R. A. Monroe, *Journeys Out of the Body* (Garden City, N.Y. 1971). During the heyday of the New Age, Monroe was interviewed by *Newsweek* (May 1, 1978) along with his star-pupil, Dr. Kübler-Ross. He told the reporters that during the seven years prior to the interview he had dispatched no less than 1400 persons on astral journeys. According to Monroe these travelers *are* publicly observable. It is regrettable that skeptics were not invited to witness these journeys and that not a single photograph was taken. Susan Blackmore, *Beyond The Body* (London 1982) may be recommended as by far the most thorough critical study of out-of-body experiences and theories about the astral body. Blackmore also discusses issues relating to out-of-body experiences in "Visions from the Dying Brain," *New Scientist*, May 5, 1988 and "Out of the Body?" in R. Basil (ed.), *Not Necessarily the New Age* (Buffalo 1988).

Philosophers have rarely discussed the astral body, but it figures prominently in a symposium on "Survival" by H. D. Lewis and A. Flew which is reprinted in Lewis, *Persons and Life After Death* (London 1978). It should be emphasized that neither Lewis nor Flew is a believer in the astral body, although Flew regards it as a less implausible vehicle for survival than either the disembodied mind or the resurrection replica. At the beginning of his discussion of immortality (selection 23) Geach dismisses the astral body on purely empirical grounds. G. McGregor, *op. cit.* chapter 11, objects to such dismissals as arbitrary and superficial. In "Questions of Survival: Some Logical Reflections," which is available in Wheatley and Edge (eds.), *Philosophical Dimensions of Parapsychology, op. cit.* J. M. O. Wheatley reaches a conclusion similar to Flew's but seems more hopeful about justifying survival by means of a "second body."

An excellent introduction to questions about the nature of the mind and its relation to the body is J. Shaffer, *Philosophy of Mind* (Englewood Cliffs, NJ 1968) and the same author's article "Mind-Body Problem" in the *Encyclopedia of Philosophy* (vol. 5, pp. 336–346). There are comprehensive and lucid accounts of contemporary work on the subject in the following three survey articles: J. Shaffer, "Recent Work on the Mind-Body Problem (I)," *American Philosophical Quarterly*, 1965, D. C. Dennett, "Current Issues in the Philosophy of Mind," *American Philosophical Quarterly*, 1978, and J. Shaffer, "Recent Work on the Mind-Body Problem (II)," in K. G. Lucey and T. P. Machan (eds.), *Recent Work in Philosophy* (Totowa, N.J. 1983). The following anthologies are useful collections of influential papers by contemporary Anglo-Saxon philosophers: S. Hook (ed.), *Dimensions of Mind* (New York 1961); V. C. Chappell (ed.), *The Philosophy of Mind* (Englewood Cliffs, N.J. 1962), D. F. Gustafson (ed.), *Essays in Philosophical Psychology* (Garden City, N.Y. 1964), G. N. A. Vesey (ed.), *Body and Mind* (London 1964); H. Morick (ed.), *Introduction to the Philosophy of Mind* (Glenview, Ill. 1970), S. Hampshire (ed.), *Philosophy of Mind* (New York 1966); J. O'Connor (ed.), *Modern Materialism: Readings on Mind-Body Identity* (New York 1969); S. F. Spicker (ed.), *The Philosophy of the Body* (New York 1970); C. V. Borst (ed.), *The Mind-Brain Identity Theory* (London 1970); D. M. Rosenthal (ed.), *Materialism and the Mind-Body Problem* (Englewood Cliffs, NJ 1971); J. Glover (ed.), *The Philosophy of Mind* (Oxford 1976); N. Block (ed.), *Readings in Philosophy of Psychology* (Cambridge, Mass. 1980, 2 vols); J. E. Tomberlin (ed.), *Philosophical Perspectives, 3—Philosophy of Mind and Action Theory* (1989) and *Philosophical Perspectives, 4—Action Theory and Philosophy of Mind* (1990), both published by Ridgeview Publishing Co., Atascadero, Calif., and D. M. Rosenthal (ed.), *The Nature of Mind* (New York 1991). The last of these, which is extremely comprehensive, gives an excellent idea of the major current controversies. A. Flew (ed.), *Body, Mind, and Death* (New York 1964) contains some contemporary papers, but most of the selections are from philosophers of the past. J. W. Reeves (ed.), *Body and Mind in Western Thought* (Harmondsworth 1958) has a long and informative historical introduction and contains some little-known pieces, but its selections do not extend beyond the nineteenth century.

As explained in the Introduction, dualism in general and dualistic interactionism in particular have been out of fashion for some time and most of the anthologies just listed are heavily weighted in favor of one or more forms of materialism. However, dualistic interactionism is far from dead. It is defended in H. D. Lewis, *The Elusive Mind* (London 1969), K. R. Popper and J. C. Eccles, *The Self and Its Brain* (London and New York 1977), R. Swinburne, *The Evolution of the Soul* (Oxford 1986), and in various of the contributions to J. R. Smythies and J. Beloff (eds.), *The Case for Dualism* (Charlottesville 1989). G. Madell, *Mind and Materialism* (Edinburgh 1988) is a vigorous counter-attack against all major contemporary versions of materialism and at the same time a defense of dualistic interactionism. C. J. Ducasse, *Nature Mind and Death* (La Salle, Ill. 1951), from which our selection 19 is taken, continues to be widely quoted. Many who do not share Ducasse's views on survival nevertheless admire the thoroughness with which he defends dualistic interactionism against its critics. A still earlier book, C. D. Broad, *The Mind and Its Place in Nature* (London 1925), has achieved the status of a classic. In the end Broad comes down on the side of epiphenomenalism, but the book strongly favors dualism in opposition to the versions of materialism current in his day, some of which are not significantly different from versions in vogue at the present time. Both Broad and Madell insist that materialism is incompatible with the phenomenal qualities of our experiences which are usually referred to as "qualia" in contemporary discussions. The quotation from John Mackie on this subject in the Introduction comes from chapter 5 of his *Problems from Locke* (Oxford 1976). Roland Puccetti's remarks on intentionality quoted on p. 27 are taken from his "The Heart of the Mind: Intentionality vs. Intelligence" which is one of the pieces in Smythies and Beloff (eds.), *The Case for Dualism, op. cit.* The passage from Searle on the same subject occurs in chapter 1 of *Minds, Brains and Science* (London 1984). Searle's statement that "mental processes are biological phenomena located in our brain" is quoted from a letter in the *New York Review* of February 16, 1989. Similar statements are found in several of his other publications. E. G. Boring's statement that "consciousness is located in the brain" is quoted from chapter 8 of *The Physical Dimensions of Consciousness* (New York 1963). Thomas Nagel's illustration concerning the privacy of taste experiences is quoted from chapter 4 of *What Does It All Mean?* (New York 1987).

A substance-theory similar to Reid's is defended by Bishop Butler in his "Dissertation of Personal Identity," which is available in vol. 1 of W. E. Gladstone's edition of Butler's *Works* (Oxford 1896). It is reprinted in Flew, *Body, Mind, and Death, op. cit.* The passage from Francis Wayland quoted on p. 32 of the Introduction comes from *The Elements of Intellectual Philosophy* (Boston 1853). J. McCosh wrote in support of the spiritual substance in *An Examination of J. S. Mill's Philosophy* (New York 1880). More recent defenses are found in vol. 1 of F. R. Tennant, *Philosophical Theology* (Cambridge 1930), C. A. Campbell, *On Selfhood and Godhood* (London 1957), and H. D. Lewis, *The Self and Immortality* (London 1973) and *The Elusive Self* (Philadelphia 1982). The foremost champions of the substance-self on the current scene are R. M. Chisholm, Richard Swinburne and Geoffrey Madell—Chisholm in *Person and Object* (London and LaSalle, Il. 1976) and *The First Person* (Minneapolis 1981); Swinburne in *The Evolution of the Soul* (Oxford 1986) and his contributions to S. Shoemaker and R. Swinburne, *Personal Identity* [Oxford 1984]; Madell in *The Identity of the Self* (Edinburgh 1981). The passage from Lotze quoted on p. 33 of the Introduction comes from vol. 2 of his *Metaphysics*, an English translation of which was published in Oxford in 1887. Lotze is almost completely forgotten, but he was very highly regarded in the nineteenth century, by William James among others. In the same chapter in which the quoted passage occurs Lotze convincingly attacks the view still widely prevalent that "only like can act on like."

The leading champion of the bundle theory in the 19th century was J. S. Mill who defended it in chapter 12 of *An Examination of Sir William Hamilton's Philosophy* (3d ed., London 1872). The passages quoted from Bertrand Russell on p. 33 are found in his *Why I Am Not a Christian* (London and New York 1957). Russell always thought of the spiritual substance as well as of its material counterpart as "grammatical illusions." "The subject," he wrote in *My Philosophical Development* (London 1959), "appears to be a logical fiction, like mathematical points and instants. It is introduced, not because observation requires it, but because it is linguistically convenient and apparently demanded by grammar." The passage from Ayer quoted on p. 34 occurs in his introduction to Ayer and R. Winch (eds.), *The British Empirical Philosophers* (London 1952). Ayer discussed the subject in several later books, including *The Origins of Pragmatism* (San Francisco 1968), *The Central Questions of Philosophy* (London 1973), and *Hume* (New York 1980). A. Quinton's reply to F. H. Bradley's jibe is quoted from *The Nature of Things* (London 1973). In Section 13 of *The Genealogy of Morals* (1887), Nietzsche presents a view that is strikingly similar to Russell's. "Behind the doing, acting, becoming," he writes, "there is no agent, no 'being.' The 'doer' has simply been added to the deed by the imagination—the doing is everything." Only the "snare of language . . . blinds us to this fact."

Philosophers have concerned themselves with the problem of personal identity—what makes a person the same at different times—ever since Locke and Leibniz, but the earlier literature is not extensive. Since the 1950s, however, the topic has become a major focus of interest among analytic philosophers and the literature is now immense. To find one's way in the maze of conflicting theories and extremely subtle arguments, one cannot do better than consult H. W. Noonan, *Personal Identity* (London 1989), which, in addition to tracing the history of the subject, lucidly and fairly explains the competing positions and offers judicious comments on the arguments that have dominated contemporary discussions. J. Perry (ed.), *Personal Identity* (Berkeley 1975) is an extremely useful anthology containing selections from Locke, Reid, Hume, and such influential contemporaries as A. Quinton, H. P. Grice, S. Shoemaker, B. Williams, D. Parfit, and T. Nagel. The book also has an excellent introduction by the editor. A. Rorty (ed.), *The Identity of Persons* (Berkeley 1976), contains papers by some of the best-known British and American philosophers as well as a comprehensive bibliography. T. Penelhum, "Personal Identity," *Encyclopedia of Philosophy* (vol. 6, pp. 95–107) is highly recommended as an introduction to the subject.

Most contemporary publications on personal identity do not spell out the implications of the theories advanced by the authors for the question of survival. There are, however, several notable exceptions. J. Perry, *A Dialogue on Personal Identity and Immortality* (Indianapolis 1978), is a delightful pamphlet written on a popular level in which the main character, a dying philosophy teacher by the name of Gretchen Weinrob, rejects the consolations offered by friends who think that survival is at least possible. The implications of theories of personal identity for survival are also explored in Flew, *The Logic of Mortality*, *op. cit.* and T. Penelhum, *Survival and Disembodied Existence* (London 1970). Penelhum also discusses both personal identity and survival in the last two chapters of *Religion and Rationality* (New York 1971).

Nobody writing on personal identity and related problems in recent years has aroused as much controversy as Derek Parfit whose "Divided Minds and the Nature of Persons" is the last selection in the present book. Parfit's first and probably most famous paper, "Personal Identity," originally published in the *Philosophical Review* in 1971, is reprinted with an additional note in J. Glover (ed.), *The Philosophy of Mind, op. cit.* He subsequently elaborated his views in "On the Importance of Self-Identity," *Journal of Philosophy* 1971, "Later Selves and Moral Principles," in A. Montefiore (ed.), *Philosophy and Personal Relations* (London 1973), and "Lewis, Perry, and What Matters," in Rorty (ed.), *The Identity of Persons, op. cit.* Parfit's fullest statement may be found in his *Reasons and Persons* (Oxford 1984), which is widely regarded as one of the most challenging and imaginative philosophical works of recent decades. Parfit has repeatedly stated that what is important is not personal identity but what he calls psychological connectedness, as exemplified in the relations between the memory of an experience and the remembered experience for example, or the intention to perform a certain action and the performance of the action. It is instructive to spell out how Parfit would react to certain of Hick's contentions. Hick believes that after our death God will create replicas of ourselves. (Parfit does not believe in God, but this is of no consequence in the present context.) Hick maintains (selection 24, pp. 240–241) that these replicas can quite properly be regarded as identical with the premortem individuals whose replicas they are. Parfit would neither endorse nor reject this claim: he would say that it does not matter whether the replicas are identical with the premortem person. What matters is psychological connectedness, and this would be present in the situation which Hick postulates. Parfit believes that acceptance of his views on personal identity and psychological connectedness has significant practical consequences. In *Reasons and Persons* he mentions that he has found his views on these topics liberating and that his own death seems "less bad" to him than it did formerly.

The following are some of the numerous critical discussions of Parfit's ideas: T. Penelhum, "The Importance of Self-Identity," *Journal of Philosophy*, 1971, the same author's "Survival and Identity: Some Recent Discussions" in B. Shapin and L. Coly (eds.), *The Philosophy of Parapsychology* (New York 1977), D. Lewis, "Survival and Identity," in Rorty (ed.), *The Identity of Persons, op. cit.*, B. Williams, "Persons, Character and Morality," also in Rorty, *op. cit.*, J. Shaffer, "Personal Identity," *Journal of Medicine and Philosophy*, 1977; D. Wiggins, "The Concern to Survive," in *Midwest Studies in Philosophy* (1979), reprinted in Wiggins, *Needs, Values, Truth* (Oxford 1987); Madell, *The Identity of the Self, op. cit.*; chapter 10 of J. Glover, *The Philosophy and Psychology of Personal Identity* (London 1988); J. Robinson, "Personal Identity and Survival," *Journal of Philosophy*, 1988, and chapter 9 of Noonan, *Personal Identity, op. cit.*

Parfit has repeatedly emphasized the affinities between his view and certain of the Buddha's pronouncements — not only endorsements of the bundle theory but also of the implications, resisted by most Western supporters of the bundle theory, that human beings are not the same persons at different times. Some relevant passages are quoted by Parfit in selection 34. Several others are found in Appendix J of *Reasons and Persons*. Parfit gives as his sources T. Stcherbatsky, "The Soul Theory of the Buddhists," *Bulletin de l'Academie des Sciences de Russie*, 1919, the same author's *The Central Conception of Buddhism*, Royal Asiatic Society (London 1923); and S. Collins, *Selfless Persons* (Cambridge 1982). Hick, in *Death and Eternal Life, op. cit.* (p. 334), quotes a verse from a Buddhist scholastic by the name of Buddha Ghosa which is a perfect summary of the Buddhist doctrine:

For there is suffering, but none who suffer;
Doing exists although there is no doer;
Extinction is but no extinguished person;
Although there is a path, there is no goer.

It will be remembered that Russell and Nietzsche use almost the same language to state their versions of the bundle theory.

The eighteenth-century debate on whether matter can think took as its point of departure Locke's declaration that there was no contradiction in supposing that God could "superadd to matter a faculty of thinking." However, several decades before Locke, Spinoza had offered a similar suggestion. "No one has hitherto laid down the limits of the body," Spinoza had written, "no one has as yet been taught by experience what the body can accomplish solely by the laws of nature." The view that the body has mental as well as material attributes was explicitly advanced by John Toland, who considered himself a disciple of both Spinoza and Locke, in his *Letters to Serena* (London 1704); by Anthony Collins in his *Letter to the Learned Mr. Henry Dodwell, Containing Some Remarks on a (Pretended) Demonstration of the Immateriality and Natural Immortality of the Soul* (1707); by Lamettrie in *Man As a Machine* (1747); by Voltaire in various of his works (selection 10), and by Baron Holbach in his *System of Nature* (1770). The story of the debates inspired by Locke is told in great detail in two books by J. W. Yolton: *Thinking Matter—Materialism in Eighteenth Century Britain* (Oxford 1984) and *Locke and French Materialism* (Oxford 1991). Both books have superb bibliographies. The French story is also told in several chapters of A. S. Spink, *French Free-Thought from Gassendi to Voltaire* (London 1960). F. A. Lange's great *History of Materialism*, originally published in 1865 and available in English translation with an introduction by Bertrand Russell, is a mine of information on the spread of materialism and the hostile reaction to it in Britain, France, and Germany. Ernest Nagel's "Are Naturalists Materialists?" which is the second piece in Nagel's *Logic without Metaphysics* (Glencoe, Ill. 1956) first appeared in the *Journal of Philosophy* in 1945, listing as authors John Dewey, Sidney Hook and Nagel. It was, however, entirely Nagel's work who was writing in response to criticisms of naturalism by W. H. Sheldon appearing in the same volume of the *Journal of Philosophy*. Dewey and Hook, who were also the targets of Sheldon's polemic, simply endorsed what Nagel had written. Köstler's claim that the brain cannot "generate" consciousness, quoted on p. 40 of the Introduction, comes from his "Whereof One Cannot Speak" in A. Toynbee et al., *Life After Death* (New York 1976); the similar assertion by Medard Boss is found in *Psychoanalysis and Daseinsanalysis* (New York 1963) and Külpe's remarks along the same lines are quoted from *The Philosophy of the Present in Germany* (Leipzig 1902; English trans. 1913). The scholastic maxim that any attribute of an effect must already have been present in its cause, or a principle very like it, is supported by Thomas Nagel in an article, "Panpsychism," in his *Mortal Questions* (Cambridge 1979). Nagel argues that the brain could produce consciousness only if its ultimate constituents possessed mental properties. Unlike Koestler and the other writers quoted on this topic, Nagel does not deny that the brain generates consciousness, but he maintains that, if we do believe this, we are committed to panpsychism. Critics will reply that since panpsychism seems absurd, one or more of Nagel's premises must be wrong.

The two outstanding defenders of epiphenomenalism in the nineteenth century were T. H. Huxley and Shadworth Hodgson. Huxley's "On the Hypothesis That Animals Are Automata and Its History" appeared in 1874. The entire essay can be found in Huxley's *Methods and Results* (New York 1902). It is reprinted with slight omissions in the third edition of P. Edwards and A. Pap (eds.), *A Modern Introduction to Philosophy* (New York 1973). Hodgson presents his version in *The Theory of Practice* (London 1870) and *The Metaphysics of Experience* (London 1898). In chapter 5 of volume 1 of his *Principles of Psychology* (1890) William James quotes Huxley, Hodgson, an "exceedingly clever writer" by the name of Charles Mercier (from whose works some especially interesting passages are reproduced), and several other nineteenth-century psychologists who favored epiphenomenalism. He himself, however, embraces "the language of common-sense," by which he means dualistic interactionism. Santayana defended epiphenomenalism in *Reason and Common Sense* (New York 1922) and *The Realm of Essence* (New York 1927). Broad supports epiphenomenalism in *The Mind and Its Place in Nature*, *op. cit.* Broad's views are criticized in W. Kneale's contribution to P. A. Schilpp (ed.), *The Philosophy of C. D. Broad* (New York 1959), which also contains Broad's reply. Epiphenomenalism is criticized in M. Maher, *Psychology* (9th ed., London 1940); Ducasse, *Nature Mind and Death*, *op. cit.* and several of his other writings; B. Blanshard, "A Verdict on Epiphenomenalism," in F. C. Dommeyer (ed.), *Current Philosophical Issues* (Springfield, Il. 1966); R. Taylor, *Metaphysics* (Englewood Cliffs, NJ, 2nd ed. 1974) and R. Swinburne, *The Evolution of the Soul*, *op. cit.* The "teaser" from J. Shaffer quoted in the Introduction appears in his "Recent Work on the Mind-Body Problem (I)," *op. cit.* Epiphenomenalism is sympathetically discussed in K. Campbell, *Body and Mind* (2nd ed. Notre Dame, 1984). In "Mind, Brain, and Causation" which appeared in P. A. French et al. (eds.), *Midwest Studies in Philosophy*, vol. 4 (Minneapolis 1979), John Mackie defends what may be described as a modified version of epiphenomenalism. Epiphenomenalism is supported without any modifications in F. Jackson, "Epiphenomenal Qualia," *Philosophical Quarterly*, 1982.

Computational materialists, to whom I briefly referred in the Introduction, are for the most part opposed to any belief in survival, but, as will be evident from the conclusions of MacKay's discussion (selection 26), some of them believe that the theory is not inconsistent with bodily resurrection. In a fascinating (and also somewhat frightening) book, *Mind Children—The Future of Robot and Human Intelligence* (Cambridge, Mass. 1988), H. Moravec, one of the most prominent figures in the field of artificial intelligence, maintains that it is in principle entirely possible for human beings to achieve an afterlife — not in a "mystical or religious sense," but by having the programs presently realized in their brains transferred to a "physically different computer," a "shiny new body of the style, color, and material of one's choice." Those interested in introductions to computational materialism may be referred to P. M. Churchland, *Matter and Consciousness* (Cambridge, Mass. 1984) and J. Haugeland, *Artificial Intelligence — The Very Idea* (Cambridge, Mass. 1989). J. Haugeland (ed.), *Mind Design* (Cambridge, Mass. 1981) and J. L. Garfield (ed.), *Foundations of Cognitive Science* (New York 1990), are extremely useful anthologies containing papers both by leading computational materialists and by their critics. *Mind Design* has an excellent bibliography. Some of the basic philosophical questions are explored in Shaffer, "Recent Work on the Mind-Body Problem (II)," *op. cit.* and more briefly, but very illuminatingly, in Dennett, "Current Issues in the Philosophy of Mind," *op. cit.*

The leading critics of computational materialism are John Searle and the mathematical physicist Roger Penrose. Searle's objections are stated in "Minds, Brains and Programs," *The Behavioral and Brain Sciences* (1980), in *Minds, Brains and Science, op. cit.* and in his contribution to C. Blakemore and S. Greenfield (eds.), *Mindwaves* (Oxford 1987) entitled "Minds and Brains Without Programs," which reprints portions of the BBC lectures and also contains additional explanatory remarks. Searle is criticized in *Mindwaves* by Richard Gregory and Philip Johnson-Laird. His original article in *The Behavioral and Brain Sciences* was followed by several critical notes. Both Searle's article and the replies to him are reprinted in G. L. Garfield (ed.), *Foundations of Cognitive Science, op. cit.* Searle's original article is also reprinted in Rosenthal (ed.), *The Nature of Mind, op. cit.* where it is followed by J. A. Fodor's reply and by further exchanges between Searle and Fodor. *Scientific American* of January 1990 contains an exchange on the subject between Searle and Paul and Patricia Churchland. Penrose's objections to computational materialism (some of them highly technical) are stated in *The Emperor's Mind: Concerning Computers, Minds and the*

Laws of Physics (Oxford 1989) and also in his review of Moravec's *Mind Children* in the *New York Review of Books* of February 1, 1990. There is a critical review of Penrose's book by Dennett in the *Times Literary Supplement* for September 29–October 5, 1989. Searle's positive views, which may be characterized as a form of "biological materialism," are stated more fully in the last chapter of *Intentionality* (Cambridge 1983). Searle clearly belongs to the tradition of Cabanis, Darwin, and Vogt (the "secretionists" referred to on p. 23 of the Introduction), but his contentions are less specific and hence not falsifiable in any obvious way.

Among Anglo-Saxon philosophers who believe in survival, resurrectionism has undoubtedly been the most widely supported version in recent decades. However, this is not true of other regions of the world and it was not true of Britain and the United States in earlier times. Protestant philosophers and theologians as well as many educated laymen found it increasingly difficult to believe in bodily resurrection. In *The Hope of a World To Come* (London 1930), Edwyn Bevan, a leading liberal Protestant of the first half of the twentieth century, remarked that "for many people today the idea of a literal resurrection of the body has become impossible." If these people can believe in survival at all, it must be survival of the disembodied mind, and there has been no shortage of writers defending this version of life after death. In a lecture on "The Soul and the Body," delivered in 1912 and published in English translation in *Mind-Energy* (New York 1920), Henri Bergson, who prided himself on being a thoroughgoing empiricist, stated that "mental life overflows the cerebral life" and hence "survival becomes so probable that the onus of proof" falls on the unbeliever. Although he did not spell this out, it is clear that Bergson did not believe in bodily resurrection but in the survival of the disembodied mind. Bergson tacitly assumed that it makes sense to talk about a disembodied mind. It evidently never occurred to him to address himself to this issue, but it is this logically prior question of whether the notion of a disembodied mind is coherent which has been the focus of contemporary Anglo-Saxon discussion. H. H. Price argued in several places that statements about disembodied survival are intelligible. His arguments are presented briefly in "What Kind of Next World?" (selection 21); "Two Conceptions of the Next World," in Price's *Essays in the Philosophy of Religion* (Oxford 1972); and most fully in "Survival and the Idea of 'Another World,'" in J. R. Smythies (ed.), *Brain and Mind* (London 1965). H. D. Lewis in *The Self and Immortality* (London and New York 1973) advances very similar reasons for regarding the notion of a pure mind as entirely coherent. It should be mentioned that while Price was an agnostic about survival, H. D. Lewis is a fervent believer. Among unbelievers there is a division of opinion on this issue. A. Flew in his article on "Immortality" in *The Encyclopedia of Philosophy* (vol. 4, pp.

139–150), a section of which is selection 22 of the present book, also in *The Presumption of Atheism* (London 1976), and most recently in *The Logic of Mortality* (Oxford 1987), and T. Penelhum in *Survival and Disembodied Existence* (London 1970) deny that it makes sense to talk about a pure mind. M. Schlick in "Meaning and Verification," *Philosophical Review* 1937; C. Lewy in "Is the Notion of Disembodied Existence Self-Contradictory?", *Proceedings of the Aristotelian Society* 1942–43, P. F. Strawson in *Individuals* (London 1959); A. J. Ayer, *The Central Questions of Philosophy* (London 1973), and J. Mackie in *The Miracle of Theism* (Oxford 1982), do not believe in survival but regard statements about disembodied existence as intelligible. An unusually interesting defense of this view is advanced by M. Scriven in "Personal Identity and Parapsychology," *Journal of the American Society for Psychical Research*, 1965. Strawson argues that survival without a body would be a greatly impoverished form of existence, something that H. D. Lewis disputes. The intelligibility of statements asserting the existence of a disembodied mind is defended by G. R. Gillett in "Disembodied Persons" (*Philosophy* 1988), and in two articles by R. L. Purtill — "Disembodied Survival," *Sophia*, 1973, and "Disembodied Survival Again," *Canadian Journal of Philosophy*, 1977. The view of B. Williams, T. Geach, K. Campbell, and A. Quinton, mentioned in the Introduction, that we cannot individuate minds or mental states except by reference to the bodies with which they are connected or to which they belong, is challenged by R. M. Chisholm who writes (*Person and Object*, London and La Salle, Ill. 1976, p. 35): "I identify myself without identifying myself by reference to my body and I identify *my* body by reference to myself." Campbell's remarks about individuation are quoted from his *Body and Mind, op. cit.*, Quinton's from *The Nature of Things* (London 1973). The BBC discussion on "Life After Death" between Quinton, H. D. Lewis and Williams, as well as Lewis, "Immortality and Dualism," are contained in H. D. Lewis, *Persons and Life After Death* (London 1978). Readers interested in the struggle of liberal Protestants to get their churches to replace belief in the resurrection of the body with survival of the disembodied mind are referred to Kirsopp Lake, *Immortality and the Modern Mind* (Ingersoll Lecture, Cambridge, Mass. 1922). Appendix I is an account of the efforts by some prominent rebels in the Church of England to have belief in the Resurrection of the Flesh excised from the Apostles' Creed.

Schrödinger's view that all minds are absorbed in the one Universal Mind is explained in *Mind and Matter* (Cambridge 1958) and *My View of the World* (Cambridge, 1964). Köstler's similar assertion is presented in his contribution to Toynbee, et al., *Life After Death, op. cit.* The body-mind dependence argument on a cosmic scale which would seem to undermine views such as those of Schrödinger and Köstler is expounded in Emil DuBois-Reymond, *Über die Grenzen des Naturer-*

kennens (Berlin 1873) and by W. K. Clifford in an essay entitled "Body and Mind" which is available in volume II of Clifford's *Lectures and Essays* (London and New York 1879). The passages from Bertrand Russell quoted on p. 52 of the Introduction come from "What I Believe" (1925), which is reprinted in Russell's *Why I Am Not a Christian* (London and New York 1957). A fuller statement by Russell can be found in chapter 5 of *Religion and Science* (London 1935). Chapter 3 of Corliss Lamont, *The Illusion of Immortality* (London 1936), contains a detailed presentation of the evidence not only from brain physiology but from biology generally in support of the negative position on survival. An early defense of the body-mind-dependence argument is found in *On the Immortality of the Soul* by the Renaissance philosopher Pietro Pomponazzi (1462–1525) who argued, in opposition to Aquinas and most other Christian theologians, that the immortality of the soul cannot be established by natural reason but must be regarded as an article of faith. Pomponazzi's treatise is available in English translation in E. Cassirer, P. O. Kristeller and J. H. Randall, Jr. (eds.), *The Renaissance Philosophy of Man* (Chicago 1948). Pomponazzi's treatise was greatly admired by the French free-thinkers of the eighteenth century who went so far as to circulate a clandestine edition of the work.

Resurrectionism is represented in this book by Aquinas, Geach, Hick and van Inwagen. Perhaps the most lucid commentary on the views of Aquinas is found in chapter 4 of F. C. Copleston, *Aquinas* (London 1955). A briefer account occurs in chapter 37 of the same author's *A History of Philosophy*, volume 2 (London 1950). Hick has stated his views in greater detail in *Death and Eternal Life, op. cit.* Flew's criticism of Hick's position quoted on p. 57 of the Introduction comes from his "Is There a Case for Disembodied Survival?," originally published in 1972 in the *Journal of the American Society for Psychical Research* and since reprinted in several anthologies and in Flew's *The Presumption of Atheism op. cit.* Hick does not merely believe in the conceptual coherence of his form of resurrectionism but also in its truth. R. W. Perrett in chapter 7 of *Death and Immortality* (Dorbrecht 1987) defends the coherence of Hick's theory without in any way committing himself to its truth. In "Survival As Replication," *Sophia*, 1988, J. C. Yates endorses Flew's objections and also rejects Hick's view that the New Testament teaches the kind of resurrection he advocates. Hick has also been criticized by A. Olding in "Resurrection Bodies and Resurrection Worlds," *Mind*, 1970 and J. J. Clarke in "John Hick's Resurrection," *Sophia*, 1971. Hick's answers to Olding and Clarke, first published in *Mind* and *Sophia* respectively, are reprinted in chapter 15 of *Death and Eternal Life*. The following are some of the articles published in recent years which explore various issues arising from belief in bodily resurrection: S. R. Sutherland, "Immortality and Resurrection," *Religious Studies*, 1967–68; G. R. Mavrodes, "The Life Everlasting and the Bodily Criterion of Identity," *Nous*, 1977; P. L. Quinn, "Personal Identity, Bodily Continuity and Resurrection," *International Journal for Philosophy of Religion*, 1978; P. Helm, "A Theory of Disembodied Survival and Re-Embodied Existence," *Religious Studies*, 1978–79; F. D. Dilley, "Resurrection and the 'Replica Objection,' " *Religious Studies*, 1983–84; S. T. Davis "Is Personal Identity Retained in the Resurrection?", *Modern Theology*, 1986 and the same author's "The Resurrection of the Dead," in Davis (ed.), *Death and Afterlife, op. cit.* Several of these writers consider the possibility of a "mixed" view according to which a person exists after death as a disembodied mind until he is united with his resurrection body on the Day of Judgment. There is an extensive literature on the question of exactly what the Church Fathers believed. K. Stendhal (ed.), *Immortality and Resurrection* (New York 1965), contains the 1955 and 1956 Ingersoll Lectures by the distinguished Church historians Oscar Cullman and Harry A. Wolfson. Cullman sharply distinguishes between the "courageous and joyful primitive Christian hope of the resurrection of the dead" and "the serene and philosophic expectation of the survival of the immortal soul" taught by Socrates and Plato. The teaching of Socrates and Plato, he concludes, "can in no way be brought into consonance with that of the New Testament." In partial opposition to Cullman, Wolfson (who was also distinguished for his work on Philo and Spinoza) maintains that there is an element of Platonism in the outlook of the Church Fathers.

The statement of the age regression problem by W. T. Stace quoted on p. 60 of the Introduction is taken from *Man Against Darkness* (Pittsburgh 1967). The same difficulty for the believer is also raised in chapter 11 of Ernst Haeckel, *The Riddle of the Universe* (1899, English trans. London 1900), and in Clarence Darrow's "The Myth of Immortality" (1928) which is reprinted in Edwards and Pap, *A Modern Introduction to Philosophy, op. cit.* This hard-hitting article, which completely dispenses with technical terminology, is perhaps the best statement in the entire literature of the unbeliever's position. St. Augustine's discussion of the issue occurs in the *City of God*, Book 22, chapters 14–15. Augustine is criticized in chapters 3 of P. and L. Badham, *Immortality or Extinction?* (London 1982), from which selection 27 is reprinted. It might be of some interest to note that when this book was written both Paul and Linda Badham were believers in survival. Since then Linda has become a "naturalist," that is, an unbeliever, which is evident from her contribution to P. and L. Badham (eds.), *Death and Immortality in the Religions of the World, op. cit.* Hick's solution of the problem is offered in chapters 15 of *Death and Eternal Life, op. cit.* The quotation from Kübler-Ross on p. 60 is transcribed from a tape of the Canadian television program in the editor's possession.

The theological argument and the classification of arguments for

332   BIBLIOGRAPHICAL ESSAY

immortality mentioned on pp. 69 and 62 respectively are found in volume 2 of F. R. Tennant, *Philosophical Theology* (Cambridge 1930). Cudworth's metaphysical arguments are contained in his *The True Intellectual System* (1678). Clarke's version of the metaphysical arguments is contained in *A Letter to Mr. Dodwell* (1706). This "Letter" as well as further exchanges are printed in the sixth edition of the same work (1731). Some of Mendelssohn's writings on immortality are available in English in M. Mendelssohn: *Selections from His Writings* (New York 1975). A lucid statement of all the major metaphysical and moral arguments appears in chapter 24 of Maher, *Psychology, op. cit.* J. H. Holmes appeals to the "conservation of spiritual energy" in his "Ten Reasons for Believing in Immortality," a sermon delivered in 1929 and reprinted in Edwards and Pap (eds.), *A Modern Introduction to Philosophy, op. cit.* There is a brief reply to this argument in Darrow's "The Myth of Immortality," *op. cit.* In chapter 5 of *The Illusion of Immortality op. cit.*, C. Lamont criticizes attempts to deduce conclusions about immortality from the goodness of God.

C. D. Broad was probably the most prominent philosopher to be seriously interested in psychical research. The last two hundred pages of his *Lectures on Psychical Research* (London 1962) are devoted to mediumship. Broad conceded that the performances of numerous mediums were fraudulent, but he was impressed by cases in which a dead person seemed to take control of the medium's body and speak in his own characteristic voice through the medium's lips. Broad made it clear that he had no wish to survive his own death and he concludes his book with the following remark: "For my part I should be slightly more annoyed than surprised if I should find myself in some sense persisting immediately after the death of my present body. One can only wait and see, or alternately (which is no less likely) wait and not see." An extremely illuminating discussion by Broad entitled "Personal Identity and Survival," first published in 1958, is reprinted in Wheatley and Edge (eds.), *Philosophical Dimensions of Parapsychology, op. cit.* Broad died before the "immortality explosion" that began with Raymond Moody's best-selling *Life After Life* (Harrisburg, Pa. 1976) and the numerous declarations by Dr. Kübler-Ross that nothing was more certain than life after death, which received enormous publicity at the time and for some years thereafter. Hence he did not discuss the "near-death" experiences which form the subject matter of Moody's book as well as books by his various successors. P. and L. Badham, *Immortality or Extinction?, op. cit.* from which selection 27 is taken surveys the older as well as the more recent appeals to psychical research. R. Heywood, *Beyond the Reach of Sense* (New York 1974), covers much of the same ground as Broad. She lacks Broad's philosophical sophistication and is less critical, but her book contains a great deal of information that is difficult to find elsewhere in such compact form.

The literature on mediumship is enormous. Summaries of the *prima facie* strongest cases of cross-correspondence are found in H. F. Saltmarsh, *Evidence of Personal Survival from Cross Correspondences* (London 1938), and two books by G. N. M. Tyrrell—*Science and Psychical Phenomena* (London and New York 1938) and *The Personality of Man* (New York 1946). G. Murphy and R. O. Ballou (eds.), *William James on Psychical Research* (New York 1960), reprints James' lengthy report on Mrs. Piper, a medium who had greatly impressed him. The book also contains the full text of James' lecture "Human Immortality" and numerous letters in which he discusses survival. In "Why I Do Not Believe in Survival," *Proceedings of the Society for Psychical Research*, 1934, reprinted in A. Flew (ed.), *Readings in the Philosophical Problems of Parapsychology* (Buffalo 1987), E. R. Dodds concedes that "neither chance nor cheating, nor any combination of the two, will suffice to account for the *whole* of the mental phenomena of mediumship." According to Dodds the knowledge displayed by mediums is due to telepathy or a combination of telepathy and clairvoyance. Dodds, who was a distinguished classical scholar, describes his interest in psychical research in chapter 11 of his autobiography, *Missing Persons* (Oxford 1977). In "Discarnate Survival," in B. B. Wolman (ed.), *Handbook of Parapsychology* (New York 1977), A. Gauld replies to Dodds and others who try to explain mediumship by the "Super ESP hypothesis."

Two fascinating books about the history of spiritualism have been published in recent years. Ruth Brandon, *The Spiritualists* (New York 1983), is a witty account by a total skeptic of the fraud perpetrated by mediums and their associates and the astounding (or perhaps not so astounding) credulity of some of the famous men who were drawn to spiritualism. The Appendix on "The Machinery in the Ghost," showing the instruments of deception employed by mediums, is particularly hilarious. Janet Oppenheim, *The Other World—Spiritualism and Psychical Research in England, 1850–1914* (Cambridge 1985), concentrates on the role of spiritualism as a substitute-religion at a period when scientists and philosophers found it increasingly difficult to believe in the tenets of Christianity. Oppenheim does not address herself to the question of whether any of the mediums or automatists provided dependable evidence for survival, but she notes that there is no plausible this-worldly explanation for the "Palm Sunday" case of cross-correspondences. One of Brandon's sources is the great magician, Harry Houdini, who was an inveterate enemy of mediums, devoting a great deal of energy to exposing their fakery. His investigations are recorded in *A Magician Among the Spirits* (New York 1924). He and his wife agreed on a message which the one dying first was to send to the other in case survival turned out to be a reality. Houdini died suddenly and tragically in 1926. No message was ever received.

The term "near-death experience" has come to refer to three classes of phenomena: (1) experiences by persons who were revived after their heart had stopped beating for a few minutes but who had not suffered brain death; (2) experiences of people who came very close to death; and (3) the visions of dying patients shortly before their death. It is by no means a recent idea that in the course of such experiences it may be possible to get a glimpse of the next world, the reasoning being that if there is another world one is never closer to it than when one is dead or near death. James Boswell, who had a morbid obsession with death, made it a practice to attend executions, some of them of his own clients for such crimes as sheep-stealing, in the hope of hearing the condemned man's last words which might be a description of the next life. James H. Hyslop, the first secretary-treasurer and research officer of the American Society for Psychical Research, expressed the same idea in a paper included in his *Psychical Research and the Resurrection* (Boston 1908). "If there be such a thing as a transcendental spiritual world and if we actually survive in our personality after death," Hyslop wrote, "we might naturally expect some connection between the two sets of cosmic conditions, at least occasionally." It would not be unreasonable to expect these "connections" to take place at the time at which a person crosses from one world to another.

Raymond Moody's *Life After Life, op. cit.* started the recent interest in the first two classes of near-death phenomena. Moody did not claim to have provided evidence for survival, but there is no doubt that his book was and was intended to be read as a defense of life after death. Fortified with an introduction by Dr. Kübler-Ross, it was on the bestseller lists for several years. Moody had two successors—Kenneth Ring, a psychologist from the University of Connecticut, and Michael Sabom, a cardiologist from Atlanta. Ring's contributions to human knowledge were published in two books—*Life at Death* (New York 1980) and *Heading toward Omega* (New York 1984). The former has a moving introduction by Moody, the latter by Kübler-Ross who describes Ring's book as "masterful." Sabom's *Recollections at Death* (New York 1982) concludes on a reassuring note. "Does the near-death experience represent a glimpse of an afterlife?" Sabom asks; "Could the mind which splits apart from the physical brain be, in essence, the 'soul,' which continues to exist after final bodily death?" The answer given on the last page of his book is a ringing "yes." Those who had a near-death experience "were touched by some ineffable truth encountered face to face at death's chosen moments." It might be mentioned in passing that Moody, Ring, and Sabom are leading figures in the International Association for Near-Death Studies, which publishes a journal, *Anabiosis*, recently renamed *Journal for Near-Death Studies*. If Ring and Sabom are Moody's sons, Karlis Osis and Erlendur Haraldsson, the authors of *At the Hour of Death* (New York 1977), introduction by Dr. Kübler-Ross, may be best described as his cousins. They express great admiration for Moody, but their own prime evidence comes from deathbed visions. We are told that many dying patients have visions of dead relatives and friends who form a kind of reception committee welcoming them into their new home. Naturalistic explanations are firmly rejected and, unlike Moody, Osis and Haraldsson explicitly claim that the survival-hypothesis is by far the best explanation of the phenomena under investigation.

There are selections from Moody, Ring, Sabom, Osis, and various others of Moody's sons and cousins, but not from any of their critics in C. R. Lundhal (ed.), *A Collection of Near-Death Research* (Chicago 1982). Bruce Greyson and C. P. Flynn (eds.), *The Near-Death Experience* (Springfield, Ill. 1984) is a more balanced collection. Moody and sons are here but so are two critics, Ernst Rodin (who had a near-death experience which he interprets as a delusion) and Ronald Siegel. D. S. Rogo, "Research on Deathbed Experiences: Some Contemporary and Historical Perspectives," *The Journal of the Academy of Religion and Psychical Research*, 1979, contains information about the predecessors of Moody and his family. Historical information is also supplied by I. Stevenson and B. Greyson in "Near Death Experiences—Relevance to the Question of Survival After Death," *Journal of the American Medical Association*, 1979. In chapter 5 of *Immortality or Extinction?, op. cit.* P. and L. Badham examine the explicit or implicit claims of Kübler-Ross, Moody, Osis-Haraldsson and several other writers not mentioned in this bibliography. They find grounds for regarding all of them as unreliable reporters, giving very specific reasons in the case of Moody and Kübler-Ross. They nevertheless conclude that because of the basic similarity of so many of the reports, near-death experiences provide *some* evidence for life after death. Other writers greatly impressed by the work of Moody, sons and cousins are D. H. Lund in *Death and Consciousness, op. cit.* and Ian Wilson in *The After-Life Experience* (London 1987). Wilson devotes rather more space to Moody's sons than to Moody himself. He evidently believes that Ring and Sabom have made a strong case for survival. As for Moody himself, it may be of interest to note that he recently moved into a branch of psychiatry known as "past-life regression therapy." In *Coming Back: A Psychiatrist Explores Past-Life Journeys* (New York 1991), Moody claims highly beneficial results for this technique. Although not committing himself to belief in reincarnation, he asserts that there are some meticulously documented cases which cannot be plausibly explained on any other assumption. It would not be surprising if this book also became a best-seller. If it does, we may confidently expect new sons and cousins to appear on the scene.

Philosophers and psychologists familiar with the work of the near-death theorists have almost without exception rejected it as without merit—at least as far as the question of evidence for survival is concerned. Their methodology is flawed, their reports of questionable authenticity, and naturalistic explanations are dismissed on the flimsiest grounds. Above all, none of the patients was brain-dead, and there is every reason to believe that the brain can go on working for some time after the heart stops beating. It should be observed that this negative verdict has been rendered by believers as well as unbelievers. Moody and relatives are criticized in J. E. Alcock, "Psychology and Near-Death Experiences," *Skeptical Inquirer*, 1979, the same author's *Parapsychology: Science or Magic?* (Oxford 1981), R. Puccetti, "The Experience of Dying," *The Humanist*, 1979, several articles by Ronald Siegel—"Life After Death," in G. Abell and B. Singer (eds.), *Science and the Paranormal* (New York 1981), "Accounting for 'Afterlife' Experiences," *Psychology Today*, 1980, and "The Psychology of Life After Death," *American Psychologist*, 1980, and D. F. Beyerstein, "The Brain and Consciousness: Implications for Psi Phenomena," *Skeptical Inquirer*, 1987–88. In the Winter 1990–91 issue of *Free Inquiry*, J. Preisinger, a California psychiatrist, writes about his own near-death experience, offering detailed physiological explanations of its various aspects, especially the euphoria connected with it. Preisinger mentioned the experience and his explanation to Moody. It will come as no surprise that Moody was not shaken in any of his views.

Several psychologists have been interested in near-death experiences without any ulterior motive concerning proof of life after death. Prominent among these is the Swiss psychoanalyst Oskar Pfister, whose "Mental States in Mortal Danger" (1930) appeared in *Essence*, 1981. (*Essence*, a Canadian journal published between 1976 and 1982, was devoted to "issues in the study of aging, dying, and death.") Pfister's paper was translated by R. Kletti and R. Noyes, two American psychologists who have published extensively on this subject. Their joint paper, "Depersonalization in the Face of Life-Threatening Danger," is reprinted in Lundhal (ed.), *A Collection of Near-Death Research, op. cit.* In "Near-Death Experiences: Their Interpretation and Significance," in R. Kastenbaum (ed.), *Between Life and Death* (New York 1979), Noyes offers a naturalistic explanation of near-death experiences and warns against "sensationalism and unwarranted claims," a warning which has for the most part not been heeded.

This bibliography would be incomplete without reference to *Search for the Soul* (New York 1979) by Milbourne Christopher. Like Houdini (about whom he wrote two books), Christopher was a magician who made the exposure of fakery one of his hobbies. As the title of the book indicates, Christopher relates the attempts of various "investigators" to produce incontrovertible empirical proof of the existence of man's immortal soul. Moody and his cousins get their due, but they are dreary compared with a Dr. Duncan MacDougall of the Massachusetts General

Hospital who in 1907 determined that the human soul weighs between one-third and one-half of an ounce. There is also a Mr. Holland who in the presence of a Chicago *Tribune* reporter saw, by means of a magnifying contraption, how vapor particles formed themselves into the double of a man who had just died. The fate of this particular double is unknown, but another gaseous replica, observed by Andrew Jackson Davis, one of the first American trance mediums, was seen to leave the room through an open door "en route to the hereafter." One is reminded of Voltaire's observation that not everything people see is really there.